AF316823

Praise

"Even from a quick skim, I could tell—this book is polished, engaging, and packed with real substance. It's the kind of book that doesn't just get read … it gets devoured. I can't wait to read it cover to cover."

—John, Software Developer

"This has been the most fun project I've ever worked on—and I've edited a lot of books. I'd burst into laughter while working on it, and my husband would ask, 'What did Dan say this time?' It's raw, it's real, and it's unlike anything else out there on leadership."
—Debra, Editor

"Leadership books usually talk at you. This one talks with you—and then hands you a wrench. I finished it fired up and with a plan."

—Rachel, Safety Director, Oil & Gas

"I read it in two sittings and handed it to my foremen. It's gritty, funny, and brutally useful. Our culture conversations changed the next day."

—Tom, Municipal Fleet Manager

"Dan doesn't hand you theory—he hands you a flashlight for the trenches. I laughed, I underlined, and I walked away sharper as a leader."

—Melissa, HR Director

"I've read a lot of leadership books, but this one feels like a conversation with a buddy who's been there, done that, and isn't afraid to tell you the truth. It's fresh, it's funny, and it sticks."

—Chris, Business Owner

"I laughed out loud, underlined like crazy, and already shared quotes with my team. This isn't theory—it's leadership in steel-toed boots."

—Angela, Small Business Owner

"After just chapter one, I was hooked and wanted to know more about Dan. The lessons are clear, the stories are powerful, and the way it's written makes it incredibly easy to put into practice."

—Chad, Safety Professional, Electric Cooperative

"*Leadership isn't forged in comfort. It's hammered out in the heat, sharpened by grit, and carried with grace.*"

Dan Greer

GRIT, GREASE, AND GRACE

Leadership Forged in the Trenches

Daniel Greer

Dedication

To the Bad Bosses

Thank you. You micromanaged, gaslit, played favorites, and promoted chaos as if it were a leadership skill. But without you, I wouldn't have half the stories or scars that forged this book. You showed me what not to do. That turned out to be one of the best leadership lessons of all.

To the Great Leaders

You didn't just lead—you inspired. You still do. Your examples challenge me daily to be better, lead bolder, and serve deeper. I owe a huge part of who I am to the standard you set.

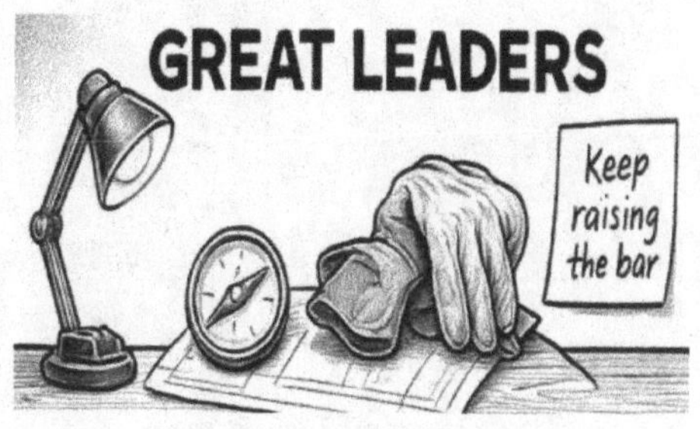

To Jenna and Our Amazing Kids

I know. I've had some wild ideas from Department of Transportation (DOT) compliance empires to writing books in the middle of road trips. But you've stood by me through it all. Your love, your patience, and your belief in me are the greatest gifts I've ever received.

No, this isn't your typical dedication, because this isn't your typical book.

Contents

Acknowledgments

Special Thanks

This book wasn't written alone, and I wouldn't want it any other way.

First, I've got to thank **the good Lord**. Every open door, tough lesson, and crazy idea that somehow worked all came from Him. He gave me the creativity to think outside the box and the courage not to care what anyone else thought. I've learned to trust that if He gave me the idea, He'll give me the grit to run with it. And He always has. I had to apply the grease, but He's the one who always reminds me of the grace.

To **my parents, Harry and Cindy,** thank you for not giving up on me or putting me on Craigslist. I was definitely a handful. I was loud, wild, and opinionated. I hated rules and always pushed limits. But you raised me with faith, grit, and a whole lot of grace. I wouldn't be who I am today without your steady hands and prayers. They likely kept the lightning from striking.

To **Bud Rousett,** you've always been a steady source of encouragement and positivity. You believed in me before there was a stage, a business, or a book. You saw something in me early on, and you never stopped reminding me it was there.

To the leaders who've shaped me: **Ezra, Brooke, Isaiah, Brad, Bobby, Bill, Mom, Dad, Don, Carlos, Chad, James, Gary, Grandpa Greer, and Grandpa Phelps.** You've made your mark. Your example, correction, and support all helped shape how I lead, think, and live. You didn't just lead me. You forged me.

Thank you, **my wife and kids,** for always being there. You've supported my wild ideas, road trips, late-night writing, and early-morning thoughts. You've supported me when I didn't deserve it and pushed me when I needed it most. I love you more than planes, tractors, and all the Rocky Mountains combined.

To **my brother Rusty,** thanks for always being there, working beside me, and having my back more times than I can count. We've built, fixed, and fought through a lot together, and I wouldn't trade it for anything.

To **my team.** You don't just support the mission—you *live* it. You show up, bring the energy, and make everything better. I'd be running on half capacity and sheer stubbornness without you. Thank you for having my back.

And to **all the others**—yes, even the ones I didn't name directly—thank you. You made a difference in my life. You shaped me with encouragement, correction, friendship, and challenge. Sometimes, just being there when I needed support mattered most. Some of you supported me in ways I never expected. Some of you spoke one sentence I'll never forget. And some of you helped carry the weight when I was running on fumes. I might

not have named everyone, but if you're reading this, I'm truly thankful for you.

Chapter 1 | Introduction

Leadership Lessons from a Feed Mill

Let me start this book by saying that I sucked at leadership. Maybe you did too, or heck, maybe you still do! This is my no-BS introduction to the book you didn't know you needed.

If you're thinking, This guy's about to drop seven perfectly polished nuggets of leadership wisdom tied up in a bow like every other business book on the shelf, toss this book on the table right now. I'm not that guy.

I'm the guy who's missed a payroll, patched a team together with duct tape and prayer, and learned most lessons the hard way—then got up and learned them again. This isn't theory from a corner office. It's the real, grease-stained, field-tested, knock-your-socks-off truth from a guy who's lived it.

When I first stepped into leadership, I wasn't a little bad at it. I was really bad at it. And I wasn't bad at it in a cute, he's-just-learning way, either. I'm talking full-blown, Olympic-level suckage (I made up that word)—the kind that's career-limiting, pride-swallowing, forehead-slap-from-your-grandma suckage. If sucking at leadership were a sport, I'd have taken home gold, silver, and bronze—and then failed the drug test for good measure. If failure had a flavor, I was the expired meatloaf your grandma wrapped in tinfoil, forgot behind the green beans, and then served with a smile three weeks later. And if Hoover vacuums ever launched a Hall of Suck campaign? Yeah—I'd be front and center in the commercial flashing a cheesy grin, giving two thumbs up next to a banner that reads: Certified Suction King Since 2005.

My first taste of leadership came when I was nineteen or twenty years old. I was old enough to be handed responsibility and young enough to have absolutely no clue what to do with it. The local agriculture co-op was in a pinch. Their feed mill guy was leaving. The co-op needed someone to step in, pick up the responsibilities on the fly, and not burn the place down in the process. Enter me.

I had a solid ag background—grew up on a farm, knew how to work, knew how to sweat, and could operate about anything with a motor and a gearshift. I'd spent my teenage years fixing broken rakes and balers in the middle of hay season, hauling feed, patching fences, chasing livestock that didn't want to be caught, and trying to convince my grandpa that baling hay at midnight built character. (It did.)

So, when they said, "Hey, we need someone who can learn this feed mill yesterday," I said, "I'm your guy," before even knowing what a pellet ration was.

They handed me the keys to this massive, loud, slightly terrifying contraption that mixed grain, filled fifty-pound bags, and expected me to keep it humming like clockwork. I had to sew each bag shut with a sewing machine—the kind that'll eat your fingers if you so much as blink at the wrong time. Then I'd stack those suckers on pallets like I was prepping for the agricultural apocalypse. The routine required part brute strength, part mechanical ballet, and part keep-your-hands-clear unless you want a new nickname like Lefty. And all the while, I was responsible for keeping local ranchers stocked with everything short of Miracle-Gro for their livestock. And suddenly, just like that—I was in charge. Me. The kid who still considered pizza rolls a food group. The guy who thought inventory management meant eyeballing the stacks and thinking, *yeah, that looks about right.*

They gave me the title and the responsibility, but no playbook. My orientation was like saying, "Here, drive this tractor—blindfolded—and through a parade."

I wasn't hired because I was a great leader. I was hired because I was available, teachable, and hardworking. Those are solid traits, and they'll take you far—right up until you realize leadership's a whole different beast than plain old hard work.

Let me be clear. I wasn't a manager. I was a teenager trusted with serious machinery and even more serious responsibility before I knew how to lead anything but a lunch break. Still, I took pride in that job. I kept that warehouse spotless. I stacked pallets of feed so tight you'd think I was building grain pyramids for pharaohs. I had the feed bags organized like a color-coded apocalypse bunker. I was, in my own head, crushing it.

From Rage Monster to Realization

Then one day, as I'm bagging grain and minding my own business, this guy from the yard jumps on my forklift. Acting like he owns the place, he starts hauling out full pallets of feed. No paperwork. No "Hey, Dan, just a heads-up." Bam—he's yanking bags off the pallets like a sugar-crazed kid digging for marshmallows in a box of Lucky Charms. No rhyme. No reason. One minute, I'm feeling like the king of inventory. The next minute, I'm watching my hard work vanish, forklift by forklift, like a bad magic trick.

Within minutes, the place went from stocked and organized to looking like we'd been looted by a crew of feed-hungry raccoons. Bare shelves. Empty rows. My beautiful system—gone. And I lost it.

When my boss walked by on his way out to his truck, I didn't ask a question. I didn't check myself. I didn't use my words like a functioning adult.

Nope—I went full-volume, sarcastic rage monster.

"Hey! It would have been nice to know about this order at 8 a.m. this morning, when you got it, instead of watching my whole day get wrecked at 4 p.m. while they're loading the dang truck!"

Loud. Sharp. In front of customers, coworkers, and anyone who had ears and happened to be within a five-mile radius. If there were a Hall of Fame for public overreactions, this moment would be a first-round inductee.

He yelled back, of course, and told me to expect that order every week moving forward. Then, he stormed off like I had kicked his dog and insulted his grandma.

Honestly, he should have fired me on the spot.

Rage Monster Unleashed

The next morning, the general manager showed up at the feed mill. Now, he was at the co-op every day, but he rarely wandered back to my corner of the operation unless something was broken, burning, or begging for attention. This wasn't a casual drop-in. He had no donut box in hand—only a serious look on his face and uttering a line I'll never forget:

"Dan, I've had to fire a few people recently. I'd really hate for you to be the next one, especially over something stupid."

And what did I do? Did I thank him for the second chance? Did I apologize for yelling across the parking lot like a teenager who just found out curfew was back on? Nope. I argued with him because this was only the beginning.

I told him it wasn't stupid. I told him the communication was trash. I told him I was right, and they were wrong.

I doubled down like a blackjack rookie with no clue how to play the hand. Looking back, I should have been handed a cardboard box and a paper check and sent home with a note that read, "Good luck out there, champ." But I wasn't. And here's the crazy thing—I still didn't learn the lesson.

I left that job convinced they were the problem. I mean, obviously, they didn't communicate. They didn't lead. They were a bunch of out-of-touch managers with clipboards, blue jeans, and titles they probably got from winning a coin toss—or just outlasting everyone else. I walked out convinced I'd just sat through a masterclass in how not to run a circus taught by the clowns.

The Cost of Blame

But what I didn't realize and flat-out refused to see was that the real issue wasn't their communication. It was a lack of ownership. Mine.

They didn't fail to inform me. I failed to take responsibility for how I responded. I blamed up the chain, sideways, diagonally—heck, if the dog walked through the yard that day, I probably blamed him too. But the man in the mirror? Nah. I wasn't ready to look at him yet.

At the time, I thought I was the smartest guy in the room. I thought I got it. I thought leadership meant barking louder, working harder, being more right than everyone else. It doesn't. Leadership is not a title. It's not volume. And it's definitely not about always being the smartest guy in the room. Leadership is taking the hit, even when it wasn't your fault. It's asking, "What could I have done differently?" It's owning your reaction, even when someone else dropped the ball. And in that moment, I failed every one of those tests.

But here's why you're still reading: You've had moments like that, too. You probably never yelled in a parking lot, but maybe you shut down in a meeting instead. Maybe you didn't storm off, but you quietly refused to take responsibility. Maybe you didn't throw blame out loud, but you blamed someone else and justified it under your breath. Maybe you didn't explode, but you stood there in your own mess, arms crossed, knowing you were wrong and not quite ready to admit it.

Or maybe—just maybe—you rage-typed an email so intense your keyboard started sweating, hovered over the send button like it was a missile launch, and thankfully hit delete before nuking your whole career. If that's you, welcome. You're in the right place.

I'm not writing this book as a guru. I'm writing it as a guy who's been there, blown it, and learned how to suck a little less every day.

No matter where you are in your leadership journey—whether you're managing a team of two, a company of two hundred, or trying to lead yourself without burning your whole life down—I've been there. I've stood where you're standing, messed up what you're messing up, and walked through what you're walking through.

And here's what I've learned—the hard way: No matter how bad it gets, no matter how far you think you've fallen, it's not over. There's more. You can grow, change, and lead, even if you suck right now. Especially if you suck right now. So, buckle up. This is just the beginning. And I promise, we're about to have one heck of a ride together.

Now, after my little parking lot performance, you'd think I would have walked away humbled. Maybe taken a deep breath. Reflected. Grown. Learned a little something about grace under pressure. Yeah—no.

I walked away mad. Not a little upset—righteously indignant. You know the feeling: chest puffed, jaw tight, already scripting your exit interview in the rearview mirror like you're the star of a workplace revenge movie.

I was convinced I was the victim. I had been wronged, and I was the tragic hero in a badly written sitcom where poor communication played the villain and clueless leadership was the bumbling sidekick.

In my head, I was the one keeping the ship afloat while management stood around with their clipboards and coffee cups poking holes in the hull of the boat. I truly believed that if everyone did their jobs the way I thought they should, the place would run smoother than a buttered slip-n-slide in a heatwave. I mean, clearly, I wasn't the issue. Right? Wrong.

But let me ask you something—and be honest: Have you ever felt that way before? Like you were carrying the weight of it all? Like, if you didn't do it, it wouldn't get done right? Like everyone else was only clocking in for the paycheck while ignoring common sense?

Maybe you've even muttered something under your breath (or said it out loud when no one was within earshot):

- There's no good help anymore.
- If I want it done right, I've got to do it myself.
- Why am I the only one who gives a crap around here?

Yeah. I've been there too. Heck, I've had entire internal monologues worthy of an Oscar—dramatic pauses and everything. Once I got so worked up, I found myself passionately arguing with an imaginary version of my boss—in the grain room—only to realize someone was behind me holding a clipboard. I'm pretty sure he backed away slowly and never made eye contact with me again.

But try explaining that to twenty-year-old Dan—the kid with enough attitude to light a fire and enough pride to dance around it shirtless, thinking it made him look brave.

Back then, I could have held a masterclass on arrogance. I had all the greatest hits on loop:

- My boss doesn't get it.

- This place would fall apart without me.
- I'm the only one who works hard.
- They don't pay me enough to deal with this crap.

Ever had those thoughts? Congratulations. We've shared the same pit. Thinking like that is dangerous because you'll start attracting people who think like that too. It's like a bitterness magnet. I ended up with my own little fan club of coworkers who nodded along with every complaint. We didn't hold meetings—we held gripe circles. Half venting, half sarcasm, and 100 percent unproductive.

Picture us standing around like we were solving company problems—really, we were trading excuses like baseball cards and convincing each other we were geniuses trapped in a world of idiots.

Victim Mode and the Gripe Circle

We weren't leaders. We were hecklers in matching uniforms. We rolled our eyes in meetings, made sarcastic jokes during toolbox talks, and said things like, "That's above my pay grade," every chance we got. We weren't building anything. We were waiting for something to break so we could point fingers.

We thought we were smarter than the people in charge. We just didn't want their responsibility. We wanted their power, their paychecks, and their titles minus the pressure.

It was a full-blown pity party with no cake or balloons. A stale bowl of blame, a cooler full of bad attitudes, and party favors made of sarcasm and eyerolls was all we had to offer. We served up second helpings of *nobody listens to me* and topped it off with a big scoop of backseat leadership—always full of ideas, never full of accountability.

Surround yourself with people who validate your excuses, and you'll never outgrow them. That's what I did. I didn't need a coach. I needed a mirror. I didn't need validation. I needed a good old-fashioned wake-up call. But when you're deep in victim mode, the truth feels like an attack. And I wasn't ready to hear it. I kept telling myself the same tired story: *I get it. They don't. I'm the leader this place needs—they just haven't realized it yet.*

But the truth? I wasn't a misunderstood genius. I was an arrogant kid with a fragile ego and a loud mouth. I had no clue what leadership really was, but that didn't stop me from pretending I had the blueprint to save the world. Charts? Check. Confidence? Check. Actual experience? Not even close. When your confidence is a Ferrari, but your maturity is a go-kart motor, you're going to crash. Hard. Like Mario Kart with my kids hard.

Those little speed demons game way more than I do. I'm thinking I'm holding my own, and boom—I'm in twelfth place in a race with eight players. That's not merely losing. That's losing with style. I don't even know how I do it. My character's still spinning out in the background while my thirteen-year-old is already collecting his trophy and trash-talking with fruit snacks in his mouth. That was me as a leader: all gas, no map, and full speed in the wrong direction.

Want to stall your growth? Easy. Surround yourself with people who let you stay small and call it support. That's exactly what I did. And yeah, I stayed stuck. If someone had walked up to me back then and said, "Dan, maybe the reason you're not being led well is because you've never learned how to follow without whining," I probably would have laughed, fired off some sarcastic one-liner, and dismissed them as another clueless suit.

But I needed someone to say it. Not gently or with a soft voice and a hand on my shoulder. I needed it delivered like Tim Taylor swinging a 2 x 4 on *Home Improvement*. You know the episode when he knocks out Bob Vila with a flying piece of wood while trying to prove a point? Yeah, that level of impact.

Maybe someone did try to tell me. I just wasn't listening. I didn't want to follow. I wanted to lead. I wanted the spotlight, influence, and the *atta boy* respect without the challenge or the character required to earn it.

I wanted to be seen as wise without putting in the work. I wanted to be in charge without earning trust. I wanted to skip humility and go straight to being the guy people listened to. But leadership doesn't work like that. I stayed stuck, loud, defensive, offended, constantly on edge, and always looking for proof that someone else was to blame. I wasn't leading. I was throwing a grown-up tantrum in steel-toed boots.

The School of Real Life

In God's infinite humor and mercy, He enrolled me in the longest, slowest, most painful school of leadership ever invented: real life.

About two years after that glorious parking lot meltdown—the one where I proved, beyond a shadow of a doubt, that I wasn't even qualified to lead a toddler across a sidewalk—I landed what I thought was my big break. This time, I would be around big machines and expectations to match. It was a real-deal opportunity. I pictured myself standing next to an excavator, my arms crossed, nodding like a seasoned pro, barking commands with gravel in my voice—somewhere between John Wayne, Mike Rowe, and a low-budget motivational speaker. This was leadership, baby. Nope.

It turns out that the guy needed a driver, not a foreman, a decision-maker, or even a what-do-you-think guy. He needed a warm body with a commercial driver's license (CDL) and a halfway decent left turn. To make things even more entertaining, he was just as Type A as I was.

So now we had two alpha personalities, one construction site, and zero chill. For ten hours a day and five days a week with no escape hatch or buffer, we were locked in like a low-budget reality show called *Extreme Tension: Highway Edition.*

It was like stuffing two pit bulls into a phone booth with one gas station burrito. Every task turned into a silent contest. Every conversation felt like a passive-aggressive chess match. He'd say, "Back it in over there," and I'd fire back, "Oh, you mean exactly where I was already headed?" He'd sigh. I'd roll my eyes.

We spent five months together chewing through frustration like day-old jerky—tough, dry, and somehow still stuck in your teeth. Eventually, it boiled over. No shouting match. No dramatic walk off. Just a slow, grinding realization that one of us had to go. And since it was his truck and his name on the door, I was the one who hit the road. That was another almost-leadership moment and another hard-earned lesson in humility.

Next stop? Pipe delivery. Just me, a truck, and the open road. No crew. No pressure. No leadership required. I was the guy hauling massive lengths of pipe to towns that barely showed up on Google Maps—places that hadn't seen a paved road since the Reagan administration. I loved it. For a while, it felt like freedom. Nobody breathing down my neck. No arguments in the cab. Just diesel, drive time, and the occasional sketchy gas station burrito.

Every week, I ran Wolf Creek Pass—twice. Rain, snow, shine, or avalanche warning, it didn't matter. That pass and I had a relationship. A complicated one. We're talking record-breaking winters. The snow that makes grown men rethink their life choices mid-shift. I'm not exaggerating when I say that one winter, I chained up my truck over 180 times. Yep. That's how awesome the snow was.

There was one day I'll never forget. I'd clawed my way up the steep side of Wolf Creek Pass. No chains. Should have had them. But hey—the signs weren't up yet, so technically I wasn't breaking any rules, flirting really hard with stupidity. I pull off at the top because nature was calling, and as I'm stepping out to take a leak, I spot the snowplow guy standing next to the chain law sign, getting ready to flip it up.

We lock eyes mid-zip. He sees me. Sees the dry tires. Sees the timing. And instead of lifting the sign, he lets it fall back down. He didn't say a word. Just gave me that quiet, you-lucky-punk look. I zipped, nodded, and climbed back in and eased down the hill, slow and smooth—like I meant to do it that way all along. I still had to pee but figured I'd stop at the bottom where my brakes had a better chance of working.

But while I was crushing it behind the wheel, I was completely coasting in life. No books. No growth. No reflection. I wasn't leading. I was delivering. I was living in cruise control, convincing myself that as long as the job got done, I was doing fine. But leadership doesn't grow in cruise control. It grows when you hit resistance and choose to push anyway. That wasn't happening. Not yet.

From there, it was back to delivering equipment and driving a lowboy semi for another company with the opportunity to run their mechanics shop. Another shot at influence. Another opportunity to lead. Another explosive argument—this time right in the shop. In front of everyone. Boom. Fired!

After that, I landed a job with the local government running heavy equipment. They handed me the keys to a shiny Caterpillar motor grader and said, "We want you shaping roads." And I was pumped. This was it—my redemption arc. My watch-me-lead-with-excellence-and-maybe-wear-aviators-while-doing-it moment. Yeah, not so much.

Five minutes in, they figured it out. I was way better behind a steering wheel than behind a blade. They yanked me off that shiny new grader faster than a toddler snatching a cookie off a table he wasn't supposed to be near—and threw me right back into a truck.

I got to run crews occasionally, which mostly meant I was the guy who knew how to load the cooler without smashing the sandwiches. But even then, I still didn't get it. I blamed my boss. the weather, the equipment, the schedule, the GPS, the full moon, Mercury in retrograde—you name it, I blamed it. I blamed everything except myself.

At that point, I still didn't own a dang thing. I wasn't leading. I was reacting. And let's be honest—reactive leadership is survival dressed up in a tucked-in button-up and a bad attitude.

Breaking the Cycle

Then, finally, something shifted. Not because I got promoted. Not because I had some lightning-bolt breakthrough or because someone handed me a "World's Best Boss" mug with confetti and applause. Nope. Things started changing when I finally asked one question—just one: "What could I have done differently to change the outcome?" Not:

- Whose fault is this?
- Why do these people keep screwing things up?
- Who messed with my perfectly stacked pallet of feed again?
- Did someone use a forklift as a bumper car again, or is that how we park now?

I asked that one question. "What could I have done differently to change the outcome?" Every time. Even if it wasn't my fault. *Especially* when it wasn't my fault.

It probably was at least partly my fault. I didn't want to admit it, like when the trash can's overflowing but you swear it wasn't you, even though you're standing there holding the last Taco Bell wrapper and have a look of guilt stronger than the Diablo sauce.

That's when things finally started to click like a bad knee before a snowstorm or like a seatbelt after the cop's already walking up to your window. The moment I stopped trying to dodge blame like a toddler caught drawing on the walls with a Sharpie and started owning my part—even the messy, uncomfortable ugh-fine-I'll-deal-with-it part—I grew.

Don't get me wrong. This wasn't some thirty-day, glow-up-style leadership montage where I stood on a hilltop with the wind blowing through my beard while inspirational music played and someone slow-clapped in the distance. Nah. This took seventeen freaking years. Seventeen years of grinding it out, screwing things up, apologizing badly, learning lessons the hard way, and getting humbled by everything from hard conversations to having to re-do something I thought I nailed.

And even after all that, most days, I still had the emotional intelligence of a used work boot—beaten up, stiff, and not quite waterproof. But I was slowly and clumsily getting better. I had to eat humble pie for breakfast, lunch, and dinner. Got demoted. Got scolded. Got a few come-into-my-office-and-shut-the-door talks that still haunt me in the shower.

But little by little, the vacuum-level suckage dropped. I went from a full-blown hydrovac truck with an eight-inch hose to something more manageable, like a beat-up shop-vac from the back of your uncle's garage. Still sucks, just not quite as violently. Progress, baby!

Leadership without Leverage

Eventually, I stepped into a real leadership role. Not because I'd earned a throne or got knighted by a CEO. But because I'd finally stopped pretending I knew everything and started taking responsibility, even when no one was watching.

And here's the twist: I had zero authority. I had no power to hire or fire and no special badge. All I had was influence. That's when I learned what leadership is. If you want to know whether you're a real leader, take away your ability to threaten someone's paycheck and see if they still follow you. That's leadership without leverage. That's when it gets real.

And now I own multiple businesses. I operate nonprofits. I coach leaders from field guys who still track mud across shop floors to boardroom execs who could season a cast iron skillet by standing next to it. I didn't arrive here because I'm a genius. I didn't skyrocket to success with a ten-year plan, a vision board, and a personal branding coach whispering affirmations in my ear. I got here because I crashed. Repeatedly. Then I stood back up, covered in sawdust and ego bruises, and asked myself, *all right, what'd I learn this time?*

So, if you've made it this far, congratulations. You know more about my failures than most of my close friends. Heck, more than some of my family. (My mom's going to read this and call me after chapter one.) And probably more than you ever expected when you picked up a leadership book.

What This Book Is and Isn't

We are now at the part where I tell you what this book is and isn't. Let me shoot straight. This book is *not* a quote-filled, highlight reel of a perfect leadership career. It's written by someone who's yelled over a diesel engine and stormed out of a meeting with steam coming out of their ears. It's not built around 4 a.m. smoothies, cold plunges, or journaling in a leather-bound notebook next to a Zen fountain. This isn't that. This is for the leader who:

- Has to win influence without a fancy title, a corner office, or anyone reporting to them.
- Works with people who think books are for college kids, corporate trainers, or someone else's problem.
- Leads with duct tape, grit, a quick prayer, and a five-gallon bucket pulled up like it's a throne.
- Solves problems with sweat, not spreadsheets, and gets more done in boots than most do in boardrooms.
- Wants to grow, but doesn't need another corporate seminar with a $12 boxed lunch and a guy in slacks saying, "Let's circle back."
- Is tired of surface-level stuff and wants the real talk. The kind that makes you better—not busier.

This book is for real leaders in the real world. Whether you run a field crew, a sales team, a kitchen, a city department, or a household full of kids who only listen when you yell, "Ice cream," you're going to find yourself in these pages. These are lessons I learned the hard way. They're stories I lived, mistakes I made, and truths I wish someone had handed me on a crumpled-up napkin fifteen years ago. So, let's make a deal.

You don't have to like me. You don't have to agree with everything I say. But if you're willing to get just a little better every day—to grow, stretch, laugh at yourself, and get back in the fight—you're my kind of leader.

By now, you've probably figured out this book isn't here to rub your shoulders, hand you a participation trophy, and whisper sweet affirmations while the leadership fairy sprinkles pixie dust all over your Outlook calendar.

This isn't a bedtime story, and it sure isn't full of leadership fables and unicorn farts. (Although for the record, I did buy a bag of those for my nephew this Christmas. They were cotton candy flavored (obviously), and yes, I'm *that* uncle. The one who shows up with something ridiculous, laughs, and somehow makes a lesson out of it.)

This is real stuff. And if no one's told you yet, let me be the first to say it: It's okay to be polarizing. In fact, if you're going to be a great leader, you kinda *have* to be. Let me explain before you throw this book across the room and mutter something about ego.

When I finally started figuring this leadership thing out (like, year twelve out of my seventeen-year transformation tour), I noticed something strange.

Not everyone liked me. And I'm not talking about the you-can't-please-everyone kind of not liking me. I mean—some people *really* didn't like me. They rolled their eyes when I spoke. They stopped inviting me to meetings. They whispered stuff like, "He's a little much," or "He thinks he knows everything."

At first, that stung because I wanted to be liked. Still do. Then I realized, I'd rather be followed than liked. When it dawned on me that standing for something—*really* standing for it, not just saying it in the safety of my truck—attracted people who believed in the same things, and repelled the ones who didn't.

And that's not a bad thing. That's what leadership does. It draws lines. It provides direction. It plants a dang flag in the ground and says, "Here's where we're going. If that's not for you, no hard feelings—but I'm not changing course to keep things cozy."

It doesn't mean you're rude or arrogant. It means you've got conviction. And conviction is what makes people trust you. It's what makes them follow you. If people don't know what you stand for, they'll never know when to stand with you.

I'll tell you something else I've learned. Real leaders don't get there by being neutral. They don't lead with disclaimers, soft edges and ten backup plans for if someone gets their feelings hurt. They lead with clarity, heart, and a little grit under their fingernails. Sometimes, that means having haters.

If you want to know what level you're leading at, count your critics. If nobody's mad at you, you're probably not doing much.

Now look—I'm not saying you should go out of your way to tick people off. Don't be that guy cutting in front of someone at the gas station to rack up a few extra haters for street cred. That's not leadership—that's being a jerk with a steering wheel. What I am saying is this: You don't need to be loud to make noise. But you do need to know who you are, what you stand for, and be okay with the fact that some folks aren't going to like it. That's part of the deal.

If you're reading this thinking, "Yeah, but Dan, I've got people who don't like how I lead." Good. You're probably doing something right. Now, if everybody hates you, it might be time for a little reflection—or at least a coffee and a reality check with someone who'll tell you the truth. If even your dog's giving you side-eye, you're probably not leading with boldness. You might be a tool with a title. But if the right people are sticking close and the wrong ones are slowly backing away, like you just mentioned you sell essential oils for wolves, you're probably right where you need to be.

Plant the Flag

Here's the goal: Be someone worth following—even if you're not everyone's cup of tea. Especially then.

The people who matter—who will go to bat for you, who will buy into the mission, who will help build something that lasts—they don't need you to be perfect. You don't need to be everyone's cup of tea. Shoot, you might not even be their cup of lukewarm truck stop coffee. That's fine. The goal isn't universal popularity—it's clarity. And the people who matter are looking for someone who doesn't change flavors every time the wind shifts. Someone who knows where they're headed, even if they occasionally hit a pothole or take a wrong exit and end up at a Taco Bell they definitely weren't aiming for.

They need you to be honest, consistent, and clear enough for them to know whether they're in or out. Be a little polarizing. Plant your flag. Say the thing. Stand for something. The moment you do, you stop leading a crowd and start leading a crew. And that's when the real magic happens.

Quick HR disclaimer (before you go full Rambo in the office): Just so we're clear—I'm not saying you should go marching into your next staff meeting, flip the conference table, and yell, "I read a leadership book and Dan Greer said I could." That's not what I'm saying at all.

Be respectful. Use wisdom. This isn't a permission slip to go off half-cocked and turn your next performance review into a WWE (World Wrestling Entertainment) monologue. What I am saying is that it's okay to have a backbone. It's okay to have a different opinion. And it's definitely okay not to agree with everyone at the table—even if that table has muffins, name tags, and someone from HR giving you the stare.

So yeah—don't blame me if you misread this book and go full cowboy. Use some discernment. Lead with confidence, not chaos. And remember, disagreement doesn't make you a bad leader. It makes you human with a spine. And guess what—people like to follow someone they can get behind!

You don't have to agree with everything I say. Shoot, you don't even have to like me. Honestly, there's a decent chance something in this book will offend you, confuse you, or make you laugh and question your entire leadership strategy mid-bite of a breakfast burrito. And that's fine. I'm not here to win a popularity contest. I'm here to tell the truth—with boots on, a little grease on my hands, and enough sarcasm to keep it fun.

But if you're willing to grow—just a little, every day—you're my kind of people. That's the challenge. Not perfection. Not a life-altering transformation by Tuesday— just a little one percent better—today, tomorrow, and the day after that.

And if you keep stacking one-percent days? The math says that makes you three-hundred and sixty-five percent better in a year, which, isn't how actual percentages work, but hey—this isn't a math book. It's a leadership book. We round up with confidence around here.

So, if you're still here, still reading, still game for more—buckle up.

Leadership with Grit

We're about to talk about leadership in a way no one else dares to; with stories that aren't filtered through a public relations (PR) team. With sweat that doesn't wipe off in the boardroom. With faith, because God's the real CEO around here. And yeah, with a little diesel smoke in the air.

Full Circle

Now, before we dive into all the grit, growth, and gut checks ahead, let's go full circle for a second. Let's go back to that parking lot. You remember me yelling like a smart-mouthed teenager who thought sarcasm was a leadership skill? The boss I called out in front of customers? The guy I assumed wasn't a real leader? Yeah. That guy.

He's now the general manager of the whole dang company. And guess who he hired to be their safety and DOT consultant? Yep. This guy. The same loudmouth kid who nearly got fired for throwing a tantrum. The same guy who thought he had it all figured out while screwing up publicly.

Not only did he bring me back—he brought me in to train his leaders. He sat me down with his board of directors for three days and said, "Dan, I don't know what we need—just bring your best and surprise us." So, I did.

I walked in, gave them the same goal setting and mindset strategies I use today with teams across the country and challenged every leader in the room to stretch beyond what they thought was possible.

You know what happened? They had one of their biggest years ever. Now, let's not get carried away. I'm not saying I was the magic ingredient in their financial casserole. There were a lot of people cooking that thing. But I was in the room. I got to stir the pot. And for a guy who once yelled across the yard like a moron with a badge and no brain, that felt like redemption.

I didn't just earn his respect—I earned a seat at the table. Not because I was perfect. Not because I nailed it the first time. Not because I read a book, memorized a quote, and suddenly became a Jedi of emotional intelligence. I got there because I finally started owning my crap. I dropped the blame. I killed the excuses. I stopped pointing fingers and started asking better questions. "What could I do differently next time?"

That question changed everything. If I can come full circle like that—from loudmouth to leader, from almost-fired to consultant—then so can you.

Leadership isn't about a title, a LinkedIn badge, or a well-lit headshot where you're pretending not to flex your jawline. Leadership is who you become when you stop blaming and start building—when you stop faking it and start owning it—when you stop chasing approval and start standing for something.

This book? It's not theory. It's not fluff. And it's definitely not written by someone pretending they've got it all together. It's real. It's tested. And it's yours now.

Before we wrap up this chapter, I want to leave you with one of the most memorable quotes I've ever heard. It didn't come from a polished author or some corporate buzzword machine. It came from a dynamite speaker I heard at a conference. He said:

> *"When you first start ANYTHING, you're going to suck. And not*
> *just a little—you're going to really suck. But if you keep going,*
> *keep learning, and refuse to quit, you'll eventually suck less. And*
> *if you stick with it long enough, one day you'll suck so little...*
> *people might actually think you're good. But make no mistake—*
> *you'll still suck compared to where you're headed next."*
> *—Garrett J. White*

I love that quote. Not because it's fancy, but because it's true. It gives us all permission to start messy, be uncomfortable, suck, and show up anyway. If you're stepping into leadership, building a business, raising kids, or diving into faith—go ahead and suck. Embrace the awkward. Swing and miss. Just don't stay there.

If you keep showing up, you'll eventually suck less. And then one day, you'll suck so little, they'll call you a pro. Deep down, you'll smile—because you'll remember the early days when you sucked big time.

If you're ready to stop sucking so bad and start becoming the leader people want to follow, keep turning the pages. This is just the beginning.

Key Takeaways from Chapter One

Own the mess before you blame the map. Leadership clicked for me the day I stopped asking "Who dropped the ball?" and started asking "What could I have done differently?" That shift turns victims into leaders.

Titles don't make leaders—temper tantrums expose wannabes. A forklift-side meltdown showed that volume is not equal to vision. If people follow you only because you sign their checks, you're a boss, not a leader.

Influence without leverage is the ultimate test. Strip away hire-and-fire power and see who still lines up behind you. If no one does, you're managing, not leading.

Be polarizing on purpose, not by accident. Plant your flag. The right crew will rally. The wrong crowd will roll their eyes—and that's healthy. Clarity beats universal comfort.

Progress = 1 percent better, repeated recklessly. Stack small wins and let the math be messy. You won't notice the compounding until someone else does.

Leadership is sweat-stained, not spotlight-polished. It's duct-tape fixes, midnight hay baling, and asking forgiveness with grease still on your hands. Boardroom theory comes second.

Victim language kills momentum. "No good help," "Above my pay grade," and similar greatest hits keep you parked in neutral. Swap them for ownership, and watch the wheels bite.

Failure is mandatory; quitting is optional. You'll suck, then suck less, then maybe get called good. Keep swinging, keep learning, and keep laughing at your cringe reels.

Faith fuels grit. Behind the diesel smoke is the deeper truth—God's the CEO. Spiritual resilience underwrites every roughneck lesson.

Redemption stories beat résumés. The same boss Dan once roasted in public later paid him to train leaders. Long games belong to people who apologize, level-up, and keep showing up.

Chapter 2 | Where Influence Lives

*Leadership isn't what the rest of the world says it is,
at least that's what my experience tells me.*

Leadership has nothing to do with your title or how many people follow you on social media. It's not about your job description, rank, or name tag. It's not even about always making the right decisions. And leadership sure isn't about how much you can get others to do for you—though, that sometimes sneaks in. To me, leadership is your ability to influence people—to help them become better than they were yesterday and to unite them in moving a shared mission forward. It's about inspiring growth, not enforcing control. Put simply, leadership is influence.

Now, I'm guessing at least one of you just pictured a slick-haired, loud-talking, 1970s car salesman with a gut the size of a spare tire, chomping on a cigar and yelling, "What's it going to take to get you into this rust bucket today?" And yeah, technically, he influenced you to buy that lemon. But was he a leader? Not even close. Sure, there are some exceptional leaders in sales—I've met a few. But like every other industry, great leaders are rare. And that guy with the cigar? He's not one of them.

Truthfully, it seems to me that most people in leadership positions aren't great leaders. Heck, many aren't even *good* leaders. Some are downright terrible. They're just people with a title and a clipboard, trying to throw their weight around like it means something. And the worst part? They often think they're amazing.

So, what is a great leader? That's not an easy question to answer because great leaders aren't usually flashy. They're not always the best speakers, the sharpest dressers, or the loudest voices in the room. Most great leaders don't even realize how great they are until someone tells them—again and again.

And that right there is one of the key traits of a great leader: humility. Great leaders are humble, because nobody wants to follow a jerk. No one wants to line up behind someone arrogant, defensive, or unwilling to admit when they've messed up. People don't follow perfection. They follow authenticity. If you want to become a great leader, the first step is simple: Be real. That's where effective leadership begins. Now that we've got that straight, let's talk about titles.

One of the most misunderstood ideas in leadership is the source of influence. It doesn't come from your title. It comes from your character. Anyone can slap a patch on their arm or get their name stitched onto a uniform. That doesn't make you a leader. That just makes you the guy who owns a shirt with a patch. You have to earn genuine influence by living it. Leadership shows up in how you treat people when there's no audience and nothing in it for you. If the only way people *listen* to you is because they're afraid *not* to, you're not leading.

I learned that lesson in a firehouse. I was barely out of high school, EMT (Emergency Medical Technician) certified, wide-eyed, and fired up to make a difference. I'd landed a shift at a small-town fire department. The setup was simple: 24-hour shifts, from 6 a.m. to 6 a.m., with the twelve hours between 6 p.m. and 6 a.m. was personal time unless a call came in. The job sounded like a dream. And for a while, it was—until I ran into a guy who confused his title for actual leadership.

Let's call him Captain Rick. That wasn't his real name, but it fits. Rick was the sort of guy who lived for his rank. When the chief and assistant chief were around, he was tolerable. But the second they left for the night, he transformed into a walking, talking ego parade. He puffed his chest, talked down to the rest of us, and treated his captain's patch like a crown. Rick tried to demand respect instead of earning it.

HIGH NOON AT STALL THREE

One night, Rick and the only other person on shift—a firefighter named Lisa—decided they were going to *go out on patrol* in the ambulance. Now, this wasn't a cop show we didn't patrol. We were supposed to stay at the station and wait for calls. But off they went—lights off, radios quiet, and enough sketchy energy between them to raise some eyebrows. Everyone knew they were in a relationship. Lisa had recently found out she was pregnant, and all signs suggested Rick was the father. It was the unspoken drama that lingered like the smell of old turnout gear.

Just before they walked out the door, Rick turned to me and said, "Greer—clean the crappers. I want them spotless when I get back." He gave no explanation or reason—just a direct order for a task to be completed during my personal time. Now listen, I've never been too proud to scrub a toilet. I believe in doing my part. But this wasn't about cleanliness. It was a power play. Rick was flexing, reminding me of my position on the totem pole. And I did what any reasonable guy with a stubborn streak would do—I cleaned the bathrooms. I gave them a solid once-over. I wiped down the mirrors, scrubbed the toilets, and mopped the floors—didn't make them sparkle like a five-star resort, but they were clean—done deal.

An hour later, they came back. Lisa's hair looked like she'd just stepped out of a convertible, and Rick's shirt had barely-holding-together vibes. Not professional. Rick marched down the stairs like a man on a mission, looked me dead in the eye, and unloaded. "What the hell is this? You call this clean? Are you joking? This is garbage!" Full-on fire and fury. Arms waving. Voice echoing. And there I stood, realizing this had nothing to do with the bathrooms.

Rick wasn't mad because the toilets weren't pristine. I entertained the idea that Rick's outrage was not at me, but an attempt to detract from his unprofessional behavior. Was he trying to bury his own guilt? He knew he had done something wrong. Not just wrong by policy, but wrong by principle. He had left the station during personal time, taken the department's ambulance out for personal reasons, and done it all under the radar. And now, back from his little field trip, he needed a distraction. A scapegoat. Someone to point at so no one would point at him.

He picked me. My best guess is that he thought if he came at me hard enough, I'd back down. Thought if he yelled loud enough, I'd forget I'd done nothing wrong. Thought if he embarrassed me, I'd stay quiet. But instead, I looked him dead in the eye and said, "Rick, I'm not your kid. I'm not your doormat. I did exactly what you asked— and I'm not about to stand here while you attempt to humiliate me to cover your own backside. You've got two choices: Cool it, or I call Chief Monroe and let him know you need a new shift mate, because I'm not sticking around for this."

And just like that, he shut up. The show was over. He didn't apologize. He didn't argue. He just walked away, because he knew. He knew exactly what he'd done. And he knew I wasn't afraid to call it out. That moment wasn't just me standing up for myself. That was me refusing to let someone use fear as a manipulation tool. It was me calling out a lie for what it was.

Turns out my gut was right. Rick was just trying to cover his own backside. But that night, something shifted in me as a leader. The same guy who used to come out swinging finally handled it with steady hands and a clear head. Funny how it played out. Rick had the title, sure—but nobody was following him. I didn't have an ounce of authority, but somehow, I had all the pull.

Rick didn't attempt to lead. He wanted to intimidate me. He didn't attempt to influence me. He wanted to silence me. Inducing fear is not a leadership strategy. It's a cover for insecurity. And that night, I exposed Rick's tactics. I will never know for sure what Rick's perspective and motivation was for his intimidating approach. I suspect he was trying to lead with fear, because he was afraid of the consequences deep down. He knew what he was doing was inappropriate. He knew it was immoral. He knew he was abusing his title and trying to protect his own reputation. And instead of owning it, he tried to bully someone into silence.

That's not leadership. That's cowardice in a captain's patch.

By pushing back on a bad boss, I shined a light on the behavior that destroys teams from the inside out. Instead of engaging in a power struggle, I refused to play the game. Real leaders don't need to lead with fear when consistency, humility, and truth are their priorities. They don't hide behind their title. They stand in front of their team. They don't bark and demand obedience. They serve to be followed.

Here's the truth most folks won't say out loud: If the only reason people follow you is because they're afraid not to—you're not a leader. You're a liability. Leadership isn't about being the loudest voice in the room or having the final word. It's about being the person others trust to do the right thing, even when no one's watching.

So, if you've been handed a title, here's your gut check: Are people following you because they believe in you, or because they're afraid of what happens if they don't? Influence lives in your choices, not your rank. And real leadership? It lives in the space where fear ends and courage begins.

You see, Rick wasn't a leader. He tried to use people for his benefit, but leadership isn't about using people. It's about serving them. It's about setting an example without barking orders.

Sadly, I've got a stack of stories just like Rick's. People with titles tried to belittle me into doing unethical things. Some folks used their authority to push me out because, according to the company president, they were jealous of the influence I had, even with people who didn't report to me. Some didn't like that I thought for myself. They wanted unquestioning loyalty. I gave them integrity instead. I don't fit the mold. Never have. And believe me, I've paid for it. I've been overlooked, shut out, and talked down to. But here's what I've come to know: God's not asking me to fit in. He's asking me to follow Him.

Real leadership isn't about climbing ladders or checking boxes. It's about stepping into who God wired you to be and using that to pull others up, not push them down.

That's where leadership actually lives. Not in titles. Not in ego. But in obedience.

DO NOT CONFORM TO THE PATTERN OF THIS WORLD, BUT BE TRANSFORMED BY THE RENEWING OF YOUR MIND.

—ROMANS 12:2

That verse isn't just about culture. It's about calling. You weren't made to blend in. You were made to be bold—to lead with guts, with grace, and with God's will driving every move you make. That's where leadership truly lives.

Influence Starts When No One's Watching

Now that we know where leadership *lives*, let's talk about where it *begins*. It starts with your character.

I was at a conference with one of my team members—not just attending but speaking. We had a booth set up, and I had one main goal: Deliver a killer presentation and build some solid relationships. (Translation: Find some high-quality leads. Let's not pretend we're just handing out hugs and handshakes here.)

Now, before I go any further, you need to know—I wasn't on the main stage. In their words, "Not all of our businesses have trucks." Translation: "Go speak in the side room while Daymond John from *Shark Tank* gets the big stage."

At first, that rubbed me the wrong way. I mean, I know what I bring to the table. I know the value I'm dropping. But hey, I get it. Not everyone sees trucks as central to their business. At least not until the DOT comes knocking. But I digress.

There I was, sitting at the booth, talking to what felt like seventy-five percent of the companies at that event. People were fired up about what we do. Still, I couldn't shake this nagging thought: *I'm speaking tomorrow, but just in a breakout session.*

That little voice kept poking at me. So, I did what I always do when that happens— I threw up a simple prayer.

"God, help me figure this out for my sanity. Please."

And just like that, God dropped an idea on me—like He usually does when I finally shut up long enough to listen.

What if you make this fun? What if you flip the script? So, I did.

I started telling people (half-joking, half-serious), "Yeah, I'm speaking tomorrow. You'll kick it off with Daymond John—he's my opening act. Then I'm generously giving y'all a lunch break to digest his wisdom—and your sandwiches—before I bring the real heat with some DOT fire." It was a game-changer. It broke the ice, got people laughing, and gave them a glimpse of who I am—a guy who's serious about helping people, but doesn't take himself too seriously.

When it came time for my presentation, I did what I always do—I over-delivered. I don't know if you've ever spoken to a decent-sized group, but sometimes, when I speak, I can feel the presence of greatness. I don't say that to sound bigheaded—I say it because I genuinely believe God shows up when you show up with purpose. I get goosebumps. I feel the Holy Spirit nudging me, almost like He's saying, *"That. Right there. They needed that."* During that session, I felt that presence multiple times. At the end of the day, they held a wrap-up session. Nothing fancy—just a few interactive polls where attendees voted on their phones. Then, the event organizer asked if anyone had any feedback on the breakout sessions. Some guy grabbed the mic. I didn't know him. I hadn't planted him (though, in that moment, I wished I had).

He said, "I have to say something because I sat through the DOT session today, and let me tell you ...."

My heart dropped. He paused for dramatic effect, and my brain hit DEFCON 5. What's he going to say? Did I tank it? Was it boring? Is he filing a complaint with the HR police?

Then he said, "It was the best DOT presentation I have ever sat through. This guy was on fire! I had to keep up just to catch everything he was throwing out. I didn't feel like it dragged at all—in fact, I wanted to record it so I could watch it again and soak up more of what he said."

Boom. I nearly melted.

Then the president of the association asked, "Is Dan in the room?"

I raised my hand—awkward as ever—feeling like a middle schooler being picked to read out loud.

And then it happened. The entire room stood up and gave me a standing ovation. Now, I've spoken on a lot of stages, but that moment hit differently because I knew I'd connected. I knew I had served well. And I knew God had answered that simple prayer I whispered the day before.

I'm telling you all this because leadership begins with character. It's not about the breakout room, or the main stage. It's about who you are when no one's watching—and even more when everyone is.

If people trust your character, they'll trust you to lead them. They'll listen. They'll lean in. They'll open up, because they know you're not out to manipulate them—you're out to serve them.

Later that night, there was a reception. I stuck around (free appetizers and networking— yes, please). The team member who came with me and I split up to cover more ground—divide and conquer.

She ended up sitting with a guy we'd met the night before on a rooftop mixer—the guy who made it pretty clear he wanted nothing to do with DOT. He'd blown us off so fast it gave me whiplash. But that night, they got to talking. No pressure. Just real conversation. And by the end of the evening, he walked up to me and said, "Dan, I've got to tell you something."

(Once again, bracing myself.)

He continued, "When I met you last night, I could tell you were a genuinely good guy. But the second you said you do DOT, I shut down. I didn't want a pitch. I didn't want another scam. But then I went to your presentation. I listened. And I realized—I need to work with you. You didn't pitch me yesterday. You didn't push anything tonight. You didn't even sell from the stage. Heck, you're not even pitching me now, but I'm over here begging to work with you. I can tell that even if I couldn't pay you, you'd help me anyway. That tells me everything I need to know about your character. And I know you're the person who can lead my team and fix our DOT compliance."

Man. After that, I almost couldn't fit my head through the door.

But again—I'm not telling you this to brag. I'm telling you to illustrate something powerful: People can see your character in how you live. Character speaks louder than anything you'll ever have to say. Your character is your brand.

People don't follow people in charge—they follow people they trust. They follow people who have their best interests at heart. That's the difference between someone who barks orders and someone others choose to follow.

And listen, if I'd gone home and never followed through on my promises, all of that influence and trust would be gone—just like that. Building character isn't an event. It's a lifestyle. You have to keep showing up. You have to mean what you say and do what you promised. Let your character shine, and you won't need to chase followers. They'll come find you.

Influence From the Middle of the Pack

Let's shift gears for a minute and rewind to a time before I started my company—back when I was just the *DOT guy* for someone else's operation.

There's something about having *DOT* in your job title. The moment drivers and operations personnel hear it, they assume you're the enemy—like you're holed up in some dark office, plotting how to ruin their week with paperwork and policy changes. I was a walking clipboard with a corporate logo and a bullseye on my back.

And to be fair, I get it. I was the outsider with the rules. I was the one saying, "Hey, we can't do that," or "We've got to fix this," and they thought I was sent down from the crystal palace to make their lives harder. Not exactly a recipe for popularity. But I was trying to keep the company out of trouble.

Like I've said before, I don't do things the way most people do. I tend to take the scenic route—the one with potholes and no GPS but a better view. So, I said *yes* when the president of that company asked me to take over DOT compliance right after they got audited, mind you.

What he didn't know—and what I barely knew myself—is that I had zero DOT experience. I'd never been in a role like that before. And you know what? That probably worked in my favor because I had to learn fast and learn by doing.

One of the first things I learned was that the operations people didn't want me at their safety meetings. They definitely didn't want me in their financial meetings. Honestly, they didn't want me near anything that mattered. I was corporate—but with absolutely no authority. I couldn't fire anyone. I couldn't pull a driver off the road. I was a compliance cop with no badge, cuffs, or backup.

But I had one thing going for me: persistence.

So, I started showing up to work at 6 a.m., to catch the tail end of the daily crew safety meetings and the weekly safety huddles that anyone who worked in the field was required to attend. At first, I didn't say much—just introduced myself and stuck around in case anyone had questions. At the time I didn't realize that I was doing the most powerful thing a leader can do: building trust by showing up consistently.

Looking back, I get why they were skeptical. I was a corporate guy who suddenly popped into crew meetings and watched everything. I'd be suspicious too if someone from HR or compliance started lurking in the back of my meetings without explanation.

But my main reason for being there was simple—I needed driver documents, and the only way get them was to track down the drivers myself. They weren't exactly lining up by my office door. If I wanted to catch them, I had to go where they were, which meant showing up at those safety meetings, clipboard in hand, pretending not to look desperate.

One day, I asked the operations team if I could share a quick DOT fact during the meeting. Reluctantly, they said *yes*. The ops manager looked at me like I had two heads and said, "Sure, Dan, but we only have two minutes."

I introduced myself again. The ops manager was in the back of the room, tapping his wrist like I was wasting air. I shared one DOT tip I had learned that week. Then I wrapped up saying, "I'll be around for the next thirty minutes if anyone wants to chat or ask questions." Crickets. Not a soul came over. I stood there like a pig in a prom dress and bright red lipstick—dressed up with nowhere to go. But I didn't quit.

The next week I went back. And to my surprise, the ops manager said, "Glad you're here. Think you can share another DOT tip with the team?" Uh … heck yeah, I can! I gave another quick tip, offered to hang around, and this time, one driver came over to chat.

His name was Joe.

Joe was … let's just say he was *seasoned*. Old-school. Gruff. Suspicious of anything that didn't involve a wrench or diesel fuel. But he walked over, grilled me for a few minutes, then walked off without a word—no high five. No thanks. Just a nod, a little grunt of approval or dismissal—and then he vanished. Progress, baby.

Week after week, I kept showing up. And little by little, things began to change.

One grunt closer to trust

The ops manager started introducing me with enthusiasm: "Hey guys, Dan's back with another DOT tip." And instead of one person coming to talk, now it was three. They'd even say "Thanks" or "Catch you later" when they walked off. I was practically a celebrity. Not Daymond John-level, but hey—I'll take it.

By the second month, folks at every level started asking me questions. Managers, foremen, laborers—even folks who didn't drive trucks wanted to know more. And I did my best to answer them. I wasn't trying to be the smartest guy in the room. I was trying to be the most helpful.

Then, about eight months into this new rhythm, something crazy happened. The division manager walked into my office and said, "Dan, I don't know how you did it, but my team likes you. They trust you. And I'm having a heck of a time getting them to follow these new procedures. Is there any way you can roll it out to them? I think they'll listen to you."

Now, this had nothing to do with DOT. It was about a new timecard system. But I said *yes*, because once you build influence, people will follow you—even outside your lane.

The next morning, I showed up at the safety meeting. I shook hands, cracked a few jokes, did my usual good-to-see-you-guys thing. The division and ops managers introduced me like I was about to drop life-changing truth bombs.

I gave it to them straight: "Hey guys, we've got a new way to handle timecards. I know change is annoying, but this one's going to make life easier once you get used to it. Let's give it a shot."

I didn't expect much. Honestly, I figured they'd ignore it and go back to the old way.

Then, a few days later, I got a call from the president's secretary.

"Dan, are you in town?"

"Yes."

"The president would like to see you in his office. Immediately."

Well, shoot. Now I'm thinking I'm in trouble. I walked in and the executive team is there—the president, vice president, and division manager—full boardroom vibes. The president looked at me and said, "Dan, I heard you've been going to safety meetings. What made you start doing that?"

I panicked a little, but I told the truth. "Sir, I needed a better way to get the documents I needed from the drivers. And I wanted to help them understand DOT better, not so they'd see me as the bad guy, but so they'd see this stuff matters."

He nodded. Then came the longest pause in the history of humanity. I swear the Grand Canyon was still a ditch when he started, and by the time he finished, it had eroded into a national treasure.

"Dan, have you seen the timecard report from last week?"

I said, "No sir, I didn't even know there was a report."

"Well, before you talked to the crew, we were getting 3-8 percent of employees to fill them out correctly. After your meeting? We hit 76 percent. What do you think about that?"

I shrugged and said, "Maybe they were just ready to change, and it had nothing to do with me." He didn't buy that for one second. He looked me dead in the eye and said, "I gave that same presentation. Nothing changed. You gave it, and now we're at 76 percent."

Once you earn influence by building trust, people will follow you—even in areas outside your job title. You don't need a badge to lead. You don't need permission to make an impact. When people believe in you, they'll listen, change, and grow.

Influence comes from character, consistency, and care. And sometimes the loudest leaders aren't on the stage. They're the ones who showed up quietly at 6 a.m., asked good questions, and earned the right to be heard.

Influence Requires Courage

Now, courage—that's a whole different conversation. The courage I'm talking about is not the action-movie style where someone runs in slow motion into gunfire and walks away unscathed (although that's great, too). I'm talking about the quiet, everyday leadership it takes when you know everyone's watching and waiting to see what you do.

Courage is not natural. It's not built in. You won't find it in your back pocket. And it doesn't supernaturally appear in a calm, confident voice and a cape. Courage shows up when your knees are shaking, your palms are sweaty, and you are scared out of your mind—and you step forward anyway. According to the *Merriam-Webster Dictionary*, courage is the "mental or moral strength to venture, persevere, and withstand danger, fear, or difficulty."

John Wayne said, "Courage is being scared to death, but saddling up anyway."

I say, "Courage is looking fear in the face, grinning a little, cracking a joke, and doing the hard thing anyway because it's the right thing to do."

Courage is the grit to lead when you feel unqualified and the faith to act even when the outcome isn't guaranteed. It's going first so others are confident following. Nobody embodies this gutsy, creative courage like Captain Dodge in the movie *Down Periscope*.

If you've never seen it, add it to your movie list—right after you finish this book. Seriously. It's required viewing for real-world leadership training. Plus, it's hilarious.

Captain Dodge, played by Kelsey Grammer, is handed command of a beat-up diesel submarine and a crew of outcasts, weirdos, and walking HR violations. It's the Navy's version of the Island of Misfit Toys. His mission is to test Navy defenses in a simulated war game.

Everyone expected him to fail. And the top brass wanted him to fail. But Dodge is built differently. One scene perfectly captures courageous leadership. The Navy's best attack sub—a high-tech, fully loaded, nuclear-powered beast—is hunting Dodge and his old diesel rust bucket. Deep in enemy waters with a storm rolling in, pressure is mounting. No one would blame him for giving up or surrendering. But he doesn't panic, yell, blame the crew, or radio for help. Dodge does what real leaders do under pressure.

He gets creative—and courageous. And here's the best part: He doesn't tell anyone the plan.

He picks up the intercom and calmly says, "Howard, I need an extension cord, a drop light, and a roll of duct tape." Understandably confused, Howard calls back.

"What is this, a scavenger hunt?"

Then Dodge looks over at Jackson, a former basketball star who had flamed out of the Navy once already, and says to him with a grin, "Mr. Jackson, you look like you could use a little exercise." In the next scene, they're topside in the middle of a raging storm. Waves are crashing. The wind is howling. Rain is coming in sideways. And there's Jackson, climbing up the periscope tower while lightning flashes behind him, like a scene out of *Braveheart at Sea.* His mission? Duct tape the drop light to the top of the periscope. That's it. That's the plan. No missiles. No sonar tricks. It's just a drop light and some creative crazy. Meanwhile, down below, Dodge tells the crew to raise the periscope and plug it in. And then, without skipping a beat, he shouts, "All hands on deck!"

Cut to the sub's hull. The entire crew and band of rejects are singing *Louie Louie* at full volume. It was painfully off-key, off-beat, and offensively bad. But the crew is all in. And it works. The enemy sub picks up the sound, sees the light flickering above the waves, and assumes they've stumbled across drunk fishermen lost in the storm.

The sonar tech proudly reports, "Captain, we've got them!"

And the other commander—thinking they've wasted all that effort on civilians—sighs and says, "Great work, crew. We just chased down a bunch of beered-up fishermen." The enemy sub turns and heads in the other direction.

Boom. Dodge wins.

He didn't out-gun, out-tech, or outrank them. He out-led them. That's influence. That's leadership with courage at the helm. Dodge never explained everything. He didn't need to. His crew trusted him because they'd seen his courage in action.

That's what makes people follow you—not the patch on your sleeve, but the grit in your gut and the calm in your chaos. That brand leadership shows up when you need it most.

That scene stuck with me because I've been that leader—out-gunned, out-matched, and standing in front of a room of people who didn't want to hear a word I had to say.

That's what it was like when I was the DOT guy standing in the back of the room at safety meetings, feeling I didn't belong. Whenever I raised my hand to speak, cracked a joke, offered a helpful tip, or made myself available by showing up early, I chose courage. One quiet act at a time.

It didn't feel heroic. Most of the time, I felt out of place and unwelcome—like a new kid at lunch trying to join the table full of guys who've been trading inside jokes since 1998. It was awkward, but I kept at it, and little by little, the guys started to see that I wasn't there to flex, catch them messing up, or throw the book at them. I was there to serve, protect, and lead from the back of the room before asking for a seat at the table.

Like Dodge's crew finally busted out singing *Louie Louie* at full blast in the middle of a storm, these guys eventually let their guard down. They started trusting me and asking questions before they made a move they were uncertain about. They cared about my heart more than my credentials.

Courage like that showed up the day I asked my wife to marry me. I'll be honest. That was easily one of the scariest things I've ever done.

I had this big plan. The sky was bright blue, birds were chirping, and flowers had started to bloom the day I took Jenna to the river bottom on my grandparents' land. There was this big pond, and the geese showed up with their babies like they'd been waiting backstage for their cue. I swear God sent them in for dramatic effect. The setting was perfect. I'm down on one knee, my heart pounding like a diesel engine. I'm waiting for her to turn around so I can hit her with the most important question of my life.

And just as she turns around—what happens? I drop the ring. More than an *oops* drop, it was a full-on lost-it-in-the-dirt, panic-sweeping-with-my-hand drop. I'm on one knee, shoving dirt around like a five-year-old making mud pies. Jenna's standing there thinking, *Aw, look at him ... playing in the dirt. He's so cute"* She didn't even realize I was proposing. Why would she?

To make it worse, I was so nervous I couldn't even get the words out. Me. Speechless. Can you imagine that? I finally found the ring, held it up, stumbled through a sentence that was supposed to be a proposal, and somehow, miraculously, she still said *yes*. That *yes* changed everything.

Here's what I learned that day: Courage doesn't wait until you're ready. It just shows up. It shoves dirt around and sweats through your shirt and hopes to heaven the moment still counts.

Courage isn't a once-in-a-lifetime burst of bravery. It's a habit. A posture. A choice you make long before the world notices. Courage is dropping the ring, brushing yourself off, and still asking the question that will change your life, regardless of the answer.

Some of the absolute best things in life only happen after you take a step that scares you. The step that has you asking, "What if I screw this up?" is the one you need to face head-on. What about you? What's the next step you're afraid to take but deep down, know you need to? You might have a crazy idea brewing. Maybe you're staring at a team that needs a new direction. Is it possible you're the one person in a meeting full of silence who's supposed to speak the hard truth? Do it. Step up. Speak up. Take the risk. Sing the dang song if you have to.

Be the guy in the sub who breaks protocol, tapes a light to the periscope, and leads his team through a storm with duct tape and off-key singing. When you act boldly, go first, and lead with courage even when it looks ridiculous, you win the crew, which matters more than the battle. And that's what leadership is all about, you hit the dirt, but the moment still matters.

Influence is Earned, not Given

We live in a world addicted to instant gratification. We want fast results, overnight success, and a crowd of followers with the swipe of a finger. And leadership? Many people treat it the same way. They expect influence to come automatically with a job title or a business card. But real influence doesn't work like that. It's not delivered with your promotion or built into your email signature. Influence is earned, and it's earned over time.

Plenty of people in my life thought they were great leaders. They talked big and carried themselves like kings. But when you stripped away the bravado, they were just bosses. And there's a huge difference between a boss and a leader. Bosses give orders. Leaders earn trust.

It takes me a while to follow someone. I don't hand over my respect easily. I need to see who they are when the pressure's on. I've worked for companies where the person in charge was merely the loudest voice in the room. But every once in a while, someone earns that title. Not because they demand it, but because they prove it. One of those people was a man named Ezra.

Ezra was the president of a company I worked for—one he built from the ground up. Over time, that company exploded to over 1,200 employees, and Ezra led it with heart. He loved the people. He loved the community. He hated the day they had to assign employee numbers, because to him, no one was ever just a number.

But I'll be honest with you. When I first started working there, I didn't like him. I didn't even know him, but I didn't trust him. Perhaps it was because of his success. Maybe it was the way others talked about him. Or maybe I wasn't mature enough to recognize what a leader worth following looked like. Whatever the reason, I kept my distance.

That went on for a year or two. I showed up, did my job, and collected a paycheck. Nothing more. However, I then reached a turning point. I began to care about the mission. I started to serve instead of coast. And when I made that shift, everything started to change.

I began to pay attention. I started observing Ezra, not just listening to what he said but watching how he carried himself. And that's when I realized: The man lived what he preached.

Eventually, I built up the nerve to knock on his office door.

"Hey Ezra," I said. "You got a few minutes?"

He looked up, smiled, and said, "Always, Dan. What's on your mind?"

"I want to grow," I told him. "I think you're someone I can learn from. Got any book recommendations?"

He didn't even hesitate. "Go read *How to Win Friends and Influence People* by Dale Carnegie," he said. "It's old, but it's gold. And you need it."

Now, in my head, I'm thinking, *I don't need any book.* But I smiled, said thank you, and left his office. Then I bought the digital-age, updated version of the book because, well, it sounded newer. I read it. A month later, I went back to Ezra.

"Hey Ezra, remember that book you told me to read? I finished it."

"Oh yeah? What'd you think?"

"It was all right. Honestly, I think I've learned more from some podcasts lately."

He grinned and asked, "Which version did you read?"

I told him. He laughed.

"Dan, you bought the wrong book. That one's okay, but the original is the one that changes lives. Go read the original one."

So, I did. I bought the first version of *How to Win Friends and Influence People,* and this time, I read it with an open heart. That book rocked me. It didn't just give me leadership principles; it gave me insight into people, connection, and influence. It gave me the wisdom I didn't realize I needed.

I went back to Ezra and told him, "Okay—you were right. That book's a game-changer. Especially for someone like me, with responsibility but no real authority."

Our relationship deepened after that. I asked questions. He gave guidance. What I didn't know at the time was that during one of the most challenging seasons in the company, and layoffs were on the table, Ezra was the only person on the leadership team who fought to keep me. Ezra saw something in me. He saw potential, grit, and the future. And he stood in the gap.

After he sold the company and stayed on in a transitional role, we kept in touch. Our relationship continued to grow. Today, I still reach out to him for wisdom and ideas. I still look for ways to serve him and his family. I still trust him. But that trust wasn't handed out—it was earned.

Ezra didn't earn my loyalty because he had a title. He earned it by showing up, telling the truth, and caring about people. And I didn't earn his mentorship by asking for it. I earned it by being consistent, by putting in the work, and by staying teachable. That's what leadership looks like.

Now I'll tell you about another leader in my life—one I *paid* to follow. Yes, you read that right. Not "licensed a platform." Not "purchased a product." I paid real money to follow a man before I even knew if I liked him. And if you know me, you know that's not something I do lightly. His name? Russell Brunson.

A few years ago, I had no idea who he was. I was following Jenna Kutcher at the time, and she was promoting a free virtual event with Dean Graziosi, Tony Robbins, and some guy named Russell Brunson. I knew Tony. Dean sounded familiar. But Russell? No clue. Looked like the kid who refills the coffee in the green room.

But I paid a couple of bucks and showed up for that event anyway. I logged in on my laptop, cleared the calendar, and told my family I was *attending a business conference*. (Translation: a meeting on my laptop at the kitchen table, clad in pajama pants, with a notebook for good measure). Tony came out and brought the fire like only Tony can. Dean was solid. Then Russell showed up. No lights. No fog machines. No big stage presence. Just a guy calmly teaching. Telling stories. Dropping value. Not flashy. Just consistent. Authentic.

I wasn't instantly sold. But I couldn't ignore how clear he was, how much ground he covered, and how easy he made it feel. So, I started digging. I found his podcast. I listened, took notes, and signed up for ClickFunnels. And then canceled it. Signed up again. Canceled it again. (You get the picture.) Not because the software didn't work—but because I wasn't sure he worked. I wasn't looking for a flashy brand or a magic trick—I was looking for a leader. And I wasn't ready to buy in until I saw consistency over time.

I bought and read one of his books, *DotCom Secrets*. That's when things shifted. I couldn't stop reading. Every chapter hit. I underlined it like it was a Bible study. I tried ClickFunnels again, joined one of his challenges, got pumped, and started seeing results.

Then, in true fashion, I canceled again. (By this point, I think ClickFunnels was waiting for my monthly back-and-forth.)

But here's what happened that made all the difference: Every single time I interacted with anything Russell did, the value was unreal. I'd walk away from a podcast episode with a page of notes. Leave a virtual event with a better plan than I had after a paid coaching session with someone else. He over-delivered on every challenge, workshop, and book.

And that's why, when it came time to invest in him as a leader, I didn't hesitate. He'd already proven he was worth it.

I bought a ticket to Funnel Hacking Live—think rock concert meets business bootcamp. Over 4,000 entrepreneurs packed into a high-energy, four-day event hosted by Russell Brunson. It's loaded with powerful content, massive inspiration, and some of the sharpest business minds you'll ever meet. And while it cost close to a thousand bucks, I wasn't there to learn funnels. I was there to see if this guy actually lived what he preached. And man, he did not disappoint.

He didn't just teach frameworks. He shared his mission. His why. He talked about his faith, family, and his values. And he cried—on stage—in front of thousands, because he cared that much about the people he was serving. That's when I stopped listening with my head and started listening with my heart.

After that, I devoured everything—*Expert Secrets, Traffic Secrets*, more challenges, more training. I rejoined ClickFunnels and joined his mastermind group. At that point, it wasn't about funnels anymore. It was about following a man who had consistently shown up with integrity and value—a guy who had earned my trust.

Which brings me to Phoenix, Arizona in July—a place where the sidewalk gives you second-degree burns and the weather app says "Don't." We attended a family mastermind event, and between sessions, my wife, kids, and I floated in the lazy river at the resort.

And out of nowhere, Russell floats up. No camera. No script. No one filming a testimonial. Just him in a tube with his family behind him.

He saw me, smiled, and said, "Hey Dan!"

Then he looked me in the eye—still bobbing in the water—and said something I'll never forget:

"What can we do better for you?"

No ego. No pitch. No agenda. Just a leader checking in with another man with full attention and sincerity.

And that's when it hit me: This guy never stopped earning the influence he already had.

He could have waved and floated on by. No one would have blamed him. But he didn't. He paused, looked me in the eye, and in front of both of our families asked how he could do better.

And it didn't take anything away from his family either. It showed his kids—and mine—what humble, service-based leadership looks like in real time. A few kind words, a little laughter, then back to enjoying the day. But that moment? It stuck. Especially for my oldest son. He saw something I'd been trying to teach for years: that real leadership isn't about always being *on*. It's about always being real.

That was the moment I stopped seeing Russell Brunson as merely a mentor and entrepreneur. That's when he became a leader I'd follow anywhere. Great leaders don't just teach from a stage. They live it in the floaties. They pause to ask the right questions when no one's filming. And they show everyone watching—especially the next generation—how to lead with heart. They never stop earning the trust they've already gained. Real influence doesn't come from being above people. It comes from being with them—even in the lazy river. So, let me ask you. Are you showing up like that for your people?

Are you coasting in leadership, or are you still paddling, still asking, still serving, still earning it? Influence isn't locked in after one good speech. It's confirmed in the lazy rivers of life—when no one expects you to ask, but you do anyway. And that's what makes you unforgettable. And if you want to build lasting, earned, loyal-to-the-end influence, ask, "How can I serve you better?" Then stick around long enough to listen to the answer. I challenge you to be honest with yourself:

Are you trying to demand that people follow you? Or are you living in a way that earns trust? Showing them you're worth following usually results in people doing so— when they're ready. Instead of focusing on how many people are following you, focus on how consistently you're showing up. Once someone decides to follow you, what you do next matters even more.

Let's Anchor This in the Word

WHEN I FIRST CAME TO YOU, DEAR BROTHERS AND SISTERS, I DIDN'T USE LOFTY WORDS AND IMPRESSIVE WISDOM TO TELL YOU GOD'S SECRET PLAN. FOR I DECIDED THAT WHILE I WAS WITH YOU I WOULD FORGET EVERYTHING EXCEPT JESUS CHRIST, THE ONE WHO WAS CRUCIFIED. I CAME TO YOU IN WEAKNESS—TIMID AND TREMBLING. AND MY MESSAGE AND MY PREACHING WERE VERY PLAIN. RATHER THAN USING CLEVER AND PERSUASIVE

> SPEECHES, I RELIED ONLY ON THE POWER OF THE HOLY SPIRIT. I DID THIS SO YOU WOULD
> TRUST NOT IN HUMAN WISDOM BUT IN THE POWER OF GOD.
> —1 CORINTHIANS 2:1–5 (NLT)

Read that again if you need to. Paul didn't say, "Hey, I showed up with charisma, an impressive résumé, and a slick five-step plan." Nope. He said, and I'm paraphrasing, "I came trembling ... but I showed up." Real leadership shows up even when you don't feel qualified.

We've all been there. Someone hands you a task, a team, or a title, and your first thought is, "Who, me? I'm not ready for this." But here's the beautiful truth: God doesn't call the qualified. He qualifies the called. Read that again.

God doesn't call the qualified. He qualifies the called. If you're waiting to feel ready before you lead, you're going to wait a long time. God's not looking for perfection—he's looking for obedience. He's looking for someone who will show up even when they are exhausted and feel like they can't take another step. That's how he helps you become a leader and gain the influence you need. It won't happen all at once. It will happen when you are about ready to give up! God will use you where you are—with what you have—when your heart is surrendered. One of the best examples of this is David—before the crown, before Goliath, before anybody knew his name.

When the prophet Samuel came to Jesse's house to anoint the next king of Israel, Jesse lined up all of his sons—except David. He didn't even bother calling him in from the field. Talk about being overlooked. But Samuel kept going down the line, and God kept saying, "Nope. Not him."

Finally, Samuel had to ask, "Do you have any more sons?" And Jesse's like, "Well, yeah. David. But he's just out watching the sheep." That's the one God wanted.

> MAN LOOKS AT THE OUTWARD APPEARANCE, BUT THE LORD LOOKS AT THE HEART.
> —1 SAMUEL 16:7

David was leading before he had a title. He was talking to God when nobody else was watching, leading sheep, writing psalms, and defending the flock. When the lion came, he didn't run. When the bear came, he didn't fold. When the giant showed up, David stepped forward while every qualified warrior backed away. But get this—he didn't step up for glory. He wasn't chasing a promotion. He wasn't trying to go viral for slaying giants. He stepped up because someone was dragging God's name through the mud.

Goliath wasn't just taunting Israel—he was talking trash about David's God. And David wasn't having it. It was like he said, "No way, José. You don't get to run your mouth about my God and leave standing."

That was the turning point. David showed up and fought for God's honor because God's name mattered more than his own. He didn't walk onto the battlefield with fancy armor or a five-star recommendation. He walked in it—because God had already chosen him. With only a sling, five smooth stones, and a heart that had already been trained in obedience and tested in faith, David went to battle for God.

And why was he able to take on Goliath? David had been leading long before anyone called him a leader. He'd been showing up in private before God promoted him in public. And here's the part that lights me up:

- If you feel like you're *just a shepherd*
- If no one's noticing what you're doing
- If you feel underqualified, overlooked, or underappreciated

Good. You're exactly the person God loves to use. He doesn't look for perfect résumés. He looks for obedient hearts. So, if you're leading in the shadows right now. If you're pouring into your team, family, and coworkers, and no one is clapping yet, keep going, because God sees what others don't.

He's developing your strength and deepening your faith. He's training you in the pasture before he sends you to the palace. Once you realize your influence is more about your character than your qualifications, you'll stop waiting to be promoted and start leading right where you are. And when that happens, you won't just earn influence with people. You'll walk in the influence that heaven backs.

Becoming a Person of Influence: Action Steps That Work

All right. We've talked about what influence is, where it starts, and how it's earned. You've seen it in my life, in Russell's story, in David's journey, and in scripture. Now let's get practical.

You're probably reading this and thinking "Okay Dan, I get it, but what do I do now?" Here's your blueprint. These aren't complicated or flashy. But they're powerful—because they work.

1. Start showing up consistently.

Be reliable. People don't follow the guy who shows up when it's convenient. They follow the one who's there rain or shine, early or late, in the highs and the lows. You want influence? Show up when nobody else does. Be the person you would want to follow. That's where trust is built, and trust is the currency of influence.

2. Lead by example.

It's easy to tell people what to do. It's harder—but way more impactful—to show them. If you want others to work harder, outwork them. If you want others to grow, let them see you growing. If you want your kids, your crew, or your team to serve with integrity, be the living, breathing example of that integrity. People follow examples more than instruction.

3. Speak encouragement, not just commands.

We've all seen leaders who bark orders. We've all ignored them. But leaders who speak life and call out the gold in others are the leaders people line up to follow. You don't need a big speech—sometimes it's as simple as, "Hey—I saw how you handled that. That was solid." You'd be amazed at what one sentence of genuine encouragement can do. So be the voice that builds others up—not the one that wears them down.

4. Stay humble and teachable.

Nothing kills influence faster than pride. The second you think, *I've got this. I don't need feedback,* is the second your leadership skill development stalls. Humble leaders are magnetic because they make space for others to grow with them. They admit mistakes, ask questions, and aren't afraid to say, "I don't know—but I'll find out." Stay teachable. No matter how far you go or how high you climb, keep learning. Even Jesus, the greatest leader of all time, served first.

5. Ask God to increase your influence for his glory, not your ego.

Let's get real here: We all like to be recognized. We all want to be seen. But true influence isn't about you—it's about who you point people toward. So, if you're asking God for more influence, ask him to make you a steward, not a superstar. Say, "God, give me the opportunity to impact people—but keep my heart aligned with you." The influence God blesses us with is the kind that honors him. You were made to lead, serve, and build. And the more you lean into that with humility and obedience, the more God will entrust with you.

The Bottom Line

You don't need to be famous to be impactful. You don't need a stage to be influential. You need to show up, lead well, and keep your heart in check. True influence isn't about being followed—it's about being *worth* following.

Wrap Up: Where Influence Really Lives

So, let's land this plane—well, submarine, in this case.

You've seen throughout this chapter that real leadership isn't about authority—it's about impact. It's not about how loud you talk or how many stripes you wear. It's about how you serve, show up, and build trust that lasts longer than titles ever will.

If you need one final picture of what that looks like, go back to Captain Tom Dodge, our unlikely hero from *Down Periscope*. Remember, it started with a crew of misfits, a rusty diesel sub, and Navy brass who wanted him to fail. But through guts, creativity, humility, and a little karaoke, Dodge led them to victory—not with brute force, but with earned influence. But it's the *end* of the movie that seals the deal.

After winning the war games and proving everyone wrong, Admiral Winslow meets Dodge at the port. It's the moment Dodge had been working toward his whole career—finally, a chance to get a modern, top-tier sub and a proper command.

And the Admiral says, "Captain Dodge, I regret to inform you, you will *not* be receiving command of a sea class submarine." You can see it in Dodge's face—he's crushed but composed. Then the Admiral continues: "Instead, you'll be attending the launch of your new Wolf Class submarine this Friday at Norfolk. And this time, I'm giving you a crew *worthy* of your leadership and tactics." Boom. The recognition. The promotion. The dream come true.

But what happens next? Dodge declines. "Sir, with all due respect, I wouldn't be in line for that command if it weren't for my current crew." He gave up the big prize of a shiny promotion and status upgrade because he refused to abandon the people who helped him get there. Let that sink in.

A real leader doesn't climb over people to rise—they bring people with them.

Dodge didn't just win the war game. He won the loyalty of his team. Sacrifice. Integrity. Loyalty. But it takes a real leader to *earn* the respect where people will follow you into a storm—even while singing *Louie Louie* off-key.

Captain Dodge didn't chase a title. He built trust. He didn't use people—he empowered them. And in the end, when the world offered him a bigger platform, he made a choice that proved what mattered most—his crew, character, and calling.

All those lessons from a military comedy hardly anyone remembers. (*Maybe I should be getting royalties for this chapter. Hahaha!*) But you know what? Maybe that's the best part, because it proves you don't need to be in some grand movie, on a big stage, or in a viral post to be a great leader. You just need to lead like Captain Dodge.

- Show up.
- Fight for your people.
- Stay humble.
- And when the spotlight hits? Shine it on the ones who got you there.

Key Takeaways from Chapter Two

 **Leadership isn't a title—it's trust.** Your patch, your position, or your popularity doesn't make you a leader. People follow character, not credentials.

 **Influence is earned, not handed out.** You can't demand loyalty—you prove you're worth it by showing up, standing firm, and serving first.

 **Humility builds more influence than hype ever will.** Nobody wants to follow a loud, arrogant jerk. They want real. Be honest. Own your mistakes. Stay teachable.

 **Character leads when no one's watching—and even more when everyone is.** The real test of leadership isn't the stage. It's the everyday moments when nobody's clapping.

 **Courage doesn't always feel brave—it just shows up anyway.** Whether it's standing up to a bad boss, taping a drop light to a periscope, or proposing with dirt under your nails—courage leads even when you're terrified.

 **Leadership doesn't need permission.** You can lead from the back of the room. From the middle of the pack. From the DOT desk nobody respects—yet.

 **Consistency creates credibility.** Show up early. Stick around late. Be the guy they know they can count on. That's how trust is built over time.

 **Real leaders serve the crew before they chase the command.** Like Captain Dodge, the goal isn't a fancier sub—it's fighting for the people who got you here.

 **God qualifies the called—He's not looking for perfect.** You don't need to have it all together. You just need to be obedient. Be faithful with what you've got, right where you are.

 **Leadership that lasts lives in the lazy river.** Anyone can give a speech. But real influence happens when you float up, look someone in the eye, and ask, "How can I serve you better?"

Chapter 3 | Extreme Ownership

Success doesn't start with pointing fingers. It starts with pointing thumbs.

Let me take you back to the county yard. I was a blade operator, but depending on the day, I could be anything from a water truck driver to a pothole patcher to the guy babysitting a giant tank of P90 oil. If you've never smelled P90, imagine the lovechild of asphalt and skunk musk that's been baking in the sun for three days. My wife hated it. I mean, *hated it*. I went through washing machine drain pumps like normal people go through socks. We kept two backup pumps on hand, because I was blowing the thing out at least four times a year. Yeah. It was that bad.

One day, right before Thanksgiving, I got handed one of those *good luck* jobs while everyone else was off enjoying our department potluck. My task was to keep the P90 oil heated over the long, holiday weekend so it didn't turn into a useless, tar-flavored gelatin. Simple enough in theory. But this wasn't a set-it-and-forget-it situation. We had a big, dual-tank setup, and you had to manually circulate the oil between the front and back tanks to keep it at the proper temperature. That meant climbing up and down the tanks several times a day, double-checking gauges, opening and closing valves, and babysitting a volatile barrel of lava. All the while, your coworkers are stuffing their faces with green bean casserole.

Now, listen. I had it dialed in. Or so I thought.

I got everything set up in circulation mode, confirmed the flow, and gave it an extra once-over before heading inside to grab a quick plate of food. I wasn't being careless or cutting corners. But, somewhere in that setup, something wasn't right. Maybe a lever didn't seat right. Maybe I fat-fingered a valve, or maybe (and this was my theory at the time) someone with the maturity level of a toddler and the intelligence of a potato came by and shut a valve to mess with me.

Sabotage at that job wasn't off the table. The place had more drama than a high school lunchroom and fewer adults than a kindergarten field trip. And I was no better than those guys. I was still learning what it meant to be a man and a leader. Anyway ... back to the mess.

By the time I got back outside, I noticed the smell first. Then the puddle. About 300 gallons of hot oil had overflowed and oozed down the side of the tank, like something out of a B-rated horror movie. It wasn't catastrophic, but it was bad enough. And trust me, there's no hiding an oil spill that big.

My boss—definitely more of a supervisor than a leader—blew up on me. He laid into me in front of the crew and made me feel like dirt. Honestly, I deserved it. Something I was responsible for had gone sideways. But here's where the story takes a turn.

I *knew* I had set everything up right. I double-checked it. I was sure of it. I was *so* sure I convinced myself someone must have messed with it. And instead of just owning the mistake, I became a full-blown conspiracy theorist.

I walked around stewing for days. Angry. Embarrassed. Playing detective in my head, trying to figure out who had sabotaged me. Replaying the moment over and over. I couldn't let it go—because letting it go meant *I* might have messed up. And that wasn't a truth I wanted to face.

But that's the thing about ownership: it's not about whether it was 100 percent your fault. It's about asking, *What could I have done differently to prevent this?*

Honestly, I could have skipped the potluck and kept watch a little longer. I could have locked out the valves or triple-checked everything after the last guy left the yard. I could have left a note that said, "Touch this and I will find you." (Okay, maybe not that last one.)

But the point is, I *could* have done something more. Leadership lives in the gap between what happened and what you're willing to take responsibility for. I wasn't there yet. I didn't want to own the mess. I wanted to point fingers, make a case, and prove I was right. I wasn't asking, *What could I have done differently?* I was asking, *Who did this to me?* It felt safer to blame than it did to reflect.

But that thinking is a trap. It keeps you stuck. And worse, it keeps you small.

Here's what I've learned since then, and it's hit me like a freight train more than once: Leadership isn't about fair—it's about faithful. Faithful leaders don't wait until every detail is sorted before they take responsibility. They don't need to win the argument or uncover the villain. They step in and say, "I'll take it from here." That doesn't mean you cover for others forever or accept mistreatment, but it does mean you stop making excuses and start making progress.

You can't lead people if you're always trying to defend your image. You can't grow if you're always waiting to be declared innocent. And you sure as heck can't gain influence if the only thing you're protecting is your ego.

Extreme ownership means choosing humility over pride. It means saying, "This one's on me," even when it would be easier to deflect. It means accepting that the outcome happened under your watch, and if you're serious about growing as a leader, you won't waste time explaining why it wasn't your fault. You'll roll up your sleeves and figure out what to do better next time.

And yeah, maybe someone closed the valve that day. Maybe they didn't. But here's the truth: Great leaders don't get distracted by drama. They stay focused on stewardship.

The oil was my responsibility. The job was mine. And I learned something that day: If I ask God to trust me with more, I'd better be ready to take full ownership of what's already in my hands. Not when it's convenient and everything's running smoothly, but especially when it's hard, messy, and unfair.

The world doesn't need more supervisors who bark orders and dodge blame. It needs more leaders who are willing to say, "If it's mine to manage, then I'll take responsibility for the results—period."

That's what makes you trustworthy. That's what builds respect. That's what earns the keys to the next opportunity. If you're too big to own the problem, you're too small to lead the solution. I want you to ask yourself: What's one situation in your life right now where you've been pointing fingers but you need to start pointing thumbs?

Take a breath. Be honest. And own it. That's the starting line for every great leader I've ever known.

The oil spill was one of those moments that sticks to your boots, literally and figuratively. I still remember the way that stuff smelled burning in the sun—like hot tar and bad decisions. For weeks after it happened, I kept replaying the incident in my head and beating myself up over it.

But what hit me harder than the mess was this quiet, sinking feeling: *I didn't handle that like a leader.* I handled it like a guy who wanted to protect his image. I got defensive. I blamed. I built a whole conspiracy theory in my head about someone tampering with the valve. And maybe they did. But the question that kept echoing in the back of my mind wasn't, *Who messed with the tank?* It was, *Why didn't I triple-check it?*

That's when something started to shift in me. Not overnight. Not in some magical moment of clarity. It was more like a slow, gritty realization: If I'm going to be a leader someday, I've got to start acting like one today—without the title, without the spotlight, and without the praise.

I remember praying one morning before work. It wasn't a fancy prayer. More like a frustrated sigh with words.

"All right, God ... I'm done chasing it. I'm done trying to be the guy. You tell me what to do and I'll do it. You open the door when it's time. Until then, I'm done striving."

That was the real turning point—not when I got a promotion or someone recognized me, but when I stopped needing any of that to show up like a leader. After that, my work didn't look much different on the outside, but I was different on the inside.

At the county, I quietly became the guy who took care of things. There was no big announcement, no name tag that said *problem solver*. Just one truck after another passed down the line like worn-out jeans. These were the trucks no one wanted. They rattled, wheezed, and had more rust than paint. If it had more electrical tape than wire, I probably drove it. And I treated every single one like it had my name on the title.

Every week, it was a new challenge—different quirks, breakdowns, and what-in-the-world-is-that noise moments. But I didn't complain. I didn't shrug it off or leave it for someone else to figure out. I handled it. If a headlight was out, I replaced it. If a lever was frozen, I soaked it and got it moving again. If something rattled loose, I tightened it up. I kept spare parts, fuses, tools, and gloves in the cab—not because someone told me to, but because I wanted the next guy who drove it to think, "Man, someone cared about this rig."

And then came the day they handed me the keys to the 1974 International with the 5 & 4 brownie transmission. Two shifters, ten gears, and one very cooked operator's seat. Every other driver had passed it over saying it was too complicated, too janky, and too much trouble in the summer heat. That thing had a transmission setup so weird that if you put both shifters in neutral at the same time, it was game over. Full stop. You'd have to clutch, cuss, and pray to get it back in gear without holding up half the county.

But I said *yes*, not because it was easy, but because it needed someone to take ownership. So, I climbed in, adjusted the seat, wiped the sweat off the steering wheel, and figured it out. I stalled it a few times and ground a gear or two. But I got the rhythm. I learned how to make it sing. And by the end of the week, I didn't just know how to drive it—I knew how to keep it running.

That truck didn't reward laziness. It rewarded focus, awareness, and humility. You couldn't force it—you had to *learn it*. And that's what made it so dang valuable. When you choose to take ownership of the things no one else wants, you don't just fix problems—you become someone people can count on.

That lesson followed me right into leadership.

It's why I back my team when something goes sideways. It's why I don't throw people under the bus. It's why I'd rather teach someone how to shift than shame them for missing a gear. Owning junk trucks prepared me for something bigger: owning the culture I lead today.

I started using every minute wisely. When I was loading water at the river—thirty minutes of downtime most guys spent scrolling their phones or napping in the cab—I worked. I'd crawl around under the truck with a flashlight and look for problems like frayed wires, loose mounts, and leaky hoses. I'd sweep the floors, wipe down the windows, and clean out the cab that smelled like fast food, sweat, and three years of bad decisions.

Nobody asked me to do that. Nobody stood behind me with a clipboard poised to hand out a bonus or gold star. But I wasn't doing it for recognition anymore—I was doing it because that's what owners do.

Owners take pride in what they touch. They don't wait to be told. They see a problem and say, *That's mine to fix.* They leave things better than they found them. Not because it's expected; because it's right. That mindset changed everything for me.

My attitude changed once I stopped asking "Why won't anyone promote me?" and started asking "What can I take ownership of today?" My confidence changed, my reputation changed, and over time, so did my opportunities.

And then, one day, something happened that nearly knocked the wind out of me. The county got a few new trucks—*brand* new and still-smelled-like-factory paint. And usually, those went straight to the guys with the most seniority—the lifers. I'd only been there a year. I wasn't even on the radar. Or so I thought. My boss handed me the keys. No speech. No ceremony. Just a quick handoff—and a look that said, *I've been watching.*

I can't even describe how that felt. Not because I needed the truck. But because I

didn't chase it. It came after I let go. After I stopped needing someone to validate me and just started owning the work in front of me.

I took care of that truck like a classic muscle car I was driving in a parade. It was the first new piece of equipment I'd ever been trusted with. Not loaned. Not rotated. Not shared. *Mine.* And I didn't take that lightly.

I shined and polished the cab floor. Every. Single. Week. I swept it out every day before I headed home—even if all I'd done was haul water and eat dust. I kept a little handheld broom behind the seat and some rags stuffed in the door pocket. If there was a smudge on the dash, I wiped it. If the windows got cloudy, I cleaned them. If the boots left footprints on the floor mats, I vacuumed them out. But the part I was most proud of? The fifth wheel.

Every week, without fail, I'd disconnect the water tanker, grab a fresh tube of grease, and crawl underneath that trailer like a pit crew tech at Daytona. I'd lay down on a tarp, grease gun in hand, and lather up that fifth wheel until it looked like it had just rolled off the showroom floor. Some guys thought I was overdoing it. I wasn't.

I was maintaining something that mattered—not because it was expensive or someone told me to go the extra mile. I did it because I knew deep down that *how* I handled this truck would determine what God could trust me with next.

This wasn't about chrome and clean cabs. This was about character and stewardship. I wanted to prove to myself and the One who gave it to me, that I could be faithful with what was in my hands.

Then, about a year and a half later, I was standing in the yard eating my lunch, when two drivers from another department walked over. They had the same truck—the same model, year, and everything.

One of them asked, "Hey, is your fifth wheel getting sloppy yet?"

I looked at him like he'd asked if I regularly drove it into a ditch. "Nope. Still tight. Why?"

They both looked at each other, frustrated. "Ours are already worn out. There's slop in the coupling."

So, I asked the obvious question: "When's the last time you greased it?"

One of them shrugged. "I think I do it ... maybe twice a year?"

The other laughed and said, "That's not my job. The shop's supposed to do all the maintenance."

And right then, the lesson slapped me across the face. That's the difference. We were all given the same equipment. The same opportunity. But only one of us took ownership of it. Only one of us said, "If it's under my care, then it's my responsibility." The others made excuses and passed the buck. And their trucks wore out faster.

They thought I was wasting my time greasing a fifth wheel. But I wasn't just greasing steel—I was building trust. I was investing in something that had been entrusted to me. And it paid off.

Here's the truth: Excuses say, "That's not in my job description." Ownership says, "If it touches my hands, I'm going to take care of it." Those guys got the same truck I did—but they didn't get the same result, because they didn't *carry* it the same way.

And listen to me—this part matters more than you might think: You don't rise to the level of your potential. You rise to the level of your ownership. How you treat what you're given determines what you're trusted with next.

If you wait to be handed a leadership title before you start leading, you'll never get one. But if you show up like an owner when no one's watching and view your role as an act of stewardship, not just a paycheck, doors open that you don't have to force.

That truck didn't make me a leader. But the grease gun did. Here's what I want you to take away from this: Leadership doesn't start with a promotion. It starts with a decision.

Before I was ever handed the keys to that new truck, I had already made up my mind: I was going to lead with whatever was in front of me. Old truck, busted equipment, no recognition—I was done waiting for someone else to *give me* a leadership role. I decided to *own one* instead.

That's what real ownership looks like. It's not a moment, it's a mindset. It's not flashy, it's faithful. It's not about who notices, it's about how you show up when nobody's watching. A title might open a door, but ownership keeps it open.

And here's the kicker. God won't trust you with more if you're careless with what you already have. He's not in the business of promoting entitlement. He's looking for people who will steward what's in their hands like it belongs to Him, because it does.

So, if you're sitting there wondering why doors aren't opening, ask yourself: Am I taking care of what's already in my hands? Am I showing up like an owner or just clocking in, waiting to be noticed? Am I waiting for a title, or picking up the towel and serving where I stand?

Here's something most people miss:

ON THE NIGHT JESUS WAS BETRAYED, KNOWING FULL WELL THE CROSS WAS COMING, HE DIDN'T DELIVER A POWER-PACKED SERMON OR CALL DOWN FIRE FROM HEAVEN.

HE POURED WATER INTO A BASIN, KNELT DOWN, AND WASHED HIS DISCIPLES' FEET—

GRIMY, ROAD-WORN, SANDAL-SCARRED FEET.

AND POURED WATER INTO A BASIN. THEN HE BEGAN TO WASH THE DISCIPLES' FEET, DRYING THEM WITH THE TOWEL HE HAD AROUND HIM.

—JOHN 13:5, (NLT)

That wasn't just about hygiene. It was a mic-drop moment of servant leadership. Jesus didn't wait for someone else to act. He led by example. No title. No spotlight. Just a towel and a purpose.

And if the Savior of the world could grab a basin and serve, you and I can stop waiting to be crowned and start showing up to be useful. That's leadership. That's extreme ownership. And that's the heart God trusts with more. You don't get handed the big things until you've been faithful with the small ones. Jesus said it best:

WHOEVER CAN BE TRUSTED WITH VERY LITTLE CAN ALSO BE TRUSTED WITH MUCH.
—LUKE 16:10

That's not just a good verse for Sunday mornings. It's a blueprint for leadership. God doesn't promote based on potential. He promotes based on stewardship. If you can't be trusted to take care of what's already in your hands, why would He trust you with more?

And sometimes, leadership starts with nothing more than a grease gun, a quiet commitment, and a fifth wheel that never wears out.

The Blame Game (When Ownership Is Missing)

I didn't get that new truck because I was the most experienced driver. I got it because I treated the trucks previously entrusted to me like they already mattered. But let's flip that around for a second, because not everyone does.

Some people get handed a good thing and wear it out in a year. It doesn't wear out because the equipment is bad. The owner's attitude is the problem. The opposite of ownership isn't laziness. It's blame. And if extreme ownership multiplies trust, *blame does the exact opposite.* It divides it.

I've seen this play out more times than I care to count. In the shop. In the office. On the job site. Even in my own company. These are the people who are quick to deflect, point fingers, and throw someone else under the bus, even when the bus was clearly in *their* lane.

Here's something most folks don't realize: Blame isn't just a reaction—it's a habit. Once it sets in, it spreads like a leak in a hydraulic line. It may start small, but left unchecked, it'll bring down the whole machine.

I had a team member, a business development rep, who I truly believed was ready for more. She was a sharp thinker and strong communicator. Her natural confidence made you believe she could handle anything you threw at her.

I wanted her to win. I really did. I was already picturing her leading a bigger role, owning part of the client journey, maybe even mentoring new hires someday. But then something went sideways.

A customer interaction didn't go as planned. The client had questions and concerns—nothing major, the usual fog that sometimes settles in when things move too fast. A hiccup, really. These things happen all the time in business.

How did she respond? Not the way I had hoped.

She didn't pause. She didn't ask a single question. She didn't even pick up the phone to get clarity. She lit the place on fire—with blame.

In the span of one morning, she had tossed every piece of responsibility onto someone else's desk. It was the sales team's fault for mis-communicating. It was onboarding's fault for not preparing the client better. It was our systems, support, and culture. Heck, I half expected her to start blaming the thermostat.

And as I read through the messages she sent, I felt this knot build in my stomach. Not just because of what she said, but because I recognized it. The panic, the pride, and the need to be right, even when things weren't. It was like watching a rerun of my old

P90 bulk tank story—but this time, in jeans and an office chair instead of boots and a safety vest.

What made it harder was that I knew that mindset. I'd lived it. I'd stood in the middle of a mess, convinced that I'd done everything right, desperately wanting someone to validate my frustration. I knew the feeling of needing the problem to be someone else's fault—because admitting it might've been mine was too heavy to carry. And that's what I saw in her.

Not a bad employee. Not a malicious person. But someone who hadn't learned the cost of blaming others instead of asking herself, *What part of this could I have done better?*

She was so focused on saving face that she lost her credibility. Instead of repairing trust, she cracked it wider. Instead of asking, she assumed. Instead of owning even a *small* part of the mess, she stood back and pointed to the damage like it was a crime scene, and she was the detective—not the one holding the muddy boots. That moment changed how I led.

I realized you can't promote someone just because they're talented. You've got to see how they handle things when the parts are late, the welder's throwing sparks, and somebody just filled the diesel truck with gas. That's when ownership either shows up or runs for cover. On that day, ownership left the building.

But I also knew how much growth I had left on the table back then because I was too busy defending myself to take responsibility. And that's exactly what I saw happening with her.

Her mistake wasn't what nearly cost her credibility—it was her *response* when things didn't go her way. Blame didn't solve the problem. It just made people defensive, shut down communication, and made the team question whether they could trust her in the long run.

Blame doesn't protect your reputation. It *punishes* it. It may feel like a shield in the moment, but it becomes a wall between you and the people you need to lead. That's why this stuff matters. Just like ownership compounds, so does blame. One excuse doesn't stay one excuse. It turns into a pattern.

That pattern becomes your posture—how you carry yourself and respond. People learn to brace themselves when something goes wrong and you're in the room. And before long, you're not just *the smart one* or *the experienced one*. You're the one no one wants to work with—not because you aren't capable, but because nobody wants to be the next name you drop in a blame email.

It's subtle at first. You start by defending yourself, trying to explain your side. But then the explanations get sharper, and the tone gets colder. You stop asking questions and start issuing statements.

Suddenly, people stop coming to you. They stop looping you in early. They stop trusting that you'll be part of the solution because they've already seen what happens when something doesn't go your way. And that's when things break down—not only the task and the process—the *team*. When someone's first instinct is to blame, they fracture culture because of damaged relationships. They create silos. They kill initiative. People start walking on eggshells instead of stepping up. And the worst part? Most people don't even see it happening—until they look around and realize no one's following them anymore. Trust me, I know. I've been both people. I've been the guy who took the hit, even when it wasn't fully mine, and earned respect that paid off tenfold. Those moments built something lasting. Something solid. Teams formed stronger. Trust ran deeper. And I walked away knowing *I led well today.*

And I've been the guy who deflected and dodged the hit, wanting so badly to *not* be wrong that I missed the chance to grow. That cost me more than a rough afternoon and a few awkward conversations.

It cost me influence and relationships. It cost me time that could have been spent leading, learning, and getting better instead of cleaning up the emotional mess I made trying to protect my pride.

You can get away with it for a while. You can out-talk people. You can deflect. You can play politics. But eventually, people stop listening and believing. And when that happens, your talent no longer matters because nobody follows someone they don't trust. So now, as a leader, I know what to look for. I don't just pay attention to what people do when everything is running smoothly. I pay attention to what they say when things break down, because when a mistake happens, and it will, your first words matter.

Do you react with any of these responses? "They didn't tell me," or "That wasn't mine," or "Nobody trained me on that." Or do you start with this question? "What could I have done differently?" That one question can change everything.

And here's the hard part of leadership: Even when you didn't create the mess, sometimes you're still responsible for cleaning it up. Not because it's your fault. You're the one who cares enough to fix it.

What Real Life Ownership Looks Like

Some mirrors aren't glass—they're moments.

Here's the thing—this story doesn't end with a pink slip. A few weeks later, after things cooled off and the dust settled, she knocked on my office door and sat down across from me. This time, I saw a different posture and a different tone. She said, "Dan, I don't get it. How do you do it? I mean, seriously—how do you keep everything together?"

I raised an eyebrow, not sure where this was going. She kept going.

"You've got multiple companies. Multiple nonprofits. Employees across time zones. You're flying all over the country—more than a commercial pilot. You're writing a book, for crying out loud! And somehow, you're still available when we need you, answering questions like you've got nothing else on your plate. I … I just want to be more like that."

Let's just say that was next-level stuff, like grade-A-salted-whipped-Kerry-gold-level butter. I mean, if words were fresh-from-the-oven biscuits, mine were dripping in melted butter.

Buried in the compliment was something real. She wasn't merely trying to flatter me. She was asking how to be better. She wanted to shift. To lead. To grow. I knew that spark needed some structure to turn into a fire. So, I gave her a few things. Nothing flashy—habits that had changed everything for me.

"Start with this," I said. "For one week, write down what you do every fifteen minutes. No judgment—just track it. At the end of each day, take five minutes and ask yourself two questions."

1. What did I accomplish?
2. Where did I drift?

She blinked. "Every fifteen minutes?"

"Yep," I said. "If you want to take ownership, you've got to know where your time's going. Most people don't have a productivity problem—they have an honesty problem."

Then I gave her the next step.

"Set goals every day. Goals are more than a to-do list. You are looking for measurable outcomes. 'I'm going to call ten people today.' 'I'm going to write five emails.' 'I'm going to follow up on every lead in my queue.' Put it on paper. Then own it."

She nodded, taking notes like I was handing her the launch codes.

"And here's the final part," I said. "When you don't hit those goals—and there will be days you won't—don't spin it. Don't blame the distractions. Don't point at someone else. Just sit with it for a minute. Ask yourself: 'What could I have done differently?' Not 'Who dropped the ball?' Not 'How do I cover my backside?' Just: 'Where did I lose the opportunity to lead today?'"

She looked at me and said, "I've never tracked my day like that before."

I smiled. "Yeah, and that's why your day's been tracking you. But that changes now."

Ownership doesn't start when things go right—it starts when you admit where you went wrong. Most people don't need a miracle. They just need a mirror. This is what real ownership looks like in real life.

Real ownership is not some dramatic apology in front of a group. It's not taking credit when things work out. It's the quiet, daily discipline of checking in with yourself and asking the hard question: *Where did I lead well today—and where did I miss the mark?*

Leadership is how you manage your minutes. It's how you respond when your plan gets wrecked. It's whether or not you own your energy, choices, and results. You don't have to be the smartest or have it all figured out. But you do have to *own your role*.

The people who lead well don't flinch or pass the buck when things go sideways. They don't say, "That's not my job." They take ownership, even when it's inconvenient, uncomfortable, and not *technically* their fault. Leadership rises and falls on responsibility, not perfection.

If you want more growth, influence, and opportunities, start with what's already in your hands and own it. Ownership builds trust. Trust builds momentum. Momentum builds impact. And that starts right now. Track it. Own it. Lead it.

Culture Shifter: How Ownership Builds Teams People Want to Be On

Ownership changes your output and your environment. It starts small. Maybe it's owning a mistake before anyone even brings it up. Maybe it's a team member stepping in to help clean up a mess they didn't make. Maybe it's someone saying, "I've got this," when it wasn't their job. And suddenly, without any dramatic announcement, something shifts.

People notice when one person steps up and quietly owns their corner of the world. They notice when someone doesn't flinch, point fingers, or duck the hard stuff. They notice when someone leads without a title and takes responsibility without being asked. That style of ownership is contagious.

It spreads across a team like a spark catching dry grass. First, one person, then another. Suddenly, the standard rises, excuses vanish, and

people start showing up differently. They're not scared or guilt-tripped, because they've seen what it looks like when someone leads with responsibility instead of ego.

The truth is you don't need a position of power to shape culture. All you need is the guts to go first. I've watched teams transform, not because we overhauled a system, but because one person took ownership. They didn't wait for a team meeting or a policy change. They saw a gap, stepped in, and made the situation better. They did what needed doing—quietly, consistently, and without fanfare. And that changed everything. But I've also seen the opposite.

I've watched teams crumble under the weight of blame. I've seen departments where everyone is constantly looking over their shoulders, wondering who's going to call them out, throw them under the bus, or pass the buck.

It always starts with small stuff—a missed email, a vague handoff, a detail dropped somewhere between "I thought you had it" and "Wasn't that their job?" But when no one steps up to own it, the tension starts piling up like unpaid parking tickets. People stop fixing problems and start covering their tracks. Morale drops. Trust leaks out. And before long, your best people—the ones who *do* take pride in their work—start mentally checking out.

And they don't check out because they don't care. They're tired of dragging the whole load while everyone else watches from the cab. The culture becomes one big collective sigh: *"That's not my job."*

Once that phrase takes root, good luck growing anything meaningful. "That's not my job" is leadership poison. It kills initiative, momentum, and turns your most capable people into quiet, frustrated spectators.

But when ownership takes root, everything changes. It's like greasing a fifth wheel every Friday—not because someone told you to, but because you know what happens when you don't. It probably won't break down today, and might not even break down next week. But it's silently and constantly wearing down. And one day, the slop shows up, and it's too late. Culture works the same way.

A little ownership regularly applied goes a long way. It keeps things tight. Keeps trust strong. Keeps friction low. And it signals to everyone watching, *"Hey—we take care of what we're given around here."* When no one's responsible, everything falls apart but when *everyone* owns their part, things run smoothly—even under pressure.

There's something powerful about a team that cares more about getting the job done right than who gets the credit. I'm talking about a team that follows up because it matters, steps in instead of stepping aside, says, "Let me fix this," not "Let me find someone to blame."

Jesus perfectly modeled this culture. He built a culture of invitation and responsibility. He didn't micromanage the disciples, nor did he build a shame-based team. He let Peter sink, then reached down and pulled him up. He let Thomas doubt, then showed up and gave him what he needed. He didn't force ownership—He modeled it. And that changed everything. He didn't say, "This isn't my fault." He said, "I'll take that." And if the perfect Son of God was willing to own what wasn't His, what excuse do we have?

Ownership culture builds teams people want to be on. It creates safety, momentum, and a standard that people aspire to. If you want that culture, don't wait for a staff retreat or a fancy mission statement. Be the one who leads it. Own the tone in the meeting. Own the email that didn't get sent. Own the awkward conversation. Own the mess, the misstep, the moment.

Culture doesn't change when everyone agrees; it changes when someone leads. And that someone can be you.

When It's not Your Fault ... But It's Your Responsibility

The other day, I had a string of one-on-one conversations with different members of the team at Eclipse DOT. Some of those chats ran deep—like, really deep. One of them clocked in at nearly two hours. Another one wasn't far behind. At some point, I stopped checking the time and just leaned in.

Now, I won't name names, but let's just say some folks really enjoy hearing themselves talk. You know the type. (And if you're wondering who I'm talking about, there's a 50/50 chance it might have been me.) It's funny how a simple "How's everything going?" can turn into a full-blown TED Talk when the right personality gets warmed up.

But buried in all those conversations were some solid gold insights. Not complaints. Not drama. Just honest, thoughtful observations from people who care about the mission and want to see us do better. And even though the conversations were mostly productive, a theme started surfacing.

It wasn't a list of complaints. It wasn't even *feedback* in the HR sense of the word. It was just small stuff. Thoughtful stuff. Observations that made me pause and think, *Dang, they're not wrong.*

"Hey Dan, that email you sent the other day came off a little pointed."

"Have you ever considered adding more context when you check in on things?"

"Sometimes when you're moving fast, we're not quite sure what direction we're supposed to go in with you."

Oof. It wasn't personal. It wasn't an attack. But it was real. And they were right.

So, in our all-hands team meeting the next morning, I served myself a heaping plate of good old-fashioned crow—extra crispy, no sauce, just straight humility on a paper plate. I looked at the team and said, "All right y'all, I've got some things to own. A few screw-ups that have my name written all over them in Sharpie. Let's dig in."

I talked about how I'm going to make some small shifts to improve communication, and how I realized I've been hitting send on some emails that read more like command-line code than a message from an actual human being.

Like this one:

Subject: (None)

Body: How's the project?

And that's it. That's the whole email. No greeting. No context. Just three little words floating in a white box.

Now, I'll be real—I wasn't typing with *tone*. I just wanted a quick update. But I admit, I can see how that might land as cold or abrupt.

I even told them about a buddy I texted early that same morning—6 a.m. sharp. I shot him a message that said, "Hey, I'm writing a book on leadership, and you keep coming up in it. Would you care if I use your real name, or would you rather I use a fake one?"

His first response? "Good morning, Dan!"

His second? "I'm honored that you'd even consider writing about me. Use whatever name you want. Some people might not like me anyway. LOL."

That text exchange reminded me that my tone may be clear in my head—but not always in someone else's inbox. So, I owned that, too. I told the team, "If it ever feels like I'm being short, pushy, or rushing you, know this: I'm just trying to get a read on where we stand. That's it. I'll work on being more clear."

But there's another piece to this. As a leader, your job isn't to always speak everyone else's language. Sometimes it's about teaching your team how *you* communicate so they're not constantly guessing or misreading your intentions. I told them, "Look, I'm a direct communicator. I'm to the point. If I shoot off a five-word email, it's not because I'm mad—it's because I've got five hundred other things in motion and I need a quick answer to keep the gears turning."

I said, "You guys don't need to tiptoe around my tone. If you ever feel like I've been unclear, ask me. Don't assume. And I'll do my part too. I'll slow down when I can and give you better context when it matters."

That moment was more than me explaining myself. It was leadership. Not because I took ownership of how I'd been communicating, but because I also showed them how to work *with* me, not *around* me.

Leadership isn't about catering to everyone's preferences. It's about communicating with clarity. It's about building mutual trust. And it's about ensuring your team knows that the door is open for feedback, honesty, and understanding how to work together better.

Then I opened the floor. I said, "If there's anything else I need to own, now's your shot. Bring it." And they did.

We talked about our new client onboarding framework—how we've rebuilt that thing at least eight times before finally landing on something solid. I acknowledged that sometimes I get so excited about launching a new thing that I don't wait for the road to be paved before I hit the gas.

"I love your energy," someone said, "but sometimes it feels like we're chasing a moving target. You're halfway down the highway, and we're still trying to find the keys to the truck."

They weren't wrong. I laughed. But then I nodded and said, "Okay—that's on me too."

Here's the thing: I didn't *intend* to cause confusion. I didn't *mean* to sound sharp in my emails. And it definitely wasn't my fault that we've had to rebuild systems while sprinting. But it was still my responsibility to minimize confusion and communicate with attention to tone. Leadership doesn't start with who caused the problem. It starts with who's willing to own it.

At that moment, I realized real ownership isn't about being perfect. It's about being *approachable*. It's about having the humility to say, "You're right—and I'll fix it." Being humble even when the mistake is small, shared, and just a ripple in the bigger picture. The people you lead don't need a flawless boss. They need a human leader who humbly listens, adjusts, and leads.

And you know what happened after that? My team started taking more ownership, too. Not because I asked them to, not because we had some checklist or policy change, but because leadership is contagious. And when your team sees you—their leader and the company's founder—stand in front of them and own it without flinching, it empowers them to do the same.

They didn't run *from* it. They ran *to* it. They saw what it looked like to lead with humility and strength, and you could see it in their eyes. They wanted that feeling too. They wanted to be trusted. They wanted to confidently say, "That one's on me," knowing they won't be thrown under the bus for it. They're ready to get better.

And I'll tell you what else—some of them couldn't help but laugh while I owned my stuff. Not disrespectfully, but in a "Yeah, I did say that," way. That's the environment we've built at Eclipse DOT.

We bust our butts like a Kenworth W900 pulling a fully loaded D8 dozer up a mountain pass. Imagine 150,000 pounds of angry, yellow steel with a blade bigger than your first apartment, turbo screaming, engine temp creeping, and every gear shift timed like a prayer. We know exactly when to lean in, when to downshift, and when to ease up just enough to keep her pulling steady. And we sure as heck don't need dispatch reminding us it's uphill—we've been climbing since sun up and still haven't touched the brakes. Just hoping our lunch doesn't vibrate off the dash before we reach the top.

We're there for our clients late into the night—and yeah, sometimes even on weekends. But our people love working here. They love the mission. They love the momentum. They love that I don't just talk about open-door leadership—I live it. They can walk into my office, tell me the truth, and not get their heads taken off.

They love that if I say I'm going to do something, it gets done.

And here's the part that means the most to me—they love taking ownership when things go wrong. In this company, when we make mistakes, we don't panic—we coach. We don't cover up. We course correct. We don't shame. We sharpen.

Owning a mistake here isn't a failure—it's an opportunity. It's a moment to learn, improve, and grow. That's what happens when extreme ownership becomes part of your culture. And that's what sets the stage for something even more powerful.

Jesus modeled this, too. He didn't sin. He didn't make the mess. But He saw it and He took responsibility for it. Not because it was His fault, but because He could and because He cared.

Leadership doesn't always look like charging ahead with a perfect plan. Sometimes it looks like slowing down, listening closely, and saying, "You're right. That one's on me." Owning what's not your fault is one of the most powerful leadership moves you'll ever make.

The Gift of Making Mistakes

Let me say this as plainly as I can: You're going to screw up. Not might. Not maybe. *Will.* Making mistakes is included in the leadership starter pack, packed right between stress and random fire drills. And I'm not just talking about rookie mistakes either. You'll mess something up six months into the job, and then you'll mess something up sixteen years into running a company with your name on the door. I've done both—sometimes in the same week.

I've launched systems that didn't work. I literally opened the gates, hyped them up like we were rolling out the red carpet, only to find out we forgot the carpet, the gate, and the instructions on how to open it.

I've forgotten to include my team in planning. One time, I was so sure I had already told them about a new project. I explained something in a meeting and looked around like, "Y'all with me?" The looks I got back were not-with-me looks. They were is-this-man-okay looks.

Do you want to know what the worst part is? I used to think admitting mistakes would make me look weak. Like, if I owned my mess-ups, people would stop trusting me or start doubting my ability to lead. So, I'd dodge the blame with all the elegance of a toddler caught with chocolate on his face, from the cake intended for Sunday dinner. Despite the frosting on his nose, he stood innocently with hands behind his back and big puppy-dog eyes looking up at you like, "Who, me?"

But here's what I found out: Owning your mistakes doesn't make you look weaker. It makes you look real. And real wins.

There was this moment recently when I stood before my team, cleared my throat, and said, "All right y'all, I dropped the ball on this one." Before I even finished the sentence, half the team was already smiling. The other half? Laughing. Not *at* me, but like, "Finally. We've all been thinking it." And right after that, they started admitting their stuff, too. No guilt—just relief. Like I'd just taken the lid off a pressure cooker.

That's what happens when you lead with ownership. It doesn't create chaos—it creates oxygen. People breathe. They stop hiding and blaming. And they start fixing what's broken instead of pretending nothing is.

At Eclipse DOT, that's how we roll. We run fast, work hard, and yeah—we mess things up sometimes. But we don't bury it under red tape or wait for someone else to take the fall. We say, "That one's on me," fix it, laugh about it (eventually), and then get right back to work.

I actually *want* my people to make mistakes because mistakes mean they're trying, taking initiative, and moving forward. You show me someone who never messes up, and I'll show you someone who's playing it safe and hiding behind a spreadsheet.

The truth is that mistakes are where the best leaders are made. Not in the polished moments, but in the moments where it all goes sideways and someone steps up and says, "All right. Let's get this back on track."

So, if you're leading a team, here's what I'll say: You don't have to be perfect. But you do have to be brave enough to be honest. Own your misses. Laugh at yourself. Fix what broke. Then go do it better next time with the team still believing in you because you had the guts to say, "Yeah ... that one's on me."

That's the gift of making mistakes. It won't ruin your leadership—it'll make it real. And people will follow real every time.

Make It Safe to Mess Up

If there's one thing that'll choke the life out of a team faster than a surprise audit on a Friday at 4 p.m., it's fear of failure.

I don't care how talented your people are, if they're constantly worried they'll get snapped at, shamed, or thrown under the bus for making a mistake, they'll stop taking initiative. They'll freeze. They'll overthink every email like it's going to be carved into stone and sent to court. They'll triple-check every move like they're defusing a bomb strapped to their keyboard.

Eventually, the only people left are the ones too scared to lead and too tired to care. But here's what I've learned: Mistakes are going to happen. That's part of the deal. You can either freak out about them, or build a culture where they're part of the process. We had a situation like that not long ago.

One of our newer team members—less than six months in—was filing a routine DOT report for one of our clients. She was still getting her footing, still learning the rhythm of our systems, still earning confidence with every form she submitted. This wasn't a seasoned vet making a careless move—this was a dedicated new hire doing her best to follow the process.

Everything was going smoothly—until she hit the payment section. There was a $20 credit sitting on the client's account. She didn't catch that it was a credit and thought it was the balance due. So, she did what she was trained to do—she sent the approval form over. The client approved it. Everything seemed fine.

Until they actually looked at the paperwork and realized they'd just authorized a payment on a $20 credit. Not $2,000. Not $20,000. *Twenty bucks.*

Now, keep in mind—this company brings in around $40 million a year. They didn't ask for clarification. They didn't come in with curiosity. They came in hot.

Full-on interrogation mode—like she'd just wired money to a Nigerian prince and personally sunk their quarterly earnings. And the pressure they brought down? It didn't match the size of the mistake—it matched the size of their ego.

So, I stepped in. I called the client myself and handled it professionally, but directly. I owned the mistake, promised we'd fix it, and then I calmly but firmly said, "Don't talk to my team that way again." I knew something they didn't. What mattered more than $20 was the culture we were building.

I could have turned around and laid into her, lectured her about slowing down, double-checking, and paying closer attention. I could have used it as a chance to tighten things up and send a message. But here's the truth: She already felt terrible. She was beating herself up the second she saw the email. I didn't need to shame her. She was already carrying the weight. And I know that feeling, because I've been there. People are hard enough on themselves when they mess up. What they need in that moment isn't a boss with a megaphone. They need a leader with their back.

So, I backed her up. I helped her fix it. And I watched what happened next. She didn't retreat. She didn't get scared. She didn't walk on eggshells from that point forward. She got better. She took more care, more initiative, and more ownership—not because she was afraid of messing up again, but because she wanted to get it right.

That's what extreme ownership looks like. It's not perfection. It's not punishment. It's pride. It's doing the work right—not because you're scared of what'll happen if you don't—but because you care about the results. You care about your contribution and the team. When you build a culture where people are allowed to fail without being humiliated, something incredible happens: They stop hiding. They start owning. They stop bracing for impact and ask, "How can I grow from this?" That's when a good team becomes a great one.

When someone messes up and knows they're safe to say, "I got this wrong," without it becoming their identity, you've created something powerful. You've built trust. You've built leaders. You've built resilience. And it all started with letting one person make a $20 mistake and not making her feel like she'd sunk the Titanic. She wanted to get it right. At Eclipse DOT, we don't just celebrate wins. We coach through the losses because though it starts with the boss, ownership isn't just for the boss. It's for everyone.

Remember that P-90 hot oil spill story? The worst part wasn't the 300 gallons of sticky, black disaster bubbling over while I was trying to enjoy a plate of green bean casserole. The worst part came afterward—the shame that showed up to work with me every day. I didn't get written up or fired. I got something worse. I was shamed for months. Every morning, that boss would find a way to bring it up—jabs in safety meetings and off-hand comments And the best part? Once a week, we'd drive past where it happened. He'd slow the truck down, stare out the window, and shake his head like I needed a visual reminder to feel worse than I already did.

He thought he was making a point. What he was doing was making me hate coming to work. I dreaded mornings. I dreaded meetings. I dreaded passing that spot on the yard.

It didn't matter how hard I worked or what else I did right—he made it clear that I'd always be the guy who spilled the oil. And eventually, I quit.

Not in a blaze of glory. I didn't flip a desk or storm out. I just quietly started looking for the door, because leadership that weaponizes shame doesn't inspire people to grow. It inspires them to get the heck out.

So now, when my team messes up, I remember that feeling, and I lead the opposite way. I protect and coach them. I make sure they walk away from that moment better—not broken, because when we allow people to fail, we empower them to grow. We give them permission to be better tomorrow than they were today. And that is what winning looks like.

Own It All

If there's one thing I hope you take away from this chapter, it's this: Extreme ownership isn't just a leadership strategy—it's a way of life.

It starts with the way you respond when things go sideways. It's marked by the way you show up when you're tired, wrong, and your brilliant plan hits a wall and everyone looking at you like, "Now what?"

You can blame, spin, duck, and dodge, making it look like someone else should have seen it coming. Or, you can say the seven words that change everything: "That one's on me. Let's fix it." That's the pivot point. That's what separates real leaders from the rest.

IMPACT OUTLIVES INCOME.

We've walked through a lot in this chapter—from the trucks I used to fix when no one asked me to, to the time I had to eat crow in front of my own team, to defending a new employee over a $20 mistake that never should have turned into a storm.

And through every story, one thing stayed the same: Ownership builds trust. Blame breaks it. When you take responsibility, you don't just protect your credibility—you create space for your team to grow. When you go first, they stop hiding. They start stepping up. They start becoming the leaders you've been praying for. That's the culture we've built at Eclipse DOT. Not one of perfection, but one of progress.

We make mistakes, but we own them and, we use them as stepping stones—not stumbling blocks.

So, what now? Here are some action steps:

- **Look in the mirror.** This week, take inventory of something that didn't go right—and ask yourself, "Where could I have led better?"
- **Call it out.** If you dropped the ball, say so out loud to your team. Model what ownership looks like, even if it's uncomfortable.
- **Coach, don't condemn.** When your team makes a mistake, use it as a chance to build them, not break them.
- **Create safety.** Let your people know that failure isn't fatal here. What matters is how we respond.
- **Ask better questions.** Instead of "Who did this?" ask, "What can we learn from this?" Shift the tone from blame to build.

And here's where we land this thing in truth: Jesus—the only perfect leader who ever walked this earth—took ownership of a burden He didn't even cause. He didn't say, "That's not my fault." He said, "I'll take that." He didn't dodge the cross. He carried it. For all of us.

So, when we take ownership, even of things we didn't fully cause, we're walking in the footsteps of the greatest leader the world has ever known. If *He* could do that for us, we can own the messes we make and lead others through theirs with grace. So, go first. Lead loud. Own it all. And watch what happens when your team stops being afraid to mess up and starts showing up like owners.

Key Takeaways from Chapter Three

If it touches your hands, it's your responsibility. Leadership isn't about pointing fingers—it's about pointing thumbs. The moment something falls into your lane, it's yours to deal with. Maybe it wasn't your fault, but if it happened on your watch, it's yours to own. That's what separates people who lead from people who make excuses.

You don't rise to your potential—you rise to your level of ownership. Potential doesn't move the needle—ownership does. The guy who says, *"That's not my job,"* eventually wears himself and everyone else out. But the one who faithfully greases the fifth wheel every Friday? He's the one trusted with more. Leaders get handed keys because they've already proven they'll take care of what's been given.

Blame breaks trust—ownership builds it. Blame is like a hammer hitting glass: it shatters teams, drains energy, and kills culture. But ownership? Ownership repairs. When a leader steps up and says, *"This one's on me,"* the team leans in. They stop hiding and start following, because they trust someone who takes the weight instead of shifting it.

God doesn't promote entitlement—He promotes stewardship. You want bigger opportunities? Be faithful with the smaller ones already in your hands. God doesn't reward shortcuts or self-pity. He rewards stewardship. If you take care of the little things in front of you, He'll hand you the bigger ones when you're ready.

Leadership shows up before the title does. You don't need a promotion to lead—you need a decision. It's not about waiting for a badge, a nameplate, or someone else's permission. It's about showing up like an owner before anyone calls you one. Lead where you are, with what you have.

Create a culture where it's safe to mess up. Fear freezes people. Grace frees them. If your team is terrified of mistakes, they'll hide their mess-ups until it's too late. But if you build a culture where mistakes can be owned and fixed, people grow faster. Grace doesn't lower the standard—it raises it by giving people the courage to step up without fear.

Own it all—even the tone. Leadership hides in the smallest details: the subject line of your email, the way you check in on a Monday, the tone in your voice when you're frustrated. Own how you show up, even when it feels minor, because those "little" things shape how your team shows up in return.

Chapter 4 | Your Brand

It's Not What You Say. It's What They Experience

I was probably in middle school the first time I realized what a brand really was—and no, I'm not talking about cattle. I grew up in farming country on a ranch, so branding wasn't a new word. But this brand wasn't about irons and livestock. This was something you couldn't see but sure could feel.

It started with a beige box in my bedroom—a Macintosh Plus. My parents were early adopters and rolled in with that thing like it was the future in a plastic casing. It had those oversized 5.25-inch floppy disks you had to slide in just right, like defusing a bomb with sweaty hands. If the stars aligned, the screen wouldn't freeze. And if luck really smiled on you, you could launch *Dark Castle*—a pixelated adventure where a tiny knight ran from bats and evil cackling crows that somehow sounded exactly like my older brother laughing when he stole the remote.

That crow noise? I can still hear it. And that Mac? It didn't just compute—it made me feel like I had access to a secret world. It was something creative and weird—different from anything else out there.

Eventually, we upgraded to a Tangerine iMac. That machine wasn't a tool—it was a *statement*. It sat out in our house like a piece of art. Not tucked in an office or shoved under a desk. We were proud of it. Even the mouse was circular, like someone in design school said, "What if computers were *fun*?" I didn't care that it couldn't run the latest PC games—I had a computer that looked like it belonged in a candy shop.

Then came the iBook. Ours was blue, curved, and looked like no other laptop. And later, the iPod. Oh, the iPod ... I owned three of them before I ever had a phone that could play music. Those little devices changed everything. I'd mow lawns for hours just to buy one. I'd build playlists like I was auditioning for a record label.

We didn't just use Apple products—we *belonged* to Apple. And that's when it hit me. A brand isn't just a thing you buy. It's an experience you step into. It's a belief system dressed up in packaging.

Apple made it clear from the start—they weren't like everyone else. They didn't want to be. They were rebels. Misfits. Round pegs in square holes. And people loved them for it.

But what stuck with me most wasn't the software or the hardware color—it was the feeling. Apple made me feel like I was part of something bigger. And that's what a real brand does—it connects with people, not just markets to them.

But here's the part most people forget. Even Apple lost its way. In the mid-90s, they fired Steve Jobs—their founder and heartbeat—the guy with the wild vision and even wilder expectations. Without him, Apple became ... average. Their products started to look like everyone else's. Beige boxes made a comeback. The fire was gone. The brand was fading. They weren't building tools for creatives anymore—they were chasing trends, playing it safe, and trying to blend in.

And you know what happens when you try to blend in? People stop noticing you. They became another confused, forgotten company on the edge of bankruptcy—until they brought Jobs back.

When he returned, he didn't just fix the product line—he brought back the *soul*. He reminded everyone who they were and what they stood for. He said, "We're not just selling tech. We're building tools for people who see the world differently." And the second that clarity returned, so did the momentum.

Here's the leadership lesson: When you lose your vision, you lose your voice. And when you lose your voice, you lose influence.

That line may be short, but it's true enough to hang your hat on. I've seen it play out in business, ministry, and even parenting. When you start drifting and forget what you're building, you stop showing up the way you were meant to. You stop leading. And whether you realize it or not, people stop following.

The reason I'm telling you all this is simple: You've got a brand, too. You may not think about it that way, but you do. Your name carries weight. Your attitude shows up before you do. Your habits, work ethic, how you treat people when you're tired, annoyed, or behind on a deadline—that's all part of your brand.

A brand isn't something you slap on a business card. It's not your title or your job description. It's what people say about you when you're not in the room and what your team feels when you walk in Monday morning. Your brand tells the story of your life, whether you like it or not.

Just like Apple, you can drift—lose your way. You can wake up one day and realize you've been trying so hard to fit in, smooth out your rough edges, and keep people happy, that you forgot who you were in the first place. You stopped being bold. You stopped leading with conviction. You got ... beige.

I know that feeling. I've lived it. There have been seasons in my life when I wasn't proud of the brand I was putting out into the world. Not because I didn't care, but because I got tired. Distracted. Burned out. But here's the good news: Apple had to bring back its founder to find its brand again. You? You need to return to yours.

God never loses sight of the leader He made you to be. He still knows your calling, wiring, and mission. You don't need a rebrand. You need a recovery of the voice and vision He gave you.

Your brand becomes powerful again the moment you remember who you are—when you stop apologizing for your convictions and start leading from the identity God gave you, not the one the world tried to assign you.

That's when people start following because they believe, not because they must. And that is a brand worth building.

Brand Check: What Do You Stand For (Besides Tacos and 90s Country)?

So far, we've talked about Apple, identity, beige boxes, and the moment you realize your personal brand might have drifted off somewhere between your last performance review and that one time you agreed to lead a meeting that could have been an email.

But what does this mean for *you*? Simple: Even if you feel like your personal brand is hiding under the deck with your old gym shorts and broken weed trimmer, you're not stuck. You've still got options. You can build a new brand. You can dust off the brand you were once proud of. Or, you can redefine your brand into something stronger, clearer, and more like *you*.

But no matter what path you take, one truth remains: You've got to build it on something. And that something is called core values.

Now, before your eyes glaze over like you're reading HR's annual mission statement (you know, the one they copy and pasted from 2003 and slapped on a wall next to the coffee pot), hang tight. We're going to do this the right way.

Think of it like this: You wouldn't build a skyscraper on the same foundation you'd use for a two-bedroom house with a carport and a questionable water heater. That'd be a disaster waiting to happen. You try stacking forty stories of steel and glass on a foundation built for a ranch-style house, and it's not a matter of *if* it topples—it's *when*.

The same thing is true in your life. If you're planning to grow—carry more weight, lead more people, make a bigger impact, or chase after something God-sized—make sure your foundation can handle it. What you believe, stand for, and how you make decisions must go *deep* before you try to go *high*.

Here's the good news: If you realize you've been trying to build big on a small slab, you don't have to tear down the whole thing. You only need to reinforce the foundation. Add new rebar. Pour deeper footings. Reevaluate what you've got, figure out what's missing, and then strengthen it.

Sometimes your foundation is too small, not because you did something wrong, but because you've outgrown it. Maybe you used to lead a team of two, and now twenty-five people are asking for your input before lunch. Perhaps you used to be responsible for yourself, and now you've got a family, business, mission, and a stack of expectations so high they're casting a shadow over your confidence.

That's not failure—that's *progress*. But progress comes with weight, and weight requires a strong base.

Your core values are more than a feel-good list. They're the blueprint for the foundation you're going to build your life and leadership on. And the stronger they are, the more you can handle without everything cracking under pressure. Now let's figure out what yours are. Let me ask you a question—and I want you to actually pause and think about this: Do you have core values?

Some of you just nodded. Some of you tilted your head like a confused Labrador. Either way, you already do. Even if you've never called them values, you're *living* by something. Maybe it's integrity and responsibility. Maybe it's caffeine and sarcasm. Either way, there's a code you're operating by.

This next part is about calling that code out of the shadows and getting it onto paper so you can lead with it. This book isn't some fluffy motivational speech disguised as a leadership manual. It's a guide to help you lead from *anywhere*—whether you've got a corner office or a corner of the jobsite trailer with half a desk and a microwave that smells like regret.

So, here's what I want you to do: Don't overthink this. Don't try to be impressive. Just be *honest*. Below is a list of values. These are the big ones—the stuff that shapes how we live, lead, and react when life punches us in the throat. Read through them. Circle the ones that hit your gut. If your heart yells "Yes!"—circle it. If it doesn't land, move on. We're not here to collect stickers. We're here to find your authenticity. Ready? Go!

Integrity	Courage	Responsibility	Gratitude
Faith	Accountability	Boldness	Perseverance
Family	Authenticity	Joy	Clarity
Extreme Ownership	Creativity	Justice	Honor
Ingenuity	Discipline	Leadership	Peace
Drive	Growth	Encouragement	Self-Control
Positive Energy	Wisdom	Stewardship	Influence
Excellence	Respect	Patience	Truth
Service	Compassion	Resilience	Forgiveness
Humility	Kindness	Empowerment	Loyalty
Grit	Generosity	Obedience	Trustworthiness

Now, don't just stare at your list like it's a menu at a new taco place. Narrow it down. Pick your top five. These should be the ones that scream "This is me," or "This is who I'm becoming." They are not who your boss wants you to be, or what looks good on a résumé. Just *you*—unfiltered. Ask yourself:

- Which of these describe who I already am (on my best days)?
- Which ones do I want to be remembered for?
- Which ones do I want my kids, team, and the guy I trained last week to say about me?

Write your answer here. Seriously. Don't skip this.

____

____

Got 'em? Good. Now we're going to take it one step deeper. I want you to define them. But not the dictionary version—that's for essays and people who use the word *synergy* without irony. I want *your* version. Ask yourself questions like these:

- What does grit look like *in my world* when I'm low on sleep and high on deadlines?
- What does humility mean when I'm managing a crew that knows *just enough* to think they know everything?
- What does *faith* mean when the numbers don't add up and the pressure's on?

Here's a quick example from me:

- Grit: I finish what I start. I show up even when I don't feel like it. I pick discipline over drama, and if something breaks, I fix it (or duct tape it until I can).
- Faith: I trust God more than I trust my comfort. I pray before I plan—and when the plan blows up, I pray again.

Now it's your turn. List your top five values:

1. ____
2. ____
3. ____
4. ____
5. ____

Bonus Round: To anchor these values in something solid, find a Bible verse that supports each one. Find something that reminds you these aren't just feel-good words, they're a foundation, because here's the truth: When the pressure is on, you don't rise to your goals—you fall back to your foundation.

Your foundation is built with these values. So don't skip this. Don't fake it. And don't pick *humility* just because it sounds holy. Choose what matters. Build a brand that reflects it. Your personal brand isn't forged on a stage—it's formed in the quiet decisions you make when nobody's clapping. Let's keep building. Here's an example for you.

My Personal Core Values

(The Stuff That Keeps Me from Going Full Sasquatch on a Tuesday)

Every strong leader either stands on something or floats around like a dollar-store balloon full of hot air and stuck to the ceiling. These seven values are what I stand on. They shape how I lead my businesses, love my family, serve my team, and walk out my faith.

And just to be clear—these weren't pulled from some corporate leadership workbook during a vision board retreat in the mountains. Nope. These were forged the real way: through prayer, failure, grit, grace, a few faceplants, and a lot of asking God, "Are You sure You picked the right guy?"

1. Extreme Ownership

I take full responsibility for my choices, my attitude, and my results. No excuses. If something goes sideways, I don't blame the guy next to me—I look in the mirror (which is never fun, especially before coffee). Leadership starts the second I stop pointing fingers and start fixing what I can actually control: *me.*

> *"Leaders must own everything in their world.*
> *There is no one else to blame."*
> —*Jocko Willink*

Translation? If there's a mess, I clean it up—even if I didn't make it. And if I did make it, I double-knot the trash bag and get after it.

2. Integrity

If I say I'll do it, I do it even if I don't feel like it later and even if it costs me sleep, pride, or a perfectly good Saturday afternoon. Integrity is doing the right thing even when you'd rather do literally *anything* else. It's walking out of the gas station to return the $5 bill the cashier dropped, even if your coffee is already getting cold in the truck.

> *"True integrity is doing the right thing, even when you're the*
> *only one who knows you did it."*
> —Dan Greer

Shortcuts are like duct tape on a leaking gas line. They might hold for a second, but eventually something's going to explode.

3. Driven

God gave me work to do—and I'm going to do it like I mean it. I don't believe in coasting, unless we're talkin' about down a mountain road in neutral to save fuel (been there). I'm wired to build, grow, and push forward even when I'm tired—*especially* when I'm tired. That's usually when the magic happens—right after the first "I'm done," but before the second wind kicks in.

> *"Opportunity is missed by most people because it is dressed*
> *in overalls and looks like work."*
> —Thomas Edison

Opportunity smells like diesel and sweat. Most folks run from it. I run toward it—with gloves on.

4. Innovative

I don't just fix problems—I redesign the whole process while I'm at it. If something's broken, I tinker. If it's slow, I streamline. If it's annoying, I automate it or hand it off to someone better at it. I'm not trying to be trendy—I'm trying to be *useful*.

> *"The competitor to be feared is one who never bothers about you*
> *at all but goes on making his own business better all the time."*
> –Henry Ford

The truth is, I get bored doing things the same old way. So, I don't. And that's where breakthroughs happen. Right after, "Wait ... what if we did it *this* way instead?"

5. Positive Energy

Listen—I'm not a fake chipper. You won't catch me handing out glitter and motivational quotes in the breakroom. But I *do* show up with grounded optimism and real, contagious momentum—the kind that gets people moving, not rolling their eyes. When I walk in, I want people to feel a little more clear, a little more confident, and a *lot* less like quitting today.

In other words: I bring the juice, not the junk.

6. Faith

God's not just a chapter in my story—He's the author. I don't separate *business Dan* from *Sunday Dan.* It's all one story. I pray before I plan, and I lean on Him when I'm about to hit a wall (which happens often). I've learned that trusting God's *timing* usually means trusting His *process*, too. And yes, that includes detours, delays, and people who test my sanctification daily.

God doesn't call the qualified; rather, He qualifies the called. Also true, from Paul, but I'm claiming 1 Corinthians 2:1-5 too.

FOR I DECIDED THAT WHILE I WAS WITH YOU I WOULD FORGET EVERYTHING EXCEPT JESUS CHRIST, THE ONE WHO WAS CRUCIFIED. I CAME TO YOU IN WEAKNESS—TIMID AND TREMBLING. AND MY MESSAGE AND MY PREACHING WERE VERY PLAIN. RATHER THAN USING CLEVER AND PERSUASIVE SPEECHES, I RELIED ONLY ON THE POWER OF THE HOLY SPIRIT. I DID THIS SO YOU WOULD TRUST NOT IN HUMAN WISDOM BUT IN THE POWER OF GOD.

—1 CORINTHIANS 2:1-5 (NLT)

And in case you're wondering—yes, I've tried doing it my way first. It never works.

7. Family

This one? It's my *why.* I don't hustle to escape them—I hustle to lead them. I want my wife and kids to know they come before success, strategy, and whatever exciting thing I'm building next. I may speak on stages, run businesses, and build systems, but I'm still the guy who changes lightbulbs, folds laundry wrong, and shows up to my kids lacrosse games in work boots.

Leading my family is my first job. Everything else is just bonus miles.

These seven values guide everything I do at Eclipse DOT—and more importantly, they guide *who I am* when nobody's looking.

Your values don't have to look just like mine. Heck, yours *shouldn't* look just like mine. But you do need to know what they are. Otherwise, you'll spend your life reacting instead of leading, chasing success instead of living purposefully, and trying to please everybody instead of standing for something.

Here's the deal: When you know what you stand for, you stop chasing everything else. And the world doesn't need more leaders who follow the crowd. It needs more leaders who know exactly who they are and live out their identities like it matters—because they do.

Now That You've Got Core Values, What's Next?

It's not framing them and hanging them over your toilet.

You've defined your core values. Look at you go. Seriously, solid work. If we were in the same room, I'd give you a firm handshake and maybe even one of those awkward half man hugs with the back slap.

But now comes the hard truth, friend: Values aren't your brand unless you actually *live* them.

I hate to break it to you, but writing *integrity* in neat cursive in your journal doesn't mean you're walking it out. Hanging *faith* on the office wall doesn't mean God's part of your meetings. And *family first* doesn't count if your kids are raising themselves while you're out chasing every shiny object that pays a deposit.

Values that aren't visible are aspirations. And aspirations without action are merely motivational fluff—like a *Live, Laugh, Love* sign hanging in a house full of yelling.

This is where most people miss the mark. They think picking values is the work. Once they check that box, they're now a certified leader with character and depth. Newsflash: Identifying your values is the warm-up. It's stretching before the workout. It's putting on your boots before you step in the mud. The real work is living those values consistently when it's inconvenient, uncomfortable, or costs you something.

That's the difference between a leader and someone who owns a bunch of leadership books they haven't read. So, let's not play games here.

If you say you don't cuss, then don't drop f-bombs when someone cuts you off in traffic—even if they deserve it. If your brand includes extreme honesty, don't start spinning half-truths because the full version makes you look a little bad. If you say, family first, but your calendar looks like a CEO boot camp and your kids have to book an appointment to get a hug, your brand is lying and not leading. Are you picking up what I'm laying down?

This isn't a do-as-I-say gig. It's a watch-me-do-it life. And make no mistake—people are watching. Your team. Your kids. Your spouse. Your coworkers. Even the random guy at the gas pump. And trust me—people smell inconsistency like a skunk in a crawl space.

When your actions don't match your values, people stop trusting your voice. Sure, they might still nod along in meetings or chuckle at your jokes (out of respect or survival). But in their hearts, they're already gone, because if they can't trust your brand, they're never going to fully buy into your leadership

Now hold up. I'm not saying you have to be perfect Nobody is. Heck, even Paul had a thorn in his side, and he wrote half the New Testament. What I am saying is this: Your integrity isn't built in your perfection—it's built in your ownership. When you mess up (and you will), own it. When you drop the ball, say so. When you act out of line with your values, apologize, and don't justify because that right there is where real trust is built. Not in your wins, but in your willingness to be real when you lose.

Your brand isn't about image—it's about integrity. It's not about impressing people—it's about influencing them. It's not about having it all together—it's about being the same person on Monday morning that you were shouting "Amen!" on Sunday.

You don't need a spotlight to build a brand worth following. You don't need a title or a corner office or a logo with a trademark. You just need to live your values loud enough that people see them—even if you never say a word. At the end of the day, a strong personal brand isn't something you show off. It's something that shows up every single day.

Your Brand Speaks When You Are Not in the Room

Core values are great. You need them. They give you direction, keep your decision-making from looking like a squirrel crossing traffic, and help you sleep at night. But let's clear something up—core values are not your brand. Your brand is what people say about you when you're not in the room.

Think about that.

When you leave a meeting, what sticks? Do people breathe a sigh of relief or say things like this?

- Man, I wish they'd stayed longer.
- She always had my back.
- He talked a big game but never delivered.

Do they remember your wisdom or your weird, backhanded compliments?

The lasting impression people carry around in their heads is your brand. Right there. No fancy logos. No slogans. I'll be straight with you: If you're leading anyone— your team, your family, yourself—there will always be someone who doesn't appreciate your style. And yes, they'll talk behind your back. I've had bosses who didn't like me, and boy, did they talk. Notice I didn't say *leaders*. There's a difference the size of Texas between a boss and a leader.

But here's what matters: the people who do know you, the ones you've served well and led with integrity, they'll carry the truth of your brand long after the noise dies down.

Now, it wouldn't be fair to tell you what your brand is without showing you how to take control of it. Warning: This next part might not be fun. If you're into the easy road, feel free to skip ahead. But if you're serious about becoming the leader people follow when you're not in the room—this is where the real work begins.

Still with me? Good. In the words of my Grandad, "Time to put your gloves on and get to work."

Ask yourself: *How do I want to be remembered?* Think beyond today. Think years from now. What will your kids, friends, coworkers, and community members say about you? What stories will they tell when your name comes up?

I was at a conference with Russell Brunson, and he asked us to do something that absolutely wrecked me—he asked us to write our own eulogy. Yeah, that thing someone reads at your funeral. Not your LinkedIn bio or sales pitch. The final chapter.

He read his eulogy out loud and then challenged us to write ours. It was one of the hardest and most rewarding things I've ever done. Writing down what I wanted my wife, kids, friends, and even my competitors to say about me when I was gone was emotional and transformational.

If you're afraid of facing death, this exercise will be uncomfortable. But leadership isn't about comfort. It's about clarity. So in true fashion of leading by example—here's mine.

Dan Greer Was Known by a Few Names

He would always say that he could tell when you met him by what name you called him. If you called him Danny, you knew him as a child—full of questions, energy, and just enough mischief to keep the adults guessing. If you called him Daniel, you probably knew him during his 20s or early 30s, when he was learning, building, pushing hard, and

discovering who God really made him to be. And if you called him Dan, you knew him as a man. The man who had weathered some storms, sharpened his voice, deepened his faith, and made peace with his purpose.

So, as you mingle today at the party after this service—because yes, he wanted it to be a party—ask people what they called him. That'll tell you a lot about how far back their story with him goes.

Dan was quite the character. As a child, he earned the nickname Bug—not because he liked insects (although he probably could have told you what they ate and where they lived)—but because he'd bug you with questions until he figured things out. He wanted to know why you did what you did. And he wouldn't let up until he understood it.

He had a love for trucks and equipment before he could walk. Anytime a semi pulled in to load cattle, Dan would beg his dad to let him talk to the trucker. Then he'd climb up in that cab like he owned it and play until the last cow was loaded. He wasn't playing pretend—he was preparing for a future that would be anything but ordinary.

He met his lifelong partner, Jenna, as a freshman in high school. They had geometry class together and sat at the same table. Dan used to joke that he loved her from the first day—but had to spend two years pleading with her before she'd say yes. Truth is, he didn't actually ask her out until the end of junior year. But once he did? Game over. They fell in love. They built a life.

Jenna and Dan raised four amazing kids. They grew up in a home where travel was a lifestyle. Dan and Jenna believed memories mattered more than money. They'd pack up the minivan, load the snacks, and hit the road—twenty-four hours straight to the Redwoods in Northern California, or down to San Diego for some warm beach time.

Dan was blessed to raise his family on the same homestead he grew up on. That land saw everything: laughter, lessons, bonfires, birthdays, wins, losses, and more faith than most folks would ever guess. And if you asked Dan what made it all work? He'd say, "Community. We didn't just live on the land. We lived with the people."

In his thirties, Dan started his own compliance business. It made sense—his parents always said, "That boy could argue with a fencepost and win." And they weren't wrong. Dan had a way with words. He could sit across from the toughest DOT officer, keep his cool, and turn the whole conversation around. But he didn't just run audits—he helped people understand. And that's what made him different.

As his business grew, so did his leadership. And so did his faith.

Dan had been raised in a house where God was present—but it wasn't until his mid-twenties that faith became personal. That's when Dan turned the wheel over to Jesus. And from that point on, God wasn't just part of his life—God was the CEO.

Dan would often stop in the middle of a meeting, mid-sentence, and just pray. Didn't matter who was in the room. He'd bow his head, ask God for clarity, and when he got the answer—that was it. Whether he liked the answer or not, he acted on it.

He knew that God protected him in everything he did.

Dan had more passions than most people have passwords. But two things topped the list: family and travel. He believed in loving big and living wide. His kids, grandkids, and even great-grandkids never wondered if they were loved. Not because of what they got, but because of what he taught.

One of his favorite lessons went like this: One time, we were walking through a national park—me, Jenna, and the kids—and one of my boys had just gotten snapped at by a stranger. Now when I say this guy was old, I mean old. Like, older than a VHS tape left in a hot truck bed. He was so old I half expected him to offer us a tour of the Garden of Eden.

Anyway, he barked at my kid about something ridiculous—probably walking too close to the trail edge or breathing too enthusiastically; I don't know. My son was rattled. I could see it all over his face. So, I put my hand on his shoulder and said, "Listen, if you had $86,400 in the bank and you lost ten bucks, would you spend the rest of the money trying to chase down those $10? Or would you take the loss, learn the lesson, and go grab lunch?"

"Never forget it—but don't be dumb enough to let ten lousy seconds hijack the other 86,390. You get a fresh batch every day—don't waste 'em all just because one moment went sideways. That's like torching your whole paycheck over a bad tip."

Now here's the kicker. As we kept walking, this complete stranger—who had apparently been right behind us the whole time—caught up to me back at the car. He looked at me and said,

"Hey, I think I'm just going to follow you around all day. That was pure gold. The wisdom you're dropping on your kids? That's the good stuff. Don't be surprised if I find you again before we leave this park."

I laughed and thanked him, but it hit me: People are always watching. Your kids. Your coworkers. Your team. And sometimes … even strangers at a trailhead. So, if you're going to be known for something— make it wisdom worth following.

Dan accomplished way too many things to list. If you knew him, you saw the fruit. But the things he was most proud of? His family, his faith, and the way he poured into others.

Dan didn't just think outside the box—he built the box, decided it could be better, tore it apart, and rebuilt it into something no one saw coming. Then he used it to carry the message God gave him—whether that meant a boardroom, a barn, or a back road.

Whether it was crafting insanely detailed artwork on leather or launching businesses that are still going strong today, he believed that if you could picture it, you could build it.

He had a way of pushing people to be better—without them realizing they were being pushed. One time, an employee told him they wanted to step up. Dan looked her straight in the eye and said, "Are you really ready for this? It's going to be hard. And I don't want you to hate me for pushing you." That was Dan. Direct. Honest. And full of heart.

He was also a chronic over-truster. He'd give you the shirt off his back and the last dollar in his wallet if you needed it more than he did. Not because he was soft, but because he believed in people. Sometimes to a fault.

But when it came to truth and follow-through? He didn't mess around.

He was a no-BS leader. If you lied to him, or failed to do what you said you'd do, he'd let you go. Not out of anger—but out of principle. He believed in excellence, ownership, and honor. If you showed up with honesty and effort, he would back you to the ends of the earth.

Dan lived a blessed life—and he knew it. He'd say it all the time: "God's given me more than I deserve." But he didn't just receive blessings. He gave them back—tenfold. He donated millions to causes he believed in. He started nonprofits that still serve today. He was always there when people needed help—and not just with money, but with time, wisdom, and presence.

He worked hard. He played harder. And he mentored anyone who wanted to grow, because for Dan, success wasn't about titles. It was about legacy.

And if he were standing here right now, he'd end it like this: "All things are possible with God! Not with a mere human, but if you include God in your plans—you will succeed."

So, on behalf of Dan—pray boldly. Dream bigger than what's comfortable. Ask God for what you want, because if you don't ask, you might miss the very thing He's been waiting to give you.

*****

Let's be clear—none of that's happened yet. That eulogy wasn't a highlight reel of my past. It was a roadmap for my future. The goal isn't to impress people when you're gone; it's to guide how you live while you're still breathing.

Now, as you read that, could you tell what my brand is? Exactly. It's integrity. Extreme ownership. Family and faith first. A life of service, prayer, hard work, generosity, and unapologetic joy. It's not a tagline. It's who I am—on paper, on purpose, and in practice.

So, what about you? What do people say about you when you leave the room? Do they light up or lock down? Do they trust you, or do they watch their back?

Someone I used to know (no names, we're keeping it clean) thought their brand was *hardworking and encouraging*. But what people actually saw was someone with backhanded compliments like, "Oh wow, you actually look like you care today!" and a work ethic that only kicked in when deadlines were burning. They thought they were respected, but in reality, they were distrusted, avoided, and quietly laughed about behind closed doors. Don't let that be you.

Now take a breath, and ask yourself: What do you think your brand is? Then ask: What do you want your brand to be? If those two don't match, it's not game over. It's go time.

I used to be seen as power-hungry, manipulative, and completely disconnected from faith. I was known as the guy who would say whatever it took to avoid blame and stay in control. That's not who I am today.

But it took intentional, uncomfortable, faith-filled work. I made commitments and kept them. And by the grace of God, I made a 180-degree turn. If I can do that, so can you.

Let's be clear: A brand isn't just something you say—it's something you live every single day. It's the code you carry, the values you refuse to bend on, and the legacy you're quietly building with every choice you make.

Back in the cowboy days, they used to say, "He rode for the brand." That didn't just mean he worked for the ranch—it meant he lived for it. Protected it. Represented it, even when no one was watching, because the brand wasn't just burned into the cattle. It was burned into *him*.

And that's where we're headed next. Now that we've looked at what people remember about you—the shadow your life casts when you're not in the room—it's time to ask a more intentional question: What brand are you actively building?

I'm not talking about the one you hope people see or the one you slapped on your business card. I mean the one that shows up in your daily actions, habits, and relationships.

If Jesus was willing to give everything—His name, purpose, and people—for His mission, then the least we can do is build a life and brand that reflects what matters.

So, let's roll up our sleeves and dig into it. It's time to define your brand on purpose.

Brand Audit: The Honest Look Most People Avoid

So, now that we've talked about the legacy you want to leave, it's time to face the mirror. Like it or not, you already have a brand. Right now. Today. Even if you've never written it down, brainstormed using a journal, or posted it in your office, it's there.

It shows up in how you handle pressure and treat people who can't do anything for you. It shows up when things go wrong, you're tired, and no one's watching. And here's the kicker: Your brand isn't defined by your best day; it's revealed on your worst.

Most people will spend years building a résumé and never stop long enough to think about what their name actually means to the people around them. But if you're going to lead—really lead—then you've got to face the reality of your current brand before you can shape the one you want. Let me break it down really simple. Your brand is defined by how you answer these questions.

- What does my team say about me after me leave the room?
- What does my spouse feel after a hard conversation?
- What do my kids think when they see me walk in the door?
- What do my crew, customers, and community trust me with—or don't.

If the answers to those questions sting a little, good. That's the sound of growth knocking.

Now, let's take inventory. No hiding. No sugarcoating. Ask yourself these questions, and don't answer them like you're updating LinkedIn—answer them like your future depends on it:

- What do people consistently trust me with and why?
- Where am I dependable? Where am I flaky?
- What's one value I claim to have but rarely live out when it's inconvenient?
- What am I known for when I'm not trying to impress anyone?

You don't need a hundred answers. You need honest answers because if the story you tell doesn't match the one you live in, your brand is broken, and people already know it. And I'll be the first to say, I've been there.

There was a season when I said the right things, but behind the scenes, I was just trying to survive. Instead of living the brand I wanted, I was managing the one I had created by accident. It looked strong but lacked roots.

But here's the grace in all of this: You don't have to stay where you are. You get to rebuild your brand, on purpose, starting right now.

Before You Write Your Brand, Let's Talk About What You *Don't* Want It to Be

Before we start carving your brand into stone, I want you to think about something first: What brand do you not want to build?

Seriously—pause for a minute. Think about a few people in your life who've left a bad taste in your mouth. The ones who made you say, "Yeah, I'll never lead like that." Maybe it was Captain Rick or my old boss who drove past that oil spill for weeks without lifting a finger. Maybe it was someone who always smiled in public but tore people down behind closed doors.

Look, even those folks had some good qualities. But their brand wasn't one I'd want tattooed on my legacy.

And that's the whole point. Brand building is about more than avoiding bad behavior—it's about refusing to become the leader you once rolled your eyes at. You don't want to be the one who talked big but led small, showed up late, blamed everyone else, and thought a title was the same as trust.

You've got to build the leader you want to be on purpose—with grit, conviction, and a willingness to lead differently than the ones who disappointed you. Nobody drifts into greatness. You define your brand with intention, or default to someone else's mess.

Let me tell you a story that'll make this hit a little deeper.

I was hired to teach a two-day company training. Day one was CDL prep, day two was all about DOT regs, vehicle definitions, you name it. They flew me in as the expert. I had a clear agenda, the company was all in, and the room was full of folks ready to learn.

Enter: Know-it-all Jack

Jack was … experienced. You know the type. He walked in like he owned the building, took a front-row seat, and spread out like he was setting up command central. Three pens were lined up on the desk like he was preparing for battle, and a legal pad so big it appeared he was planning to rewrite the government regulations handbook from memory.

He wasn't mean. He was *a lot*—like a double shot of espresso mixed with a handful of Pop Rocks. Loud, confident, and constantly commenting, he was the guy who would correct your grammar mid-sentence and then mispronounce *axle*. He came in hot with a let-me-tell-you-how-this-works attitude, before I'd even opened the slide deck.

It was barely five minutes into day one, and Jack was already pushing back.

We weren't even in the classroom—we were out by the trucks doing the walkaround inspection in the hot sun heavy with diesel fumes. This was the setting where most folks shut up and learn because they *know* they're about to get gold. Not Jack.

I'd just finished showing the group how to walk through the pre-trip inspection— exactly how the examiner wants to see it for the CDL test. I've done this hundreds if not thousands of times. I know what works. What passes. What fails. This wasn't theory— this was proven.

And right then, Jack throws his hand up like he's in a town hall meeting and says— loud enough for the folks across the yard to hear— "Well, that's not how I was trained at my last job."

Now, what I *wanted* to say was: "Well, Jack, this isn't your last job—and thank the good Lord above for that. So why don't you stop polishing your participation trophy and actually pay attention? Or better yet, if your old way was so fantastic, why are you standing here needing *my* help? Or (*and this is my favorite*) do you just want a cookie for being confidently wrong in front of everyone?"

But instead, I took a slow breath, looked him right in the eye, and said, "That's nice, Jack. If you follow what I'm showing you here, I can almost guarantee you'll pass the test on your first try. If you stick to your way, well, all I can say is good luck."

He smirked like he'd just won something. But what he didn't realize was that the room had already shifted. Guys started glancing sideways. One rolled his eyes. They all knew exactly what I knew: This wasn't going to be the last time Jack spoke up. And it definitely wasn't going to be the most helpful thing he said.

My response should have ended it.

But no, Jack kept going. For every lesson, step, and statement, I got the "I'm not saying you're wrong, but …" routine and outline. The whole room cringed a little more every time he said it. He was trying so hard to impress the company owner, but he only drained the energy out of the room like someone pulled the plug.

Day two comes, and now we're in the classroom, diving deeply into DOT regulations. Jack's back at it—interrupting, questioning, and side-commenting. And then, out of nowhere, he hits me with this gem: "So, what happens if a plane taxis across a freeway?"

Wait. What?

I looked at him like he just asked if squirrels need to signal before crossing the road. The room went silent. People glanced at each other. One guy actually dropped his pen in disbelief. Then Jack launches into a full story about a state patrol officer who supposedly pulled over a jet on the tarmac after it crossed a freeway with its flaps down. I kid you not.

I didn't even respond. I just stood there and let the silence do the work. The room knew Jack was full of it. And what's wild is that he probably took more notes than anyone else in the room. He was *trying*. He really was. But because of the way he showed up, no one could hear what he was saying anymore. And that's the *branding lesson.*

Jack wanted to be seen as knowledgeable and experienced. But his behavior screamed, "I already know everything, and you can't teach me squat." He didn't build credibility—he buried it under ego.

Here's the truth: Even if you have something valuable to say, your brand determines whether people listen.

So, before you write down the brand you *want*, take five minutes and write down what you *absolutely don't*. Think of the Jacks, the Ricks, and the bosses who led by fear, laziness, and arrogance. List the traits you want to run from like a blown steer tire on I-70. Then commit—right now—not to carry those into your leadership. Knowing what to avoid is just as important as knowing what to pursue.

You still with me? Good. Now that we've cleared the air, let's build something worth following.

But first, here's my list. This isn't hypothetical. This is straight from my own experience. From people I've worked with… and from times I've had to look in the mirror and admit, *I don't like what that version of me stood for.* So, when I think about the brand I'm building, I also think about what I *refuse* to bring with me:

- **Dishonest** – I want my word to mean something. Period. If I say I'll be there at 3 p.m., I'm there. And not *on my way* from forty-five minutes out.

- **Unteachable** – If I ever start acting like I know it all, hand me a gold-plated congratulations-you've-peaked trophy and send me home.

- **All Talk, No Follow Through** – I don't want to be the guy who promises steak and delivers a cold hot dog.

- **Ego-Driven – Edging God Out (EGO)** – That's what ego really stands for. I've been there—thinking I had to carry everything on my own shoulders. I don't. And neither do you. The second I start building a brand that makes me the hero instead of God, I know I'm off track. No amount of chest-pounding can outwork obedience.

- **Fake** – And I don't just mean fake on social—I mean *fake* fake. Like those high school cowboys who wore boots, had a dip can ring in their jeans, but had never touched a horse unless it was made of plastic at the county fair.
- **Fake Humble** – "Oh, I'm nothing special," says the guy who just spent ten minutes telling you about all twelve of his awards. Nah, I'll pass.
- **Always Right** – I'd rather be the guy who learns from every argument than the guy who wins and ends up wrong with confidence.
- **Judgmental** – I don't want to be the person who raises an eyebrow every time someone tries something new. Unless it's a tuna hotdog—then all bets are off.
- **Checked Out** – I've seen leaders who were more emotionally distant than a teenager at a family reunion. I don't want to be that guy.
- **Emotionally Volatile** – Your team shouldn't have to consult the *Farmer's Almanac* to figure out if today's a good day to talk to you.
- **Insecure and Loud About It** – Confidence doesn't have to yell. If I ever start being the loudest guy in the room, just know—I'm probably covering up the fact I forgot what the meeting was about.

That's what I'm running from. Not because I've got it all figured out. Not because I've nailed every one of these every day, but because I've lived and led long enough to know exactly what I don't want my name attached to.

I've seen what the wrong brand can cost in business, marriage, and faith. And I've watched too many good people lose influence because they didn't take the time to define what they stood for.

Now it's your turn. Before we write the brand you want, let's discuss where that desire actually comes from. Whether you realize it or not, this isn't just about leadership—it's about identity. Identity is something God's been serious about since page one.

The Bible doesn't use the word *brand*. But flip through a few pages, and you'll see God cares deeply about what we're known for. What matters is our name, reputation, and fruit in business and how we show up, serve, and lead when no one's looking.

Proverbs 22:1 says, "A good name is more desirable than great riches; to be esteemed is better than silver or gold."

That right there should stop Christian leaders in their tracks. God's not saying a good name is *nice* to have—He's saying it's *better than money*. Let's face it. We've all known people who had wealth, power, and position, but their name was not worth much. They weren't trusted, respected, or remembered for the right reasons. That's a bad brand, plain and simple.

Your brand is the story people tell about you when you're not around. It's your character on display, the legacy you leave, and what your team says at the water cooler. It's what your spouse and kids tell others about who you are. And whether you realize it or not, you're building that brand every day—one decision, conversation, and act of integrity at a time. But here's where it gets bigger.

As a Christian, you don't just carry your *own* brand—you carry the name of Jesus. That's not some cute phrase you put on a bumper sticker. That's your identity. You're a CEO, manager, parent, or community leader and *an ambassador of Christ.*

In the second book of Corinthians 5:20 we read, "We are therefore Christ's ambassadors, as though God were making His appeal through us."

Let that sink in. When people see you, hear you speak, and experience your leadership, they get a picture of Jesus, whether they know Him or not. That's a weighty responsibility. But it's also a beautiful invitation. You carry His values into your company, home, and friendships. You are a walking billboard for grace, truth, hope, and love.

Now, Jesus didn't build His brand with flashy miracles or catchy slogans. He built it by showing up for people, healing the broken, standing for truth, forgiving the guilty, and loving the unlovable. Climbing the ladder is something we do, but Jesus never sought status. He did the opposite, and washed feet instead. That's a brand rooted in humility and purpose. And people followed Him because of what He said and how He lived.

Philippians 2:5–7 reminds us of this: "In your relationships with one another, have the same mindset as Christ Jesus: who, being in very nature God, did not consider equality with God something to be used to His own advantage; rather, He made Himself nothing by taking the very nature of a servant."

That's our example. That's the brand we're supposed to reflect.

Let's not pretend this is easy. You're going to mess up. I have botched things up more times than I can count. I've been prideful, short-tempered, and more focused on business than the people in it. And I've had to hit my knees and ask God to realign me with what matters.

Psalm 139:23–24 has been one of my go-to prayers:

"Search me, God, and know my heart; test me and know my anxious thoughts. See if there is any offensive way in me, and lead me in the way everlasting."

That prayer right there? It'll wreck you in the best way. It'll shine a light on the places where your brand and your beliefs don't line up. It'll reveal where you've been building your name instead of His.

Here's the reality. Your brand isn't about being perfect. It's about being consistent. It's about aligning your values with your actions. It's about owning your mistakes, showing grace, and leading with humility. And when your brand reflects Christ, it becomes a beacon for others. It draws people in—not to worship you, but to wonder about the One you follow.

Matthew 5:16 says, "Let your light shine before others, that they may see your good deeds and glorify your Father in heaven."

That's what a God-honoring brand does. It shines, serves, and points people straight to Jesus.

So here's my challenge to you: Take inventory. Ask yourself, "What does my brand say about Christ?"

If you don't like the answer, don't beat yourself up—just do something about it. Pray. Repent. Realign. Rewrite the story starting today. In the end, what matters is who you served, how you lived, and whose name you carried. No one cares about how big your business got or how many followers you had. If you carry the name of Jesus, make sure your brand reflects Him well. That brand is the one worth living and dying for.

Write the Brand

Look, I didn't drag you through this chapter to hand you a gold star and tell you "good job for thinking about leadership." Nope. This isn't about thinking. It's about doing. If you've made it this far and still haven't started writing your brand, what the heck are you waiting for? Permission? Cool. You've got it.

Let me remind you of something you already know but probably haven't said out loud: Your brand already exists. Right now. In this moment. With every text you send, decision you make, second you choose pride over your purpose, you're either building a brand that earns trust, or one people are silently stepping around. And let's not pretend like we've got unlimited time to figure this out. The truth is, your legacy is under construction whether you like it or not.

And people are watching you build it like it's an HGTV show. Some are rooting for you, others are waiting to see if it all collapses. A few are standing

RIDING FOR THE BRAND

back saying, "Man, I hope he figures it out before it's too late." So, here's my advice: Don't wait until your funeral to find out what people really thought.

Write it now. Shape it now. Live it now. And hey—don't try to perfect the whole thing in one sitting. Remember: the only way to eat an elephant is one bite at a time.

So take that bite. Messy or not. You can't live a brand you never define. If you want to be remembered for something that matters, you've got to start on purpose.

Write the five words you want people to say when your name comes up in a room you're not in. Then go out and *earn* those words—every day, one action at a time. This isn't a branding exercise. It's a defining moment. So shut the book, pick up the pen, and write your brand like your life depends on it. The truth is, it does.

Key Takeaways from Chapter Four

Your brand is the feeling people get when you show up (or don't). It's not your title, your logo, or what's printed on your business card—it's the experience you create. People follow what they feel, not just what you say.

Lose your vision, you love your voice. When you drift from who you are and what you stand for, your leadership fades. Bold influence comes from living anchored, not beige and blended.

You're already building a brand—on purpose or by accident. Every action, attitude, and reaction is telling a story. Whether you mean to or not, you're building a reputation every single day.

Core values are the foundation, not wall decor. Picking words is easy. Living them out when it's hard, inconvenient, or humbling? That's where leadership gets forged. If it's not visible, it's not a value—it's wishful thinking.

If you don't define your brand, the world will do it for you. Your name means something—especially to the people who count on you. If you're not intentional, someone else's version of you becomes the story that sticks.

Brand isn't perfection. It's consistency with ownership. You're gonna mess up. But when you do, own it. People trust leaders who are real, not polished. Integrity isn't found in the wins—it's proven in the cleanups.

You don't just represent yourself—you represent Jesus. As a believer, your brand carries weight beyond your business. You're a walking billboard for Christ. Build a brand that points to Him—not just your hustle.

Don't just write your brand. Live it loud enough they don't need to ask. The goal isn't to be impressive. It's to be real, consistent, and trusted—even when you're not in the room. Your brand is showing up whether you're watching or not.

Chapter 5 | When No One's Watching,
You're Still Leading

Leading in the Absence of Applause

I still remember the day my boss called me into his office. He had that salesman smile on his face—the kind that usually meant I was about to get a compliment right before getting handed something that would wreck my calendar.

"Dan, you've done a great job getting our compliance program in shape," he said. "And that defensive driving course you built? Top-notch."

"But now," *here we go* … he leaned in like he was about to tell me a secret, "I need you to start helping out our water hauling division too."

Before I could ask a single question, he tossed me a set of company truck keys like I'd just won a prize at the county fair. "You'll keep doing your current job, but I need you over at the state line yard. Those guys start early—like 6 a.m. early."

That's when I started doing the math. Wait a minute … *Isn't that place like an hour and a half from my house?* Yup. It was. I checked later. And just like that, my mornings got a whole lot earlier. Then he added, "Oh, and we hired a guy to manage them, but … he's struggling."

So now I was keeping my full-time role, jumping into a second one, driving three hours a day, and inheriting a team's problem child. And I was supposed to do it all with a smile. Translation: Dan, go fix a dumpster fire, but make sure you don't step on the guy who's supposed to be running it, and do it while still doing your regular job.

I nodded and smiled like an idiot. I mean, this *offer* came with a company truck, salary job, and company credit card. I felt like I had finally made it. As I turned to leave, he dropped the cherry on top—the one that would stick with me forever.

"Dan, you're going to have to be the sheriff down there. That means sometimes you'll need to be a prick. You're representing corporate now." I laughed. "Not sure I'm good at being a prick," I said. *Guess I got better. Just kidding. Sort of.*

The truth is, I wanted to impress him. I wanted to prove I could lead. I thought leadership was about being noticed and getting the title, the truck, and the card. I didn't know yet that real leadership has nothing to do with what's in your pocket and everything to do with what's in your heart.

The next morning, I felt like a million bucks. I fired up my new company truck, rolled the windows down, cranked up the radio, and headed toward the yard like I owned the world. Giant coffee in one hand. Pride in the other. Head held high.

I pulled into the yard around 8 a.m., ready to show them all how it's done. Only, the place was a ghost town. The drivers had been gone for hours. It turns out, that in the water hauling world, if you show up at 8 a.m., you're already three hours behind and half an inch deep in mud.

I stayed late that night. I sat in that yard past 7 p.m., waiting for drivers to limp back in with mud-caked trucks, weary eyes, and a few looking at me like I was a ghost. Nobody expected the compliance guy to stick around past lunch, let alone until sundown.

The next morning, I was up at 4 a.m., backing out of my driveway under a sky full of frozen stars. It was the cold that bites through your jacket and makes your steering wheel feel like a block of ice. But I rolled into the yard by 5:30 a.m.

That's when I saw it. Some guys—*a few*—were doing solid, legit pre-trips. Walking their trucks, checking tires, popping hoods, lights on, gloves on—they had their heads in the game. And then, there were the clipboard cowboys, as I like to call them. You know the type. Slap the hood. Click a pen. Pretend to squint at a tire like it owes them money. Maybe wiggle a light and then walk off like they just finished a NASA launch inspection. I stood there watching the whole thing and not saying a word, just soaking it in.

If I'm being honest, I started to wonder what the heck I'd gotten myself into. I wasn't the boss. I wasn't even from their division. I was just some dude with a company truck, a clipboard, and a long drive. Still, I tried doing what my boss told me—play sheriff.

So, I marched over to a few of them, chest puffed out, trying my best gruff voice like I was auditioning for a role in a low-budget cop movie.

"You call that a pre-trip?"

"Pop that hood back open."

"Tell me what you're checking or go park it."

It worked—until it didn't. Let's just say, if leadership were measured by how fast people ran away from you, I would have been Employee of the Year. They didn't respect me. They didn't even dislike me. They *avoided* me

Leadership Lesson #1: Fear Doesn't Build Loyalty. It Builds Distance.

So, I pivoted. I went to the yard manager and asked if any extra budget was lying around. It turned out there was enough for gift cards and small bonuses.

I started hiding little tags around the trucks. Notes that said, "If you find this, come see me." The first one who found it got a $100 cash bonus at the next safety meeting. No shaming. No scolding. Just quiet wins for doing the right thing. Suddenly, they weren't dodging me anymore. They were looking for me. I didn't have to be there at 6 a.m. every day. But I was still showing up when it mattered.

September and October had been beautiful—golden leaves, crisp mornings. And then, December hit, bringing snow, ice, and mud that could swallow a pickup whole. Chains snapping. Trucks buried axle deep. The cold chewed through your gloves and laughed at your jacket. There were mornings when I left my house at 4 a.m. and never made it home that night. I slept in the shop more nights than I care to count, curled up on a plastic couch. Still wearing my boots, I wondered if this was really what making it looked like. No cameras. No applause. There was just me, a shovel, a flashlight, and a whole lot of stubbornness.

There was one night in particular I'll never forget. I had just made it home. After dinner, I tucked my kids into bed and read them a book to help them fall asleep. The house was finally quiet, and I was finally starting to settle in, when my phone rang. I looked at the clock—8:30 p.m. *Who in the heck is calling me at 8:30 p.m. at night?*

I looked over at Jenna and asked if I should answer. She smiled that knowing smile and said, "You're going to answer it anyway." She knew me. She's always known me. I'm built to help. It's stitched into my bones.

It was one of our water truck drivers. He said, "Dan, we're still missing three trucks. They haven't come back to the yard yet." Without even thinking, I kissed Jenna goodbye, grabbed my truck keys, and jumped back into my company pickup.

This was supposed to be my night off, but I was throwing myself right back into the mess. The hour-and-a-half drive back to the yard was harrowing in the pitch-black night with roads slick from fresh snow melting into mud. When I pulled into the yard, another guy was waiting for me. He wasn't even a supervisor in the water division. He just ran one of the hydro vac crews.

If you've never seen a hydro vac, it's basically a vacuum cleaner the size of a semi-truck. It'll suck rocks, mud, even small trees through an eight-inch hose. Wicked cool. He climbed into my truck, and we took off into the dark, heading toward the last GPS pings from the missing drivers. There is no cell service. No radio communication. No backup. Just two guys, a pickup, and a prayer.

The first driver we found was already limping his way back in. He looked like he'd been through war. He told us he'd gotten stuck two or three times but had managed to dig himself out every time. No complaining. No whining. Just grit. We waved him through and told him to get back to the yard. One down. Two to go.

We kept pushing deeper into the reservation access roads. These weren't even real roads. They were mud trails barely wide enough for a single truck. Out here, even in the middle of the day, you might see five cars in twenty-four hours. At night? It was us and the coyotes.

I could feel my pickup slipping even in four-wheel drive. Every rut felt like it wanted to eat my truck whole, and every puddle looked like it might be a sinkhole disguised with just enough surface tension to ruin your night. We were crawling, headlights barely cutting through the blackness, scanning every ridge and ditch for any sign of a truck or taillights.

And then, just off the main trail, I spotted a faint glint of chrome reflecting in the brush.

"There!" I hit the brakes and slid sideways a bit. We bailed out of the pickup and walked into the mud—boots instantly sinking. His water truck was tilted at an angle, buried up to the frame in slop thick enough to swallow a man's pride.

He was standing outside, covered in mud, sleeves soaked, hands raw from digging. No radio, no signal, no backup. Just a guy doing what he could with what he had. No complaints. No drama. Just old-fashioned grit.

We didn't waste time with questions or blame. We were just three men with two shovels and one shared mission. Frozen hands hit frozen mud. The cold sliced through our gloves like razor blades. My fingertips went numb so fast I wasn't even sure if I was holding the shovel or just pretending. But we dug him out. No cheering. No pats on the back. Just a nod and a wave as he climbed back in his rig and started the slow crawl toward the yard.

Two recovered. One still missing.

We pressed deeper into the dark. The roads weren't even roads anymore. They were just suggestions where trucks had once tried to drive. Finally, we found the third truck, buried all the way to the axles. Not going anywhere.

The driver stood there, headlights lighting up the endless mud, looking half defeated and half frozen. We didn't scold him. We didn't yell. We didn't say, "Why didn't you do this or that?" We just grabbed the chains and shovels and got to work. Cold mud clung to everything—our boots, our gloves, and his pride. Our boots were sinking deeper into the mud by the second, and the truck wasn't going anywhere on its own.

Our hands went numb so fast it felt like we were digging with frozen sausages instead of fingers. Every time we took a step, the mud tried to suck our boots off like it was hungry. We slipped. We grunted. We let a few words fly under our breath but most were *way* too loud. But we were the only ones out there. Who was going to get offended? The coyotes? The elk? We laughed at the absurdity and kept digging.

Quitting? Yeah, that wasn't an option. Not out there. Not with people counting on us to get it done. We threw boards under the tires. We chained up the rear end. We pushed and pulled and rocked that truck for what felt like forever. In reality, it took us three hours to move that truck less than half a mile. Every twenty feet, we got stuck again. Every twenty feet, we dug again. Hooked up again and pulled again. We fought that mud like it was alive.

Finally, we got that truck down to the main gravel road where it could sit safely. We locked it up, loaded the driver into my pickup, and started the long drive back to the shop. By the time we rolled into the yard, it was 4 a.m. I crashed on the dirty office couch, still wearing my boots, still covered in mud, too tired to even care. A few hours later, the truck boss strolled in—fresh, well-rested, coffee in hand—and looked at me crashed out on the couch. He chuckled and said, "Man, you're here early today."

I looked up at him, eyes burning from exhaustion, and said, "No. I'm still here. I came back out last night when your drivers called me because they knew I would answer, and they trusted me to come. Why are they calling me instead of you? Why am I the one out there dragging trucks out of the mud while you're asleep in your bed?"

He didn't say a word. He didn't have to.

The drivers knew who was really leading—not the guy with the title and fancy office. The leader was the guy who showed up, answered the phone, and stayed until the last truck was safe. That night changed everything for me. I wasn't the sheriff or the boss. I wasn't trying to be anything except someone they could count on. Little by little, the drivers noticed. Not because I gave speeches or demanded respect. I lived leadership.

They saw the guy who didn't brag about leadership. He just picked up a shovel and started digging. They saw the guy who didn't bark orders. He just topped off their coolant when they weren't looking. They saw the guy who wasn't too proud to chain up a rig at 2 a.m. in a snowstorm without asking for anything in return. Six months into it, they trusted me more than they trusted the guy with *manager* on his door. And the crazy part is, I wasn't trying to be trusted. I was trying to do the right thing.

Meanwhile, back home, Jenna was leading too. She was raising our kids while I was chasing down missing trucks. She was folding laundry, paying bills, and making sure our part of the world didn't fall apart when I wasn't there. She was doing it without applause, backup, a trophy, or a title. That's leadership, too.

It doesn't happen under the lights. It doesn't happen in the applause. Leadership happens in the mud and cold. It happens when you stay one more hour, dig one more truck, and take one more phone call nobody else wants to answer. It happens when you drive one more mile, chain up one more rig, stay one more hour, and help one more person with no promise that anyone will ever say thank you.

The world tells you leadership is about being in charge. Real leadership is about showing up when it's dark, freezing, you're bone tired and lonely, and the only ones watching are heaven, your wife, and the mud stains on your boots.

You earn your calling in the shadows, and God shines the light when you're ready. The leader you become in the shadows, is the leader God can trust in the light.

The Myth of Public Leadership

When most people think about leadership, they think about the spotlight. They think occupying a corner office with a gold engraved nameplate on the door and scoring a reserved parking spot makes someone a leader. Leaders are the experts standing at the front of the room with a microphone, saying the right things made more credible by flaunting their title. They think it's getting called up to the stage, shaking hands, posing for pictures, and holding a plaque while people politely clap over a cold chicken dinner.

The world has spent a lot of money selling us that cheap, plastic version of leadership. It's the one that says you're a leader because somebody gave you a title. It's the one that says you've made it when people know your name. It's the one that says leadership is about being seen. Real leadership has never been built under the lights. It's built in the dark.

Real-world leadership is built in the moments nobody sees—when your alarm goes off at 2 a.m. and you drag yourself out of bed because someone out there needs you. It's built when the phone rings late at night, and you could pretend you didn't hear it, but you pick it up anyway. It's built when you kneel in freezing mud with a shovel and frozen chains, shoulder to shoulder with people who barely even know your name because whether they know it or not, they're counting on you.

Leadership isn't made the day they hand you the truck keys, a new title, or a raise. Leadership is made the thousand days before that when nobody knew your name or cared if you showed up, but you showed up anyway.

Flash fades. Titles come and go. Nobody cares about your business card when the wheels fall off, and the mud is swallowing their truck whole. What they care about and remember is whether you were there when it mattered.

You don't lead because people recognize you. You lead because people can rely on you. If you're only willing to lead when someone's looking, you were never leading. Leadership isn't something you get handed. It's something you fight and bleed for. The proof isn't in how many people follow you on LinkedIn. The proof is in the nights you stayed when it would have been easier to leave. It's in the miles you drove when it would have been easier to go home. It's in the people who trust you because they watched you keep showing up when everyone else found an excuse not to.

Leadership is proven when the crowd is gone, the lights are off, and you're still standing in the mud, fighting for the people who can't fight for themselves. The truth is simple: Leadership isn't proven when things go right. It's proven when a leader is still standing when everything goes wrong.

If you're willing to keep showing up when no one's watching, a day will come when the people you quietly served—the ones your fought for without recognition— will know exactly who to follow when the pressure's on and the stakes are real.

That's leadership. It's what the world is desperate for. And it begins with the decision to show up—not for applause, but because you've been called to lead.

The Hard Places Where Leadership Grows

The other day, I was driving across Red Mountain Pass with two of my boys. We were headed to my youngest son's lacrosse tournament. The three of us were packed into my truck with a couple of bags thrown in the backseat, chasing a sunset over the Rockies.

Red Mountain isn't the road you take by accident. It's a narrow strip of winding blacktop, chiseled into the side of some of the steepest, wildest mountains Colorado has to offer. If you don't like heights, or if hairpin turns with thousand-foot drop-offs that make your palms sweat, Red Mountain Pass is probably not going to be your favorite part of the family road trip. But if you can stomach it, it'll give you some of the most jaw-dropping views you'll ever see. We had already climbed up through the mining town of Silverton, crawling along roads so narrow you could reach out the window and touch the cliff walls if you wanted to. We twisted through a handful of switchbacks near the summit, barely doing fifteen or twenty miles an hour, the truck hugging the edge like it knew better than to slip.

Above us, the mountains shot straight-up—walls of jagged rock that looked like the hand of God had just slammed them into the earth. Below us, the cliffs dropped off so sharply that if you stared too long, your stomach would turn somersaults. And somewhere between all that, the sky stretched wide and blue, so clean it made you feel like you were breathing for the first time.

It's funny. We call those *hills* out here in Colorado. Back east, they call them *mountains*. If you ever get a chance to drive from Ouray to Silverton, buckle up. Those aren't hills. Those aren't even friendly mountains. Those are God's skyscrapers. As we started winding our way down the far side of the pass, threading through the switchbacks like a needle through cloth, something caught my eye.

Growing right out of the cliff face—and I mean *straight out of the rock*—were trees. At first, you almost don't believe what you're seeing. There's no soil up there— no real ledge. There is no safe spot for roots to nestle in and hide from the storms. Just jagged rock, sharp enough to slice your hands open if you tried to climb it, and there— sticking out like a miracle—were towering trees. They weren't little twigs either. They were eight to twelve inches thick at the base, standing twenty, thirty feet tall, waving in the mountain wind like they belonged there. It was the sight that makes you stop talking, worrying, and thinking and just sit there with your mouth hanging open like a kid seeing fireworks for the first time. As we kept winding down the pass, my youngest son leaned over and stared out the window, his nose almost pressed against the glass. "Dad," he said, his voice filled with wonder, "How in the world is that tree growing there? There's no dirt. I couldn't even hang onto that cliff with my fingertips. How does a tree even find enough to live?"

I laughed quietly, but inside, something bigger than a laugh stirred. Standing there on the side of that impossible mountain was a living, breathing picture of what leadership really looks like.

I kept driving after my son asked the question, but his words stuck to me like a splinter under the skin. I couldn't shake it. How *does* a tree grow in a place like that? How does *anything* survive, clinging to the side of a cliff with no soil, shelter, or easy way to get what it needs?

We wound lower down the pass, the sun radiating light over the peaks, casting shadows that seemed to stretch all the way into tomorrow. I kept stealing glances at those trees, rooted in places where life had no business surviving. Somehow, against all odds, they were thriving. Their sturdy trunks supported branches reaching for the sky like they owned it—silent proof that something had fought through every storm, winter, miserable howling night, and decided to live anyway.

The more I thought about it, the more it hit me deep down in that place where no speeches can reach: That's where leadership grows. Leadership grows in the cracks, cliffs, and the barren places nobody else thinks are worth planting in. Not in the easy places. Not in the rich soil where everything comes easy. Not in the spotlight where the applause is loud and the critics are few.

Anybody can look strong when the ground is soft, and the rivers run easy. Anybody can lead when the weather is fair, and the crowds are clapping. Only a few can lead when the wind is trying to rip you off the side of the mountain, and you've got nothing but a few stubborn roots and the grace of God holding you there.

It's forged in the mornings when you drag yourself out of bed at 4 a.m. when everything in your body says to quit. It's built on the nights you stay out till 1 a.m. draining contaminated diesel out of trucks and your hands freezing to the metal, because if you don't do it, the job doesn't get done.

People always say pressure makes diamonds. That's true. But they never tell you what pressure feels like when you're under it. It doesn't feel heroic. It feels crushing, like you're stretched so thin you're one bad day away from shattering. It feels like you're hauling weight you were never built to carry, but you carry it anyway, because the people behind you depend on you to stay standing.

I've lived it. There have been times when I thought for sure God had me confused with someone stronger. I've sat alone in my truck, head against the steering wheel, telling Him, "I'm at the end, Lord. There's nothing left in the tank." And still, somehow, He'd give me just enough strength to dig deeper.

And maybe you feel like that sometimes too. Maybe you feel like the odds are against you. The ground's too hard, the rain's too late, and the storms are too strong. The hard places aren't where you fail. The hard places are where God grows leaders.

Those trees on Red Mountain didn't survive because they were lucky. They survived because a seed found the tiniest crack in the rock, dug deep, and refused to let go.

God doesn't waste the struggle, long nights, tired mornings, or the moments when quitting sounds a lot more reasonable than digging in one more inch. He uses every bit of it to shape you, not into someone who looks good under soft lights, but into someone who can stand tall when the storms hit. Leadership is about standing tall when it's easy and when everything else crumbles. It's about planting yourself when the wind howls, the sky falls, and the ground shakes—and refusing to be moved.

That's what those trees taught me that day. That's what the cliffs of Red Mountain preach to anyone willing to listen. You don't need perfect conditions to lead. You don't need a smooth path or a friendly breeze or a whole valley cheering you on. You need one crack. One place to dig in. One stubborn, God-given refusal to give up.

Rooted, weathered, and unshakable, someday when the winds rage, the mountains roar, and everyone else looks for shelter, you'll be the one still standing. These conditions don't scare you. You didn't grow in the easy places; you grew in the hard ones. And that's where the strongest leaders are made.

When You're Built in the Dark, You Can Lead in the Light

There's something about those trees on Red Mountain that stuck with me long after we rolled down the far side and the peaks disappeared in the mirror. It wasn't just that they were growing where they shouldn't. It was that they were thriving where nobody even thought to look.

Most people driving through those switchbacks probably never noticed them. Maybe a few gave them a quick glance and thought, "Huh, how's that tree standing there?" But nobody pulled over, clapped, or marveled at the battle those roots had to fight every single day to survive. They just grew. Day after day. Storm after storm. Quietly. Fiercely. Faithfully. That's how real leadership grows, too.

Everybody loves to celebrate the leader once they're standing tall, when the lights are shining and the world is paying attention. But almost nobody sees the years spent clawing for every inch of ground, the early mornings when quitting would have been easier, or the silent fights to stay rooted when the storms came screaming. There are so many people in the Bible who demonstrate this kind of leadership.

David wasn't crowned king the day the oil ran down his head. He went back to the lonely field to tend the sheep. Nobody applauded his work in the wilderness marked by long, dirty days.

Joseph didn't jump from dreams of leadership to running a kingdom. He went through betrayal, slavery, and years of being forgotten in a prison cell.

Even Jesus—the Son of God—spent thirty years living quietly in a town nobody cared about, building tables with his hands, obeying his parents, walking dusty streets, and waiting for a time no one else could see coming.

No stage. No applause. No shortcuts.

Faithfulness first. Obscurity first. Darkness first.

Sometimes that kind of leadership shows up in the most unexpected places, like the sidelines of a lacrosse field. Last year, my youngest son Jacob, showed me more about leadership in one weekend than most corporate training seminars taught me.

He played on a U12 team, meaning everyone on the field was supposed to be twelve or younger. Kids are still wiry and scrappy at that age, trying to figure out how their arms and legs should work together.

U14 is a whole different world. By fourteen, boys start looking like grown men. They're faster, stronger, and heavier—sometimes a full foot taller than the twelve-year-olds still learning how to tie their cleats right.

We showed up at that tournament thinking we were ready for a long day of U12 games. Then we realized only two kids from Jacob's team had shown up. That's a problem. No full team. No subs. No rest. Most kids would have pouted and packed up while their parents threw a fit.

But Jacob just tightened his cleats and grabbed his stick. The coach scrambled, finding other teams who could use an extra player. Jacob played five games with five different teams and wore five different jerseys with the same fight, grit, and heart every time he stepped on the field. By the end of it, one team from Salida claimed him. "You're ours tomorrow, Jake!" they said, laughing and pounding him on the back after the final whistle.

And they meant it. The next day, Jacob played every single game with them—U12 and U14—against kids two and three years older than him. Those kids could have flattened him without breaking a sweat. But Jacob didn't flinch.

He's not the biggest kid on the field, but he's got a move we call the *can opener*. He wedges his stick between an opponent's hands and his stick, sits down hard on it, and pops their grip loose like yanking the lid off a stubborn can—fast, messy, and completely wrecking their hold.

That weekend, he pulled off the can opener so many times the Salida boys gave him nicknames: *Jake the Slayer* and *The Can Opener*. You could hear them yelling from the sidelines, warning each other like it was a matter of survival. "Don't let the Slayer near you!" "Watch the Can Opener!" They weren't laughing. They meant it.

Later that season, we packed up the truck and headed to another tournament—back to Salida. Jacob's U12 team showed up in full force this time, ready to grind through their schedule. They had three games spaced out across the day, giving just enough time to catch their breath between matchups.

But not long after the first game, it became clear that the U14 team from our club was in trouble. They were short on players. They needed more bodies, or they'd be playing with no subs and no real chance to last through the day.

Jacob didn't blink. He volunteered. My twelve-year-old stepped up to play against kids two years older and a whole lot bigger because the team needed him. He didn't just dip in for a game or two, either. The schedules overlapped, and Jacob pulled off something nobody else did that day.

He played a quadruple header—four games back-to-back—bouncing between his U12 team and the U14 team without a real break. One game ended, and he sprinted across the field to start another.

After that stretch, he caught his breath—barely—and jumped into a double header. Then, one more game meant Jacob played seven games total that day. Twelve years old. Seven games. Two divisions. Playing 75 percent of the time every game.

He didn't complain or hesitate. He played with all heart. He didn't just survive against the older boys—he thrived. Jacob has always played bigger than he is. He's never been afraid to swing his stick, throw his weight around, or go toe-to-toe with somebody twice his size if that's what the team needed. Playing up with the U14s just gave him more targets.

He didn't waste this opportunity to play against bigger and faster boys who could have flattened him if they wanted to. Jacob kept showing up, battling, and smiling. When his U14 team faced off against the Salida boys again—the same ones who had once claimed him—you could hear them across the field, hollering warnings: "Whatever you do, avoid the little monster!" "Stay away from the Can Opener!"

They weren't afraid of his size. They were afraid of his heart. But the thing that made me prouder than anything he did during the games happened when the whistles stopped. Most kids, win or lose, would have huddled with their own teams, licking their wounds or bragging about the scoreboard. Jacob wasn't wired like that. With his helmet off, stick dragging behind him, he was already pulling players from both sides together. Jacob's laughing and back-slapping was building brotherhood, and that's bigger than a game. Jacob didn't have the loudest voice, tallest body, or the flashiest talent. He had the willingness to show up, dig deeper, play harder, and lift people higher. That's leadership.

Why This Style of Leadership Matters Most

Before I ever had a title next to my name or a business card with fancy letters, I was sitting in the cab of a four-axle semi, teaching guys how to drive the right way. Not in some parking lot with cones. Not five times around a building until they could memorize the turns. Real driving. Your hands sweat and your brakes start to smell funny halfway down the pass. Most trainers would hand a kid a book and a pat on the back and call it a day. But not me. I wasn't interested in raising drivers who *thought* they could handle the road. I wanted drivers who *knew* they could—because they'd already been through it.

So, when it came time to get serious, I didn't just talk about the San Juan Mountains—I pointed at the rig and said, "Get in." We drove up two of the meanest mountain passes you'll ever find between Durango and Silverton. Twisting roads barely wider than a semi, sheer cliffs waiting to teach you about consequences if you got sloppy.

I let them drive it themselves—every terrifying curve, every screaming downhill grade. You haven't lived until you've watched a rookie white-knuckle their way around a hairpin turn with nothing but Jesus and forty-eight feet of trailer behind them.

And Red Mountain Pass? Forget about it. I didn't even let them touch the wheel on that one their first time. I drove it myself—slow and steady—talking through every insane switchback as their eyes got bigger and bigger, realizing what a real mountain pass looked like.

Then when it came time for night driving, I didn't lecture them about visibility and safe following distances. I met them at 10 p.m.—headlights cutting through the dark— and we climbed Wolf Creek Pass in the pitch black. Just an eighty-thousand-pound rig, a mountain road, and the reality that out here, mistakes don't get second chances.

Every single driver I trained went through it. Every one. Not because it was fun or easy. It wasn't. But it mattered. If they were going to earn that CDL, they needed to be ready when it wasn't pretty. They needed to learn how to react when the brakes got hot, the lights disappeared, or the fear hit somewhere deep down in their gut and started whispering that maybe they weren't cut out for it.

I wanted them to beat that voice, and you don't do that sitting in a classroom. You beat it out there where it's real. Anybody can show up when it's easy. Anybody can talk tough when the sun's shining, the brakes are cool, and the road is smooth. Real leaders keep the wheel steady when the cliffs are inches away, the engine's screaming, and sweat's running down their backs.

If you can't lead when no one's looking—if you can't show up in the shadows— you won't be trusted to lead when the lights come on. Private victories come first. The public victories are the echo.

God's in the grind. He's in the early mornings, late nights, those moments when it's just you, the mountain, and a prayer. He's asking if you're willing to lead when it's hard, lonely, and costs something. If you can say yes to that—if you can show up when nobody sees—you'll be ready for the battles most people run from.

Leadership isn't about standing tallest. It's about staying longest. It's chaining up one more rig when you're dog tired. It's about driving one more pass when your hands are trembling. It's about pouring into someone when there's nothing in it for you but the satisfaction of knowing you made them better. It's doing the right thing in the dark—long before the spotlight shows up.

If you can lead there, you can lead anywhere.

The Leadership Nobody Sees (But Changes Everything)

You don't have to climb Red Mountain at midnight to be a real leader. You don't have to be pulling water trucks out of the mud at 1 a.m. or playing seven back-to-back lacrosse games against kids twice your size just to prove you have heart. Real leadership isn't always wrapped in heroic headlines or big, dramatic moments.

Most of the time, it happens quietly. Leadership opportunities appear in the small places and choices that never make it to Instagram. They are in the sacrifices nobody throws a trophy party for.

Leadership shows up when a boss sees something good in a tired, worn-down kid and pulls him aside—not with a mic in his hand, not with a laminated five-step leadership manual—but with a simple word of encouragement. "Hey, I saw how you handled that today. You're better than you think you are. Let's sharpen it." It shows up when a parent gets out of bed before sunrise—not shouting orders at their kids to work harder while they sit and drink coffee—but leading by example. Parents who lead roll up their sleeves and show grit with their hands and words.

It shows up when a manager stands between their team and the chaos coming down from corporate, taking the heat without dragging their people into the fire. Leadership fights battles nobody else knows about because it's the right thing to do.

Real leadership doesn't always come with medals or recognition. Most days, it looks like ordinary people choosing faithfulness when quitting would be easier. Leadership chooses to show up when they could easily blend in and it's carrying weight when nobody else realizes there was a burden to carry.

It's not the stage that makes a leader. It's the silent, stubborn, everyday choices behind the scenes that build someone the world can trust when the pressure finally hits. Most of the time, leadership shows up when you least expect it; unscheduled, unpolished, and inconvenient. Real leadership happens when life hits you in the face, and you choose people over plans.

If you want to lead in the light someday, you have to get comfortable leading in the shadows first. Quiet leadership starts with simple decisions anybody can make. If you want to build real leadership when nobody's watching, here are seven places you can start

1. Be Positive. Loudly and Quietly.

About six years ago, I made a decision that changed more than I realized at the time. I decided I wasn't going to be negative on social media anymore. I abandoned complaining, jumping on whatever outrage bandwagon was rolling through town, and dragging people down because it felt easy in the moment.

I decided that every comment, photo, and caption I posted would be positive, uplifting, and encouraging—not fake sunshine and rainbows, but real hope and real life without bitterness.

For a while, it felt like nobody noticed. No fanfare. No viral moments. It was just me plugging away, trying to put a little light out into a world that felt pretty dark most days.

But then something started happening. People started pulling me aside, sending messages, and stopping me at events. "Man, I love seeing your stuff. It's the only thing in my feed that doesn't make me want to delete the app." "I know when I see your name pop up, it's going to be something good." "Thanks for being a bright spot."

It wasn't overnight or flashy. It was slow, authentic, and steady—like most leadership in the dark is. My stupid little social media posts—half the time written from a tractor seat or the front seat of a pickup truck—somehow started shining a little light. They brought joy, not because they were fancy, but because they were faithful.

Be the light. Stay loudly and quietly positive, even if you feel like nobody notices. Do it even if it seems like nobody cares. Do it when the world keeps screaming into the void. Stay positive because somebody out there is scrolling through darkness. Your little post, word, and choice to stay hopeful might be the thing that reminds them there's still some good left out there.

2. Lead to help, not to be recognized.

It happened a while back. But it's one of those memories that feels as fresh now as it did then. I was driving a lonely country highway toward an early morning, company-wide meeting. That made it a button-up shirt day. With a fresh cup of coffee riding shotgun, my mind was already half-worried about seating charts and PowerPoint slides. I crested a small hill, and that's when I saw a car upside down in the bar ditch.

Steam was curling up into the cold morning air. Glass was scattered across the shoulder. Tires were spinning slowly and helplessly in the air like the wings of a dying bird. And cars kept flying by.

People were whizzing past, probably on their way to work, likely telling themselves somebody else would stop. They probably told themselves they didn't have time and couldn't risk being late. But here's the thing about real leadership: You don't schedule opportunities to display leadership. Opportunities show up in the moments that blow up your calendar and schedule.

Without even thinking, I pulled over. I threw my flashers on, grabbed my old turnout gloves from behind the seat—because, of course, I still had them—and ran toward the wreck.

Nobody else was there yet. No flashing lights. No sirens. It was just me, the twisted car, and the scared eyes of the people trapped inside. The first thing I did *after* calling 911 was call my boss. He answered with that tone—you know the one—the one that says, "Why are you bothering me already?"

"I'm going to be late," I said.

There was a heavy sigh on the other end of the line, thick with disappointment. And then I said why. "There's a wreck. No emergency responders on scene yet. I'm staying until help arrives." There was a long pause—long enough that I thought maybe he hung up. And then, everything about his voice changed.

"Take all the time you need. Just stay there until they don't need you anymore," he said.

That's leadership, too.

This time, leadership wasn't about the meeting, schedule, or carefully crafted agenda. This time, leadership meant choosing people over plans—messy, inconvenient, and wrecked-up people-serving tasks. If you only lead when there's a reward, you're not leading—you're performing. Real leadership shows up when nobody else does. When the world speeds by, pretending to not see the need. The cost is real, and the reward is invisible.

That's why you must do it to help—not for recognition. True leaders don't pull over because they think it'll look good later. They pull over because someone needs them right now. And they know that's enough.

3. Speak life without needing a microphone.

The world doesn't need another loudmouth leader looking for a spotlight. It needs more people willing to show up quietly, faithfully, and speak life into others without needing a parade for it.

Sometimes leadership isn't about standing in front of the room with a microphone. Sometimes it's about standing unnoticed in the back, and making sure the room stays standing. I spent a lot of time early in my career doing just that. I showed up at safety meetings though I had no official role—no speeches, plaque presentations, or atta-boys for sitting in the corner. Sometimes it's your presence that speaks louder than any speech you could give.

I'll never forget one night when our drivers came back in dragging bad news behind them. Every truck was lined up with a tank full of contaminated fuel, and the whole yard was a mess. It wasn't technically my problem. I didn't cause it. I didn't even get the call that made it my responsibility. But there I was.

I could have gone home. I could have said, "Not my circus, not my monkeys," and punched out. Instead, I grabbed a tool, rolled up my sleeves, and started draining tanks right alongside the management team. Nobody took a picture, made an announcement, or said *thank you*. I didn't care, because leadership is about seeing what needs to be done and stepping into it without waiting for someone else to notice.

Catch people doing something right—and tell them. Catch a need rising—and meet it. Catch a team about to break under the weight—and carry some of it for them. Most people are dying for someone to believe in them, see them, and remind them they're not alone.

Real leaders don't need a stage. They just need a heart that notices needs and a little bit of grit that's willing to act. Stay late, show up, and believe when nobody else will. That's enough.

4. Show up when it's inconvenient.

Real leadership isn't always recognized at awards banquets with the nice steak dinners. Most of the time, it's digging chains out of the mud at 2 a.m., showing up at midnight to pull a stuck truck off a snowy mountain pass when you could have easily said, "Not my problem," and dragging yourself over Wolf Creek at 10 p.m. because you promised a trainee you'd show them the real thing. If you only show up when it's easy, you're not a leader. You're a spectator. I learned that in a way I'll never forget.

I had a group of six drivers coming down for CDL training. Traveling eight hours away from home, they were all counting on us to get them across the finish line. They had taken time off work, made sacrifices, and put real miles behind them to show up. As they were heading down, my grandfather passed away. The funeral was scheduled smack in the middle of their trip. I had one other trainer at the time, and he was good, but one guy serving six drivers was not enough.

I was torn up about it. Family is everything to me. And my grandpa? He was one of the men who shaped me into who I am. The morning of the service, I sat with my family. I stayed through the funeral, honoring the man who had lived his life full of grit, grace, and quiet leadership. But then, after lunch, the hugs, and the prayers, Dad pulled me aside. He didn't guilt or lecture me.

He just said, "Dan, you need to be there. This is your business. This is your calling. Grandpa would have wanted you there more than he would have wanted you here." He was right. Grandpa would have understood. He would have expected it, because real leadership doesn't flinch when it's inconvenient. So, I hugged my family, hit the road, drove back to work.

I showed up for those six drivers. Still wearing the weight of goodbye with a tired and heavy heart, I kept my promise, because those drivers mattered. Leadership is built on the days you have every reason to stay home, but you lace up your boots anyway.

5. Protect people without needing credit.

Real leadership is about quietly doing the work behind the scenes that makes somebody else stronger—even if they never know how much you carried for them. Taking bows under the spotlight isn't part of the deal.

That same weekend I drove back after my grandfather's funeral, running on fumes and heartache, I found myself staring at another choice. One of the women in our CDL group was struggling—especially with backing. It's the struggle you can't fix with one more YouTube video or a few quick pointers. She needed real help, the kind that requires a time investment from someone else.

Nobody would have blamed me if I said, "Hey, it's been a long day. We'll work on it tomorrow." Nobody would have thought less of me if I headed back to the hotel and got some badly needed rest. But that's not what leaders do.

So, after everybody else packed it in for the day, I stayed three extra hours on the range in the fading light. I walked her through every step of the process, over and over, until she could feel it, not just think about it. When we finished, I didn't just wish her luck and send her on her way. I climbed into the truck riding shotgun and had her drive back to the hotel, coaching her every turn, gear, and brake check along the way.

No audience, no boss standing there taking notes, and no customer writing it up in a glowing review. In fact, the owner of her company doesn't even know I did that. That's fine, because real leadership is going the extra mile when nobody's keeping score. The extra mile is digging a little deeper, carrying a little more, and investing in people's futures without expectations of a bonus or shout out is what leaders do. When you do those things, you're growing as the leader God can trust with more.

6. Stay faithful in the small stuff.

Real leadership is sending that extra email, making that extra call, finishing that file right when you could easily let it slide because nobody's checking anyway. It's not glamorous or exciting, but it's where the real foundation is laid.

Faithfulness in the small things—the invisible, the boring, the uncelebrated—is what makes you strong enough to carry the weight of real leadership later. If you're faithful in the little things, the big things won't crush you. But if you cut corners now, you'll find yourself with no foundation when the storms hit.

Leadership is built in the faithful, stubborn decision to show up every single day. Regardless of how insignificant the task may seem, stay faithful and steady. You're not wasting your effort. You're building something storms can't tear down.

7. Trust that God sees it all.

Joseph knew what it was like to be unseen. He was faithful in places nobody would have chosen. He was betrayed by his own brothers, thrown into a pit, sold as a slave, hauled off to a foreign land where nobody even knew his name.

He did more than survive—he served in Potiphar's house. He showed up every day and worked like it mattered. When he was thrown into prison for something he didn't do, he showed up there too. He lead, served, and staying faithful when there was no one to impress, and no crowd to cheer.

Nobody was standing outside the prison gates handing Joseph gold stars for his faithfulness. Nobody was writing a leadership book about the slave boy who kept stacking bricks when life kept knocking him down. But God saw every act of integrity, quiet decision to do the right thing, and moment when Joseph stayed faithful when it appeared faithfulness was getting him nowhere.

When the time came that Pharaoh and the nation needed a trustworthy leader who could handle the pressure, Joseph was ready. God was still working, even when Joseph couldn't see that He had prepared him for leadership. Leadership didn't come by luck or because Joseph played the political game better than everyone else. Leadership is trusting that the same God who sees you stacking bricks in prison is the God who calls you to the palace when the time is right. Leadership is built when you:

- Pull a driver out of a ditch at 1 a.m.

- Drain diesel tanks long after everyone else has gone home

- Drive all night after a funeral because a handful of people are counting on you to show up

- Miss the meeting but make it to the wreck

- Whisper encouragement to someone who doesn't even know how badly they need it

Stay faithful. Stay steady. God sees the work you're doing in the dark. And while you're out there showing up with no spotlight, He's building something *bigger* than you can imagine. It's something you might not see yet, but it's coming.

If you're feeling overlooked, unseen, or like none of it matters, you're not forgotten. You're not invisible. You're being *forged*. God sees every mile, late night, and quiet act of faithfulness. He's not wasting a second of it. While you're out there with calloused hands and quiet faith, He's laying the foundation for something you can't see right now. One day when the pressure rises, the storm hits, and the world needs real leaders, you won't have to scramble to become one. You'll already be standing.

Become the leader storms can't knock over—one who can step onto any field, stage, or battlefield—and already be prepared. You weren't waiting for the light to make you real. You were already real in the dark.

The world may not see the roots you're building right now. But heaven does. And when the time is right, you won't have to fake it. You'll just keep doing what you've always done. Those roots will hold up the life and leadership that changes everything. That's the leadership the world desperately needs now.

Key Takeaways from Chapter Five

 **You're always leading—especially in the shadows.** The most powerful leadership doesn't happen on a stage—it happens when no one's clapping, no one's watching, and you show up anyway.

 **Fear gets compliance. Trust builds loyalty.** Trying to lead with power, pressure, or a title will only make people avoid you. Real influence comes from service, not swagger.

 **Leadership happens in the mud, not the meetings.** It's built at 2 a.m. with frozen hands and a stuck truck—not in a boardroom or a conference call. If you're not willing to sweat with your people, don't expect them to trust you.

 **Recognition is nice. Reliability is leadership.** People won't always applaud the leader who answers the call in the middle of the night. But they'll remember who showed up when everyone else bailed.

 **Faithfulness in the dark prepares you for the light.** God forges leaders in the lonely, hidden places—so when the pressure comes, you're already built to stand strong.

 **The hard places are where leaders grow roots.** Leadership isn't born in comfort. It's grown where the conditions are rough, the odds are stacked, and quitting would be easier.

 **Lead like Jacob—heart over hype.** Leadership isn't always loud. It's grit, hustle, and heart—like a twelve-year-old earning the respect of kids twice his size by just showing up and playing his guts out.

 **Do the right thing—even when no one's keeping score.** Leadership is pulling over for a wreck, staying late to help someone finish, or draining tanks after a long day—when nobody's watching and nobody's asking.

 **God sees what the spotlight misses.** Even when the world forgets, God doesn't. Every mile, every sacrifice, every quiet act of integrity—He sees it all and is shaping you for something bigger.

 **The leader you are in private is the one they'll trust in public.** You don't become a leader when you're given the mic—you become a leader when your everyday decisions, done in silence, earn the right to be followed when it counts.

Chapter 6 | The Power of Prayer for Leaders

Make Prayer Your Strategy, Not Your Backup Plan

I was sitting in my hotel room in Las Vegas, preparing to speak at a conference, and struggling. I kept asking myself, *Why the heck am I even here?*

I do a lot of public speaking, and I often donate my time and services in exchange for them to pick up the cost of my travel and hotel and give me a booth. That kind of arrangement is pretty standard stuff. They invited me. They wanted me and were excited for me to speak. But this time, I did something I almost never do. I said, "Hey, I'll cover my flight. Just give me a booth and cover my hotel." I thought I was being generous, but maybe I was a little too trusting.

One month before the event, I sent the organizer a quick email: "Hey, just checking—you got my hotel booked, right?" She replied, "Yep! Here's your confirmation number." Cool. Easy. No red flags. Yet.

Then I landed in Vegas. I was tired but ready to roll and go to check into the hotel. The lady at the front desk says, "Okay, I just need a card for the full stay." I blinked. "Wait. What? I thought the event organizer booked and paid for the room." She gave me that classic Vegas smile. "They booked it, but they didn't pay for it."

So there I was, swiping my card at a Vegas casino hotel, wondering if I'd just become the most underpaid keynote speaker in the history of conferences. Still trying to be optimistic, I went to the organizer and said, "Hey, I checked in, but they charged me for the room. I thought you guys were covering it?" She was super sweet and said, "Oh, let me look into it." She promised to follow up.

Meanwhile, I told my amazing assistant to keep an eye on the credit card. If it went through, she'd follow up. And sure enough—cha-ching. It posted. So, my assistant sent the email, and the reply comes back: "Well, the agreement doesn't say we were covering the hotel." Insert jaw drop here.

Now look—I know how this sounds. "Oh, Dan's just mad because he had to pay for a hotel." But hang with me for a second. It's not about the money. Okay, it was a little about the money. It was Vegas, and this wasn't a run-down budget motel off some forgotten exit in the middle of nowhere. My bigger issue was about principle. I'd built a brand of leadership. My expertise was valuable to them, and my time was valuable to me.

I gave up time with my family, left my business, and showed up to serve. This event and experience was misaligned with the leader I strive to be and the brand I've worked so hard to protect. I was frustrated and felt disrespected. I wondered if I should pack up my booth and head home.

I tossed and turned all night. You know those nights wrestling and arguing with yourself like a courtroom drama in your head? Yeah, it was one of those. Then the next morning, I pulled open the curtain to witness the Nevada sunrise peeking over the mountains. And God gently asked me, "Did you pray about this?" Oof. Nope. Sure didn't.

So, right there in that hotel room, I said, "God, you're the CEO of this business. You lead; I follow. This is your deal. What do you want me to do?" And man, He answered. He reminded me that if I left, it would tarnish my name. That's not who I am. I don't ghost people or walk away from my commitments. I show up and overdeliver. Period.

He reminded me that the money was just money. And maybe this was my donation to an organization that needed what I had to offer. He reminded me to talk to them. To be clear, respectful, and honest. And yeah, to make sure every detail is in writing next time. Lesson learned.

And last, He reminded me of something huge: I underpriced myself. Again. They brought in other speakers at $20K+ and I was out here paying for my own room. That's not on them—that's on me. It's my fault for not negotiating better and not sticking to my standards.

But after that prayer, I had peace that allowed me to stand tall, walk in purposefully, and speak powerfully. So, I unpacked my bags, walked into that event with my head high, and gave a dang good presentation. I served the heck out of those attendees, because that's what real leaders do. They lead with obedience, not ego, and when in doubt—they pray.

Why Prayer Matters for Leaders

We're wired to rely on our own wit, knowledge, and understanding. Or at least I know *I* am. I've spent a good chunk of my life believing that if I just thought, worked, or stressed about it deeply enough, I'd find the answer. But here's what I've figured out over time (don't tell my wife I said this): I don't know it all.

Yep. It's true. I don't know everything. I don't always understand why things happen. I don't have the future mapped out, and sometimes I barely have the present under control. But I've come to live by this truth: Everything happens for a reason. I may never know the reason. I might not even like the reason. But I trust that God has a plan, and He's leading me in the right direction—even when it doesn't make sense.

Let's go back to the story I started this chapter with—the one where I wrestled with a decision for hours. I paced, analyzed, and overthought the whole thing until I was mentally worn out. And then, I finally stopped, paused, and prayed.

It wasn't some long, dramatic speech. It was a short, honest prayer lasting all of thirty seconds that changed everything. God didn't speak with a booming voice or announce his appearance with flashing lights. Instead, He delivered peace, clarity, direction, and a calm confidence I didn't have before. That's why prayer matters. When we lead without prayer, we carry burdens we were never meant to hold. We move too fast, react out of fear, and lead from pressure instead of peace. But when we lead with prayer, everything shifts. We slow down, surrender control, and make space for God to speak and for us to hear.

Prayer shouldn't just be something we do before dinner or during emergencies. It's our lifeline. It's how we stay aligned with the one who does know it all and is not surprised, overwhelmed, or confused. Prayer reminds me that I don't have to pretend to have all the answers. I just need to be humble enough to ask for help. So next time you're stuck, don't start with the spreadsheet. Start with surrendering.

He's not sitting up in heaven scanning for résumés with no red marks, mistakes, and questionable decisions. He's after purpose, not polish. He's after leaders who are willing to show up, get their hands dirty, and follow even when the directions seem fuzzy. He pursues leaders who'll say *yes*—even when they've got no idea what they just said *yes* to.

Real leadership is more than charging ahead and getting things done. It's more than being the loudest voice or the fastest worker. Real leadership is about stopping long enough to climb the tallest tree and look around. And that's when it hits you. "We're in the wrong forest."

That realization doesn't usually come in peaceful moments with birds chirping and soft music in the background. For me, it usually shows up in a full-blown, all in, already-committed moment where I've poured everything into a specific direction, only to realize it's not where God told me to go.

It happens like this: I get a big idea—the kind that hits like lightning, makes you want to call ten people and yell, "This is it! This is the thing we've been waiting for!"

So, I make big, bold plans. Before you know it, I've got full-blown event-level stuff—dates, venues, topics, and ticket prices—the whole nine yards. Then I go to work building the presentations. I spend days—sometimes weeks—putting together slides, outlines, and content. I hype it to the team, book the venue, fire up the marketing, and call people to get them excited like I'm selling the next life-changing event.

And then ... nothing. I check the registration page, and there's no one there. I refresh the browser like maybe it just glitched. Still nothing. No signups. No buzz. No "I can't wait for this!" emails. Just me, staring at a blinking cursor in an empty inbox. I start making excuses. People haven't seen the ad yet, it's bad timing, Mercury's in retrograde. But deep down, I know what's really going on. I didn't pray. I didn't ask God if this was something He wanted me to do. I just assumed, "Hey, it's a good idea, and I'm passionate about it, so it must be God's plan." That's not how this works. So, I finally slow down, drop the pride, and pray. And you know what He says? "Dan, this is a great idea. But it's not My idea."

That'll hit you like a brick to the chest. All that energy, planning, and excitement, and now I've got to go back to my team—the same team that's been working their tails off—and say, "Hey, uh ... we're pivoting." You can feel the air get sucked out of the room. It's like telling your kids you're not going to Disneyland after all—you're going to the DMV.

It's emotionally and financially painful. It's hard to watch thousands of dollars go down the drain. Venues don't refund because you forgot to check in with the Holy Spirit. And I sure haven't found a marketing platform that offers a God-didn't-greenlight-this-one clause. It stings. In that moment, I always ask myself some hard questions. Maybe you should, too.

Why didn't I pray first? Why did I assume God would just bless whatever I was passionate about? Why did I think I could outrun bad direction with good hustle? Maybe you've done the same. Maybe you've been charging full steam ahead—shoulder to shoulder with your team—clearing trees like a bulldozer on a mission only to look up and realize you're not even in the forest God asked you to go to. You've been pushing so hard you never stopped to ask if the destination was even right.

If that's you—I get it. I haven't just been there and bought the T-shirt. I've worn it proudly, stained it, and ripped it on a tree branch. I even tried to iron it with a hair straightener and still have it hanging in the closet as a reminder of what not to do.

I've got a long list of great ideas that went nowhere because I never paused to ask for God's input. But, I've got an even longer list of times I prayed, asked for direction, and waited for clarity. I tuned in instead of charging in, and every single time, God revealed a path forward that worked and had purpose. Don't get me wrong. He didn't make it easy. I still had to work, sweat, and push through challenging moments. But what He promised, He delivered. Every time.

So, now, before I start anything big—before I rally the team, spend the money, or dream up a killer campaign—I pause and pray. I ask God for wisdom, direction, favor, and the guts to listen if He tells me, "Not that one."

Do I still forget sometimes? You bet. I get excited and jump the gun. My tunnel vision leads me to convince myself that, because it feels good, it must be right. But then I look around at my family, my business, the people I've been trusted to lead, and I remember something that grounds me every time: God doesn't just build forests. He builds leaders to walk through them. And sometimes, the only way He teaches us how to truly lead is by letting us get a little lost first.

I brought Gary Chapman, the author of *The Five Love Languages,* to Durango, Colorado. Sounds impressive, right? This all started with a fire-in-my-belly idea. I wanted to do something bold for our community—something faith-based, inspiring, and different. I thought, *What if we hosted a marriage event? What if we brought in someone with real wisdom? What if we brought in Gary Chapman?*

Now, I should have paused and prayed. I should have climbed the tree and asked, "Lord, is this the forest You want me in?" But instead of praying, I took off like a squirrel on a Red Bull bender—wide-eyed, twitchy, and one hundred percent convinced I could change the world before lunch.

You know that squirrel from those viral videos? The one that hits the spinning bird feeder, gets flung halfway across the yard, then dusts himself off and launches right back at it like a furry little missile of determination? Yeah. That was me. No plan. No prayer. Just raw ambition and blind faith in my own to-do list.

I skipped the whole pause-and-ask-God part and went straight into action like I was starring in a one-man Broadway show called *Dan Takes the Stage* (and also the catering, lighting, and ticket sales). I emailed Gary's team, got a response, and before I knew it, we were talking dates, contracts, and hotel reservations like I had a full event crew and a planning budget larger than $47.

Gary's fee was shockingly reasonable. He didn't have a list of outrageous demands like a private jet. The man wasn't asking for a bowl of avocados massaged by monks or a playlist of whale sounds. All he wanted was airfare, a hotel, and a room full of people who cared about their marriages. And I thought, *how hard could that be?* For the record, that's the last thing you should ever say before planning an event, building an ark, or assembling IKEA furniture without the manual. So, I picked a date without praying about it, running it by anyone, or checking a single local calendar. I didn't ask God. I didn't even ask Google.

Now I had to find a venue. We didn't have much money in the nonprofit account, so I started calling churches around town hoping someone would say *yes* to hosting it for free. Thankfully, a local church agreed, and even though we didn't attend there, they were kind enough to open their doors. That part worked out.

Then came the advertising push. I had visions of 200, maybe 300 people filling those pews. I was pricing tickets at $25, doing back-of-the-napkin math (which was probably wrong because, fun fact—I'm terrible at math). I was dreaming of breaking even, having a little left over for future ministry, maybe even kicking off a series of events. And then, the silence started.

With just a couple of weeks to go, we'd sold around seventy-five tickets. That might sound decent, but in a room that holds four hundred, it's basically a well-attended staff meeting. Gary asked, "How many people are you expecting?" I replied confidently, "We've sold seventy-five, but we're pushing hard the next two weeks. Walk-ins, day-of buzz—just you wait!" Except, they didn't wait, because they didn't come.

The day before the event, I picked Gary up at the airport and gave him the full Durango tour—Silverton, the mountains, and the scenic drive. He was gracious, calm, full of stories and wisdom. That one-on-one time with him was worth the entire experience. He spoke into my life in ways I didn't even realize I needed.

But then came the event. The youth event on night one was solid. Not packed, but meaningful. I got to speak, Gary spoke, we encouraged young people—and I felt like, "Okay, maybe we'll turn this thing around tomorrow."

The next day was the main event—the couples' seminar. About sixty people showed up. Standing in front of a sea of empty chairs when you've poured your heart, time, money, and reputation into something pierces your soul.

I opened for Gary and shared how his book changed my marriage—how it helped Jenna and me reconnect in a season when we were just surviving. It was raw and honest. And then Gary, being the pro he is, gave an incredible talk to a room that should have been full.

The only staff member who showed up was the secretary. The pastor and youth pastor didn't even send a late apology text. Not a word. And get this—the youth pastor barely even showed up for the youth night. The event was hosted in their building, and if the secretary hadn't been there, I'm not even sure we would have gotten into the room.

After the event, the secretary walked up to me. She looked me in the eye and said, "Dan, I'm so sorry. We didn't do our part. We should have promoted this. People needed it. We dropped the ball." She didn't make excuses or blame anyone. She just owned it with grace, humility, and heart. That moment stuck with me.

Her husband was outside parking cars like a pro. I knew this guy from outside church. We'd worked together before. He was a solid guy with a good reputation—blue-collar grit and no fluff.

She told me, "Before we agreed to host this, I asked him what he thought about you." And her husband said something I'll never forget: "I don't know what the event's going to be like, but I know Dan will show up. And if he shows up, it's going to be worth it." That hit me hard, because he was right. I did show up—not just physically—I showed up in heart, faith, and service. I showed up even when the turnout was low, the pastors bailed, and the seats were emptier than my email inbox after launching the event.

The secretary and her husband showed up too. She didn't need a title. He didn't need a spotlight. Together, they led better than anyone on staff that weekend. They were all in, from parking the first car to locking the doors after everyone left. That couple modeled leadership that doesn't need applause because they weren't doing it for praise. They were doing it for people. Meanwhile, the folks with all the titles and the nameplates? Silence. Look, I'm not trying to be harsh. But this part matters because leadership is more than a title. It's a presence. It shows up or it doesn't.

I wasn't mad at the church. I was mad at myself. I didn't pray before I planned. I didn't ask God if the timing was right. I didn't ask if this was His vision or just mine. It wasn't a bad idea. It was a great idea. But it wasn't the right idea, and it wasn't the right time. And the hardest part is that I knew it. I knew deep down I was doing too much. I was torn between running Eclipse DOT and pushing our ministry, God First Life Next, forward at the same time—trying to carry two full-time callings with one body, one brain, and one soul that hadn't stopped to rest or listen. I was in the wrong forest.

I thought I could build something big *and* beautiful, but I skipped the most important step: asking God if this was the place He even wanted a trail. God will still use it. He'll still show up. He'll still speak to the sixty people in the room. But if you're trying to force something because it feels holy or sounds exciting—without praying first—you're not leading. You're just swinging your axe in the wrong woods.

That event wasn't a failure. It was a reminder to stop, climb the tree, and ask the question: "Lord, is this where You want me?" And more importantly—wait for the answer. It's tempting not to plow ahead because the idea sounds holy. It's hard not to proceed with an event because you already booked the room and ordered the banner. But slowing down long enough to let God speak is critical. When He does, even if the answer isn't what you wanted, it's always what you *needed*. And trust me, I've learned that the hard way.

This brings me to something I want to unpack with you: I have a list of things I once believed held me back from being a leader. These weren't wild, evil ideas. They sounded wise. They looked like hustle. They felt right in that moment. But looking back, they were steering me off track.

If I can help you avoid a few faceplants, parking-lot prayers, and awkward pivot meetings, then I'll gladly give up my pride and share what I've learned. So, let's break down a few things I used to believe that sounded spiritual but left me stuck, tired, or spinning in circles. You might recognize some of them, and you might be living one of them right now. That's okay, because the moment you learn better, you lead better.

Thing I Used to Believe #1: "I'm too busy to pray."

This one feels logical at first—especially when your calendar looks like it was built by a caffeinated octopus. I used to tell myself, *"Dan, you don't have time to pause and pray—you've got stuff to do!"* You've probably said it, too. "I've got deadlines, employees, phone calls, payroll, kids, meals, invoices, that weird email I've been ignoring for a week. How am I supposed to stop and pray like I'm sitting on a front porch sipping sweet tea with Jesus?"

But here's what I've learned: If you think you're too busy to pray, it probably means you *really* need to. Let me give you an example. We were planning two major events. I had three speaking engagements coming up next month. I was on the road in northern Colorado, juggling client calls from hotel rooms and squeezing in presentation prep between fast food and spotty Wi-Fi. My team was onboarding new clients left and right, and we were in the middle of expanding—new team members, processes, and systems. On top of that, my oldest son was about to ship out for the Army. My head and my heart were both full. It felt like I was carrying a backpack loaded with rocks and still trying to run a marathon. Then, right in the middle of that whirlwind, I felt this tug— *You need to plan a Train-the-Trainer event.* And I'll be honest, my first thought was, *Absolutely not. Nope. Not now. Have you seen my schedule?*

But the tug didn't go away. It got louder, heavier, and clearer. So, I paused and stepped out of the chaos. Not for an hour-long quiet time, not for a retreat in the woods— just long enough to pray and ask, *"God, is this You? If it is, I'll move. But I don't want to force something that's not mine to carry."*

If you have time to worry, you have time to pray.

And right there—somewhere between the hotel carpet and cold coffee—I got the peace I needed. It didn't make everything easier. It didn't erase my to-do list. But it gave me clarity. I knew I was supposed to do it, and I knew I wasn't doing it alone.

That event ended up being one of the most powerful things we've ever done. The timing made no sense. I had no room in my calendar for it. But it worked because I made space for God to lead it.

Prayer needs to be real, not long-winded. Sometimes, I still whisper quick ones between Zoom calls or in the truck. Something like, *Lord, I need Your help. I don't want to mess this up. Please guide me.* Then I go lead. I take the next step. But I don't skip the conversation anymore, because I've learned that speed without direction is exhaustion. Leading without prayer is like swinging an axe while blindfolded. You will hit something, but it probably won't be what you hoped for.

So no, I'm not too busy to pray. I'm too busy *not* to.

Thing I Used to Believe #2: "Prayer doesn't belong in business."

I've heard these suggestions more times than I can count:

- Dan, you've got to keep faith and business separate.
- Don't scare off your clients.
- Religion and professionalism don't mix.

Well, maybe that works if you're running a soulless conglomerate where people are line items on a spreadsheet, and values are printed on posters no one reads. I'm not running that kind of company. We're in the trust, leadership, and service business. If you can't show up with your faith intact, what are you leading with?

I remember sitting across the table from someone I trusted early on—someone who was seasoned in business, and I looked up to. He'd just pulled up my brand new website and scrolled through it between bites of lunch. Then he looked at me and said, dead seriously: "Dan, there are two things you avoid in business: faith and politics." I laughed. Then I realized he wasn't joking.

He had noticed the Bible verses at the bottom of each web page—different ones on every page, each one intentional. To him, it looked risky. To me it looked like alignment. I smiled and said, "Well, I am who I am. And I'm not going to change that for a client." I'm not sure he loved that response. I'm pretty sure he was halfway into writing me off. I wasn't bluffing. And you know what's wild? Having those Bible verses on the bottom of each page has done more for our businesses than I ever imagined.

They've started conversations, encouraged people, and helped our clients know exactly who they're dealing with—and that's built more trust, not less.

Some folks warned me it would scare people away. And maybe it has. But here's the thing: if someone's scared off by a quiet verse about peace, integrity, or courage, they're probably not our ideal client anyway. And real leadership means showing up as *you*, not some watered-down version you think the world will accept.

I'm not shy about my faith. You don't have to believe what I believe. But I'm not going to pretend my faith doesn't lead me. Like Aaron Tippin crooned in his country hit back in 1990, "You've got to stand for something, or you'll fall for anything." I've got kids, my team, and me watching. So, yeah—I stand.

I remember being at a trade show once, chatting with a guy at the booth next to us, when he started trash-talking the president. Now look, I wasn't there to argue. But he kept going—loud, snarky, and mocking his faith. I finally cut him off and said, "Well, my son is currently in the military, and we're proud that our leader isn't afraid to pray and put God first." That shut him up faster than a flight delay on a cold Denver morning. Faith isn't a gimmick. It's not something I tack on to look noble. It's the foundation for how I lead, serve, and show up.

So, yeah—prayer belongs in business. It belongs in boardrooms, budgets, decisions, and how we treat our people. The minute you start separating who you are from how you lead, you've already lost something far more important than a sale.

Thing I Used to Believe #3: "I'll pray when things get bad."

Oh man. This was me. Waiting to pray until everything hits the fan is a bad strategy.

It's like standing on the wrong side of a box fan at the family reunion, watching that *one cousin* grinning like a lunatic as he winds up with a shovel full of horse apples. You know exactly what's about to happen. He's locked and loaded, and you're standing there like a deer in dress shoes.

And to make it worse? You're in your Sunday best—the nice clothes your mom *specifically* told you not to get dirty. You didn't even do anything, but you're about to wear that mess like it's part of your wardrobe, and you know she's going to kill you for it. That's what it feels like when you wait to pray until after everything goes sideways. I'd cruise through the day doing my own thing, running on caffeine and confidence, and only hitting the brakes to pray when everything was already smoking.

One time, I almost hit an elk while driving a Kenworth over a snowy mountain pass. I was straining to maintain control of a fully loaded truck, skidding around a blind corner, and bam—there's Bullwinkle, standing there like he owns the place. That's when I prayed. Hard.

Or how about when my relationship with Jenna was on the verge of falling apart? I love that woman more than life and wouldn't trade her for the world. And I'm pretty sure—*most* days—she still likes me. I'm *positive* she mumbles *best husband ever* under her breath at least once a day. I don't pay attention to the sarcastic tone. Details, right? But seriously, rewind the tape, and you'll see a version of me that only prayed *after* the fight. Once I realized I couldn't fix it with another *my bad* and a quick dinner out, I prayed.

I didn't pray when things were going well. I didn't pray when the truck was cruising fine or the relationship was strong. I only prayed in crisis—when I was forced to. But I'm not that guy anymore.

Now, I try to pray throughout the day, not just at bedtime or when I'm desperate. I pray when I'm driving, thinking, and breathing. Yes, I still forget and get distracted. But I've learned that when I make myself aware of God's presence, I *want* to pray more. It's like momentum—it builds.

One of the biggest shifts for me came after reading Napoleon Hill's *Outwitting the Devil*. In that book, Hill talks about the power of gratitude—starting your day by being genuinely thankful, not fake-thankful. Not the thanks-for-the-sunshine stuff—like *really* thankful. Now, every year, I do something that's changed my mindset. I take inventory. I pause and look at where I was this time last year—mentally, spiritually, relationally, financially—and I compare it to where I am now. I count *everything*. I'm not just talking about stuff, though if God blesses me with a private jet one day, I will be thankful for the plane, crew, and especially the snacks. I take stock of the progress I've made during the last year. How far have I come? What has God brought me through this year? How have I grown as a man, husband, dad, and leader?

And when you lead people—whether it's your family, your crew, or a whole dang company—you have a responsibility to check the course *before* you drift too far off. Leadership isn't like driving down a marked highway. It's more like flying a plane. I'm a pilot and I fly multi-engine airplanes. In the air, there are no road signs, painted lines, or red lights. You rely on your heading, instruments, and a whole lot of trust. You can be just two degrees off and end up a hundred miles from your destination.

Now imagine that in your leadership. You don't notice it at first. But over time, you end up in the wrong city, state, and mission. Fortunately, prayer keeps you on course. More than a panic button, prayer is your navigation system. So now, I pray like a pilot checks his heading.

God, am I still going the right way? Do I need to adjust? Do I need to land and rework the flight plan altogether?

A course correction made early is leadership. A crash landing because you didn't check in is ego. So, no, I don't wait until things get bad to pray anymore. I pray *before* the turbulence, because the best leaders don't just react to problems, they stay ahead of them. They listen to the One who sees the whole sky.

At the end of the day, prayer isn't just a pause button—it's your compass. It's the system check before takeoff. It's the voice in your headset saying, *Adjust heading. You're drifting.*

As Proverbs 3:5-6 reminds us: "Trust in the LORD with all your heart, and lean not on your own understanding; in all your ways submit to Him, and He will make your paths straight."

I don't know about you, but I've leaned on my own understanding more times than I'd like to admit, and that path wasn't straight. It looked more like a toddler drew it with a crayon during a sugar crash.

Think of your leadership journey like flying a plane. Your decisions are your heading. You wouldn't take off without checking your instruments, trusting your navigation, and knowing where you're supposed to land, right? So why in the world would you lead without tuning into the One who designed the skies?

You start with good intentions, great energy, and the right people behind you. But if you skip the pre-check, ignore the compass, and try to fly on instinct alone, you're setting yourself up for a long detour—or worse, a crash landing.

Now, I'm not perfect. I forget to pray. I rush decisions. I blurt things out I probably should have run through a Holy Spirit filter first. I've taken off without clearance more than once—and paid for it with lost time, money, and a bruised ego.

But every time I pause—every time I take that deep breath and pray, "God, is this where we're headed?" I get clarity. Sometimes it's a quiet nudge. Sometimes it's a full-on reroute. But it always comes with peace, because prayer doesn't just reset your mind. It realigns your mission. It's about being humble enough to admit you don't have the whole map—and bold enough to ask for directions.

And let's be honest. If you're not laughing and praying along the way, you're probably flying blind holding on to the yoke with everything you've got and hoping turbulence doesn't find you first. So, before you make that big decision, change direction, onboard that new hire, launch that new project, or walk into that hard conversation pause, pray, and check your heading.

God's got the full view. He sees what you can't. And He's not trying to keep you from flying. He's just making sure you land where you're supposed to, even if it means making a few course corrections that hurt your pride and budget. Trust me. A humbling mid-flight adjustment is much better than a blind crash landing.

Practical Ways to Pray as a Leader

All right, before we dive into the how, let's clear something up: Don't be weird. If you work at a place that has a strict no-religion policy, or you're not able to lead spiritually in your organization—don't go grabbing the intercom and preaching Leviticus in the breakroom during lunchtime. Nobody needs to hear about ancient mold protocols while they're trying to eat a tuna sandwich. Now, if you're in a company culture where faith is welcome—or you *are* the company culture, then let your faith lead you. Boldly. Humbly. And with a little wisdom.

You don't have to roll in with a megaphone and a pulpit. You don't have to gather your staff in a circle and drop a "thus saith the Lord" before every meeting. But you *can* lead with prayer in a way that's natural, real, and makes people feel safe and seen.

Your prayers matter—whether they're whispered at your desk, spoken over your team, or said in silence before you walk into a tough conversation. With that in mind, here are a few practical, no-nonsense, totally non-weird ways to make prayer part of your leadership rhythm:

1. Pray Before Big Decisions

Hiring someone? Starting a new project? Thinking about investing in that shiny new software that promises to solve all your problems (but will probably crash the first time you log in)? Pause. Pray.

I've learned that some of my worst decisions looked amazing on paper—but didn't have God's stamp on them. That's how you end up hiring the guy with the résumé of a rockstar and the character of a raccoon.

Prayer doesn't have to be dramatic. You don't need to light candles and hum. Just say something like, "God, give me wisdom. Help me see what I can't see. And please—don't let me mess this up."

Sometimes God gives a green light. Sometimes He gives a *no*. And sometimes He gives silence, because He already told you and He's waiting for you to remember.

2. Pray With Your Team (If You're Comfortable)

Now, I'm not saying you need to bust out a Bible study before every Monday morning meeting. But if your team knows you're a person of faith and it fits your workplace culture, it's okay to let them see that part of you. It doesn't have to be preachy or weird. Just a simple, "Hey, before we jump in—God, bless our work today. Give us clear minds, good attitudes, and at least one win before noon. Amen."

People don't remember your fancy strategies. They remember how you made them feel. And a moment of prayer can bring peace, unity, and a little bit of heaven into a high-pressure day. When someone on your team is personally or professionally struggling, don't be afraid to offer prayer.

Pray privately, respectfully, and without strings attached. You're not there to convert anyone or trying to win spiritual bonus points. You're just showing up with empathy and offering what you believe has power. And if they say no? That's okay. Respect it. But they'll remember that you cared enough to offer. Just don't be that person—the one who says, "I'll be praying for you," and really means, "I pray a flower pot falls from a window sill and knocks you in the head like I'd like to."[1]

We're not doing that here. This isn't passive-aggressive prayer. This is servant-hearted leadership. If it's done in love, not ego, people feel it, and that's where the real impact is.

---

[1] Lyrics from *Pray for You* by Jaron and The Long Road to Love (Jaron Lowenstein)

3. Pray in a Crisis and After the Win Too

This one's personal. For years, I treated prayer like a fire extinguisher I only used in case of emergency. Smoke, flames, elk in the headlights while I'm hauling the freight in a loaded Kenworth over a mountain pass in a snowstorm? *Now* I'm ready to pray. And trust me—when a bull elk is staring you down mid-curve and your brakes are giving you side-eye, that "Dear God, save me now," prayer gets real specific real fast. But over time, I realized something: God isn't just the tow truck. He's also the cheering section. We're quick to pray when everything's falling apart, but what about when it all comes together?

When the client signs, when the crew crushes it, or when your kid randomly calls and says, "Love you, Dad," and you didn't even have to send them money first. That's when I've learned to say, "Thank You, God," just as quickly as I used to say, "Help me, Lord."

Gratitude changes your posture. It reminds you that you didn't get here alone. And it keeps your ego from getting so big it needs its own office. So, yeah, pray when the wheels fall off. But also pray when they're spinning smoothly, the sun's out, and you somehow got the green light at every intersection. That's not coincidence. That's a reminder: He's with you in the chaos and the cruise control.

And celebrating with Him along the way? That's where the real joy is. Plus, He deserves a fist bump now and then, too.

4. Track the Prayers, Because You'll Forget

I used to think journaling was for teenage girls, poets, and people who own more than one essential oil diffuser. But leadership will humble you real quick.

There came a point when my brain was so overloaded that I couldn't remember what I'd prayed about three days ago, let alone three months ago. So, I grabbed a plain ol' notebook—no leather, no quotes on the cover, just lines—and started jotting things down. Not full paragraphs. Not emotional rants. Just quick, bullet-point prayers.

- "God, help me know if I should hire this guy."
- "Give me patience with this team. They're driving me nuts today."
- "Is this the right time to launch the new program?"
- "Please fix that client situation before it explodes. Or before I do."
- "Thank You for today. It worked. Somehow."

And here's the wild part—when I went back and looked through it later, I could see how God had shown up. Prayers were answered. Stuff was resolved. Decisions were made with clarity, and I knew I couldn't take credit. That notebook became proof.

I'm not leading alone. He listens, and even when I feel stuck, He's still working. When you're tired, foggy, and running on fumes, that journal is like a highlight reel of answered prayers and divine plot twists. Trust me. It beats the heck out of trying to remember it all in your head. So no, it's not lame or soft. It's one of the most tactical leadership tools I've ever used. I still scribble in it between meetings, truck stops, and flights. It works, and more importantly, He works, even when I forget He does.

5. Use Your Drive Time, Flight Time, or Tractor Time

If you commute, you've got a built-in prayer closet with cupholders. Use it. Instead of scrolling through emails at red lights or letting talk radio raise your blood pressure, just turn it off. Use that time to talk with God. I've prayed some of my most honest prayers behind the wheel. God hears you just fine in a Ford Super Duty or a John Deere cab. Just don't close your eyes. I can't stress that enough.

Prayer isn't limited to church pews or quiet corners. You can pray on the move— while you work – anywhere really. When you start bringing prayer into your everyday rhythm, things begin to shift, not because your problems disappear, but because your perspective gets aligned with the One who already sees the solution. You don't need a theology degree or sound like Morgan Freeman to get it right. You just need a willing heart, an honest word, and the guts to ask for help.

When you lead with prayer, you're not leading alone. That, my friend, changes everything.

Prayerful Leadership in the Bible

(A.K.A. You're Not the Only One Trying to Do This Right)

If you ever feel like you're the only one trying to lead with prayer in the middle of a chaotic, noisy world, I have good news: You're in great company. Some of the boldest, most influential leaders in the Bible weren't powerful because they were the loudest, the most talented, or the best dressed. They were powerful because they led from their knees. They knew what many modern leaders forget: Prayer isn't your backup plan. It's your first move. Here are a few who will light a fire under you

Nehemiah—The Silent Prayers of a Strategic Leader

Nehemiah didn't just rebuild walls. He rebuilt confidence. He was calm under pressure, sharp in planning, and tough enough to lead people who kept trying to give up halfway through the project. But the real kicker? Before he picked up a hammer, he prayed. When the king asked him what he wanted (let's be honest, this was a don't-say-the-wrong-thing-or-you-die moment), Nehemiah whispered a quick prayer right then and there (Nehemiah 2:4). No long monologue. Just, "God … help me not blow this." (That's the Dan paraphrase.) The takeaway: Prayer and strategy are not enemies. They're teammates. You need both.

Moses—The Guy Who Kept Going Back to God

If you think your team is tough to lead, imagine Moses with a million people in sandals complaining every time lunch was late. This guy faced plagues, parted seas, and still got yelled at for bad water pressure. But he never stopped going back to God.

Over and over, whether it was the Red Sea, the golden calf, or his own doubts, he prayed. He didn't just talk to the people about God. He talked to God about the people. Even when they were acting like ungrateful toddlers, Moses stood in the gap for them.

The takeaway: Leaders don't just talk *to* people. They talk to God *for* them.

David—The Warrior with a Worship Playlist

David wasn't just the guy who wrote psalms. He was a *beast* in battle. He took down a giant with a rock, led elite warriors, and ruled as king. But he also cried out to God like a man who knew his strength wasn't enough on its own.

He was tough and tender. Savage in combat, and soft in prayer. He could lead men into war by day and write a gut-wrenching prayer by night. He prayed in caves when he was running for his life. He prayed in the palace when the crown got heavy. And yeah, he failed big time. Moral failure, family drama, and personal loss were his rock bottom. But he always circled back to God. He didn't just show up at the temple when things were good. He prayed when he was broken, embarrassed, and cornered. And somehow, despite everything, God called him *a man after My own heart*.

The takeaway: God doesn't need flawless leaders. He uses fiercely honest ones who lead hard, repent fast, and never lose the connection that matters most.

Jesus—The Ultimate Model of Prayerful Leadership

Jesus wasn't passive. He didn't tiptoe around hard conversations. He walked into temples and flipped tables when people were out of line. He looked Pharisees in the eye and called out hypocrisy. He led crowds, healed the broken, raised the dead, and trained up a team of wildly underqualified guys to change the world. And He *still* prayed more than anyone else.

Before choosing His disciples, He prayed. Before performing miracles, He prayed. Before going to the cross, He dropped to His knees and wrestled with the weight of it all. And in John 17? He didn't just pray for His team. He prayed for you, your faith, leadership, and legacy. Jesus didn't pray because He was fragile. He prayed because He was focused. He knew where the power came from, and He never led on autopilot.

The takeaway: If Jesus, the literal Son of God, stopped to pray before every major move, then who in the world do we think we are to lead without it? Prayer wasn't His backup plan. It was part of the mission strategy.

*****

These leaders weren't great because they had perfect records or polished résumés. They were great because they stayed connected to the One who never fails. So whether you're leading a company, a crew, a team of tired interns, or a small-town shop with more heart than budget, lead like Nehemiah. Pray like Moses. Worship like David. And follow Jesus. The world full of noise, pressure, and people is expecting you to have all the answers. The most powerful thing you'll ever do as a leader is pray.

Lead with Prayer or Lead with Pressure

Every leader leans on something. For some, it's gut instinct. For others, it's spreadsheets, coffee, or the advice of that one guy on YouTube who swears you can scale to $10 million using nothing but mindset and a vision board.

But if you're leading with pressure instead of prayer, you're cruising for a breakdown. And it's not the good kind where you cry a little and then feel better. I mean a why-is-this-fan-covered-in-something-awful-and-how-did-I-end-up-standing-directly-in-front-of-it moment. Trust me, I've been there.

I've been the guy white-knuckling it over a mountain pass in a Kenworth, locking eyes with an elk that looked like it was daring me to keep going. I've been the guy launching an event in the wrong forest, hyping it like it was the Super Bowl, only to check the signups and realize my mom didn't even register. I've been the guy who only prayed when the wheels came off, and the guy who finally learned to pray before turning the key.

Here's the truth most leaders won't admit: Leadership is heavy. There's no off switch. There's no just-go-home-and-forget-about-it setting. You carry the weight of the vision, the people, the payroll, and the problems, and the pressure never stops knocking. So let me ask you: Do you want to carry all that with your own strength, or with God's? Those are your options.

You can lead with pressure, grit your teeth, fake the confidence, and tell yourself, "I've got this," even when you know deep down you don't. Or, you can lead with prayer. You can pause in the truck, in the bathroom stall, in the middle of the jobsite, and say something as simple as, "God, I don't know what to do. But I know You do. Help."

And that moment changes everything, not because it makes your life easier, but because it reminds you, you're not flying blind. You're not steering the ship solo. You've got the Creator of the universe in your corner. And He's a better chief operating officer (COO) than you'll ever be. So here's the challenge. Before you make that decision, answer that email, flip out on the guy who just backed into your trailer for the third time this month, pray.

Ask God to check your heading. Ask Him to show you if you're still in the right forest, or if you're halfway through building a treehouse in the middle of someone else's calling. Ask Him for peace when the pressure's high and clarity when everything feels foggy.

He's not looking for fancy words. He's not grading your grammar. He's just waiting for you to show up because leadership without prayer, is guesswork with a clipboard. And yeah, you're going to forget sometimes. You'll get caught up in the chaos and realize halfway through the week that you haven't talked to God once. Welcome to the club.

We're figuring it out too. But every time you remember, that's a win. Prayer is the most powerful leadership tool you'll never see in a board meeting. When you use it consistently, intentionally, and humbly, God will move in ways your spreadsheets never saw coming. So lean on it. Trust it. Lead with it. Then, when the fan starts spinning, you'll be ready, because the moment you let God lead, everything changes.

Key Takeaways from Chapter Six

You don't get to lead without failing. But you do get to choose how you respond. Everyone gets knocked down. Leaders decide whether they stay down or get back up and rebuild.

Your worst moment doesn't have to be your last chapter. The enemy wants you stuck in shame. God wants to use it to sharpen you. Which story are you gonna live out?

Leadership isn't proven when you're winning. It's revealed when you're wrecked. Crisis doesn't destroy leaders—it exposes what's already in them.

Stop spinning. Start owning. Blame-shifting and damage control kill trust. The moment you say, "That's on me," is the moment you start leading again.

Grace is the leadership tool most people forget to use on themselves. You've handed out second chances to everyone else. Now it's your turn to receive one—and actually believe it's real.

Apologies don't fix trust—actions do. Words are easy. Consistency is costly. The people around you are watching what you *do*, not what you *say*.

God's not done just because you screwed up. The same God who used David after Bathsheba and Peter after denial still uses broken leaders. If you're breathing, He's still building.

You can't lead people well if you're lying to yourself. Self-deception is leadership cancer. Be honest about your mistakes so you can lead from healing—not hiding.

If you're willing to walk through fire, you'll lead people who trust you through theirs. Your scars become someone else's survival guide. When they see you own your story, they'll believe they can do the same.

Chapter 7 | Servant Leadership

Lead Like Nothing is Beneath You

Not long ago, a local oilfield outfit called us in a full-on panic. They had received a letter from the state auditor, and it hit like a pipe wrench to the face. No warning and no preparation—just "Surprise! We're coming to dig through your files!" Full-blown panic mode had set in. You could hear the fear in their voices. They knew they had a lot of work to do and had no idea where to start.

My team member who answered the call could feel the pressure before finishing the standard phone greeting—voice strained, no small talk, just a straight shot of panic like someone already knee-deep in you-know-what and looking for a way out. My team brought the matter straight to me.

I called the company back, and the moment I got on the line, I felt the stress, too. With the tight words and shaky breath, it felt like the client was holding everything together with duct tape and desperation.

So, I cleared my schedule and told them, "Here's what we're going to do. First, upload all your driver files to this secure folder. Your team can scan them in. Mine will take it from there. We'll digitize, sort it, and get your house back in order."

That call came in around 6 p.m. on a Friday. By Sunday, their office team showed up and uploaded documents. No whining. No clock-watching. Just heads down, getting it done. By Wednesday at 5 a.m., my team had every single file digitized, labeled, and ready to go. I was beyond proud of how hard they hustled to make it happen.

I'd already cleared the rest of my week to back them up, so we scheduled a face-to-face for Thursday to tackle the rest. I hopped in the truck and headed out to their office. I met with the owner and the two women from the office who looked like they'd been carrying the weight of the whole company on their shoulders. We kicked things off by walking through what to expect during the audit, what the auditor would look for, how to stay ahead of the curve, and how to handle it if things went sideways.

After five hundred plus audits (eight-six the year before), I had a pretty solid read on how it would all play out. I shared some horror stories, not to scare them, but to prepare them. It helped. You could see the tension ease a bit. Clarity has a way of doing that.

Then, I sat down with the owner and dove into their FMCSA (Federal Motor Carrier Safety Administration) portal.[2] We made major updates to their DOT number—stuff that had been sitting untouched for too long. Once that was cleaned up, I helped him get his Clearinghouse account properly linked and verified.[3]

After that, I sat with the two women in the office and we talked through their vehicle files. They were stressed, like stomach-in-knots-can't-sleep stressed. But once I looked through the stack, I told them, "Honestly, y'all are in way better shape than you think." You could see the relief hit their faces. We built a checklist together of what still needed attention, and suddenly, the mountain didn't seem so high. Most of my time there wasn't spent teaching DOT regs. It was spent calming nerves, setting expectations, and being present. That's leadership, too.

Now, at this point, you might be thinking, "Dan, that's great, you did your job. Want a gold star?" Hold up. I'm getting to the servant leadership part.

I left their office, headed back to mine, rolled up my sleeves, and sat down with my team. We went file by file to make sure every detail was lined up properly. Then, like most of my best ideas, it hit me at 7 p.m. on a Friday that we needed to reclassify them in the portal. So, I logged back in, made the changes, and was about to shut down when I saw something that didn't look right. So, I stayed longer and dug deeper.

By 9 p.m., I'd found the issue. Something in their forms wasn't correct. I fixed it, but the longer I stared at the screen, the more something else gnawed at me. I pulled up the invoice we'd sent them, and it didn't sit right. What we sold them didn't match what they needed. It was off. And not in their favor. In ours.

So, I made it right. I adjusted the invoice to match what would help them succeed. First thing Monday, I called the salesperson who handled the account and explained what I'd changed and why. They weren't thrilled. It meant a smaller commission. But I told them straight: "We live by our core values. Extreme honesty means we do what's

---

[2] The FMCSA Drug and Alcohol Clearinghouse is a secure online database that tracks commercial drivers' drug and alcohol program violations and return-to-duty status.

[3] A secure online database that gives employers, FMCSA, licensing agencies, and law enforcement real-time access to CDL/CLP holders' drug and alcohol program violations

right, even when no one's looking. And our customers come before our personal gain. Period."

That Saturday, I emailed the client to explain the change and how it would help them in the long term. The owner called and said, "Dan, you've seen our operation. What do we need to do to get this right?" I told him, "Let's get through this audit first. Then we'll walk with you long term and build a rock-solid program together."

Fast-forward a month. The audit wraps. They passed with flying colors—just a couple of minor non-critical dings. But here's the part that stuck with me. The owner called and said, "Dan, there is no chance in hell we could have gotten through this without you and your team. You saved our bacon in more ways than one. I'm so dang glad you do what you do. If there's ever anything we can do to help you out, say the word."

Today, they're one of our full-service clients. They've sent multiple leaders through our leadership boot camp. And the owner? He's in my inner circle now, working on growing his company and leadership the right way.

All that happened because we didn't just sell them a service, we served them when it mattered most. Now they tell everyone they know about us, because it wasn't only about passing the audit. It was about showing up, being honest, and serving with excellence, even when it cost us something. That's servant leadership.

Most people don't want to serve others, they want to serve themselves to get ahead. However, leadership that lasts, changes people, builds loyalty, and builds a legacy always starts with service. When you serve first, you earn trust, build people, and create impact. And yeah, you grow a business that people never want to leave. That's the style of leadership I'm committed to. Not the type that takes the stage, the kind that picks up the trash on the way to it.

I learned that servant leadership is more than a strategy. It's a calling. It's about showing up when it matters, even though nobody's watching, and it's time to clock out. Servant leadership is especially evident when you could choose comfort over commitment but don't.

I could have passed that customer off to someone else. I could have said, "Well, they paid for this package, and that's what they get." I could have stuck to the invoice, ignored the portal issue, and never gone the extra mile. And sure, we might've still gotten them through the audit. But we wouldn't have earned their trust or built the relationship that followed.

See, true servant leaders go beyond fixing problems. They carry burdens. They take ownership of the whole picture because it's the right thing to do, not out of obligation.

And yeah, going the extra mile with our client came with a price. It cost us some commission, some late nights, and sore eyes. But we gained a client for life who has made more referrals to us than we could have imagined. And there was a cultural benefit, too. My team witnessed their leader practice what he preached.

When I say, *serve first*, I'm not talking about some cheesy motivational slogan. I mean, get your hands dirty, lead by example, and humble yourself enough to put someone else's success above your own short-term gain. Read the words of Jesus:

WHOEVER WANTS TO BECOME GREAT AMONG YOU MUST BE YOUR SERVANT.

—MATTHEW 20:26

That's good Sunday preaching and the secret to leading a business people want to work for. Servanthood builds lasting relationships and creates a brand that reflects Christ. So, if you're going to lead like a lion, start by serving like a shepherd. When you serve others with no strings attached, you build a legacy and trust. My friend, legacy is the only brand worth building.

What Is Servant Leadership (In Plain English)?

The easiest way I can explain servant leadership is this: You put the needs of your people ahead of your own. That's it. That's the whole game.

When Jesus was exhausted and running on empty, He still healed people. He still fed crowds, showed up, and served when no one else would. Instead of making excuses, He made a difference.

We're not healing the blind or walking on water, but the heart behind it is the same. Servant leadership shows up in the real stuff. It's giving your team the win when they crush it, even if it was you holding it all together behind the scenes, and owning the screw up when something slips through, even if it wasn't your mess. Staying late to help someone hit a deadline, though the missed deadline wouldn't affect you. Or, simply grabbing a plate for the guy who doesn't walk so well and wouldn't dream of asking for help. It's not flashy. But it's real, and it matters. Servant leadership shows up in the little things more than the big ones.

One question I am often asked is, "How do you measure that?" Easy. Look for the leader who stacks chairs, remembers names, wipes the whiteboard, grabs the cooler, hands out water bottles, or stays late to clean up, not because it's their job, but because it serves the team.

You measure it in how they treat the janitor. Do they offer the last donut to someone else, listen without interrupting, and ignore their phone to tend to someone else's' need when they've got a hundred fires to put out.

Big gestures are easy to spot, and they usually come with recognition. But real servant leadership isn't about the spotlight. It's about the shadows. It's revealed in the margins. It's built in moments so small, most folks miss them, unless they've been trained to lead from the middle, not the top.

The heart of a servant isn't loud. It doesn't demand attention. It shows up quietly, consistently, and without the need for applause. And that's what makes it powerful. When someone leads like that—through the unnoticed, unglamorous, blink-and-you-miss-it actions—they lead and influence people. They build trust, earn respect, and change the culture without needing to change the title on their nameplate.

The other day, we were at my in-laws' house talking about leadership, and they mentioned how impressed they were with our kids. Then they told a story I'll never forget.

My oldest was about two or three years old and playing in the living room. His grandpa, pushing 70, accidentally knocked over a full cup of milk in the kitchen. He let out a long, tired sigh. Nothing dramatic. Just that quiet sigh that says, "Here we go."

Without a word, my son heard it, jumped up, ran to the towel drawer, grabbed a towel, and started cleaning up the mess. Nobody asked him. Nobody told him to do it. He only saw someone in need and stepped in. After cleaning it up, he walked the towel over to the washing machine, tossed it in, and went right back to playing like nothing had happened.

That's servant leadership. He saw the need and met the moment. He didn't wait to be asked and didn't expect a thank you. He only served. That's the goal. We help people because we care; we're wired to serve, and it's right. Sometimes, we are applauded, but we don't serve for recognition. Servant leadership is not about what *I* need. It's about what *they* need. It's about how I help them move forward, even if they don't realize they need it yet, and not about how I will get ahead.

That's servant leadership. And it's simpler than most people make it. Jesus said it plain as day in Matthew 20:26–28 (ESV): "But whoever would be great among you must be your servant." He didn't just say it, He lived it. And if we want to lead like He did, we've got to follow that same example. When we serve, we grow. And when we grow, so does everyone around us.

False Beliefs About Servant Leadership

As I travel around the country, talking with leaders, business owners, and managers, I hear a lot of opinions about servant leadership. Most resistance comes from people afraid of what it might cost them. They'll fight it tooth and nail and throw out every excuse in the book.

Speaking of excuses, my big brother once told me,

"Excuses are like butt holes. We all have one, and they all stink." He didn't use that exact verbiage, but I had to clean it up a little for this use. So, let's eliminate some of these excuses based on false beliefs, one at a time.

False Belief #1: "If I serve my people, they'll walk all over me."

Horse-pucky. This belief comes from a fear of being taken advantage of. And yeah, I get it. None of us want to be the doormat. But real servant leadership isn't about letting people walk over you. It's about showing them how to walk *with* you through example, consistency, and genuine care.

Years ago, we had a new hire on the team. He was young, full of energy, smart as a whip, but clearly nervous about stepping into a world he didn't fully understand. During his first week on the job, he was assigned to help organize a massive stack of files from a DOT audit. It was tedious, overwhelming, and the job most people would pawn. Instead of sending him off alone, I grabbed a chair, rolled up my sleeves, and said, "Let's do this together."

We spent hours at that table. I didn't preach to him or micromanage his work. I just worked beside him. We cracked jokes and shared stories, and when the files were in order, so was his confidence.

The following week, I overheard him talking to another struggling team member. He said, "Hey, I'll help you with that. I've got time." And I smiled. He had caught the spirit of servant leadership and paid it forward. Leadership by example works. Control doesn't.

Now, let me give you an example of the opposite.

My youngest son once played against a youth basketball team whose coach apparently hadn't read the chapter on servant leadership. He ran his team through fear. I heard him yell during a game, "If you're tired and not going to hustle, I can take you off the court anytime!" His whole tone screamed, "Obey me, or else."

Instead of being encouraging and empowering, he belittled his players, expecting better performance. Not surprisingly, The kids hated playing for him. Their body language gave it away. Heads down, sullen faces, eyes avoiding contact—no joy, no passion, just pressure. That leadership gets short-term compliance, but never long-term commitment.

A real leader inspires people to hustle because they believe in what they're doing. A real leader knows that tearing down a team will not build it up.

Servant leadership doesn't make you a doormat. It makes you a foundation. When you serve with strength and lead with heart, people don't walk over you, they walk with you. They are the people with whom something meaningful can be built. And that's where the real magic happens.

False Belief #2: "Real leaders shouldn't have to do the grunt work."

Bull. If you think being a leader means you're above hard work, you misunderstood the assignment. Real leaders don't hide in the office when things get messy. They're the first ones to roll up their sleeves, dig in, and ask, "Where do you need me?"

One of the best examples of this concept is a general manager I know at an agriculture co-op. Every spring, like clockwork, his fertilizer department gets slammed. And I'm not talking a little busy. I'm talking full-throttle chaos. His crew is working twelve to fourteen-hour days, six days a week, moving two to five semi-loads of fertilizer a day. It's a logistical beast.

As the general manager, you'd think he would stay in his office, sipping coffee, pointing fingers, and asking why it's taking so long. Nope. This guy jumps in with both boots. He shows up early, walks down to the yard, and asks, "Where do you need me most today?" And then he does it.

If they need someone to run the bobcat and scoop fertilizer into the mixer, he's on it. If they need a cart delivered, he hooks it up and gets it there. If they need someone to run a semi-load to a farm two counties over, he grabs his CDL and gets behind the wheel. His people respect him because they know he won't ask anything of them, that he isn't willing to do himself.

And you know what's even cooler? The customers love it. I've had more than one farmer tell me, "I couldn't believe Don delivered my fertilizer. That meant a lot." That's what servant leadership does. It earns respect on both sides of the fence.

The same goes for me. If a client texts on a Saturday and my team's off, I'll jump in and pull the permit. Do I want to? Not really. Do I do it? Absolutely. Leadership doesn't clock out.

My team sees that. They know I care enough to answer those emergency texts on weekends. Slowly, without me ever asking, they check the phone line on Saturdays and Sundays, too. Not because they're on the clock, but because they're bored, maybe just hanging out at home, and they think, "Hey, I'll check and make sure no one needs anything." If something pops up, they jump on it. The customers are happy, the team members are proud they got to help, and I'm thrilled because I didn't have to jump in that time. That's a win-win-win.

I've watched it happen. Someone notices a last-minute permit needs to be pulled, and before I can reply, they've got it handled. The employee's proud. And I didn't have to touch it. That's what a win-win-win culture looks like.

There is no such thing as *grunt work* in servant leadership. If it's work that helps the mission, it's worth doing. And if you want a team willing to go the extra mile, you'd better be willing to take the first step.

False Belief #3: "You can't lead and be their friend."

Let's quickly clear something up: I'm not telling you to be their buddy. I'm saying be someone they can trust, someone who serves with integrity and leads with a backbone.

That's how Jesus did it. He wasn't worried about being popular. He was focused on being present.

Right now, I've got someone on my team learning the ropes of business development. This team member has great potential but thinks the same perks I have as the owner should be available to her, too. Let me be real. She hasn't earned them yet. And she won't get privileges just because she thinks she deserves it.

Her misguided expectations don't prompt me to treat her like trash. I don't book her into a shady motel or fly her on a sketchy discount airline just to make a point. I put her somewhere I'd stay and on a flight I'd take. Accommodations and travel are safe, clean, and decent. But no, I'm not booking her a penthouse suite or giving her first-class upgrades. There's a fine line between serving and spoiling.

If she complains, I coach her and walk her through the *why*. She's free to find another opportunity if she still doesn't get it and thinks she's entitled to more. Not everyone has to be a fan, and that's okay. But here's the thing, I go out of my way to show her how much I care. I don't just say, "I care." I prove it with action. That's what real leadership looks like.

The other day, this team member and I were heading to Las Vegas for an event. I brought her along so she could learn how we travel, do business, and show up as a company. She had no responsibilities. Attending this event was for her benefit, not mine.

But instead of being thankful for the opportunity, she sent me a frantic stream of texts throughout the day.

"My flight's delayed. I don't land until 1 a.m. my time now! Going to go straight to the hotel and check in when I land. Going to be exhausted!!!"

"When do I check into the motel?" (She called it a *motel*.)

"I don't like this motel. It's in a shady part of town. I wouldn't personally stay here, and I can't believe a business would book this. I'm not comfortable staying here."

All this melodrama stemmed from her expectations not being met. She didn't get a direct flight since it cost three times as much). She wasn't staying in a strip-front hotel that runs four times the price. It was overreaction after overreaction. She acted like a spoiled little kid, and I'll be honest. I could have gotten frustrated, snapped back, or ignored her altogether. But I didn't. I chose to be a real leader.

I took thirty seconds, googled her flight, and found it was delayed sixteen minutes. That's it. She was originally landing at 6:45 p.m., and now it was scheduled for 7:01 p.m. I took a screenshot of her updated flight info and sent it to her. My goal wasn't to be rude but to say two things: one, don't lie to me, and two, I care enough to look into it and get the facts.

She ended up landing early and was at the hotel by 7:15 p.m. Pacific time, 10:15 p.m. in her time zone, not 1 a.m. as she claimed.

Then came the *shady part of town* comments. She had even convinced the Uber driver it was dangerous. The truth is that her hotel was one block off the Strip. So, what did I do? I walked from my hotel (the one the event organizers booked for me) to hers.

I passed a Top Golf, the Grand Prix Hotel, a bunch of families with strollers, and couples walking hand in hand. Totally safe. Totally normal. And when she arrived, I was already standing at the check-in desk, waiting. I told her about my walk and how safe it was, face-to-face. And just like that, all her worries disappeared. Her stress melted off her like butter in a hot skillet simply because I showed up.

That's not spoiling someone or caving in. That's servant leadership. I didn't give her what she wanted. I gave her what she *needed*: support, reassurance, and someone who cared enough to meet her where she was.

Servant leadership means you lead with empathy, even when they're not where you are yet. It doesn't mean you blur boundaries or let people walk all over you. Show them the standard by living it, not preaching it.

You don't have to be their best friend. But if you want to be a great leader, you *do* need to care. Listen when something doesn't feel right. Validate what's real and hold your ground when it's not. If someone brings you a legit concern, fix it. If they're upset they didn't get special treatment, give them the truth and move on.

Leadership isn't about winning popularity contests. It's about earning trust. And trust means people will follow you anywhere, even when they question your decisions. That's the strength of servant leadership. It doesn't lean on fear or titles. It's built on credibility, consistency, and authentic connection to others.

And it doesn't just apply to business. It applies to parenting, too. Jenna and I raised four strong-willed, hardworking kids, and it wasn't always easy. Saying *no* was tough sometimes, but we stuck to our values. Our kids knew that when we said *no*, we meant it. But they also knew they could come to us with anything. We didn't belittle them. We didn't shut them down. We listened, cared, and created a space where they felt safe being honest.

They trusted us, not because we gave them everything they wanted, but because we consistently gave them what they *needed*: structure, support, discipline, and love. That's servant leadership at home. You don't have to be their best friend. You just have to be someone they can count on.

Servant leadership works in the boardroom and the living room. And when you live it out, it transforms everything around you. And the best part? It works in business, family, and every other part of life where people matter more than positions.

False Belief #4: "I earned this role; I shouldn't have to do the hard work anymore."

Man, this one gets me fired up. Yes, you earned the role. But if you think that means you're done digging in, you're not a leader; you're just someone with a title. There's a big difference between being in charge and leading.

I've earned a lot in my life. When someone on my team quits or drops the ball, I don't sit back and cry about the extra work. I roll up my sleeves and get to work. I double down. I wake up earlier. I stay later. I fill in the gaps and do whatever it takes to keep us moving forward.

Not long ago, we went through a major shake-up at Eclipse DOT. We started holding people accountable, really accountable, in ways we hadn't before. And you know what happened? Some folks walked. They weren't bad people, but they didn't align with the new standard.

Yeah, it stung. I'd invested a lot into some of them, years of mentoring, coaching, second chances. I wanted them to win. I still do. But they weren't ready to rise to the challenge when the bar was raised.

Instead of blaming them, I asked myself the tough questions: "Where did *I* fail them by setting clear expectations? Why didn't they know what was expected? And how can I make sure this doesn't happen again?"

So, I got to work. I revisited our onboarding system, rewrote our procedures, and refined how we train new hires. It was a grind. It meant going back to the same work I did five years ago when I was doing it all myself. But it was also one of the best things that ever happened at our company.

Now, when I bring on a new person, it's about one-third the effort it used to take to get them up to speed. I took the time to fix what was broken. I got in the trenches, identified the gaps, and built a better system.

If I were merely a boss, someone with a title, I would have hired someone new, let them fail, and then blamed them for not figuring it out. But that's not leadership. That's laziness. Real leaders step into the hard stuff and get their hands dirty. Once you do the work, you make it better for the people who follow you.

Whenever someone on my team has a question or needs help, I stop what I'm doing, jump in, help them figure it out, and then explain the *why*. Then, the next time it comes up, they can handle it on their own. That's how leadership becomes part of your business's DNA. The real goal is to raise the next generation to lead with more clarity, confidence, and ownership than you had when you started.

So yeah, you earned your spot. But now it's your job to earn your people's trust day in and day out. Showing up, doing the work, and building systems and standards that serve you also serve the people who come after you. That's leadership. That's legacy.

Real leaders raise people who are better than they are. And if you do it right, someday you'll look around and realize you're surrounded by a team of rockstars who are smarter, faster, and stronger than you ever were. That's the power of servant leadership. And that's the perfect setup for what comes next—*how to live it out every day.*

The Bible and Servant Leadership (Through the Eyes of Daniel)

If you're seeking a powerhouse example of servant leadership straight out of the Bible, you don't have to go much further than Daniel. This guy is a legend. He didn't walk around with a crown, a sword, or an army, but he had influence that changed kingdoms.

Daniel wasn't a king or top-tier executive. He was a servant captured from his homeland and placed in service to the Babylonian King. And yet, through his character, courage, and commitment to God, Daniel became more respected than most of the king's advisers.

Now, here's where it gets really good.

When the king ordered all the young men in training to eat the rich food from his table, Daniel made a bold move. Here's what's worth noticing. He didn't throw a fit. He didn't demand his way or make a scene. He didn't scream about his *rights*. Instead, Daniel made a respectful request to eat differently. He honored the authority he was under while still honoring the God he served.

He approached the chief official and asked, "Hey, can we just eat vegetables and water for ten days? Let's see how we look compared to the others." The official listened because of how Daniel carried himself with respect, humility, and confidence in his convictions. He agreed. And what happened next? After ten days, Daniel and his buddies

Serve with honor. Stand with conviction.

looked healthier, stronger, and sharper than all the other guys eating the king's rich food. Boom. That's servant leadership.

And it didn't end with food. Later, when King Nebuchadnezzar had a disturbing dream none of his advisers could interpret, Daniel was called on. And what did he say? He said, "I can't do this, but my God can." Right before the most powerful man on Earth, Daniel acknowledged that the wisdom didn't come from him. It came from God. He was serving the king, but he served the Lord first. That's the courage and clarity that authentic servant leadership demands.

He didn't throw his title around or rely on force. He led by example and by faith. He served his captors, honored the system he was placed in, and never compromised who he was or who his God was.

Daniel kept serving. He kept honoring. And because of that, he earned the trust of the king—multiple kings. When others sought ways to take him down, they had to admit: "We can't find any fault in this man unless it's something to do with his God."[4] That's influence and integrity, leadership people notice.

But don't miss this. Daniel didn't gain influence by chasing power. He earned it by staying faithful and serving well. He didn't compromise his convictions. He didn't

---

[4] This is a partially paraphrased quote from Daniel 6:4-5 (NIV)

cave to pressure. And he stood firm when things got heated, like we're-throwing-you-into-the-lions'-den heated. He knew who he served first.

And that's the message I want you to walk away with: True servant leadership means standing strong while lifting others when caving in is tempting. Daniel trusted God with his future and proved that a servant could lead the way despite a secular, broken system. Not by force. Not by fear. By faith.

This hits home for me as a business owner, parent, leader, and friend. You don't have to scream to be heard. You don't have to dominate to influence. You have to walk in truth, stand in integrity, and serve others like it matters.

When you do that, like Daniel, your life becomes the message. And that's a brand worth living by.

Servant Leadership Gut Check

When my oldest son was getting ready to ship out for the Army, just weeks after turning eighteen, we were driving home from a trip to town. It was just the two of us. The windshield time, which any dad knows is the best time for real talk, gave us a rare opportunity. I looked over and said, "Hey bud, what's one thing your mom and I could have done better to help you prepare for this transition from being our kid to becoming an adult?"

He didn't have to think long. He said, "Well, you could have looped me in more on how to pay bills, like what that even looks like. Or, had me add a new phone line to the business, so I'd know how to do that on my own someday." He continued, "You could have helped me with utilities, insurance, and avoiding gas station sushi."

And then, right when I was starting to feel like a total failure, he hit me with this: "But, you guys did a lot right, too. You always included us when we picked out beach houses for vacation. We had to help choose based on budget, location, and what we'd enjoy. When we were on road trips, you'd say, 'Where are we going to eat?' and make us Google places and find one everyone would like. You taught us how to cook, do laundry, and manage a calendar. You even taught us how to compare gas prices and grocery shop without blowing the budget. That stuff mattered."

That conversation hit me hard, because as a dad, I was doing my best, but I still missed some big things. I couldn't go back and fix it for him, but we *did* change how we prepared our other kids for their transition to adulthood. And that only happened because I asked, and then I listened. *Really* listened.

Leadership, at home, in business, church, or community, is like that. You'll miss the mark if you don't evaluate how you're doing. You'll think you're crushing it when you're coasting. Or worse, hurting the people you think you're helping.

So, here's your chance to take a hard look at yourself, not to beat yourself up, but to grow. Make the shifts you need to move your leadership from good intentions to real impact.

Grab a pen, open a note on your phone, or just sit with this and reflect. Let's go.

1. Who are you serving, and how are you serving them?

Think about your spouse, kids, team, church, and community. List names and dig into how you are serving them. Are you intentional in your time and effort? Are you present and reliable when they need you, or only when it's convenient? When's the last time you made their priorities your priorities without grumbling or rolling your eyes? Are you listening when they talk and helping when they struggle? Do you show up before they ask? Are you someone people can consistently count on? Now rate yourself: On a scale of one to ten, how well do you think you're doing?

Want to get even bolder? Ask *them,* "On a scale of one to ten, how well do I serve you?"

Be careful with this one. They might hold back if they care about you because they don't want to hurt your feelings. So, remind them that truth is a gift, and you're asking because you want to grow.

2. When was the last time you did something, expecting absolutely nothing in return?

Jesus said in Matthew 6:3, "But when you give to the needy, do not let your left hand know what your right hand is doing." That's the spirit we're talking about here. No pat on the back. No applause. No social media post. Just you, doing something good and walking away.

So, think back. How many times in the last week, past month, and last three months did you do something with no expectation of reward? Really think about it.

What counts? Maybe you made dinner for the family without announcing it. Maybe you picked up someone else's trash without calling them out. Perhaps you wrote a sermon that nobody applauded. Did you help your kids with their homework even though you were exhausted? Maybe you gave a ride to someone who didn't say *thanks.*

It doesn't count if you tell everyone how generous you are or posting about your good deeds to get likes. Helping so you can complain later or doing the dishes loudly so everyone hears you doing the dishes, (Yeah, that one's for all the dramatic dishwashers out there.) those are non-starters too.

Now ask yourself this. If someone watched your last three months like a reality show, would they see a servant or someone who wants to *look* like one?

3. Are you lifting others or holding them back?

Servant leaders don't hoard the spotlight, they lead others into it. They celebrate when someone else starts shining. Are you giving your team space to grow? Do you let your kids take on challenges and cheer them through the process? Are you giving your people opportunities to prove themselves, or are you keeping them small so you can feel big?

Servant leaders coach, challenge with kindness, and correct with care. They don't embarrass; they empower. They don't build their legacy by climbing over people. They build it by lifting them up.

What do you want to be known for? Do you want to be known as someone who helped others rise or as the person who always had to be the most intelligent person in the room?

Here's a good gut check: Ask yourself, *When was the last time I handed someone else the mic, the credit, or the opportunity on purpose? How did I feel about it?*

This is truth time. Doing something to help people grow means letting someone else shine. Did you feel good about it, or did it sting a little because they got the praise? That feeling will tell you exactly where you stand. True servant leaders don't just tolerate others succeeding; they fuel it.

4. Are you coaching someone to be better than you?

If your vision dies with you, you weren't leading. You were controlling. Real leaders generate leadership qualities in others.

Who are you coaching right now? Who are you pulling up beside you and saying, "Watch how I do this, now you try?" Are you walking with them as they learn, or standing off to the side, waiting to say, "I told you so," when they mess up?

If you want to look good, you'll always be spinning your wheels. But if your goal is to grow leaders, you'll gain the traction to get unstuck from old patterns.

Let me give you an example from inside my company. One of the things we do exceptionally well at Eclipse DOT is train our people to train each others. I coach every team member on a different piece of DOT compliance. Then, once they master it, they teach it to the rest of the team, not just once but often. You might *learn* something when you do it, but you *own* it when you teach it.

I always tell my team. "Don't just do something for someone. Show them how to do it." We don't tolerate people who hoard knowledge or hold it over others. Instead, we create a culture where teaching is the standard. It's built a strong, confident, and ridiculously capable crew.

There have been times when I thought I had a process down pat, until I tried to explain it to someone else. That's when I realized how many little things I do without thinking, things I wouldn't have passed along if I hadn't tried to teach it. That's the real power of coaching. It refines *you* just as much as it builds *them*.

So ask yourself this: If I stepped away tomorrow, would the people around me be better off because of what I poured into them, or scrambling because I kept it all to myself?

5. Is your leadership something people can feel and hear?

Talk is cheap, titles are temporary, but *impact* lasts. Without comparing yourself to Jesus, you can absolutely be inspired by how He led. Jesus didn't hand out business cards that said *Messiah* or manage a LinkedIn page full of accolades. He led with His actions. He served with His hands. He washed feet, listened, fed the hungry, and calmed storms. He spoke the truth when it was hard and stood for people when no one else would. He didn't do it for attention. He did it because it was right.

What would it feel like to be led by you?

If we interviewed your spouse, kids, coworkers, and church family, what would they say? Would they describe you as steady, patient, and present, or someone too busy, distracted, or caught up in your own storm to notice anyone else's?

Would they say you lift burdens or that you *are* the burden?

Do you lead them with intentionality? Do they trust you?

People have experienced your leadership when they can feel it. So ask yourself: If I disappeared tomorrow, would people feel the absence of my leadership in a good or bad way? Would they miss my wisdom, steady hand, and encouragement or just say, "Well, maybe now we'll be heard."

Your deeds, not your declarations, define your leadership. It's the same with faith. Going to church doesn't make you a follower of Jesus. Living like Him does.

So, live it out. Let your leadership be something people feel in the best possible way—something that brings peace, clarity, momentum, and support. That's what servant leadership looks like in real life. Leadership is how people experience you. And if you want to be known as a servant leader, it starts by living like one, even when no one's watching.

Bonus Challenge:

Ask three people you serve this question: How could I serve you better? Ask a family member, someone on your team, a friend, or a church member. Be prepared to listen and say *thank you,* without defending or explaining. That's it.

I'll warn you. This isn't easy. You might hear something you weren't expecting. You might even want to jump in and say, "Yeah, but …" Don't. Just zip it, and take it in. Leadership is about being real enough to grow.

When I asked my son this question, right before he left for the Army, he gave me a few answers that stung a bit. Not because they were harsh but because they were true. And it reminded me that I don't want to lead people in a way that looks good from the outside but leaves them feeling unseen.

This challenge is your mirror. It reflects how others experience your leadership, not just how you think you're doing. You might be crushing it more than you realize. Or you might find a few blind spots. Either way, this isn't about beating yourself up. It's about leveling up.

This is how real leaders grow:

- One honest conversation at a time
- One humbled heart at a time
- One simple question at a time

Ask. Then buckle up, because your next level of leadership starts there.

My amazing wife (amazing even when she voluntells me into things) got us roped into a youth retreat our church wanted to do. When she first got the text about it, the person organizing said the church wasn't behind the idea. And in classic Jenna style, she replied, "We don't do drama, so we're out."

About two days later, she got another message clearing it up. It turned out the church was 100 percent behind it. They wanted to bring in a speaker, someone from the film industry, for about $5,000. Our second oldest son was interested in film and TV at the time, so Jenna thought this person might be able to help him navigate the Hollywood circus. So, what did she do? She volunteered us to help.

They had five weeks to pull the whole thing together. The goal was to get a hundred and fifty people to a retreat in the middle of nowhere and somehow be selective about who they invited. We went to the first meeting. The lead organizer had about four pages of notes, but they were, let's just say, a little all over the place. They made sense to her, but no one else could follow.

So, I asked what felt like a fundamental question: "What is this event for?" Crickets. Then I asked, "Who is this event for?" Still no clarity.

I had already researched the speaker they wanted to bring in. I wasn't impressed. She didn't seem to connect with youth in any of the videos I found. She spoke to adults, not teens. And with three teenagers at home, I knew firsthand you better have some fire in your talk to hold their attention.

About thirty minutes into this meeting, there is still no traction. So, I shifted gears. I started asking questions to guide the group. "Who are we serving?" After a bit of back-and-forth, they settled on youth and young parents. Cool. Now we're getting somewhere. Next question: "What's the theme?"

I did a quick Google search on my phone and pitched a few options. We landed on one I really liked: *Behind the Scenes: Unplugged from the World and Plugged into God.* The underlying message? *Never stop praying.* Simple. Powerful. Clear.

From there, I asked, "What's next?" They said, "We need to talk to local churches and get them involved." Perfect. But if you want churches to join in, you need to make it easy. "What if we all said the same thing?" I offered. "How about a script and an agenda?"

While everyone was chit-chatting about lunch plans, I quietly drafted a sample agenda based on our conversations. Then I said, "How about this?" and read it out loud. They all nodded. "Yeah! That works."

I asked, "How about a flier for the churches? Something simple and clean?" I offered to write it. I had it drafted before the meeting even ended.

Then I asked, "What else needs to happen to make this a success?" That's when something amazing happened. A guy at the end of the table spoke up and said, "Dan asked the right question at the beginning. 'Who are we serving?'"

They had all been arguing over what to cook for lunch at the event, but it all clicked once we focused on the kids we were serving. "Let's keep it simple," he said. "What do kids like to eat?" And the drama melted away.

I didn't show up that day looking to lead. But it was killing me to sit there watching time and energy wasted. So, I asked questions that brought focus. I wrote down the answers. I repeated what they were saying in a way that unified everyone. I emailed the agenda and scripts out that night. I made the fliers the next morning and sent those, too, with everyone's suggestions folded in.

And just like that, my part was done. Except for speaking at the event. But I knew God would guide me through that.

Here's the point: Leadership is about serving others in a way that helps them move forward. It's about guiding, not controlling—supporting, not overshadowing. And when you do that well, people rise. They take ownership. They move from chaos to clarity. That's what a servant leader does.

You don't always need to be in charge to take charge. You just need to be willing to serve and lead others to success without needing the credit.

The Truth About Servant Leadership (And Why You'll Probably Suck at First)

Here's the truth that most leadership books won't tell you: You're going to suck at servant leadership. Not forever, but at first, for sure. You'll say the wrong thing, drop the ball, lead with pride instead of patience, and wonder if you're cut out for any of it. That's how it works.

Now, fair warning, this next part comes from a guy's perspective. So if you're a woman reading this, hang with me. It may not be your exact experience, but the point still stands.

Think about the first time you made love to your spouse. (Yep. I said it. Sorry, Mom. And probably sorry to my kids too. Just skip this part, okay?) Let's be honest, it probably wasn't the stuff of romance novels. You were nervous. Sweaty. Overthinking everything.

You had a sock half-on, half-off, clinging for dear life like it was afraid of what was coming next. A weird elbow angle, and a brief moment where you wondered if you were supposed to say something motivational like, "Let's do this," or "For freedom!" You might've even apologized afterward. Heck, I've been married over twenty years, and I still apologize afterward half the time. (Sorry if I overstepped again. LOL!)

But here's the thing: You get better.

Real intimacy, just like real leadership, doesn't start perfectly. It's messy and awkward. But it grows. And when it's built on trust, service, and showing up consistently, the magic happens. It happens by listening to your spouse and learning what they need to make them feel loved. My wife once told me, "I love it when you cook dinner and clean the kitchen afterward!" I know. Super sexy talk right there. Now I know what makes her feel seen, heard, and valued, and that changes everything.

Leadership is no different. At first, you'll fumble your way through it. You'll overtalk, under-listen, and try to impress instead of invest. But if you keep at it, stay humble, hungry, and committed to serving others, you'll start to suck a little less. Then, one day, you'll realize you're pretty dang good at it.

Servant leadership is about being present, showing up day in and day out, and saying, "I'm here to make life better for the people around me." When you do that, whether in your home, business, community, or church, you're doing what Jesus modeled. You're leading in a way the world desperately needs. You are leading from the trenches with dirt under your nails, love in your heart, and your ego in the backseat

Now, that's leadership worth following. What are you waiting for? Get out there and start serving the people who follow you. Give more than you get every day!

Key Takeaways from Chapter Seven

Servant leaders don't wait for recognition—they show up and do what needs to be done. Whether it's sweeping floors or taking the late shift, forged leaders lead from the front, not the corner office.

You'll never lose influence by being the one willing to get your hands dirty. When your team sees you pick up the tools, not just point fingers, they'll follow you anywhere.

Leadership isn't proven in public—it's revealed in the unseen, thankless moments. The hallway cleanups, the quiet corrections, the extra miles? That's where real leaders are made.

If you want to be great, serve harder than anyone else. Jesus said it best: "The greatest among you will be your servant." And He backed it up by washing feet.

Your team won't remember your speeches—but they'll never forget how you showed up for them. You can preach excellence all day long. But it's your actions that tattoo trust on people's hearts.

The fastest way to earn loyalty is to make your team feel seen, supported, and safe. Servant leadership removes fear and builds faith. People thrive when they know their leader's in the trenches with them.

When you serve from the heart, authority shows up naturally. You don't have to flex. When you serve with grit and grace, your team gives you permission to lead.

Forged leaders take ownership of problems they didn't create—because that's what real service looks like. It's not fair. It's not easy. But it's what separates the boss from the leader.

If Jesus could wash feet, you can clean out the back of the work truck. There's no task beneath a leader who understands what they're really called to do: serve others well.

Chapter 8 | Creating and Owning the Vision

Leading Someone Else's Vision

The safety manager's boots pounded the cracked concrete floor, every step too loud in a place fueled by whispered rumors and stale coffee. He wasn't smiling. He wasn't carrying a clipboard, a folder, or anything helpful. But the weight on his shoulders before opening his mouth was obvious.

He marched straight-up to my cubicle. I didn't even have a door, so my space was a far cry from a corner suite. My cubicle was a half-walled patch of carpeted exile wedged between two filing cabinets that smelled like burned coffee and broken promises. He didn't sit. He didn't lean. He just stood there, arms crossed like a man about to hand off a grenade with the pin already pulled.

"Dan," he said, low and tight, "we got audited." He didn't have to tell me it didn't go well. You could hear it in the way he said my name. He paused and took a heavy breath that tasted like panic. "I want you to take it over."

I stared at him, waiting for the punchline, and wondered. *Take what over? The audit? The violations? The entire dumpster fire that nobody else wanted to approach with a ten-foot pole?* I didn't say anything. Just nodded once, slow and deliberate, the way you do when you feel the floor shift under your boots, but you're too proud to fall.

He kept going, voice too casual to be real. "We had ninety days to fix it. It's been forty-five. You've got forty-five days left." Then, like he couldn't stand the silence, he threw in the kicker. "You can always go back to driving a truck if you want."

Translation: Fix it, or you're done.

I didn't answer him. Not right away. There wasn't anything polite or professional I could say that would have been honest. So, I just nodded again and watched him walk away. The weight he'd just dumped in my lap slowed my breathing.

Pause. Rewind.

You need to understand something about me. When I started at this company, I wasn't some compliance guy or a desk jockey. They hired me to build a CDL training program from the ground up with no blueprint, guidebook, or safety net. Just me, a handful of trucks that barely ran, and a clock that ticked louder every day. And somehow, by the grace of God and a whole lot of stubbornness, I didn't just build it. I dominated it.

While the rest of the industry had clunky eight-week driver programs, I sliced it down to five weeks without losing an ounce of grit. My students didn't just sit through lectures. We trained them at night, in storms, on dirt roads, four-lane highways, and winding goat trails where cell service was a rumor. They hauled real loads over treacherous mountain passes and white-knuckled their way through fog, black ice, and blind curves before they held a CDL in their hands. When they walked out of my program, they didn't just pass a test. They survived something. And they were better for it.

I didn't just meet the goals they set for me. I set goals that they hadn't even thought to dream of. This program was my vision. The program would be fully operational within a year, with three trainers and two trucks in place. I beat that timeline by five months. I built that program like a man building his own house with his bare hands, every nail driven straight through my heart. My blood, sweat, and signature were etched into every student who left better than they came. Now, they wanted me to walk away from it. They wanted me to pick up someone else's broken mess and dropped ball—someone else's failure.

I sat across the dinner table facing my wife that night, the weight pressing down harder than I could explain. With my fork half-raised and dinner untouched, my mind was racing like a freight train with no brakes. Jenna listened, as she always does, with a calm, steady, and patient spirit, knowing full well that I'm always one smart comment away from flipping the kitchen table.

When I finally ran out of words, she leaned back in her chair, tipped her head, and smiled that half-smirk that's somehow both comforting and challenging at the same time. "Well," she said, stabbing a green bean like it had personally offended her, "their compliance can't get any worse. You might as well see what you can do."

Sometimes, God doesn't shout from burning bushes. Sometimes, He speaks through your wife, armed with a fork and an impish grin. I lay awake most of that night, staring at the ceiling, fighting every part of my pride that wanted to walk away

It wasn't my mess. It wasn't my responsibility. I didn't owe them anything. But somewhere, deep in the quiet, God whispered a different truth. *It's not about who made the mess. It's about who's willing to clean it up*

I got up the next morning and made my decision. I took the job. I took their broken, limping vision of being one hundred percent DOT-compliant and made it my own. I didn't dabble. I didn't half-commit. I threw myself into it like a man who didn't know how to do anything halfway.

I ate DOT regulations for breakfast. I bled into every spreadsheet, checklist, and training manual. It wasn't glamorous or celebrated. There were no fireworks, accolades, or banners hanging from the ceiling. But I didn't need any of that because real leadership isn't about the applause. It's about the assignment.

I set a goal to have every driver file in compliance by February. When I told my boss, he didn't even try to hide his amusement. He might have mustered a polite chuckle, but instead he produced a full-throated, belly-clutching laugh that echoed off the walls, which told everyone in the building how little faith he had in me. "Good luck," he said between laughs. "You won't be done in two years."

Perfect. Fuel to the fire. I worked like a man possessed. I worked early mornings, late nights, Saturdays, and Sundays. Not a scrap of time was wasted.

I poured over file after file after file. I learned DOT regulations by flashlight because the office lights shut off at 8 p.m., and I wasn't about to go home just because the building quit before I did.

I fixed paperwork that looked like a drunk raccoon had filled it out, chased missing documents like a bounty hunter, and built systems that didn't exist. I invented processes on the fly just to survive the next round of inspections.

There were nights when I seriously considered throwing the entire filing cabinet into the parking lot and setting it on fire. There were moments I sat at my desk, forehead pressed into my palms, praying the same prayer over and over. *God, just help me not quit.*

By December, six months later, I had the driver files sitting at 98 percent compliant. That was no easy feat. If you know anything about DOT, you know that's basically chasing a unicorn riding a Harley-Davidson down a dirt road in a blizzard. I didn't just clean up a mess. I built something more substantial than what was there before, something that would stand even if I walked away tomorrow. And here's the crazy part: Through all the mess, long nights, mistakes, and late-night prayers, God wasn't just fixing their company. He was fixing me.

He was teaching me that leadership isn't about planting your flag on a mountaintop. It's about grabbing someone else's flag out of the mud, wiping off the dirt, and carrying it like it was your own all along.

I didn't create the vision or dream of putting my name on it in neon lights. But God asked me to be faithful with it anyway. That's what leadership is. Taking ownership and demonstrating stewardship of what you didn't even ask for. Before you ever get your own stage, your own crown, and your own vision, God will test you with someone else's. And if you're too proud to carry it, you're not ready for what's next.

Why Leaders Must Own a Vision That Isn't Theirs

I had many role models growing up. But if you had asked little Dan Greer who he would have given just about anything to meet, it wasn't a rockstar or an athlete. It was Tim Allen.

I didn't even like reading back then. I mean, if you handed me a book, I would have handed it right back and gone outside to build a treehouse with a hammer, three bent nails, and a whole lot of wishful thinking. But somehow, I read both of Tim Allen's books cover to cover multiple times, like they held the secret to life itself.

When *Home Improvement* came on Tuesday nights at 8 p.m., there wasn't a force in this world strong enough to pull me away from that TV. It didn't matter if homework was piling up or dinner was still on the stove. When that theme song hit, I was parked in front of the screen like it was Sunday morning church.

And when Tim Allen showed up as Buzz Lightyear in *Toy Story*, you better believe I was in that theater. Probably still wearing a flannel shirt, too. I might've even walked out of there thinking I could fly if I believed hard enough. I'm not saying I jumped off the back porch yelling, "To infinity and beyond!" But I'm also not saying I didn't.

I could, and still can, if you catch me in the right mood, pull off the classic *Tool Time* grunt. The chest-thumping, caveman grunt that somehow said everything a guy needed to say about horsepower, power tools, and doing something you probably shouldn't be doing without adult supervision.

Tim "The Tool Man" Taylor was it for me. Cars, power, family, building stuff, and blowing stuff up, while somehow keeping the people that mattered most close to him appealed to me. Tim Allen wasn't just a funny guy on TV. He was a blueprint for the man I wanted to become. He messed up, laughed it off, and kept swinging anyway. He built a life out of love, laughter, and a little bit of duct tape. And here's the thing about *Home Improvement* that stuck with me even more once I got older:

Tim Allen didn't create that show, pitch it to the networks, or write the pilot. He didn't design the *Tool Time* set, invent the characters, or choose the costumes. It was an idea someone else dreamed up, loosely based on his stand-up comedy. When Tim Allen stepped onto that soundstage, *Home Improvement* wasn't his vision. It started as just another job. But somewhere along the line, Tim Allen grabbed it.

He grabbed that half-built, halfway-thought-out vision, and he made it his. He owned every flubbed line, broken prop, exploding dishwasher, and misfired nail gun. Planting his flag in the middle of that mess, he said, "This is mine now." And because he owned it, we owned it with him.

Tool Time wasn't perfect. Half the time, it was a disaster waiting to happen. Tim burned down kitchens, launched lawnmowers into traffic, and supercharged everything until it either caught fire or fell over. But you know what? We loved it. We tuned in week after week to watch him try, fail, and try again. He believed he could do anything, and his belief was contagious.

Not every leader gets to paint the original masterpiece. Sometimes you're handed a cracked, half-colored drawing and told, "Here. Make it beautiful." Sometimes you step into a project, a department, a business, or a life that's already mid-construction with blueprints you didn't approve and nails sticking out in every direction.

And you know what? It doesn't matter. You don't have to be the architect. Lead by being the builder. That's the lesson right there. When I stepped into that DOT compliance disaster, it wasn't my baby or proud brainchild. It was a fiery mess—a grenade somebody else threw in my lap. Everything in me wanted to stand back and say, "Not my problem." But God was building me. It was as if he said, "Pick it up anyway. Own it. Fix it. Carry it like your name's written on every file folder and every policy manual, even if you weren't the one who wrote them."

You don't just earn trust by creating visions. You earn trust by carrying them.

You gain influence by walking into burning buildings with a fire extinguisher and a smile. You demonstrate leadership by seeing the mess, rolling up your sleeves, and stepping into it as if it were the most important job on earth. If you're too proud to carry someone else's vision, you'll never be trusted with your own.

Tim Allen didn't invent *Home Improvement,* but he carried it to the top. Real leaders don't need to invent the dream to make it matter. They just need the guts to pick it up, breathe life into it, and build something everyone else wants to be part of.

Leadership isn't about how a project started. It's about how you finish it. And if you finish well, maybe someday, someone will read your story, dreaming about being the leader you became.

Pride at War with Purpose

Owning a vision that isn't yours sounds noble when you say it fast. But living it? That's where the real war begins, because if you're anything like me, the second you pick up someone else's mess, pride starts murmuring in your ear: *You could have done it better. If they had just listened to you in the first place, you wouldn't even be here. You shouldn't have to fix this. It's not your fault. You're too good for this.*

Pride doesn't shout. It whispers. And it sounds remarkably like common sense. It's easy to think you're being logical when, you're just being prideful. And protecting yourself looks a lot like hiding from the purpose God put in front of you.

I'd love to tell you that when I walked into that DOT compliance disaster, I did so as a servant-hearted superhero. The truth is, I almost walked in with both middle fingers raised. Everywhere I looked, there were problems. Paperwork disasters. Inspections that looked like a toddler checked the boxes. Files were missing basic information. Medical cards were expired. Equipment inspections hadn't been touched in years. If anyone had been paying attention, none of this stuff would have been an issue And that's precisely when pride tried to set the hook. It wasn't fair. It wasn't my job. It wasn't supposed to be this way.

Before I could even start sorting through the chaos, I had to do the obvious thing first. I needed access to the files. You'd think that'd be a simple ask. Walk down the hall. Talk to HR. Get a key card or a password and start digging. Nope. Not even close.

When I asked, they didn't just say *no*. They said *heck no*. They weren't even polite about it. The folded arms and raised eyebrows spoke for themselves: "Who do you think you are?" Turns out, the guy who had been trying to fix this mess for the past forty-five days before me had burned every bridge on the way out. His miscommunication and broken promises undermined my efforts. So when I showed up asking for access, I wasn't just some new guy trying to help. I was carrying his baggage whether I wanted to or not.

Starting from scratch would have been easier. At least then I wouldn't have had to fight suspicion on top of chaos. I stood there, hearing the *no*, feeling the door slam shut, and every part of my pride wanted to fire back. But purpose, the part of me God had been quietly building, nudged me in a different direction.

So, I smiled, thanked them for their time, and walked out. And then I did what Dan Greer does when a wall shows up in the middle of the road. I found a side door. The next day, I walked into HR and asked everyone what their favorite drink was at Durango Joe's, our local coffee shop where every drink tastes like angels handcrafted it. I asked the HR manager, the payroll lady, the guy stapling things in the backroom, and everyone in between. And when they told me, I wrote it all down.

The next morning, I showed up at the office carrying the biggest cups Durango Joe's sold, overflowing with their exact favorites. I quietly dropped them off on their desks, no notes or announcements, and went straight back to my cubicle. I did it again two days later. And again after that. What started as an impulse became a pattern repeated three times a week. No look-at-me-being-nice moments. Just quiet, consistent kindness.

Two weeks in, the HR manager wandered into my cubicle. "You still need access to personnel files?" I looked up, shrugged a little, and said, "It would make my life easier. But I'm working through it. Two hours later, the IT guy showed up and told me to log out of my computer. He said he needed to move me to a different system. I followed him down the hallway, logged into the new station, and waited. "There," he said with a grin. "You've got access now. You might want to work fast. Not sure how long it'll last." I kept my face straight, but inside, I grinned so big it hurt.

The coffee was a tool for rebuilding trust. It didn't seem fair that I should have to do anything to get what I needed, especially when I didn't make the mess in the first place. But this simple act of kindness, and the proof that I keep my promises, paid off. I kept the coffee coming once a month until the day I left that company. Leadership is about winning the right to lead. If you use your brains and creativity in the process, you get bonus points.

Pride tempted me to walk away when HR slammed the door. Purpose told me to build a bridge they couldn't ignore. Demanding respect rarely works. If anyone had the right to demand respect, it was Jesus, the Son of God Himself, capable of commanding the oceans, healing the blind, and raising the dead. He chose to kneel and wash dirty, tired feet.

He didn't say, "Do you even know who I am?" He didn't throw down His heavenly credentials. He served. And if the Savior of the world could wrap a towel around His waist and serve men who would run away when things got tough, then maybe, just maybe I could hand someone a cup of coffee without needing a thank you.

Leadership is about building something new and healing what's broken. It's winning back what was lost and doing it without needing your name carved into a plaque at the end is a battle with the ego. That's leadership, and half the time, the fight is against the person staring back at you in the mirror. Pride wanted me to believe that stepping in to fix it was beneath me. Wasting my time cleaning up someone else's disaster was stupid. Find something new, something better, and mine was a better idea.

But somewhere, underneath all the noise and anger, there was a quieter voice. The one that said, "This isn't about you." It reminded me a lot of an old *Home Improvement* episode. Tim and Al got into a competition to see who could build a house faster and better. Now, if you watched the show, you already know how this goes.

Tim, full of swagger and horsepower, assembled a team comprised of professional athletes—big names and muscles with egos to match. These were guys who knew how to score touchdowns and hit home runs, but nothing about framing a wall or hanging drywall. Meanwhile, Al, good old boring Al, picked a team made up of actual tradesmen and women. Among them were plumbers, carpenters, and electricians—folks who knew their craft and showed up ready to work.

Let's just say if you were house hunting, you'd better pray you didn't end up living in Tim's house. Crooked windows, wobbly doors, and lights that flickered like a haunted house special were some of the tell-tale signs. Meanwhile, Al's house was solid, straight, and done right. Both houses used the same material. However, the difference in the finished project reflected the attitude.

Tim let pride pick his team. He valued flash over foundation and trophies over trust. He wanted to look good more than he wanted to build something good. And because of that, he lost. Leadership is the same way.

Pride says, "Stack the deck to make yourself look awesome." Purpose says, "Stack the deck to get the mission done, even if you don't get all the credit."

When Jesus washed His disciples' feet, He didn't pull them all together and say, "All right, boys, gather round. Quick reminder—I outrank every single one of you." He didn't point at Peter and say, "You wash Andrew's feet, I'll supervise." He knelt, took their dirty, calloused, dusty feet in His hands, and washed them. The same hands that carved oceans into the earth wiped the road grime from the soles of fishermen and tax collectors.

If anyone had the right to say, "You should be washing *my* feet," it was Jesus. But He didn't. Instead of flexing His authority or demanding a title, He modeled what real leadership looks like—humble, faithful, and focused on the mission, not the spotlight.

Pride tries to convince us that leadership is about getting to the top. Purpose reminds us that leadership is about serving where you are. Pride says, "You deserve better." Purpose says, "You were made for this." Pride says, "Make it about you." Purpose says, "Make it about the people you're here to help."

If you can't kill your pride in the small assignments, you'll never survive the big ones. When I stood there in that cubicle and was handed a stack of problems that didn't have my name on them, I had three choices—let pride win, grumble my way through it, or roll up my sleeves, pick up the mess, and build something that mattered.

Pride didn't die all at once. It fought dirty. I battled pride in late nights when no one saw me working, in meetings where I was overruled, and in moments where I *knew* I could do it better if they got out of my way. But every time pride whispered, purpose whispered louder. *This isn't about you.*

Leadership is about picking up a towel when you could be sitting on a throne. It's the hammer you swing even when it's not your dream you're building yet. And if you're not willing to do that, you're not ready for the dreams you're asking God to trust you with.

How to Create Buy-In When It Feels Foreign

Getting buy-in when it's not your vision feels a lot like getting thrown into a role you did not sign up for, like co-hosting a cooking show when your usual idea of *meal prep* involves a blowtorch and a bag of beef jerky. Yep. That happened.

There's a *Home Improvement* episode where Irma, the calm, casserole-loving host of *Cooking with Irma*, calls in sick and the network ropes in Al to fill in. Not Tim. *Al.* The flannel-wearing, code-quoting sidekick from *Tool Time*. But here's the twist. Tim's there too, playing Al's assistant. And from the get-go, it's a mess.

Al's trying way too hard to be funny, tossing out lines like he's on stage for the first time. He's copying Tim, but it just doesn't land. It's like watching a puppy chase its tail—lots of energy, no results.

Tim, oddly enough, is the one keeping it together. He even leans over at one point and hits Al with his own line, "I don't think so, Al." Something shifts.

Al stops trying to be Tim. He settles into his own rhythm. And when he does, the show gets surprisingly good. The good that only happens when everyone stops trying to *steal* the spotlight and starts trying to *support* the vision.

Then the full-circle moment hits. Tim lobs out a joke, something offbeat, and Al, without missing a beat, tosses back: "I don't think so, Tim." And just like that, it clicks. The roles are flipped. The magic lands. And they both find their groove in someone else's kitchen.

Now, here's why that moment matters: Leadership doesn't always mean being the one holding the spatula (or the mic, or the plan). Sometimes it means showing up in the background, holding things steady while someone else figures it out. Sometimes it means biting your tongue. Other times, it means saying one well-timed thing that pulls everyone back on track.

You don't need to be loud to be a leader. You don't need to be in charge to be influential. You just need to show up with humility, plant seeds with intention, and help others feel confident in their role, especially when the vision wasn't yours to begin with.

Great leaders don't need the credit. They just want the mission to win. When I was handed the DOT compliance nightmare, there was no mission statement plastered on the wall. No fireworks. No motivational speeches. The vision was simple: Fix it. Make it right. Make us compliant again so they don't shut down our business and make us park all the trucks.

I didn't wake up dreaming about driver qualification files. I didn't stitch "DOT Compliance King" onto a leather jacket. But when I stripped away the mess, I saw the why: People's livelihoods depended on getting it right.

Families counted on their sons, daughters, husbands, and wives getting home safely. Good men and women could lose their careers and their futures because of one missed signature or one overlooked inspection. It wasn't about paperwork. It was about protecting people. And once I understood that, the mission mattered.

That's when it clicked. I didn't need a grand speech or a laminated vision statement. I just needed clarity. The mission mattered, not because it was glamorous, but because it was good. Once I saw that, I was all in. But seeing the value is just the beginning. Getting others to see it is a form of leadership. It begins with a few key steps.

Step One: Anchor to the why behind the what.

Before you can champion a vision, you've got to understand what's at stake. You need to understand the task and the impact. Tim didn't care about hosting a cooking show. I didn't care about binders full of DOT regulations. But when you strip away the surface, there's a why that matters. For me, it was protecting the careers, livelihoods, and lives of people. If the vision seems tedious or frustrating, you're probably looking too shallow. Dig deeper. Ask what problem this solves and who benefits if it succeeds. You can't lead what you haven't anchored in purpose.

Step Two: Tie it to your own wiring.

You need to tie the vision to your own wiring. You don't have to fall in love with the vision to fight for it. You just have to connect it to something you do care about. I didn't love regulations for the sake of regulations. But I cared about excellence. I cared about honoring the people who trusted us. I cared about leaving things better than I found them. That's where buy-in starts. You don't have to love every part of the vision, but you should see something within it that resonates with your own heart. That's the key. Find a thread that ties the mission to your principles and wiring.

Step Three: Own it like you wrote it.

Ever hear someone say, "Well, this wasn't my idea, but ..."? That's a one-way ticket to eye rolls and disengagement. You can't lead a vision while distancing yourself from it. Whether you created it or inherited it, you've got to carry it like it came from your gut, not a memo. You don't have to agree with every detail, but you do have to discuss it as if you believe in it. If you sound like it's someone else's bad idea, no one's following you.

It's like a relay race. Maybe you didn't pick the route. Perhaps you hate the shoes. But once that baton hits your hand, it's your race now. Leaders carry it like they were born with it in their grip, and they run like the finish line has their name on it.

Step Four: Make space for others to find their place in it.

You got on board. Great. Now help others find their *why*. Great leaders don't just carry vision. They translate it. Show people how their role connects to the mission. Help them see how their effort matters. Buy-in spreads when people feel seen, valued, and trusted.

That's why I didn't just fix DOT paperwork. I fought for buy-in across the entire company. I wasn't doing it alone either. The president, the vice president, the whole safety team, and I locked arms and started working one division at a time. The goal was getting the entire operational leadership team to believe in doing DOT the right way, first time, every time.

It wasn't easy. I still remember one manager down in West Texas. He was the toughest nut I ever tried to crack. This guy wasn't exactly rolling out the welcome mat. When I visited, he made sure his schedule was so full that I couldn't get even five minutes of face time if I tried. It almost became a game. He'd fill up his calendar, and I'd just smile and keep showing up anyway.

The West Texas division was the biggest and most dangerous one we had at the time. It couldn't be ignored. And if he wasn't going to invite me to the table, I'd build my own. I started working with his team. One by one, I treated them to lunches, dinners, morning coffee runs, and afternoon snacks, whatever worked, you name it. I listened to every complaint, frustration, and problem they thought no one cared about. But I didn't stop at listening.

If I could fix it, I did. If I could connect them with someone who could help, I made the call. If I could offer guidance or just sit in the mess with them, I would stay. Brick by brick, conversation by conversation, I earned their trust. And eventually, there was only one person left on the outside: that manager. Then, one day, out of nowhere, he called me.

He said they were having a big operations meeting next week and wanted me to be there—said he'd love to have me in the room. No one told him to do it. No one forced it. He chose it because trust had done what paperwork never could, and buy-in, once earned, changes everything. From that point forward, he was all in on DOT.

He was all in on protecting the drivers, building something better, and a vision he didn't even create because now he saw why it mattered. It was the same as what happened with Tim in Irma's cooking show. Any real leader rises to the challenge even when the dream isn't their own, but the mission still matters. You don't have to be the guy who drew the blueprint. You just have to be willing to pick up the hammer and build like your family's moving in tomorrow.

Leading Others When You're Carrying Someone Else's Torch

Leading when you're carrying someone else's vision isn't just about swallowing your pride. It's about carrying weight that sometimes feels heavier because it wasn't yours to begin with. Sometimes that weight feels a lot like standing next to a friend whose dream is burning down right before their eyes.

There's an old *Home Improvement* episode that I can't think about without feeling a little lump in my throat. Al, good ol' steady, reliable Al, finally stepped out from Tim's shadow and took his swing. He built something with his own two hands—a board game based on *Home Improvement*—tiny houses, sheds, and tool sheds you could make with dice rolls and cards. It wasn't just some silly game to Al. It was his dream and his big leap asserting himself as more than a sidekick.

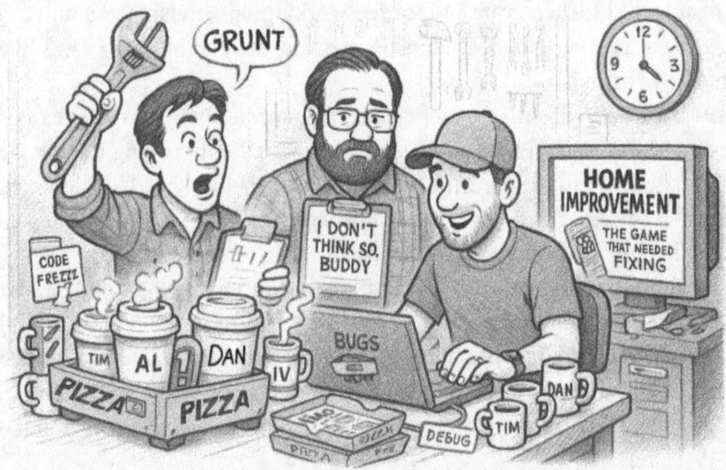

He put every dollar he had into manufacturing those games. It took every ounce of faith he had in himself and built it into those tiny plastic pieces. But dreams don't always get delivered without dents.

Tucked inside one of those tiny houses was a little flaw—faulty wiring, that under the right conditions, could spark a fire. Tim found it, and just like that, all the hard work, late nights, and hope Al had built were smoking in front of him.

If you've ever built anything you care about—staked your name, future, and heart on something—you know precisely how Al must've felt. Your stomach drops out, and you think, "This might break me." Tim had a choice right then. He could have laughed, pointed fingers, and told Al he was an idiot for missing something so obvious. After all, it wasn't Tim's dream on the line, his money in the fire, or his name stamped on those boxes.

Tim didn't walk away. He pulled his whole family together—Jill, Randy, Brad, and Mark—and showed up with sleeves rolled up and hearts open. With no cameras or audience applause, they quietly rebuilt every single game. House by tiny house, wire by tiny wire, and piece by piece, they painstakingly rescued Al's dream.

That's what leadership looks like when it's real, messy, difficult, and costly. Leadership is being the person who still sands the rough spots when everyone else has gone home, not standing in front of the line and getting your picture taken.

When I stepped into that DOT compliance disaster, I wasn't the dreamer who built the company. My name wasn't on the sign. I didn't cause the mess, but there I was, standing in the smoke. Like Tim, I had a choice. I could have walked around with my arms crossed, smirking at the wreckage and said, "Not my circus, not my monkeys." I could have done just enough to get by and protect my name. But every time pride whispered, purpose whispered louder. *This isn't about you.* So, one by one, I picked up the broken pieces. Coffee by coffee. File by file, policy by policy.

And somewhere along the way, something inside me shifted. In addition to fixing someone else's dream, I was helping save something that mattered—something that affected real people, families, and futures. When you carry someone else's vision like it's your own, get your hands dirty fixing what you didn't break, and stay when it would have been easier to leave, God starts building something in you.

He builds character, compassion, and strength. Characteristics of leadership shine when the house is half-burned and the world says it's not your problem. Real leadership is born in the ashes.

It's easy to lead when you're holding a trophy. It's harder when you're cradling someone else's shattered dream. Tim helped save Al's dream. That's more than fixing his mistakes. He helped mend his friend's heart. Whether anyone noticed or not, that's leadership that changes the world.

What Happens If You Don't Own It

You can fake a lot of leadership qualities, energy, confidence, and even results. That works for a little while if you've got people covering for you. But you can't fake ownership. And once your team senses you don't believe in the mission, it's over.

Losing the support of your team doesn't always happen at a definitive moment. It's not a dramatic explosion you can point to and say, "There. That's where we lost it." No, it's quieter than that. It starts with little things—a hesitation, a shrug, or a joke made at the wrong moment. Or, it could be a comment like, "Well, corporate wants us to do this," instead of, "This is where we're going." The once tiny crack spreads when nobody patches it.

People stop leaning forward, raising their hands, and pushing a little harder when things get tough. They don't get mad. They get tired and quiet. Eventually, without even realizing it, you're not leading anymore. You're managing ghosts.

I watched it happen once to a guy who had everything going for him. He was handed a division poised for explosive growth. He had the team, resources, and the trust. What most people have to earn over the years was given to him on the first day. All he had to do was own the vision. He didn't even have to invent it. He just had to believe it and carry it like it mattered. But he didn't.

Every conversation he had about the new direction came with a side of sarcasm. Every meeting started with a joke about how "They're making us do this," or "Corporate wants it this way." At first, people laughed, because laughing is easier than admitting you're scared your leader isn't leading. But the cracks grew.

Deadlines were missed, projects stalled, and momentum was lost. And the same team that was ready to run through a wall for him started pulling back. They started protecting themselves and keeping their heads down, doing just enough to get by.

It all came to a head one afternoon during a division-wide meeting. The VP asked him in front of everyone if he believed in what we were building, if he was bought in, and ready to lead the charge. He smiled that half-smile people use when they don't want to say what they're thinking, and he shrugged. "Well," he said, "it's not like I have a choice, right?"

The second he said it, you could feel all the oxygen sucked out of the room. You could see it on people's faces. Their shoulders slumped, heads dropped, and eyes rolled. In one sentence, without even meaning to, he told them everything they needed to know. He wasn't in. And if he wasn't all in, why should they be?

It was over. Nothing effective happened from that point on, regardless of how many meetings he called or how many new policies he tried to enforce. The one person who needed to carry the vision had dropped it at their feet. He didn't lose his team because the strategy was wrong, the people were bad, or he had a bad plan. He lost them because he never really owned it.

Leadership without ownership is a death sentence with a delayed funeral. You might still sit at the head of the table, receive emails, and polish your nameplate on the door, but you're not leading anymore. You're just taking up space.

It's a hard thing to watch. It's a harder thing to live with. Deep down, every team is asking the same question when they look at their leader: "Are you willing to believe in this before you ask me to?" If the answer is anything less than *yes*, trust starts leaking out of the side of the ship.

I think about that guy sometimes, not because I'm better or I figured it out perfectly. He reminds me of how fragile leadership is. It's easy to lose the one thing that matters most—the hearts of the people you're called to serve.

You don't have to be perfect, the smartest, or the most experienced. However, you must fully, openly, and relentlessly own it. If you won't carry the vision, someone else will. And when they do, your chance to lead is gone.

When It's Your Turn to Build the Vision

There comes a moment in every leader's life when the game changes. At first, you're carrying someone else's dream. You're fixing messes you didn't make and fighting battles you didn't choose.

That's precisely what you're supposed to do—for a while. It's in the trenches of serving that you learn the grit, humility, and wisdom it takes to carry something bigger than yourself. But if you stay faithful long enough—if you keep showing up, serving, and carrying someone else's flag with honor—one day something shifts.

One day, God hands you a blank sheet of paper and says, "Now it's your turn." That's how Eclipse DOT was born. It didn't start with a boardroom, a business loan, or a grand master plan. It started with me sitting at my kitchen table, worn out from years of fixing problems for other people, staring at a cup of coffee going cold, and one simple, stubborn thought: *There's got to be a better way.*

I had spent years inside companies that used trucks. I had seen how brilliant men and women, skilled in their craft, could build, create, transport, and transform, yet they kept getting crushed under the weight of paperwork and regulations. They didn't fail because they were lazy or stupid. They failed because nobody was standing in the gap to help them carry the invisible load.

Nobody was saying, "Let me handle the compliance so you can go build your business." And in that moment, the vision for Eclipse DOT lit up inside me like a fire I couldn't put out. Our vision wasn't to become another DOT consulting company.

Our vision was to serve companies that use trucks—to make their lives simpler and handle the back-office chaos so they could stay focused on what matters: building their business, taking care of their people, and going home to their families at night without worrying about what paperwork they missed.

We weren't just going to fix problems after they exploded. We were going to build a better road before they even hit the pothole. If that meant walking yards in the rain, climbing into dusty file rooms, and learning regulations backward and forward, then so be it.

The vision was never about us. It was always about them. That's what real vision does. It pulls you outside of yourself and forces you to dream bigger than your comfort zone. It demands that you build something other people can believe in, and even fight for, because it's not just about your success. It's also about their survival, growth, and legacy.

Identifying your vision isn't about creating something flashy to put on a website. It's about staring at the broken things around you and asking, "What if I could build something better?" It's about sitting in the middle of the mess and deciding, "I don't know how yet, but we're going to find a way." It's about crafting something real enough that people want to carry it alongside you, not because they have to, but because they believe in it too.

You have to believe and live it before anyone else can see it. You have to be willing to bleed for it. When Eclipse DOT was just an idea, nobody was clapping or cheering me on. There were no lights, cameras, or guarantees. There was a stubborn belief that companies using trucks deserve a partner who cares about them more than just checking boxes to avoid fines. They deserve a partner who builds systems that let them grow, thrive, and lead for the long haul.

A vision without people is just a dream. But a vision that people can rally around— that they can see themselves inside of—that's the beginning of a movement. If you want to lead people into something great, you can't just talk about what you want to build. You have to invite them to build it with you. And you can't invite them into something you don't believe in enough to fight for yourself first.

One day, if you stay faithful long enough, carrying someone else's vision, you'll feel that nudge. You'll feel God handing you the blueprints for something new. And in that moment, you'll realize it's about more than proving yourself and survival. It's about creating a space where others can thrive.

Eclipse DOT became more than a company. Eclipse DOT was a vision for a better way. And if you step into the same calling for your life and leadership, you won't just change your career. You'll change lives, maybe even your own.

It's one thing to talk about vision. It's another thing to live it when your boots are in the mud, the paperwork's piling up, and people are looking at you like, "So, now what?" Whether you're carrying someone else's dream or standing at the starting line of your own, vision is worthless without action.

It's not enough to have a great idea or feel inspired after a meeting, reading a book, or engaging in a stimulating conversation. You have to move. You have to build. You have to step into the mess, plant your flag, and start fighting for something that doesn't even exist yet outside your own chest.

And here's the hard part nobody tells you at the leadership conferences: Sometimes you're carrying a vision you didn't create. Other times, you're building one from scratch. Both demand the faithfulness from you—faithfulness to the mission, the people depending on you, and the calling you might not even fully see yet. So let's get real about it. Whether you're picking up someone else's blueprint or drawing your own, here's how you start building something worth following.

Building and Implementing Your Vision

Start by Solving a Real Problem

Your vision isn't supposed to sound cool. It's supposed to matter. Real leadership doesn't start with, "What sounds impressive at a networking event?" It begins with, "Where's the real pain? Where's the real need?"

When I started Eclipse DOT, it wasn't because I thought compliance sounded like a great sales pitch. It was because I saw good companies getting crushed under mountains of invisible paperwork. I saw families losing their businesses over mistakes they didn't even know they were making. I didn't create a vision around what made me look good. I created a vision around what was needed.

You don't pick your vision—you find the place where people are bleeding and build something that stops the bleeding. Plant your flag there. That's how real visions are born.

Write It Down So Clearly a Twelve-Year-Old Could Understand It

If you can't explain your vision without using corporate buzzwords, you don't own it yet. Visions aren't supposed to be complicated. They're supposed to be clear enough that a twelve-year-old eating a peanut butter sandwich at the kitchen table could nod and say, "Got it." If you can't get it on the back of a napkin, you're not ready to build yet. When we built the vision for Eclipse DOT, it boiled down to one sentence:

> "We make companies' lives easier by handling the DOT
> paperwork so they can focus on building their business."

That was it—no smoke, mirrors, or five-syllable business words. If you can't say it simply, you can't live it strongly.

Live It Before You Preach It

Nobody follows a leader who's too busy talking about the dream to live it. You can have the best vision statement in the world, but if you're not sweating for it, nobody's buying in. When Eclipse DOT started, I wasn't giving keynote speeches about compliance. I was walking through yards in the rain, digging through dirty filing cabinets, and helping drivers find missing medical cards before audits arrived. You want people to buy into your vision? Show up first. Stay late. Take the ugly assignments. Walk the talk when no one's filming you. Vision without sweat is just marketing. Vision with sweat? That's when people start following you because they trust you.

Invite Others to Build It with You

You can't shove a finished vision down people's throats and expect them to fall in love with it. People don't want to be handed a castle someone else built and be told to clean the floors. They want a hammer in their hand. They want fingerprints on the walls. They want to build something too. When we started building Eclipse DOT, I didn't come down from the mountain with stone tablets. I listened. I sat across tables with customers, friends, industry veterans, and said, "If you could wave a magic wand and fix DOT compliance, what would it look like?" They helped me shape it. They still help me shape it. When you let people put their fingerprints on your vision, they don't just support it. They own it.

Celebrate the Mission, Not Just the Milestones

Milestones are important. You hit one hundred customers. You land a major client. You get your first big paycheck. Those are worth celebrating. But if you stop there, you've missed the point. The mission is bigger than any milestone. Every time Eclipse DOT grows, we don't just high five over numbers. We go back to the mission. We remind ourselves: We're here to serve companies that use trucks. We're here to make their lives easier. We're here to take invisible weights off their backs so they can run harder.

That's what we celebrate. That's what keeps us anchored when things get messy. If you forget the mission, you'll eventually lose the milestones too.

Protect It from Drift

Over time, visions lose their edge if you're not careful. People start cutting corners. They forget why you started. They turn a living, breathing mission into just another slogan on the website. Drift doesn't happen in one big moment. It happens in a hundred small compromises. Take a shortcut here. I missed a conversation there. That's why you have to fight drift like it's your biggest enemy. Keep sharpening the mission. Keep pruning the dead branches. Keep pulling the weeds before they choke the life out of it. Protect what makes the vision dangerous, the part that changes things. If you don't, the vision dies while you're still busy pretending it's alive.

Hold It Loosely Enough to Let It Grow

The best visions outgrow their original creators. If you build it right, it'll become bigger than you ever imagined. It'll stretch in ways you didn't predict. And if you're too busy needing all the credit, you'll suffocate the very thing you were supposed to protect. I didn't build Eclipse DOT so my name could be in lights. I built it because I wanted companies to thrive without getting crushed by invisible battles they didn't know they were fighting. And if someday Eclipse DOT becomes something bigger than me—if it grows into places I never dreamed—it'll be the proof we built it right. Real leaders build visions they're willing to let other people make even better.

Carrying and Implementing Someone Else's Vision

Understand the Heart, Not Just the Words

It's easy to memorize a mission statement. Anyone can read a plaque on the wall and recite a few nice-sounding phrases. But real leaders go deeper. They don't just know what the mission says. They know why it matters. They understand what's at stake if it fails. When I first stepped into the compliance world, it wasn't enough to realize we needed better paperwork. I had to understand that behind every missing signature was a driver, family, and life that could be wrecked if we missed something. Understanding the heart behind a vision turns it from another task on your list into a cause worth bleeding for. If you don't feel the heartbeat, you'll never fight for it the way you need to.

Own It Like It's Yours

You can't fake ownership. People can tell in about three seconds whether you believe in what you're asking them to do. I've watched leaders destroy their credibility by shrugging and saying, "Well, this is what they want us to do." Let me be clear. No one follows a shrug. They follow belief. They follow fire. When you're carrying someone else's vision, you have to hold it like your future depends on it. You have to talk about, defend, and build it like you'll personally answer for it at the end of the day. In a way, you will.

Tie It to What Matters to You

Sometimes the vision you're carrying wasn't crafted in your own heart. And that's okay. You don't have to fake passion about every single line of the mission statement. However, you do have to find something inside it that resonates with your own wiring. Maybe it's excellence. Perhaps it's loyalty. Possibly it's serving people who lack the power to resolve their own problems. Find your thread and pull it tight. When I was carrying visions I didn't create, I didn't focus on the parts that bored me. I anchored myself to what mattered—protecting people, doing hard things the right way, and building something worth believing in. If you don't tie it to something inside you, you'll eventually drift away from it when things get hard.

CARRY IT LIKE IT'S YOURS (AND MAKE IT BETTER)

Lead With It in Every Conversation

Vision isn't something you talk about once a quarter at a company meeting and then shove back in a drawer. It should bleed into everything you do—every conversation, meeting, and random hallway chat over burned coffee. When you're carrying a vision, you have to make it the standard, not the slogan. You talk about it when it's easy. You talk about it when it's awkward. You talk about it when people are tired of hearing about it. You know that if you stop carrying it, no one else will. A vision that's alive is a vision that's constantly being spoken out loud.

Help Others See Themselves Inside It

People rally around ideas when they can see a place for themselves in the story you're telling. A great leader doesn't just say, "Here's what we're doing." A great leader says, "Here's where you fit. Here's why you matter." When I was carrying the compliance vision, I didn't just tell drivers to fill out their logs better. I sat down and showed them how it protected their jobs, kept their families safe, and gave them security. They were free to focus on doing what they loved without worrying that paperwork would sneak up behind them. When people see themselves inside the mission, they fight for it harder than you ever could alone.

Defend It When It's Under Fire

If you're carrying a real vision, it's going to get attacked. People will mock and misunderstand it, trying to water it down until it's safe, easy, and useless. Your job is to stand up and be the shield. You have to hold the line when it would be easier to fold. People watch more closely when things are hard, more than when things are easy. It costs you something to stay loyal. Leadership isn't proven by what you say when everyone agrees with you. It's proven by what you defend when you're standing alone.

Leave It Better Than You Found It

You might not have written the original vision. You might not have been there the day they drew the first blueprint. But you still have a chance to leave it stronger than you found it. A vision should never stay stagnant. Great leaders bring life, clarity, and strength to the visions they carry, even if they didn't create them. The legacy is sharpening the mission so that when the next person picks it up, it's even stronger than when it was in your hands.

There's a moment every leader faces, when it stops being about looking good, having the right title, and getting applause at the next meeting. It becomes about responsibility.

Carrying the vision, whether you built it from scratch or picked it up from someone else, isn't about getting credit. It's about standing in the gap when things get heavy. It's about fighting for something bigger than yourself. It's about doing the hard, dirty, thankless work, because deep down, you know the mission matters more than your comfort.

Leadership isn't a costume you put on. It's a weight you choose to carry. If you can't carry it like it's yours, bleed for it when it gets ugly, or lead people with conviction instead of obligation, then for the sake of the mission and the people counting on it to survive, you need to have the guts to step aside. Leadership is too important to fake.

People follow conviction. They follow leaders who carry the mission so deeply inside their chest that it feels like it was etched on their bones. They follow leaders who don't need to be the center of attention, because the mission is the center. They follow leaders who show up, who fight, who stay when others would leave.

That's the leader you're called to be when you create the vision and when you're asked to carry one someone else handed you. Carry it like it's yours, or step aside so someone else can, because the mission deserves better than a halfhearted leader.

And so do the people following you.

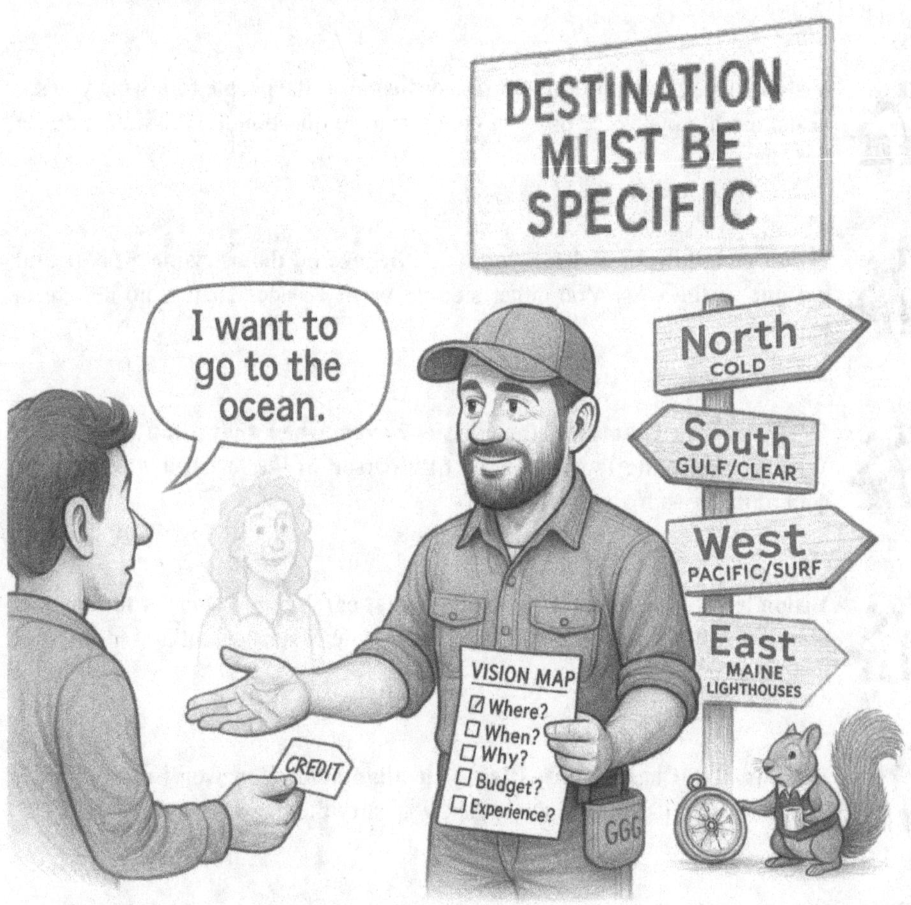

Get Clear On Your Vision

Key Takeaways from Chapter Eight

If you don't own the vision, you'll eventually fight it. You can't halfway lead someone else's mission. It'll wear you out, burn you out, or make you resent the one who cast it.

Leaders don't just repeat vision—they carry it. Anyone can echo a goal. But forged leaders *own* it like their name's on it—even if it started with someone else.

Vision without ownership creates confusion. If the people following you see hesitation in your voice or eyes, they'll start to question the mission. You set the tone.

If you're following a vision you don't believe in, do everyone a favor and get out of the way. You either step up or step aside. There's no neutral in leadership.

Great leaders champion the mission, even when they didn't create it. Whether you're the founder or the fifth person in line, what matters is your commitment—not your credit.

Vision leaks—leaders are the buckets that catch it and carry it forward. If you're not filling up on the mission daily, you'll start operating out of habit instead of purpose.

It's not about agreement. It's about alignment. You won't always see it perfectly—but if you trust the leader, you carry the flag anyway.

Forged leaders model the mission so clearly, others step up without being asked. When you live the vision out loud, your team doesn't just hear it—they start to believe it's theirs too.

Chapter 9 | Influence in Every Direction

Leading Up, Across, and Down

I was barely old enough to be trusted with a garden hose, but there I was, doing everything I could to earn my place in the volunteer fire department. My dad had been the department chief long before I was born. Around our house, volunteering in the department meant something. When my brother turned sixteen, he joined, too. He threw himself into it—boots, gear, pager on the hip—the whole deal. And like any younger brother who thought the sun rose and set on his big brother's shoulders, I wanted in, too.

I asked if I could join. But the department had a rule: You must be fourteen to start as a junior firefighter. Looking back, they had a point. Most twelve-year-olds can barely roll up a hose without turning it into a knotted mess. So, I waited. Impatiently.

At twelve and a half, I couldn't take it anymore. I marched straight-up to the chief, stood a little taller than usual, sounding as responsible as possible, and asked if I could attend trainings. He agreed.

I was in—sort of. My brother drove me to and from training because I wasn't old enough to drive myself, but I didn't care. I sat through every class, soaked up every word, and hung around afterward, hoping to learn more.

After a few weeks, I asked if I could have a pager to hear the calls and start learning how the real-world side of things worked. They rummaged around in a dusty closet and found the oldest, clunkiest pager you've ever seen. It looked like a big red brick and squawked like a dying goose anytime someone talked. But I clipped it to my belt like a badge of honor.

When summer break rolled around, I convinced the chief that if a brush fire popped up close enough to home, I could help. My grandpa, who loved me more than he loved common sense, let me use his extra four-wheeler for the summer. I paid him by raking and mowing his yard once a month, but I think he gave me the better end of that deal. It was good that he loved me because I essentially stole that thing.

I was ready. An old duffel bag I found behind a mall dumpster held my gear. It consisted of an ill-fitting hard hat, holey leather gloves handed down by my grandpa, and a set of fire gear so old it should have been in a museum. But to me, I was geared up like a Navy SEAL.

My pager went off the first time on June 14, 1:27 p.m. A brush fire had started a few miles from our house. I grabbed my gear, hollered to Mom that I was going, kick-started the four-wheeler, and shot down the dirt road toward the call. I got there fast and waited. No junior firefighter ever went in alone.

After a few minutes, the ancient army brush truck rolled up, driven by the grumpiest old firefighter we had. He didn't support the junior program. He didn't think kids should be out on calls at all. "Greer, what the hell are you doing here? You don't have permission to be here. I don't want you here. Go home."

At that moment, I had two options: I could tuck my tail and go home, or I could find a way to earn my place. I glanced at the smoke rising in the distance, then back at my four-wheeler.

"Sir," I said, swallowing hard, "looks like the fire's a mile or so in. You could use my four-wheeler to get to it faster."

He looked like he was deciding whether it was worth arguing. Finally, he reluctantly said, "Fine. Grab a piss pack, two shovels, and the Pulaski." If you don't know, a piss pack is a 15-gallon water bladder worn like a backpack, and a Pulaski is a tool with an axe on one end and a digging implement on the other.

Not wasting a second, I loaded two piss packs onto the four-wheeler, strapped the tools to the front, started it up, and said, "Let's go. I'll be careful."

We wove through deer trails, bouncing and dodging branches for approximately fifteen minutes. Finally, we found an old big tree, still smoldering from a lightning strike the night before.

It was just him and me, and I knew he didn't want me there. But I worked like my life depended on it. He yelled at me when I didn't swing the Pulaski correctly and snapped when I wasn't hitting the embers how he wanted. Every time he corrected me, I adjusted without arguing. I hustled, careful not to step where I shouldn't and not to make more work for him.

For four hours, we worked clearing, digging, and dousing embers. By the time we finished, I could barely lift my arms. When it was time to head back, I knew I couldn't ride that four-wheeler all the way to the station. It wasn't meant for long hauls.

I swallowed my pride and said, "Sir, if you're willing to pick me up at my house on the way by, I'll help you clean everything up. I'd like to help. I can figure out how to get home after." He stared at me for a long second, unsure whether to laugh or grunt.

Finally, he said, "If you want to clean up, get in." We swung by my house, dropped off the four-wheeler, and headed to the station in silence. The tension in that cab was thicker than molasses.

When we got to the station, I didn't ask what needed to be done. I started washing every dirty hose, scrubbing every tool, and restocking supplies while he worked quietly across the bay. No praise. No pats on the back.

Once everything was squared away, I shook his hand and said, "Thanks for letting me help." He nodded and forced one grunt. That was it.

Training night rolled around two days later. I showed up ready to lie low and stay out of trouble. But right away, I could feel something was different. The old firefighter was standing beside the chief, arms crossed, and staring at me with a look I couldn't read.

The chief's voice boomed across the bay. "Little Greer! Get in my office. NOW!"

My heart hit the floor. I walked into his office, figuring this was it. I'd get a short speech, a handshake, and a *thanks, but no thanks*.

The chief leaned back in his chair and said, "Close the door."

I braced myself. But then he said something I'll never forget.

"I was talking to the lieutenant. He told me what happened at that fire the other day."

My stomach twisted.

"And, he said something I didn't expect," the chief continued. "He said you didn't know what you were doing, but you listened. You adjusted. You worked hard. And when it was over, you didn't run off. You volunteered to help him clean up."

The chief leaned forward. "He said he went by the station later and saw every hose perfectly laid out. Tools cleaned. Truck restocked. All by you."

I didn't know what to say.

And then the chief smiled and said, "He said, 'That kid is mine. I want him on every call I go to because he's coachable.'"

By that time, I was thirteen years old; I didn't have a title, seniority, shiny new gear, or a résumé. What I had was a willingness to show up, listen, hustle, and stay when most people would have gone home. It turned out that's when I started leading from the very bottom.

Looking back, it's funny how clear it appears. At thirteen, I thought influence meant being the fastest and strongest and the guy with the coolest gear. I thought you had to prove you were worth listening to. But that wasn't it at all. My strength and knowledge didn't open that door, and neither did my determined swings of a Pulaski. It showed up with a heart saying, "You can count on me."

I listened, adjusted, stayed and worked with no need for applause. Influence is built on credibility, which moves people to trust. Rank is irrelevant. You can influence people who report to you, your peers, and your superiors if your character is consistent.

Jesus modeled this for us. He didn't flash his résumé or demand people follow Him. The only crown he wore was made of thorns. He was influential enough not to have to bribe crowds or threaten governors. The fishermen dropped their nets because His life was magnetic.

The tax collectors abandoned their tables because His presence made everything else look cheap. Governors squirmed, and kings raged because they knew deep down they were standing in the presence of real authority.

Who He was and how He lived revealed His authentic leadership heart. His example is our aspiration. Live like Jesus and show your heart for leadership and influence everyone watching.

Influencing Up (Bosses, Owners, Leaders)

I wish I could tell you leadership got easier after that first fire. Earning someone's respect is a worthy goal, and unless you mess it up, it stays with you forever. But influence works differently.

Influence doesn't come with lifetime memberships. You earn it one situation, sacrifice, and moment at a time—especially when you're trying to lead up. Years after that day in the woods with the grumpy firefighter, I found myself in a whole new world:

DOT compliance. Sounds glamorous, right? Let me paint the picture.

Imagine being buried under paperwork late at night, crawling around trucks and drivers who barely want to look at you early in the morning, and operations managers too busy to talk to you. They had enough to do just keeping the company alive and didn't care to deal with one more compliance guy here to tell them what they were doing wrong.

When I got handed the role, I knew the drill. No one had reason to fear me without an important title or authority to order anyone around. Most operations teams didn't trust me farther than they could throw me. (I was a chunk, so that wouldn't be far!) They had been burned before. Compliance guys who only cared about red tape and safety guys who only showed up to wag their fingers when something went wrong, made their jobs harder. To them, I was just another new guy who was supposed to fix things. Yeah. Right.

Knowing the culture I was walking into, I knew going in with guns blazing and throwing manuals on desks would not be received well. I needed to give them what they needed and not what they expected. If I wanted to lead up, I had to make their lives easier, not harder.

So, I devised a new approach. Instead of telling them, "Send me your paperwork," I said, "Don't worry about it. I'll come to you." Instead of sending long emails about what they needed to fix, I drove to their divisions, walked into their chaotic offices, and quietly started digging through their files myself. Instead of demanding they attend training sessions on my schedule, I asked them what worked for them.

"What time do your drivers usually come in in the morning? I'll be there fifteen minutes before that." "What time do they get back at night? I'll be back an hour before the first guy pulls in and thirty minutes after the last one leaves." I stopped expecting them to rearrange their world for me. I rearranged my world for them.

Read that last line again.

I rearranged my world for *them*.

That strategy cost me. It cost me sleep, family dinners, weekends, and energy I didn't always have. Some mornings, my alarm went off at 3:30 a.m. because the drivers started rolling in before sunrise. There were nights when I was sitting in a truck yard at 9 p.m., my breath fogging up in the cold, awaiting the last driver to limp back in after a fourteen-hour shift. Some weeks, it felt like I lived out of a gas station with no other possessions than a coffee cup, a wrinkled clipboard, and a pair of steel-toe boots. There were plenty of days when I wondered if any of it mattered.

But slowly, something changed. One by one, the drivers who wouldn't look me in the eye started waving when they saw me in the yard. Operations managers trusted I was there to make their jobs easier. Division leads who once saw me as an outsider pulled me into their offices, asking for advice before problems became chaotic.

Somewhere along the way, they stopped seeing me as the *compliance guy*. They started seeing me as a teammate who understood the grind. They knew I respected their time, work, and reality. Instead of making them listen to a fancy pitch or sitting through boring PowerPoint presentations, I showed up and served. Over a decade later, some drivers still call me when they change jobs. Many of the operations guys still recommend Eclipse DOT to their new companies.

To influence people above you, ask yourself, "How do I make it easier for them to say *yes*?" I made it easier for them to win. That's the secret to leading up.

Influencing someone above you differs from influencing peers or people who report to you. It's a whole different ball game with unique rules and expectations. If you go in swinging the same bat you use with your peers or team, you will strike out faster than a barefoot dude in a cactus-kicking contest.

I learned a lot while pursuing excellence and leading upward. These battle-tested lessons from the real world were honed through early mornings and late nights, sometimes banging my head against the wall until I figured out what works.

Truth #1: Think, "How can I make it easier on them?"

Listen, I get it. You think you're busy. You think you get a lot of emails. And I'm not saying you don't, but let's be honest, you think you're drowning in emails. But you're really paddling in the kiddie pool.

Occasionally, one of my team members will come to me, wide-eyed, like they stormed Normandy, and say, "Dan, I got like a hundred emails over the last two days!" I'll smile and say, "That's cute. I get that by noon every day." And I know people who get even more and are higher up the ladder than me.

When trying to influence someone above you, remember: They are busy, even if they don't act like it or don't tell you. That's why your first thought should always be: *How can I make this so simple for them that saying yes feels like a break, not a burden?*

When I started working in DOT compliance, my brilliant idea was to have drivers come to my office so I could help them knock out their paperwork. It worked. Sort of. Approximately 22 percent showed up and got it done. I was thrilled for about five minutes. Then reality set in. Twenty-two percent won't cut it when you're getting a whole company compliant.

So, I had to think creatively. Instead of waiting for them to come to me, I flipped the model. I went to them. I said, "What if you let me do the heavy lifting? I'll gather and organize all the documents. Then, all you need to do is review and sign."

What used to take an hour per driver, and felt like pulling teeth, became a streamlined process. I knocked out fifty drivers in just two mornings, four hours total. The more I simplified things for them, the more they saw me as someone on their side.

Real influence starts when people realize you're there to improve their lives.

Truth #2: Talk to them, not at them.

Every once in a while, someone asks me, "Dan, why do people listen when you talk? When I talk, they glaze over like I'm reading the side effects of a medication bottle." After about five minutes of listening to them, the reason becomes clear. They talk *at* people instead of *to* them.

They bark orders, issue demands, and insist they're right, justifying why the audience needs to listen. This approach is like teaching a cat to fetch. It's technically possible, but you're left feeling like an idiot when the cat walks away.

Tone matters. That's one thing I quickly learned when I had a team of DOT compliance folks. Walk into a yard full of tough, blue-collar folks with a clipboard and a tone like you're about to ground them—you'll get about as much cooperation as a toddler at naptime.

Think about it. If I tell you, "Do not touch that stove," what happens? Be honest. You immediately want to touch it. You weren't even thinking about stoves five seconds ago, and now it's the only thing on your mind. You're practically leaning over, hearing the sizzle, wondering, *"Is it gas or electric?"*

You might be thinking, "Dan, nobody's dumb enough to touch a hot stove." Yeah? Well, I didn't say it was hot. I just said, "Don't touch it." And now your brain is like a rebellious toddler going, "Why not? What does it do? Is it dangerous? Or is Dan just being dramatic?"

But if I say, "Hey, a heads-up, that stove's hot. If you touch it, you'll fry your fingerprints off and regret it every time you clap for the next week," suddenly you're not so curious anymore.

That's the power of talking *to* someone instead of *at* them. One sparks resistance. The other sparks wisdom.

When dealing with leaders above you, the same thing applies. You can't roll in swinging your finger around like you're the Smartsville Sheriff. Instead of, "You must do this!" try, "If we do it this way, we boost efficiency, lead the industry, and dodge heartburn if we're ever audited. What do you think?"

Changing a few words and your tone changes the outcome.

Truth #3: Ask empowering questions.

This one's a game-changer. Asking questions isn't about tricking anyone. It's about helping people see what they need, just from a better angle. It's leadership without ego. Influence without control.

When you frame ideas as questions, you're not giving up the wheel. You're inviting them into the front seat. You're saying, "I trust you to drive, and here's a route I think we should consider."

Instead of pushing, prompt:

- What do you think would happen if we tried this?
- How do you feel about this direction?
- Would it make sense to look at it from another angle?

You're not forcing them into your plan, you're walking alongside them as they discover it's a better plan for *them*.

Now, I'll be honest: empowering questions take practice. Done wrong, they can sound awkward, or worse, condescending. It's not a script, it's a skill. The best way to get better is to try it at home. Just don't tell your spouse you're *practicing influence techniques* unless you enjoy sleeping on the couch. Trust me.

Let's say you want steak for dinner, but your spouse likes picking the restaurant. Instead of charging in with, "We're getting steak," you ask: "Would you be up for something with hearty meals, protein-packed, where we feel awesome afterward?"

Boom. Now you're not bossy, you're thoughtful. Then you casually drop: "What do you think about the steakhouse? It's got that killer salad bar, too."

See what happened? You didn't manipulate. You guided. And that's the whole point. You can do the same thing with people above you:

"What if we gave this approach a shot? I'm happy to take the lead on it, and if it flops, you can mock me publicly. I'll even bring the T-shirts."

Empowering questions aren't about getting your way. They're about unlocking better ways together.

Truth #4: Plant seeds and nurture them.

Plant the right seeds. Protect the sprouts. Share the harvest.

Sometimes, I call myself a farmer—not because I can grow a good tomato (I can't). But I plant seeds all day, every day. When I meet people, I'm planting seeds:

- Imagine the extra time you'd have if we managed your DOT compliance.
- Imagine never worrying about an audit again.
- Imagine spending your Saturdays fishing instead of filling out maintenance logs.

(See, I just planted 3 seeds right there, hahah)

Planting seeds is helping people envision the future in a new way, even if they aren't ready to pursue it yet. And just like garden seeds, you can't plant and forget. You must nurture them with just enough water to help them take root and grow faster.

When I worked in DOT compliance, I always planted seeds with division managers. I'd ask, "How would it feel to be recognized at the annual operations sync-up for having the safest drivers in the company?" Suddenly, they weren't thinking about the headache of paperwork. They were dreaming about standing on that stage, getting a plaque, and soaking up the applause.

Planting seeds works, but you must be patient. (And if you know me, patience is not my superpower. I'm the guy who thinks microwave minutes feel like years.) But over time, those seeds grow. Some clients needed three years to appreciate the value of what I offered. Every time they came around, it traced back to the day I planted that vision in their mind.

Truth #5: Speak their language.

Every leader has a different language. And no, I'm not talking about English, Spanish, French, or Pig Latin. I'm talking about their *leadership language.* Some leaders want short, sweet, to-the-point bullet points. Other leaders want all the details and every step outlined in elaborate explanations. It's up to you to learn and speak their language fluently if you want to earn influence.

If a leader writes three-sentence emails and makes decisions in thirty seconds, guess what? You better not send them a five-page memo with a flowery introduction and a PowerPoint. They'll never even open it. Instead, keep it simple:

- Bullet points
- Pros and cons
- Quick, decisive answers

On the other hand, if a leader loves to talk through every angle, possibility, and scenario, you better be ready to dive deep. Walk through the plan and answer the questions before they even ask them. Let them marinate in the details because that's where they feel safe.

The higher a leader climbs, the less time they tend to have. That means you need to be efficient. Respect their time and style. Adapt your communication to them, not the other way around.

That's it. Those are my five keys to influencing leaders above you. They aren't complicated or flashy. You don't need a six-figure degree or corporate jet to pull them off. But they are powerful if you're willing to do the real work behind them. Influence with leaders isn't won by shouting louder or having the smartest ideas. It's won by showing up every day and making their life easier, not harder.

If you remember nothing else from this section, remember this: Make it easier on them. For every idea you pitch, every project you start, and every conversation you have, ask yourself, "Am I making this easier for them or putting another rock in their backpack?" I promise that if you become the person who lightens their load instead of adding to it, they will move mountains to have you around.

Leadership is about trust, which isn't distributed because you ask for it. It's earned—one decision, sacrifice, and moment at a time.

You will find loyalty when you make life easier for people without grumbling, keeping score, or making it about you. Loyalty leads to open doors you never have to force open. You will be pulled into conversations you used to dream about being a part of.

You'll discover the truth all real leaders learn eventually: Trust is the real currency of leadership. Charm, credentials, and loud opinions are overrated. Being trusted is the most significant advantage you will ever have. Once you've earned trust, you're building something that lasts.

Influencing Across (Peers, Coworkers, Partners)

Influencing your peers might be the toughest leadership move you'll ever make. Honestly, I think it's even harder than influencing those above you. At least you know the game with leaders—you expect to earn their trust and approval. There's a built-in ladder. You climb it. They pull you up or push you down. Simple enough.

But influencing peers is a whole different animal. There's often a quiet competition buzzing under the surface. Nobody says it out loud, but you both feel it. We're all climbing a ladder, and sometimes your win feels like their loss, or vice versa. That tension, even when it's invisible, makes peer influencing trickier than most people want to admit.

I'll be honest. I've bombed this more times than I can count. There were seasons when I crushed it and built real teams grounded in trust. But there were also seasons when pride got the best of me. I let competition cloud my vision and cared more about winning than building anything that mattered.

The shift came when I stopped seeing my peers as competition and started seeing them as teammates. Everything changed when I let go of the fear that someone else might get promoted before me. Suddenly, influencing across wasn't a giant emotional dodgeball game anymore. It became, believe it or not, fun.

I learned this the hard way during a company merger. At the time, I was handling DOT compliance for a company with 783 drivers and the entire DOT team was me, myself, and I. The company that acquired us had 198 drivers and a three-person DOT team. Yeah, the math didn't add up.

I was on the road 75 percent of the time, living out of hotels and helping yards across the country. They rarely left the building. Yet, somehow, we all had the same title. Same *manager* on the business card. There are apparently no bonus points for hustle.

At first, I carried a chip on my shoulder that was so big it needed its own zip code. I knew my numbers were better. I had stronger relationships in the field. I was outworking them by a country mile. And the more I saw the gap between my effort and theirs, the more I let it harden my heart. I didn't respect them, and truthfully, I wasn't interested in trying.

Then, one day, the president of the company pulled me aside. He looked me straight in the eye and said, "Dan, you know what I like most about you? Your humility. Don't lose that." Man, that hit me like a ton of bricks. It didn't matter how *right* I thought I was, arrogance was rotting everything good I'd built. That simple reminder snapped me out of it.

From that moment on, I decided I wouldn't measure myself against my teammates anymore. No more invisible scorecards. No more worrying about who got the credit. I was going to show up as a teammate. Period.

And wouldn't you know it? That's when the real influence started. When I brought ideas to the table, it wasn't *my* plan anymore, it was *our* plan. When I spoke, it wasn't "Listen to me because I'm smarter." It was, "What if we win this together?"

Influencing your peers isn't about titles or tactics. It's about mindset and what's happening in the six inches between your ears.

Michael Jordan once said he had an eight-inch advantage over every other player on the court, not in wingspan or vertical leap, but in his mentality. Leading across is no different. It's mental. It's heart work. You must win the battle inside before gaining influence outside.

When I finally dropped the competition mindset, everything changed. We stopped working in silos and started meeting weekly. We started brainstorming weekly. We shared ideas, backed each other up, and created momentum. Drivers noticed. Managers noticed. Even the corporate suits noticed.

Healthy peer leadership spreads, and when it does, it spreads like wildfire (in the best way). Here's the thing: Influencing across may look like influencing up, but people blow it in some significant ways. The first is telling people how the cow ate the cabbage.

The first way we lose influence: telling people how the cow ate the cabbage.

Now, if you didn't grow up hearing that phrase, *telling someone how the cow at the cabbage,* let me explain. It's when you roll into a room and lay it all out there like you're the great keeper of all knowledge. "This is how it is. End of story. You're welcome."

I've been guilty more times than I care to admit. It usually goes something like this: I spot the problem. I see the solution. I know exactly what needs to happen. So naturally, I do what any brilliant, logical, self-aware leader would do. I storm in like a rodeo clown with a clipboard and start declaring how things will be. You can probably guess how well that worked.

As it turns out, people don't like being bulldozed, *especially* when you're right. There's something wired deep in all of us that resists being told what to do, no matter how good the advice is. It's like telling a toddler, "Don't touch that!" You might as well paint the thing neon orange and put a spotlight on, because now it's all they want to touch.

People don't follow orders. They follow ownership. And ownership only happens when they feel like they've got a stake in the idea, not when they're handed marching orders from the *Smart Guy Committee.*

Even when my plan was faster, better, cheaper, safer, you name it, if I didn't invite people into the conversation, it backfired. Hard. Instead of nodding along, they'd undermine progress. They dragged their feet and poked holes in the plan, waiting for me to fail so they could say, "Told you it wouldn't work."

At first, I thought these people were difficult. They don't want to change. Nope. They didn't want to be steamrolled—big difference. It took me a long time, and more than a few busted relationships, to learn this: If I wanted people to follow the plan, they needed to see their fingerprints on it. They had to feel like it was *our* idea, not *mine.*

Instead of kicking in the door with, "Here's what we're doing," I had to start saying, "Here's what I'm seeing. What do you think we should do?" Instead of handing out a completed playbook, I showed up with a handful of puzzle pieces and asked, "How do we fit this together?"

At first, it felt slow and messy. It made my Type A, checklist-loving brain twitch. But then something crazy happened: People started owning the solutions. They didn't just follow a plan, they *fought* for it. They defended, protected, and cared about it. And all it took was treating them like they mattered—like their input wasn't merely tolerated, it was needed.

That's the thing about influence. It's not about proving you're the most intelligent person in the room. It's about being smart enough to know you're better *with* people than without them.

If you want to lead across, you've got to stop telling people how the cow ate the cabbage. Invite them to the table. Hand them a fork and say, "Let's figure out how to make this the best dang meal we've ever had." When people help build it, they'll fight to protect it. When people feel ownership, you don't have to push them, they'll run. And that's how real influence grows.

The second way we lose influence is by tearing our teammates down instead of building them up.

And I'll be honest, this hits close to home. I've lived it from both sides. I've been the guy who got torn down in front of others. And I've been the guy who wanted to bite back instead of build someone up. Neither one feels good. And neither one builds trust.

I still remember one day like it was yesterday. I was visiting a division yard with a teammate. I'd thrown on a sport coat. I figured I'd try to look like I belonged in the boardroom and the truck yard.

He showed up in boots and jeans that, at first glance, looked like they had seen a few hundred brake jobs. But it didn't take long to figure out that his jeans were brand new—still stiff and creased like he'd pulled them off the rack that morning. The boots were barely broken in. No scuffs. No dirt. Heck, you could tell by the awkward way he stood there that he wasn't used to wearing them. It was apparent he had bought the whole outfit for this trip, and this was probably the first time he had ever worn it.

Real field guys don't think twice about their clothes. They grab a pair of jeans from the drawer and a shirt from the hanger and hit the ground running. Their work clothes look the same—broken in, stained up, and ready for action. This? This was a costume. And the drivers smelled it a mile away.

The first driver we ran into took one look at me and said, loud enough for the whole yard to hear, "What's with the jacket, Dan? You look like some corporate stooge!" And before I could even get a word out, my teammate, *my teammate*, laughed right along with him and said, "Yeah, no kidding!"

Man, I was hotter than a firecracker in July. I could feel the heat rising up the back of my neck. There I was, standing in the field, doing the work, showing up, wearing something clean for once, and I got clowned. Then double clowned by the guy who's supposed to be on my team.

At that moment, I wanted to swing back. Not physically (though I won't lie, it crossed my mind), but with words. With sarcasm. With a comeback sharp enough to remind everyone exactly who had the better audit scores and the field relationships to back it up.

But I didn't, because I've learned something over the years: When you tear someone down in front of others, even if they deserve it, you lose more than they do. You lose trust. You lose respect. You lose influence. So, I kept my cool.

A few minutes later, another driver said he liked the jacket. Then, a second driver flagged me down with a paperwork issue. Jacket and all, I got in there and helped. I didn't need to prove anything. I needed to serve. And it wasn't long before everyone in that yard could tell who came to get something done and who came to hang out.

Here's the part I'm proud of: I didn't throw my teammate under the bus even after getting laughed at. When the conversation shifted, and drivers started talking about who shows up and who doesn't, I bragged on him. I pointed out what he was good at, not because he earned it that day, but because that's what leaders do.

Real leaders don't take cheap shots or use someone else's mistake to elevate themselves. Real leaders lift people up, even when it's hard, not fair, and the other guy tried to knock you down. That response doesn't come naturally. It comes from practice and deciding who you want to be when the heat turns up.

And here's the wild part: Word of that moment got around. It made its way back through our team. People heard how I handled it. And it built trust, not with the field, but with the folks sitting around the table back at corporate.

So the next time someone on your team makes you look bad, pause before you hit back. Ask yourself: *Do I want to be right, or do I want to lead?* Tearing them down might feel good for ten seconds, but lifting them up builds influence that lasts for years.

The third way we kill influence is by being unreliable.

And I'm telling you straight. It doesn't matter how brilliant your ideas are. You could have invented electricity, taught pigs to fly, or built a time machine from duct tape and a green lawn tractor. But if you're the person who drops the ball, shows up late, forgets the details, and blames everyone else when things fall apart, nobody's going to listen to you.

Reliability isn't flashy or glamorous. Nobody throws a party because you showed up on time. There's no trophy, banner, or plaque that says, "Congrats, you did what you said you'd do." But reliability is *everything*. It's the foundation your entire influence is built on. You can have charisma. You can have brilliance. You can even have fantastic hair. But if people can't count on you, you'll never lead them anywhere that matters.

It's like my kids' middle school group projects. If you're a parent, you already know where this is going. Every one of my kids has had a partner who talked a big game. "Oh yeah, I'll totally help! I'm great at making PowerPoints!" and then disappeared the moment the deadline got close. Poof. Gone. No text. No explanation. Vanished like a magician's rabbit.

And every single time, guess who carried the whole project across the finish line. My kids. They did 90 percent of the work while their *teammates* coasted—then had the nerve to show up on presentation day acting like they'd invented sliced bread. Do you think my kids ever trusted those partners again? Not a chance. And it's the same in real leadership.

The moment people realize they can't count on you to follow through, show up, and do what you said you'd do, you might as well look for a new team. This team won't follow you across the street, let alone into anything that matters.

Reliability isn't flashy. It's not what people notice when it's there. But the second it's missing? Oh, buddy, it's *all* they see. It's like the wheels on a car. When they're working, you don't think about them. But the second one falls off, you notice real fast.

You don't have to be perfect. You don't have to get everything right the first time. But you must be there. You must be the one your team can lean on when things get heavy, shows up when it's inconvenient, and finishes the project, even when it's boring. You must carry your share of the weight without needing a marching band and a fireworks show for doing your job.

People won't remember every brilliant idea you pitched. They won't remember every meeting where you dropped a clever one-liner. But they *will* remember whether they could count on you when it mattered. Be that person. Be the one who keeps your word, especially when it's hard. Be the one who finishes strong, especially when nobody's watching.

Influence isn't earned by being impressive. It's earned by being dependable.

The fourth way we blow it is by stealing credit or ignoring other people's contributions.

Nothing tanks your influence faster. Do you want to see trust evaporate quicker than water on a Texas highway in July? Take someone's hard work, slap your name on it, and act like it's no big deal. Trust me, people notice. They might not say it to your face, but you better believe they're keeping receipts.

I learned this the hard way at a church event I volunteered for. I wanted to help. So, I stayed up late one night, designing fliers, creating agendas, and organizing sign-up sheets. All the behind-the-scenes stuff nobody loves doing, but everybody needs.

I sent everything out early, took feedback, and made a few tweaks. I wanted to make it great for the team. Then, a couple of weeks later, the organizer sent out a mass email to the whole group: "I made some fliers. They're not as good as Dan's were, but oh well."

Wait. What? She didn't use the fliers I made. She scrapped them completely. After all that time and effort, she threw my work in the trash, made her own version, and then gave me a pity shout-out like that made it okay. It was like getting kicked in the shins and then being asked if I'd like to come back for seconds. And right after that email? She had the nerve to ask if I could help with even more. Yeah, no. Hard pass.

You lose influence when disrespecting someone's time, energy, or gifts. Not eventually. Not *if* they find out. Immediately. When someone gives you their effort, they give you a piece of their pride, creativity, and heart. When you brush past it, or worse, claim it as your own, you're not just stealing work, you're stealing trust. You're telling everyone around you, "Your effort doesn't matter here." Nobody sticks around long in a place like that.

If you want real influence, you honor the work people bring to the table even if it's not perfect and you could have done it better.

You say:

- Hey, thanks for knocking that out.
- You crushed it on that project.
- This wouldn't have happened without you.

You don't lose the spotlight when you lift others up, you make it brighter.

Leadership isn't a solo act. It's a team sport. And if you can't celebrate the people in the trenches with you, don't be surprised when you end up leading a ghost town.

And finally, the fifth way we torch our influence is by not guarding our words.

Trash-talking your teammates doesn't make *them* look bad, it makes *you* look small. You might think you're getting people to rally around you when you bad-mouth others, but you look like a toddler trying to win an argument by throwing a shoe. People don't admire you. They're embarrassed for you. They back away, wondering when they'll be the next one under your bus tires.

I saw this play out firsthand at our local volunteer fire department election. A few board seats were open, and nothing reveals someone's character faster than a little small-town power on the line. I couldn't make it to the *Meet the Candidates* night because I was driving home from one of my kids' lacrosse tournaments—family first, always— but I heard all about it.

There were five candidates. The first guy gave a short and powerful speech about why he wanted to serve, what he hoped to bring to the department, and how he planned to work with the community. People clapped. Heads nodded. He earned respect by being real.

Then, the second candidate, a woman, got up. She delivered an incredible speech. You could tell she put deep thought into it. But when she finished, there was dead silence. No applause. No excitement. Why?

For the last two months, she had been lighting people up on social media. She'd been trashing volunteers, tearing down the current board, and complaining about how everything was broken. So, even though she said all the right things that night, nobody forgot the poison she'd been spewing online. The damage was already done.

Then, the third guy stepped up. Based on what everyone said, he spent his whole speech swinging a hammer at everything and everyone. No vision. No solutions. Just a running list of what everyone else had done wrong. He probably thought he was coming off as bold and honest, but it had the opposite effect. People didn't leave thinking, "Wow, what a truth-teller!" They left thinking, "Man, what a jerk."

The fourth candidate was a current board member. He started strong—stayed positive for about thirty seconds and then spent the rest of his time defending every past decision like he was in a courtroom trial. Everybody in the room was drained and ready to nap when he wrapped up.

The fifth and final candidate gave a solid, uplifting speech. He talked about working together, improving communication, and building on the good already there. People smiled, clapped, and commented, "That's the leader we need."

Now, if you're reading this, based on what you heard, who would you vote for? Exactly. The guy who stayed positive and didn't trash anyone else to make himself look good.

That's how it works. When you trash others, you don't raise yourself up. You dig your own hole. When you tear your team apart with your words, you're torching your ability to lead them.

A cord of three strands is not easily broken. That's what Ecclesiastes 4:12 says. It's as true for leadership as it is for friendships. If you want to build real influence across your peers, be the one who strengthens instead of shreds it because your ego can't take a backseat.

Leading across isn't about outworking, outshining, or outsmarting them. It's about out serving them. It's about being gritty enough to lift others up even when nobody's clapping. It's about celebrating their wins, even when you're still waiting for yours. It's about choosing to be the leader who carries the team forward, not the anchor that drags them down. It's about showing up as the teammate you wish you had and letting the scoreboard take care of itself.

And if you can walk into the messy, pride-bruising, ego-bruising battlefield of peer leadership with grit, humility, and humor, you will influence and inspire them.

Influencing Down (Teams, Staff, Followers)

Leading people who look up to you isn't easier than leading your peers—it's a different weight. When you're influencing a team, a staff, or anyone who counts on you for direction, the stakes feel even higher. These aren't just coworkers or colleagues anymore. These people tie their confidence, energy, and sometimes even their family's future to your leadership. Whether they say it out loud or not, they're looking to you for what's next. They're trusting you to be more than a manager. They're hoping you'll be a leader worth following.

And here's the kicker: When you're leading down the ladder, you don't just carry your own reputation, you carry theirs, too. You affect their growth, success, confidence, and their dreams. All of that sits, at least partly, on your shoulders. No pressure, right?

Most people think leading a team means issuing orders and getting stuff done. And sure, there are moments when you set the pace and make the calls. But real leadership, *influence that matters*, isn't about throwing your title around. It's about building something inside the people who follow you that makes them want to run faster, aim higher, and believe bigger than before they met you.

Influencing down isn't about getting people to fear you. It's about getting them to trust you. It's about building people, not processes. It's about lifting them up, even when it would be easier to sit back and let them sink.

Sometimes, the ones who look up to you will be the ones who drive you the craziest. They'll make mistakes, miss deadlines, and frustrate you in ways that make you want to take a long walk off a short pier. But they're still your responsibility. They're still your team. And if you're willing to lead them with grit, patience, and heart, you won't just build followers, you'll build future leaders.

Leadership isn't measured by how many people serve you. It's measured by how many people you're willing to serve first. And when you get that part right, the whole game changes.

One of the biggest mistakes leaders make when influencing down is swinging too far to one side or the other. Either they turn into control freaks, where everything has to be exactly their way, or they completely take their hands off the wheel and wonder why the whole bus is on fire by lunchtime. Real leadership is about finding the middle ground. It's about giving your people enough guidance not to fail and enough freedom to make and learn from mistakes.

If you want to grow real leaders underneath you, you can't just bark orders and expect them to figure things out magically. But you also can't hover over their every move, correcting them like a backseat driver who thinks they're helping by screaming "Brake! Brake!" after you're already through the intersection. People need structure and expectations, but they also need room to stretch, fall, and get up again without being shamed.

When someone makes a mistake, and trust me, they will, it's not a license to unload on them. It's not an excuse to embarrass them in front of the team or to fire off a "How could you be so dumb?" speech that leaves them questioning why they even try.

Mistakes are some of the best leadership moments you'll ever get if you know how to handle them. Mistakes are not an indictment. They're an invitation to coach, build trust, and say, "All right, let's look at what happened. What would you do differently next time?" instead of, "You blew it, and now you're on my bad list forever."

One thing I always try to remember when I'm leading is this: If the people under me are afraid to fail, they will be too scared to succeed. You must create an environment where messing up isn't the end of the road—it's part of the road. You've got to be the leader who says, "Hey, I know you missed it here. I've missed it, too. Let's figure out how we both get better because of it."

That leadership doesn't just build better workers, it builds better warriors. It builds loyalty, confidence, and future leaders who can fall, learn, and get back up swinging. Leadership isn't about making sure nobody ever messes up. It's about making sure when they do, they're standing taller on the other side of it.

Model Before You Mandate

People don't follow orders, they follow examples. You can bark commands all day, but you're adding to the noise if your actions don't back up your demands. Like I said earlier, the fastest way to get someone burned is to point at the stove and yell, "Don't touch that!" I guarantee the second you say it, something in their brain wakes up and starts thinking, "I wonder how hot it really is?"

I laugh every time I think about it. Years ago, my kids showed me this legendary mashup video of the Crocodile Hunter—Steve Irwin in all his wild, khaki-wearing glory. It's still a running joke in our house.

The video's just this old, cut-together reel of Steve gettin' himself into one ridiculous situation after another, narrating it all in that thick-as-a-wall Aussie accent. And thank goodness you can't hear me tryin' to type it out—because when I attempt an Aussie accent, it sounds like a British pirate got lost in Texas.

But in the video, he's full tilt. First clip, he's crouched down in the dirt next to a massive snake and says, "Crikey! Wot we've got 'ere's the most poy-s'nous snake in all the world, mate. One bite'll paralyze ya almost instantly … I've gotta touch it."

Then it cuts to him standin' next to a crocodile that looks like it could flip a bulldozer and he goes, "This beauty right 'ere is the largest croc in the world! Eighteen feet long, mate, with a bite force stronger than an 80-ton car crushah. One chomp and me arm's gone. I've gotta touch it."

Then, boom—cuts again. Now he's next to a spider the size of a dinner plate. "This lil' fella is the hairiest, scariest spider known to man. The three-legged, seven-eyed Silver Typhoon Spider! One nip from 'is fang'll paralyze an elephant. I've gotta touch it."

Every time we tell our kids not to touch something, whether it's a hot pan, a sharp tool, or a mystery button, they slip into their best Steve Irwin impersonation, throw on a thick Aussie accent, and say, "I've *gotta* touch it." It's hilarious. But it's also painfully true. When you tell people not to do something without a real reason, it makes them want to do it even more.

Our followers, our teams, staff, and the people who look up to us are wired the same way. If all we ever say is *no* without backing it up, we're not leading. We're daring them to go in the opposite direction.

That's why modeling before mandating matters so much. People are way more likely to listen if you show them the *why* before you give them the what. If you live it before you preach it, they'll trust you when it matters most.

Dale Carnegie, one of the best leadership teachers of all time, hammered this point home long before it was trendy. Paraphrasing one of his timeless principles, people are more likely to change when they're led gently by example than when they're cornered by criticism. You can tell someone they're wrong until you're blue in the face, and all you'll get back is a brick wall. But if you model a better way first and let them see it working in real life, they're more likely to move that direction on their own.

It's true with your team, your kids, your coworkers—it's true everywhere. Telling people not to touch the stove doesn't work. Showing them why it's hot, and modeling how to avoid getting burned, does.

Modeling the behavior you want to see minimizes mistakes and builds trust. You're creating a culture where people aren't scared into obedience; they're inspired into excellence. Nobody wants to follow a boss who points and shouts from a mile away. They want to follow someone in the trenches with them—someone who lives it first.

We don't send memos—we show up.

Get in the Trenches with Them

If you want to build real influence with your team, you can't lead from a throne. You've got to meet them where they are, roll up your sleeves, and get in the trenches with them. When people see you as another member of the same team but with a different role, everything changes. Leadership that follows a caste system is divisive. People don't want to be ruled. They want to be fought for.

It reminds me of this hilarious episode of *The Big Bang Theory*. Howard's girlfriend drags him along to volunteer at a soup kitchen during a busy holiday. Howard's already feeling sorry for himself, grumbling about washing dishes instead of doing something more glamorous. Then, out of nowhere, Elon Musk walks in, not as some special guest, but as a fellow volunteer. The next thing you know, Howard's standing there elbow-deep in dishwater, scrubbing trays next to one of his heroes. And suddenly, washing dishes doesn't seem so lame anymore. It feels legendary. That's the magic of leadership in the trenches.

When people see someone they admire getting their hands dirty, not because they have to, but because they want to, it flips a switch inside them. Ordinary work becomes something bigger, resentment turns into pride, and compliance transforms into commitment, all because someone said, "I'm with you."

That's a massive part of how we lead at Eclipse DOT. It's not uncommon for a team member to bring me a problem—something complicated with the FMCSA, a ridiculous audit request, or a messy situation a client landed in. Before they've even finished explaining, I'm already in it with them. Instead of sending some memo from my *desk of wisdom*, I'm in the thick of it—swinging the sword, battling the bureaucracy, and trying to find the best solution for our clients.

I've taken on more FMCSA cases personally than I probably should at this point in my career, but you know what? It matters. It shows my team that when the going gets tough, leadership doesn't run. Leadership leans in.

It's easy to talk about servant leadership when writing a mission statement. It's harder to live it when you're three hours into a miserable paperwork mess, getting a client's DOT number reinstated after forgetting to file their MCS-150 for the third year in a row. But that's where trust, loyalty, and leaders are built.

Be willing to pick up a dish rag, and maybe even a few *dirty jobs*, if you want to lead people who would go to war for you. Real leaders show up in the trenches, wash dishes, get muddy, and don't complain about it. When you're willing to serve, you're not just building a team, you're building a family.

Make Them Feel Seen, Heard, and Valued

One of the deepest needs every human being has—whether they're sitting in a boardroom, behind the wheel of a truck, or somewhere in between—is to feel seen, heard, and valued. And if you're going to be a leader people want to follow, it's your job to ensure they do. A great example happened recently when a company hired us to help them prepare for a DOT audit.

If you've never been through a DOT audit, let me explain it in technical terms: It's like inviting the world's grumpiest hall monitor to dig through your junk drawer and judge you for it. And one of the first things they're going to pull out? Your DQ (Driver Qualification) files.

If you don't know what a DQ file is, think of it like your driver's diary. Except instead of sweet memories and doodles, it's full of government-mandated paperwork, missing signatures, and silent judgment. Every driver needs one, and if that file's missing pieces, or missing altogether, you're about to feel the heat.

This company knew they were in trouble, so they brought us in. We started by digging into their DQ files. My team crushed it, digitizing thirty-five files in three days. That's a ton of work. It's like cleaning out a hoarder's garage with a toothbrush. And, somehow, they made it happen.

After we cleaned up the digital files, I went to their offices to see exactly where they stood. I didn't storm in throwing around citations and scare tactics. I walked in like a coach, not a cop. I looked at what they had, sat down with their team, and listened. I helped them see the simple things they could do to make a big difference, like backing in all the trucks neatly before the officer arrived. Minor stuff, right? But those little details send a silent message: "We're prepared. We take this seriously. We care."

They took what I said as gold. Not because I barked at them or made them feel stupid. I respected them and their success mattered to me.

When the audit week finally hit, it was a brutal one. The officer was going to be in town for five full days. That's the DOT for you. When they come, they come hard. Normally, I would have camped out and fought with them in the trenches. But I was scheduled to be in Dallas with another client for an inspection I couldn't reschedule. I felt terrible. But I didn't leave them hanging.

Instead, before I left, I coached them through what to expect. I gave them a plan, a checklist, and confidence to know they could handle it. I didn't go dark. Every night, from 800 miles away, after finishing my client work in Dallas, I called them. I listened as they told me how the day went. I answered their questions and reassured them that they weren't alone in it.

And you know what happened? They were prepared for the next day. But more importantly, they felt seen, heard, and valued. Without that follow-up every day, they might have felt like just another client. They fought harder, stayed calmer, and walked through that audit with confidence you can't fake.

Leadership is being the voice reminding people they matter, especially when the pressure's on. When people know you see, hear, and value them, they'll run through a wall for you. And they'll remember who stood with them long after the paperwork is filed away.

Talk to Them, Not at Them

If you want to lose influence fast, start talking at people instead of to them. Honestly, this one's so important that I almost made it the title of the whole chapter. When it comes to real leadership, how you communicate is everything.

Most people don't even realize they're doing it. They think they're helping. They believe being direct and bossy is the same as being clear. It's not. Talking at people is when you bark orders, lay down ultimatums, and issue demands without bothering to invite them into the conversation. You tell them what to do, how to do it, when it needs to be done, and you expect them to snap to attention and say, "Yes, sir." But real life doesn't work like that. People aren't soldiers in your private army. They're human beings with brains, hearts, and pride. And when you talk at them instead of to them, you lose them, fast.

Before we dive into this next part, I need you to brace yourself. We're going to have a little fun. It will probably feel awkward, but that's the point.

Let's set the stage first: Picture me, the kid who barely read a book unless it had tractors, trucks, or explosions in it, now writing a book. If you had told my third-grade teacher that I'd be sitting here pounding out chapters one day, she probably would have spit her coffee out laughing. Heck, sometimes *I* can't believe it. *Author*. Man, that still feels wild to say out loud. I'm grinning like a goofball while I type this.

All right, now that you know the backstory, here's where it gets fun. I'm about to give a live example of what it feels like when someone talks *at* you instead of *to* you. Ready? Deep breath. Here we go.

As the author responsible for your success, I am requiring you read this book cover to cover without complaint. You must take notes on every chapter. You must implement every strategy exactly as directed, without hesitation or deviation. Completing daily recaps and sending them to my email for review is mandatory. Every day, you must post on social media about how much this book has improved your life. I expect you to tell every friend, coworker, and neighbor to buy a copy immediately. All tasks must be completed by the end of the week, no matter what. Noncompliance will result in being left behind by those who follow directions. No exceptions. No excuses. I require you to be tattooed with an image of the book cover in a not so discreet location on your body.

So, how did that feel? Not great, right? Maybe you felt your stomach tighten up a little. Maybe your brain started looking for the nearest exit. Perhaps you even thought about slamming this book shut and throwing it across the room. I hope so, because that's precisely the point.

When you talk at people, even with the best intentions, you make them want to back away. They start to feel small, like a cog in your machine instead of a partner in your mission. And the second people feel that way, they stop caring. Instead of giving you their best, they start looking for a way out.

How we talk matters more than we think. Tone, posture, and heart matters. When you talk *to* people, you pull them in. You invite them to bring their ideas, effort, and heart to the table. You don't just give them a job, you provide them with a reason to care about doing it well.

Leadership invites: "Let's build this together." When people feel like you're *for* them, not *over* them, they'll run through walls you didn't even know existed. And it all starts with how you talk.

Celebrate Their Wins More Than Your Own

If I'm being honest with you, I struggle with this more than you could ever imagine. I don't do well at all in celebrating my wins. I don't know why. There's something wired deep inside of me that says if I celebrate a win, I'm being arrogant. If I stop and acknowledge something good, I'm flaunting it and showing off, acting like I'm better than someone else.

It doesn't seem to matter if I make $10, $1 million, $10 million, or $100 million in a year, something inside me whispers, "Don't celebrate. Stay humble. Don't talk about it." Internally, it does something weird to me. It messes with my head. Every time I even *think* about celebrating something I've accomplished, it feels wrong, like I'm crossing some invisible line from confidence into cockiness.

Even with huge personal milestones, I didn't stop to celebrate. When I got my pilot's license, you'd think I would have earned a steak dinner or a victory lap around the hangar. But nope. I passed the check ride and walked out of the airport like I'd finished grocery shopping. Instead of celebrating, I was already eyeing the next thing: my twin-engine license.

Now, to be fair, when I go in, I go *all in*. In my first year of flying, I logged more hours than most students rack up after two full years in commercial pilot school. I had more hours than a seasoned private pilot I knew who had a plane and hangar and had been flying for over a decade. Nice guy. Great mustache. But I had more time in the sky than he did watching *Top Gun* on repeat.

When I say I flew myself *everywhere*, I mean *everywhere*. If I had a meeting in another state, it was wheels up. Training to run? Let's take the scenic route from 10,000 feet. I was racking up flight time like Delta hands out Biscoff cookies.

And then, plot twist, I realized that, for now, commercial flights saved me time and money. So, I swallowed my pride, traded the cockpit for seat 1A and told myself, *One day, I'll buy a jet and hire a pilot. Maybe then I'll stop and celebrate.* But knowing me? I'll nod, check the next thing off my list, and mutter, *Cool. What's next?*

That's how deep it runs. Celebration doesn't come naturally to me. So, when I first started trying to celebrate my team's wins, it felt weird, awkward, and forced. I kept thinking, *Man, they're going to think I'm blowing smoke. They're going to get arrogant and stop working hard.* But something amazing happened. The more I celebrated their real, hard-earned wins, the more they grew. I wasn't bragging *about* them. I was building *into* them.

I started calling out real victories: So-and-so made this many sales this week. This person got a client to 100 percent compliance for the first time. Someone else crushed their first audit with flying colors. Another team member brought in three new leads in one week. Another nailed a cross-sell opportunity that helped a client stay safer on the road.

At first, it was me pushing myself to acknowledge them. But then something flipped. They started celebrating each other's wins. And then, this is the part that still floors me. They started celebrating *my* wins, too.

I'd come back from speaking at a big event, or land a tough client, or roll out a new program, and before I could even get back to my desk, someone on the team would holler out, "Hey Dan, what'd you win at this week?" It became a thing. I'd ask them, "What did you win at this week?" And they'd fire the question right back at me. "Dan, what about you? What did you win at this week?"

It turned into a giant cycle of momentum, a rolling snowball of wins and positivity. It created an energy that wasn't fake; it wasn't forced, it was real. It all reminded me of something Brandon Dawson says: "The only emotion that belongs in business is celebration."

And I think leadership is the same way. If you let frustration, fear, and anger drive your leadership, you punch holes in your ship. But if you let celebration drive your leadership, if you find a way to keep the wins front and center, you make people want to keep chasing bigger wins with you.

What I'm suggesting is that celebration should be organic. Programs like Employee of the Month, Golden Stapler Awards, or VIP parking spots aren't *bad*, they're just not the whole picture. Recognition doesn't need a nameplate or a PowerPoint slide to matter.

What makes people feel seen is real, personal, genuine celebration. Looking someone in the eye and saying, "I see what you did. I see the fight you put in. I'm proud of you." That hits harder than any framed certificate ever will.

Leadership is about lifting up what went right and building on those successes until the wins stack up so high that everyone believes they can win, too.

Do you want a culture where people run through walls for you? Start by celebrating when they climb one. Celebrate their wins louder than you ever celebrate your own, and you'll build a team that wants to survive and win together.

Celebration is the only emotion that multiplies leadership.

Give Them Room to Succeed and Fail

If you're going to lead people, you must give them room to fail, and you must mean it. It's one thing to slap a motivational poster on the wall that says, "Failure is a stepping stone to success." It's another thing to watch someone crash and burn in front of you and still believe in them. Keep coaching and investing in them like you did before they stumbled.

That's the difference between a leader and a boss—between building people up and burning them out. And it's one of the hardest things you'll ever do. Generally speaking, the world views failure as a death sentence. We grew up in school systems where one bad grade meant you were dumb. We grew up around adults who thought if you lost, it meant you weren't trying hard enough, or worse, you weren't good enough. Somewhere along the way, we swallowed the lie that you are not meant to stand if you fall. And we wonder why so many people stop trying. Real leadership throws those lies in the trash where they belong.

When I lead people, whether my team, clients, or kids, I tell them: FAIL stands for First Attempt In Learning. If you're not failing, you're standing still and trying to look pretty. You're trying to protect your image at the expense of your growth. No real leader was ever built playing it safe.

The first time I ever shot a video for the public, I cringed so hard I almost deleted it before anyone else could see it. It was awful. I'm talking full-on aliens-would-cancel-Earth-if-they-intercepted-this bad. My lighting was terrible, pacing was awkward, and delivery sounded like I was reading a script written by angry robots. Even with all that, I put it out there anyway. I didn't quit or hide. I kept filming, learning, and sucking, less and less each time, until one day, people started telling me they liked my videos. They felt authentic, and people trusted me because I *wasn't* polished, I was human.

That's what most people forget about growth. Nobody sees the messy middle. Nobody sees the bloopers, failures, and nights you're questioning if you're even cut out for this. They only see the wins. Remember the messy middle for yourself and your team.

It's like teaching a baby to walk. No baby pulls themselves up and immediately sprints a 5K. They roll around like little logs first. They crawl, bump into walls, and faceplant into coffee tables. And every time they fall, what do we do? We clap. We cheer. We celebrate the crash because we know what it means: They're learning. They're getting stronger and doing exactly what they're supposed to do.

Now imagine if every time a kid fell trying to walk, we shook our heads and said, "Guess you're not meant for this. Better stick to crawling through college." Picture a world full of adults dragging themselves across the floor, covered in carpet burns, because no one believed in them long enough to let them fall and get back up.

It's ridiculous, right? And yet, that's precisely how too many leaders treat the people under them on the org chart. They expect perfection and punish imperfection. They destroy the spirit they were supposed to grow.

At Eclipse DOT, we lead differently. When I hire someone, I don't sugarcoat it. I tell them right up front, "You're going to screw up. You're going to make mistakes that cost me money. You'll do things that make me slap my forehead in frustration. And it's okay. I've got your back."

I tell them, "If you fall, I won't kick you out the door. I'm not going to shame you in front of the team. I'm going to help you up. I'm going to fight for you, not against you. I'm not quitting on you as long as you don't quit on yourself."

There's one thing I won't tolerate, though: quitting. You can fall. You can fail. You can mess up so badly that we both have to sit there afterward and wonder how it all went sideways. But you do not quit on the mission, the people who count on you, or the person you're becoming.

And when you screw up, and trust me, you will, you own it. You face it and learn from it. Pick yourself up, dust off the bruises, and try again. If you can learn from your mistakes, you're already ahead of 88 percent of the world. And if you can learn from somebody else's mistakes without repeating them yourself, you're ahead of ninety-nine percent. (Now, I pulled those percentages straight out of my back pocket. Not scientific or peer reviewed. Individual results may vary.)

Imagine a world where every leader expected people to fall and prepared them for it. Imagine a world where stumbling wasn't treated like a failure but like training. Imagine teams, families, businesses, and churches built not on perfection but on perseverance. That's the leadership that changes lives and builds legends.

Influence in All Directions

If I'm being candid, I wish I had one glamorous story about leadership. One perfect story where I swooped in, led the team, changed lives, and rode off into the sunset. I have so many stories I couldn't begin to fit them all into this book. I led from the middle and the front, and I didn't even realize I was leading until someone later said, "You have no idea how much you changed my life." That's when you know you're truly leading—when there are so many success stories that you can't even pick a favorite. Leadership is about creating a life so packed with wins for others that you forget to keep score.

One night, I was sitting in the bleachers watching my youngest son play basketball, and that simple game showed me more about leadership than most boardrooms ever could. My son's coach was everything you'd hope a coach would be. He was positive, patient, and in the trenches with those boys. When a kid missed a shot or blew a play, he'd briefly pull them off the court, wrap an arm around their shoulder, and coach them. You could hear him calling it out on the sideline, "That's okay, we'll get the next one!" "Hey, watch that kid. He's a shooter. Stay tight on him, but keep it clean." "That guy? He camps under the hoop. Don't let him get the easy layup." Every correction came with encouragement. Every mistake was a learning opportunity. The kids didn't just play for the scoreboard. They played for him because they trusted him.

And then, across the gym, the other coach was the polar opposite. Watching him was like watching a live demonstration of everything leadership should never be. His team was good. I'll give them that. They had a kid who could drain threes from anywhere on the court. They had energy and grit. But how that man coached them made your stomach turn. The moment his kids showed any sign of slowing down, and mind you, this was the second half of a doubleheader, he was all over them. "If you want to walk, walk your butt to the bench!" he bellowed across the gym. "If you don't hustle, I'll find someone who will!" There was no encouragement or grace. Just belittling and fear.

I couldn't take it while sitting there as a parent, even though none of those boys were mine. I had to move to the other side of the gym to stop hearing it. And the saddest part? Some of the parents behind him thought he was great. "Man, I wish I could make my kid hustle like that," I heard one say. "He knows how to get effort out of them!" another chimed in. But they missed what was really happening.

Those boys weren't running because they loved the game. They weren't hustling because they believed in their team or trusted their coach. They were hustling because they were terrified of being screamed at, punishment, and how much running they'd have to do at practice the next day if they lost.

Fear will make people move for a while but never make them loyal. It will never make them proud to be part of something bigger or fight for you when it gets hard. That coach wasn't building a team. He wasn't building leaders. He was out there taking a walk, barking orders into the air, while kids tried to outrun his anger.

I don't care if he won some games. I don't care if the team had a winning record. Now sure—he had influence. But it wasn't the kind that builds people. It was the kind that breaks them. And that's not leadership. That's noise with a whistle.

When you lead with fear, you might get compliance. But when you lead with trust, you get commitment. When you lead gracefully, you get something fear could never produce; loyalty, belief, passion, and heart.

I challenge you to not be that coach. Don't be the leader who has to scream to be heard. Don't be the one walking alone while everyone else follows out of obligation, not inspiration. Be the leader who builds something people want to be part of. Be the leader who leads with influence, in every direction, up, down, sideways, and everywhere.

Leadership is demonstrated in how you treat people at their best, and especially how you treat them at their worst. It's about building trust so deep that when you say, "Follow me," people move, not because they're forced to, but because they know you're not looking for credit. You're looking out for *them*.

That's exactly how Jesus led.

He didn't bark orders. He didn't dominate with titles or status. He simply said, "Come, follow me," (Matthew 4:19).

One of the most powerful examples is right after Peter denied even knowing Him *three times*. Jesus didn't cancel, shame, or replace him. After the resurrection, He met Peter on the beach, cooked him breakfast, and simply asked, "Do you love me ... feed my sheep," (John 21:15–17).

No guilt trip. No power play. Just grace, restoration, and a mission. That's leadership. Jesus gave everything before He asked for anything. And because of that, billions have followed Him, not out of fear, but out of love.

That's real influence. That's the leader you're called to be.

Influence Isn't a Title, It's a Trust You Earn

Influence in all directions isn't just a nice leadership theory—it's the battle-tested truth of every real leader who's ever made a difference. You can lead from the bottom, the middle, or the top. You can lead from the front or the trenches. You can even lead without realizing people are watching you, because, believe me, they are.

Real leadership doesn't wait for permission. It doesn't need a title. It doesn't need a bigger office or a louder microphone. Real leadership is influence, and influence is trust, earned one conversation, one sacrifice, one real moment at a time.

If you've been paying attention, you've seen how leadership lives or dies based on how we treat people. You've seen that people don't follow fear for long. They don't rally around arrogance, and they don't trust someone who talks down to them. They follow leaders who get in the trenches, believe in them, and give grace. That's the difference between a boss and a builder—between a manager and a movement.

You don't have to be perfect to be a leader. You don't have to have it all figured out. You do have to show up with a heart that says, "I'm here to fight for you, not command you." You must be the coach who believes even when the game is ugly and celebrates others' wins louder than your own. Be the leader who isn't afraid to pick somebody up after they fall, because you remember what it was like to fall yourself.

Wherever you are right now, whether you feel like you're at the top of the mountain or buried under it, lead. Lead up. Lead across. Lead down. Lead beside. Lead how Jesus led, with hands ready to serve and a heart willing to sacrifice.

The world doesn't need more bosses who use fear, pressure, or position to motivate others. We need leaders who use grace and grit to encourage people to perform.

The next half of this journey will take us deeper into how to build leadership, layer by layer and moment by moment. But none of it will matter unless you decide right now that you're going to be the one worth following.

The Circle of Influence: A Family Story

When I think about influence in every direction, up, down, and across, I can't help but think about my own family. It's one thing to talk about leadership inside companies and teams. However, influence is leadership, and it starts at home. It begins with the people who know you best and still choose to follow you anyway.

I still laugh thinking back to when my brother and I were little. We were in a Dairy Queen after a soccer game, arguing like cats in a sack about who would sit next to Dad. We fought like it was the last piece of chocolate cake on the planet. One minute, we shoved each other under the table, the next, Mom would sigh, grab our ice cream cones, and make us switch sides halfway through to keep the peace. We didn't care about the food. We cared about being close to Dad. We wanted to be near him because he was the influence we looked up to.

And now, years later, I see the same thing playing out with my own kids. They don't fight over Dairy Queen booths anymore, but they sometimes fight over who gets to work with Dad. Who gets to ride along on the job? Who gets to be part of the projects I'm working on? That's leadership at its purest. It's about creating a relationship where people *want* to be near you and feel safe, challenged, seen, and valued enough to want to be part of what you're building.

When we're parents, we influence *down* to our kids. That's natural. But something beautiful happens when your kids grow up. You start leading *across*. You see them as peers, leaders in their own right, making their own choices and building their own lives. My oldest son, Billy, is nineteen now as I write this. He's stepping into adulthood, owning his journey. I can't command him the way I could when he was nine. I didn't then and I don't want to now.

I want to influence him with respect, not control. I see him making decisions, taking risks, and chasing dreams. I know he'll make mistakes, as every great leader does. And now, my role isn't to shield him from every fall. My role is to be the voice he knows will be there when he needs it—to influence by presence, not pressure.

I still influence him, and he influences me, too. Watching Billy step into manhood reminds me daily that leadership isn't static. It grows, shifts, and changes shape with time.

One of my favorite examples is when Billy decided to become a certified falconer. At fifteen years old, he wasn't dreaming small dreams, he was thinking about partnering with a hawk. Falconry isn't a simple hobby you pick up at the local pet store. He had to pass a state falconry test, get inspected, and build a hawk house from scratch—all while balancing school, work, and the usual chaos of being a teenager.

At one point, he had to stop studying for his falconry exam to cram for his driver's permit test, then turn around a month later and ace the falconry exam, too. I still remember the day he passed both. He didn't stop there, either. Once he got certified, he had to convince me to help him build a hawk house. He didn't demand it. He came prepared with excitement and a plan. I couldn't say no. That's influence. No force, just passion, preparation, and earned trust.

Leadership inspires the people around you to want to step into something bigger with you. Whether it's a little boy fighting for a seat next to Dad, a teenager building a hawk house, or a grown son walking into his own life, it's always been about the same thing: influence born from love, trust, and respect.

Leadership doesn't end when the office closes. It doesn't end when the kids move out. It doesn't end when you're no longer in charge. It changes shape. And it echoes through the people you've loved, led, and built up.

Challenge: Your Circle of Influence

Now it's your turn. Where are you strongest right now? Is it leading up, across, or down? Where do you need to grow?

If you're brave enough to be honest with yourself, you're strong enough to change it. If you're humble enough to see where you're weak, you're already stronger than most.

Real leadership isn't about who answers to you. It's about who listens when you speak, and why.

Key Takeaways from Chapter Nine

 **Credibility beats titles.** Rank might open doors, but character keeps them propped open when the shine wears off the badge.

 **Lighten your boss's backpack or lose the hike.** Rearrange your world for theirs and watch *no* turn into *heck yes*.

 **Peers aren't opponents—they're coauthors.** Drop the scoreboard, invite them to the table, and they'll fight for the plan they helped write.

 **Reliability is louder than brilliance.** Show up, finish strong, and folks will trust you with the keys—even if you can't spell *Pulaski*.

 **Guard the locker-room talk.** Public praise builds armies; public cheap shots build exit strategies.

 **Model, then mandate.** Live the lesson first—people copy actions faster than they process bullet points.

 **Trench time trumps throne time.** Scrub the hoses, dig the ditches, and your team will charge the hill with you—no megaphone required.

 **Celebrate like confetti is free.** Spotlight their wins louder than your own and momentum snowballs without a payroll line item.

 **FAIL = First Attempt In Learning.** Give room for faceplants; coach the comeback, not the cringe.

 **Influence starts in the Dairy Queen booth.** Lead at home with presence and respect—if family won't follow, why should anyone else?

 **Run every idea through the backpack test.** Are you pulling a rock out of their pack or shoving one in? Choose wisely; trust is heavy cargo.

Leadership in the middle: where "ROI" meets 'Wrench'.

Chapter 10 | When It's Lonely in the Middle

Leading When You are Caught Between Two Worlds

Sometimes being a leader flat-out sucks. And not in the spoiled, oh-no-my-private-jet-was-delayed way, but the way that grinds on your soul. I'm talking about the weight no one sees and decisions no one understands—the pressure of knowing you're responsible for your own work and everyone else's. And somehow, you're supposed to keep everything running smoothly like a freshly tuned engine, even when every gasket leaks.

Most people don't see that side of leadership. They think it's about power, pay raises, and calling the shots. But here's the truth. No where is the pressure to lead greater than being in the middle position. It is the loneliest place in leadership.

You're not just one of the crew anymore. And you're not the top dog, either. You're smack in the middle, holding it all together. Let me tell you a true story to make my point. My dad worked at the same shop for over forty-five years, and my brother has been employed there for almost twenty-five years. They worked together for over two decades, side by side, turning wrenches, rebuilding engines and generators, and carrying the quiet pride you don't see much anymore.

My dad was an engine guy. My brother is the generator expert. Both are insanely good at what they do. But here's the deal. Neither one of them wanted leadership positions. They were capable enough, but they knew who they were. They didn't want to mess with office politics or sit in meetings about meetings. They wanted to work with their hands, fix things, and go home. And I respect the heck out of that.

At family gatherings, they'd talk shop. I mean *deep* shop talk. We all knew who Randy was, even though we had never met the guy, because his name came up *every* time. They'd go off about new policies or decisions from upper management that made their jobs harder. I'd sit right beside them, griping like the third musketeer. Back then, I wasn't leading anything. I was working and throwing my own stories into the conversation.

But that changed when I started my business.

I don't say much in those conversations anymore. I just listen, because now, I see both sides. I *am* the guy making hard decisions. I *am* the guy trying to make things work with limited info and a hundred moving parts.

About a year later, the leadership team at the shop where my dad and brother worked invited me to do some training. I walked in, and guess what? Their bosses complained about employees not listening, understanding, or seeing the big picture. I just sat there, torn, because I loved the guys on the shop floor. But I understood the folks at the table, too. That's leadership isolation in a nutshell. You see both sides and don't fully belong to either one.

The Loneliest Guy in the Room

Eventually, I asked them, "Have you talked to your team about this? Asked them for their ideas?" Silence.

Then, weeks later, at another family dinner, my dad looked up from his plate and said, "Guess what happened? Jeremiah came up to us in the breakroom and asked what we thought. He didn't correct us or push back. He listened. And when he walked off, we all felt like we'd been heard for the first time in a long time."

That moment mattered. And it proved something: Isolation shrinks when communication grows.

Later on, at another meal, they started griping again. (I love them, but it's a tradition.) This time, I pushed back. "Have you thought about why leadership made that change? Maybe they're trying to help the whole company." They both paused and did that confused-dog head tilt. Yeah, exactly that. Then my dad said, "Danny, I haven't really thought about it like that. I still don't like it, but yeah, I can see it now."

Boom. Perspective.

Here's what most people don't realize about leadership isolation: It means being professionally isolated. No one shares the weight. You're part of the team, but the hard calls are yours alone.

You can be in a crowded room, standing in front of your whole crew, or sitting at a conference table with six other decision-makers and still feel like the loneliest person in the building. Everyone's talking. Ideas are flying. And you're sitting there with a smile on your face and a storm in your chest. You're thinking about the next move, hire, and decision that will tick somebody off because no matter what you choose, someone won't like it. And guess who's still going to be responsible for the outcome?

Yep. You.

Regardless of how many people surround you, what matters is that they understand you. And sometimes, the hard truth is, no one really does. You might have ten people you could call, but most just don't get it.

You start to open up about the stress, and what do you hear? "Well, that's what you signed up for." Or the classic: "Must be nice being the boss!" And you're sitting there thinking: *Are you serious right now? Do you think I like carrying all this? Do you think this is fun?*

They don't feel the burden like you do. They don't lie awake at 2 a.m. running mental spreadsheets on payroll. They don't look a good employee in the eye and say, "We have to let you go," even though it kills you. They don't sit in the office staring at the wall after everyone's gone home, wondering if you did the right thing, or if you're screwing it all up one mistake at a time.

It's not just about being misunderstood. It's about being responsible for stuff no one else even knows is going on. It's making calls to protect people who will never know they were at risk. It's paying for things behind the scenes that your team doesn't even realize exist. It's thinking six months ahead while they're still questioning this week's schedule.

Leadership is like juggling flaming chainsaws while people critique your form, complain about the heat, and suggest you should *just relax*. You're holding up the roof, and everyone's arguing about the color of the shingles.

And then comes the part that no one warns you about: Sometimes, the *very people you're sacrificing for*, the ones you stay up late for, pray for, bleed for, are the ones who question your heart the most. You make a tough call to protect the team or the company, and someone accuses you of being selfish. Set a boundary needed for everyone's good, and they call you controlling. You say *not yet* or *no* because you see the whole field, and they accuse you of holding them back.

That'll mess with your head if you let it. You'll question your motives. You'll shrink back just to keep peace. Or worse, you'll start leading like a people-pleaser instead of the God-called leader He's shaping you to be. Listen, this isn't pity-party territory. This is just the truth. Leadership is lonely, especially in the middle.

You're neither the entry-level guy nor the CEO. You're stuck between the boots on the ground and the suits in the office. You're translating in both directions, hoping to keep the machine moving without someone throwing a wrench in it.

And yet, this is precisely where God does His best work. He's there when the noise fades, and it's just you and Him in the quiet of your truck cab, office, or living room after everyone else is asleep. He sees you. He knows. And He's not overwhelmed by the weight you're carrying.

The middle may be the loneliest place on Earth, but it's also where God meets leaders, and we hear him say something like this: "You're not alone. I put you here on purpose. Let's lead together."

Why It Feels So Lonely

When we get the call to be a leader, sometimes we expect things to go smoothly. I mean, come on, God called me into this role, right? Isn't that supposed to come with some divine favor, a few angels singing backup, maybe even a personal assistant who brings me coffee and shuts down stupid ideas with a holy head shake? But then life hits, and you realize real leadership isn't just about titles or being blessed. It's about *serving people,* many of whom are unprepared, ungrateful, uncommitted, or unaware of what it takes to get things done. Let me give you a prime example.

The other day, I met with a group of great people. What made them great is that this wasn't a bash-fest. The person who organized it is a wonderful human with a heart for ministry. She can lead when she's dialed in. But that day? She wasn't prepared, and I had little extra time to waste. Between business, travel, ministry, and, most importantly, being a present husband and dad, I guard my time like it's a limited-edition John Deere.

People are asking me to fly across the country to speak, and I've got a teenage daughter who needs me to teach her how to drive without crashing my truck. (If you've never taught a teenager to drive, buckle up. It'll make you a prayer warrior overnight.) Anyway, back to the meeting.

We got going, and you could feel it. Nobody wanted to speak up. I've been in enough of these volunteer-type meetings to know the vibe. Everyone's afraid that if they open their mouth, they'll get *voluntold* to do something they don't want to do. So, it

stalls. The leader's trying, but the wheels aren't turning.

So, after about fifteen minutes of silence and side glances, I decided to jump in and get things moving. I asked questions, helped bring some structure, and tried to nudge things forward without taking over. I was careful not to sign up for too much because I don't believe in saying *yes* to something I can't deliver on. I'd rather do one thing well than half-bake five things and let everyone down.

We ended the meeting about an hour and fifteen in. I agreed to speak to the youth at the event and help wrap things up with a message. I also volunteered to make a poster and a script that churches could use to help invite people. While folks were still arguing over what to cook for lunch, I was already sketching the agenda and creating a mock-up of the flier. I didn't volunteer to cook. I can handle dinner at home, but I'm not out here feeding two hundred people like I'm Gordon Ramsay. I know my lane.

That night, I knocked out the deliverables I said I'd handle. Posters—done. Agenda—done. I sent it all out, feeling good we were finally gaining momentum.

And then the feedback started. "We need to change this photo." "Can we use a different font?" "This color won't print well at my church." "We need a black-and-white version for churches without color printers." *What century are we in?*

Now here's where the loneliness hits. Nobody else offered to create anything. Nobody had a plan or graphics ready, but once I put in the work, they had opinions. Suddenly, everyone was a design expert with zero design effort. And I'll be honest, my flesh wanted to fire off a spicy email. "Oh, you don't like it? That's cool. Show me what you've created so far. Oh, wait, you didn't volunteer for anything. Got it." But I didn't. I sat on it. Said nothing.

And you know what happened? The next day, one person replied, "Dan, thanks for creating these. I'm going to start sharing them today." And just like that, everybody flipped. "These are awesome!" "Love this!" "Thanks so much!" Classic.

Here's the takeaway: When you step into any leadership role, people will complain, nitpick, question your motives, and try to make you feel like what you did wasn't enough.

Whether you're building a company, running a youth event, leading a ministry team, or just putting together a dang flier, you'll feel lonely. You'll feel misunderstood, second-guessed, and underappreciated. You'll wonder if you should have just stayed quiet and let the meeting stay stuck. You'll question whether your effort was worth it. When that happens, leadership gets *real* because that's the moment you choose:

- Do I get bitter or better?
- Do I clap back or stay steady?
- Do I quit because it's hard, or dig in because it matters?

It's lonely not because you're failing but because most people aren't wired to lead. They're wired to follow. And that's okay. But it means when you're the one out front, *you will feel the wind first.* You must learn to be confident in your calling, even when the crowd is silent or critical.

Even if *they* never say thank you, see what you carried, and pick apart the posters, *God* saw it. God called you to it. And He's the one who'll reward your faithfulness when no one else does.

It feels so lonely sometimes. Not because you're doing it wrong, but because you're doing it right.

Flip the Script: This Isn't a Curse, It's a Calling

Let's get one thing straight. You're not leading in the middle because you're weak or were the last one standing when everyone else ran. You're not forgotten. You're not being punished. And you're not cursed. You're called.

You're in this chaotic middle ground between doing and deciding, and God built you for it. He built you to carry what others can't, see what others don't, and hold steady while everything else is shaking.

Leadership doesn't always feel like a blessing. Oftentimes, it feels like a burden, and it should. Leadership is heavy. It's costly. And it's uncomfortable because it's refining. Anytime you do heavy lifting, you get stronger. Let's be real, this leadership life isn't what most people think it is.

People see the trappings of position, title, influence, followers, and the corner office, but they don't know about the battle behind the scenes:

- The hours you pray over decisions you can't afford to get wrong
- The pressure of knowing one bad call could ripple out and hurt good people
- The isolation when you're the only one in the room who sees the bigger picture

You get home at night, and your brain won't shut off. You're replaying conversations, recalculating budgets, and rehearsing tomorrow's meeting in your head while you're trying to enjoy dinner with your family. And maybe no one says it, but deep down, you're wondering, *Is this what I signed up for?* Let me answer that.

Yes. It is. But it's not a curse. It's a *calling*. Everything changes when you start viewing the pressure, silence, and waiting as your *assignment*. You stop asking, "Why is this happening to me?" and start asking, "What is God doing through me in this?" That shift is everything.

Let's be honest for a second. We all want leadership

to look like the highlight reel. We want the David-on-the-throne moments, the Moses-parting-the-Red-Sea moments, and the Joseph-ruling-Egypt moments. But we don't talk enough about the process to get them there. God doesn't develop leaders in spotlights. He develops them in the shadows.

- In the yard at 5 a.m. when it's ten degrees, and you're the only one checking tire tread depth

- In the back office when you're sorting through driver files that look like a toddler got ahold of a filing cabinet
- On job sites where the radios are loud, trucks are louder, and you're trying to keep everyone safe and legal
- In the late nights second-guessing a high-risk decision made with limited info
- In the moments you're sweating in a safety vest instead of giving a speech because you know cutting corners could get someone hurt

Leadership is forged while cleaning up someone else's mess, stepping in after the manager ghosted, the driver quit, the paperwork's missing, and the inspector's pulling up. It's shaped in shops and steel-toed boots. Leadership is grown in the people patching processes together with duct tape and prayer, wondering if anyone even sees the work you're putting in. That's where God develops the leaders He plans to use.

Not in comfort. Not with applause, but in the uncomfortable and invisible places most people avoid where it's just you, the grind, and God. And just when you think you're the only one who's ever had to lead through chaos with a clipboard in one hand and a compliance manual in the other, boom, the Bible rolls up like, *hold my scroll.* That's precisely where we find some of the greatest leaders, in scripture.

Joseph

This guy didn't just have a dream. He had a God-given vision. A calling so clear he believed it with his whole heart. So, he shared it with his brothers. And how'd that go? They sold him into slavery! His life spiraled. One thing after another. Just like that, he went from being the favorite son to a foreign servant. One moment he's managing Potiphar's house; the next, he's falsely accused and imprisoned.

There he stayed, forgotten and abandoned. Years went by, and the people he helped forgot him. If that was me, I might have started questioning the dream. "Hey God, was that vision real?" "Did I miss something?" "Why am I still in this pit?"

But Joseph didn't fold, lash out, post a bitter comment on social media about his toxic work culture, or sit in the corner of his cell complaining about how unfair life was. He faithfully served, *using his gift in the shadows.* He interpreted dreams in the dark when nobody noticed. God was preparing and training him to rescue a nation. That's patience and purpose under pressure.

David

David was a teenager when the prophet Samuel anointed him king. The prophet poured oil on his head and said, "You're the guy." (Obviously, I'm paraphrasing here.)

And what happened next?" Did he march into the palace and take his place? Nope. He went back to the sheep. And when the next opportunity came, it wasn't a throne, it was a giant named Goliath. David fought him, won, became a war hero, and then ended up on the run. Saul, the current king, was so threatened by David that he tried to kill him.

David spent years running for his life, hiding in caves, sleeping in forests, and living like a fugitive. He led a ragtag group of rejects and misfits, basically a band of guys with nothing left to lose. And in the middle of all that, he worshipped, wrote psalms, and *refused to kill Saul,* even when he had the perfect opportunity—twice.

David understood something that's easy to forget: You don't get to skip the process when you're called to carry God's promise. You don't get the crown without the cave.

God was using those cave years to shape him, not just into a king with a crown, but a man after God's own heart. David learned to lead people and follow God in his life's worst, loneliest, most dangerous season. The pressure, not the palace or the praise, made David God's guy.

Moses

Now, this dude had everything. He was raised in Pharaoh's palace, enjoyed the riches and respect reserved for royalty, and benefited from a royal education. He had the best life Egypt could offer, and he blew it.

One act of misplaced passion, trying to defend a Hebrew brother, and he runs for his life into the desert. His status changed instantly from prince to fugitive, and his residence from palace to pasture.

He didn't bounce back quickly. He spent forty years out there. That's four decades of dirt, heat, and sheep. Gone was the fame, glory, and stage. All he had now was time. Lots of it. God used that time to strip away Moses's pride, unlearn what Egypt taught him, and learn how to shepherd people by shepherding animals.

And when the moment finally came, when God lit a bush on fire and called Moses into his real purpose, you know what Moses said? "Not me. Send someone else." He didn't even want it anymore. He felt disqualified, too broken, slow, and forgotten. Done

But God saw something different. God saw a man who had been *humbled,* a man who knew how to depend on Him, capable of leading without relying on himself. The man who once relied on status had finally learned to rely on God.

Deborah

She didn't come from a palace or flee to a pasture. She led right where she was planted. Deborah was a prophet, a judge, and a fearless leader in a time when Israel was a mess. The men were afraid, the people were oppressed, and no one wanted to step up. But Deborah did.

She sat under a palm tree and settled disputes like a boss. She spoke for God, led with clarity, and when it came time to go to battle, she didn't flinch. The army commander, Barak, wouldn't even go to war without her. That's how much weight her influence carried.

She didn't lead loud, but she led strong. No crown, no title parade, no social media fanfare. Just grit, wisdom, and obedience. That's what real leadership looks like.

*****

So yeah, when you feel stuck in the middle, overlooked, underappreciated, or just flat-out tired of waiting, you're in good company. You're standing where Joseph, David, Moses, and Deborah stood. Not one of them was cursed. They were called. And so are you.

God's not punishing you. He's preparing you. He's not ignoring you, He's shaping you. He's not delaying you, He's developing you.

That frustration you feel? That's God stretching your capacity. That silence from others? That's God tuning your ears to hear His voice. That loneliness? That's not a red flag, it's a refining fire.

Leaders God trusts with the most are the ones who've been through the cave, the wilderness, and the prison, and still came out worshipping. So, flip the script. This isn't punishment. It's preparation. It's God saying, "If you can handle this season with humility and grit, I'll trust you with more."

So here's the challenge: Don't waste the middle. Don't complain your way through it. Don't coast. Don't check out. Don't tap out just because no one's clapping. Lean in.

What looks like a holding pattern might just be a launching sequence. While the world celebrates titles and trophies, heaven is watching to see what you do when only God is watching. To bring this home, let me tell you a story about a guy who thought he was a leader but was just a boss with a badge.

We'll call him Joe. That's not his real name, but if he reads this and thinks it's about him, well, maybe take the hint.

I was working DOT for a massive oil and gas company—4,800 vehicles, roughly 6,000 employees, and about 4,000 DOT drivers. We had yards, rigs, and job sites all across the country. And guess who they flew all over creation to keep it all DOT-compliant? This guy.

Now, when I say I traveled a lot, I don't mean a couple of comfy trips a quarter. I left on November 1, the day after trick-or-treating with my kids, and didn't return home until the Tuesday before Thanksgiving. Then, I flew back out the Sunday after Thanksgiving. That was my whole November. Gone. I spent more time with TSA (Transportation Security Administration) agents than with my wife and kids that month.

I wasn't out sightseeing and collecting hotel points like a corporate tourist. I was boots on the ground, in the shops by 6 a.m., working side by side with the drivers, helping HR, talking shop with operations, and eating every meal with someone in the field. If I wasn't in a meeting, I was riding in a work truck, visiting job sites, walking yards, or helping folks get files straight.

Then, I'd head back to the hotel, open my laptop, and work until 11 p.m., trying to catch up on everything I missed at the office. It was brutal. I didn't realize it then, but that season almost blew up my marriage. I'm not saying that for drama. It was real. I was trying to be a good provider but missing out on everything that mattered at home. It was hard on me, hard on Jenna, and hard on our four amazing kids.

Yet, even in that grind, something unexpected was happening. I was building relationships with division managers and ops supervisors, HR clerks, shop leads, field safety guys, and anyone who needed help. I wasn't networking. I was caring. I later realized I had been leading without a title or authority. I was leading by being consistent, helpful, and present.

Eventually, our DOT manager quit. I didn't apply for the job. They wanted it based in Houston, and I wasn't about to drag my whole family to Houston just to chase a title I didn't need. One of my coworkers filled the role temporarily and then—enter Joe.

Joe was a retired state cop with the Texas Department of Public Safety. He was the guy who probably wrote people tickets for driving too slow *and* too fast on the same road. He walked in like he owned the company, puffed out like he'd just been promoted to General Patton of DOT.

At first, I didn't dislike him, but I didn't trust him. He didn't know the people. He didn't build relationships. He carried his authority like a sledgehammer. And apparently, he didn't like me.

Once settled, he started visiting all the same sites I'd been pouring into for years. Instead of asking what was working, he started running his mouth. Telling people I was wasting company money, wasn't getting anything done, and they needed to stop listening to Dan.

Here's the twist: It didn't work. HR, ops, and safety teams pushed back. They said, "Hold on. Dan's helped us. Dan shows up. Dan answers when we call. You're not going to talk about him like that."

I hadn't built trust by being the loudest voice. I built trust by listening, helping, staying late, and answering dumb questions respectfully and patiently. I built it by treating the HR assistant and the ops manager with the same level of importance.

Joe didn't understand that. He thought leadership was a position. But I knew leadership is presence, integrity, and, service.

Now, fast-forward.

I'm finally on a real vacation; fishing, breathing, and recovering with my family for three weeks in Canada. It was the first time I'd taken a break like that in years. Then the phone rings.

It's Tim, the VP of Safety, Joe's boss, and mine.

Now, I could have let it go to voicemail. But being the guy I am, standing next to a lake in a different country and on vacation, I answered it.

Tim starts laying out what's going on. Joe had kicked off a full-on campaign to get me fired. He'd made accusations, saying I was misusing travel, not getting results, and burdening the company. Tim wasn't just checking in. He was investigating.

He tried to fire me. The evidence boomeranged.

I could have panicked and gotten defensive. But I stayed calm. I said, "Tim, you don't have to believe me. You don't even have to call the people I suggest. Call *anybody* I've worked with at any location. Ask them if I've helped. Ask them if I've made a difference. Ask them if they trust me." Then I prayed. Hard.

Let me be honest with you. As I write this right now, I still get choked up thinking about it. That season nearly broke me. It wore me down and tested every ounce of faith I had. I thought I was done, and I'd come back from vacation to a pink slip. But I didn't.

Instead, Tim called and offered me the DOT manager position. He said, "You'll have to move to Houston if you want it." I thanked him and turned it down. By then, I had learned something Joe hadn't: You don't need a title or corner office to lead. You just need to care more about people than your position. Joe tried to bury me, but God used it to validate me. Not because I was perfect but because I was faithful. I showed up when it was hard and lonely. That's what leadership looks like. And yeah, it can be *really* lonely.

Stay steady, trust God in the dark, show up, and serve people. You'll look back and realize you were leading long before they gave you the title. God's not calling the comfortable, He's calling the faithful. Keep walking in that middle you're stuck in. It'll become the foundation of your influence because the middle is where the willing become the warriors.

Think Differently: Use Isolation as Innovation Fuel

Let's talk about isolation for a minute. This goes beyond sitting in a meeting pretending to take notes while you daydream about what's for dinner. Your phone stops ringing, invites stop coming, and your inbox gets quieter. Your thoughts and a stack of work are your only company, except for God if you let Him in.

Most people panic when that season hits. They think they've been forgotten—lost their place. But let me challenge that idea. What if that lonely season isn't punishment? What if it's permission to think, breathe, and create?

When people, noise, and opinions constantly surround you, it's hard to hear what matters. The loudest voices aren't necessarily the wisest ones. And when you're in a leadership role, everyone's got ideas until it's time to take responsibility for them.

But when it gets quiet, there's room for the good stuff to bubble up. I've had some of my best ideas when surrounded by silence. Lonely hotel rooms, 4:30 a.m. flights, and sitting in a pickup waiting for an inspector to show up are where the gears start turning. That's when I can hear God speaking. That's when I start asking questions again.

- What are we building?
- Why does it matter?
- What's the real problem, and what would it look like to solve it?

Loneliness can be a curse or a canvas. When the noise dies down, and the meetings stop stacking up, you're finally free to hear what God's been whispering all along.

During one of those seasons when I felt like nobody really needed me, and those feelings sneak in whether you're a DOT manager, dad, business owner, or all three, I had to start doing something with the space I was in. I started going on prayer walks with God. With no plan or agenda. I'd talk a little and listen a lot. Sometimes, I'd walk and be quiet. Something about that rhythm cleared my head like nothing else could.

I started dumping my thoughts into journals. Forget the stereotypical, elegant, poetic journaling. These were straight-up brain dumps. Like, "Today was hard. I feel tired. But I had this one idea ...." It wasn't pretty, but it got things out of my head and into a place where I could do something with them.

Then, I got a whiteboard for my office and started scribbling ideas, thoughts, notes, and systems—anything that popped into my head. At first, it looked like a toddler's art project. But over time, some of those scribbles became trainings, frameworks, and strategies that now help companies nationwide.

Here's the point. Most people try to cope with loneliness by using distractions like scrolling mindlessly through social media and filling their days with busyness. But what if you didn't just cope with it? What if you saw silence as a sacred space and a chance to build something lasting without the pressure of everyone watching? That's the beauty of the middle. You're free to create, innovate, fail a little, and fix what didn't work in a way nearly impossible when the lights are on and the pressure is high.

And maybe, most importantly, you're free to hear God. Instead of speaking to us through a sign in the sky or a prophetic word in front of a crowd, God nudges us in new directions. We get ideas we know aren't ours and the conviction to follow through. Nothing compares to the peace we experience with God's guidance when everything else says you should be panicking.

If you're in that space right now, don't waste it. It feels like everyone else is building, growing, and shining while you're stagnant. Get going. Walk, write, and scribble on that whiteboard like your breakthrough depends on it because it might. And when your daughter comes downstairs and draws a picture on that whiteboard, do not erase it. I don't care if it's a crooked heart with stick figures or a cow with five legs;

leave it there. I promise you, on the days life feels heavy, and ideas aren't flowing, that doodle will remind you why you're still fighting.

The quiet season isn't a setback. It's a setup for what's next. And if you treat this time right, you'll come out with ideas, clarity, direction, and something solid that God planted in the middle of what felt like nothing. When no one else is calling and the world's not watching, that's your chance to build something no one can take from you.

And that, my friend, is innovation fuel. Use it.

Don't Lead Alone. Build Godly Support Systems

You weren't built to lead alone. Leadership is heavy enough without trying to carry it with one arm tied behind your back. But let's be honest. Most of us have tried it. We think asking for help makes us look weak, or worse like we don't have it all together.

So, we put our heads down and keep pushing, thinking, "I'll reach out when things slow down," or "I don't want to bother anybody." Next thing you know, it's been three months. You're emotionally drained, spiritually dry, and have been eating gas station burritos like they're part of your self-care routine.

There's a difference between strength and stubbornness. I've learned the hard way that you can't pour from an empty cup. You can't lead well if you're spiritually, mentally, or emotionally running on fumes. There aren't bonus points in heaven for burning out. You don't become a better husband, father, or business owner by white-knuckling through the storm. That's not strength. That's pride with a nice haircut.

God designed us to live and lead in real community, not just small talk after church. That means having people in your life who know your calling and weaknesses and aren't afraid to speak into both.

You need a circle of builders, not just cheerleaders. The cheerleaders are great. They'll clap for your wins, like your social media updates, and toss a "You got this!" your way occasionally. But, when the weight is too heavy, and you're unsure how to pray anymore, you need builders. You need burden-sharers.

These people will look you in the eye, remind you who you are, and point you back to the One who called you. These truth-tellers support you when your world is falling apart, and all you do is lie in bed wondering if you're still cut out for this. I've seen it play out over and over again. Your circle determines your ceiling. That's more than a catchy quote, that's real life.

To grow as a leader, surround yourself with people who don't flinch when it's time to challenge you. Do you

want to stay grounded in your faith while running full speed in your calling? Walk with people who will anchor you when the wind picks up. If you look around and realize you don't have people like that in your life, it's time to build that circle intentionally.

Since I started growing, I've told my kids this: If you want to be a millionaire, hang out with five millionaires. People like that will challenge, stretch, and push you to grow. On the flip side, if you hang around five potheads, guess what? There's a good chance you will be the sixth. Who you surround yourself with will raise or lower your standards. It's one of the most important leadership lessons you'll ever learn, and sadly, one of the most ignored.

So, how do you start? Find mentors. Look for people more advanced than you in life, faith, and business who've been through the fire and didn't come out bitter. You want people who walk peacefully because they've walked with God through things you haven't faced yet. Don't be distracted by flashiness or loudness. Focus on who has been consistent, who shows up when it's inconvenient, listens more than talks, and stands still when life gets crazy.

Find spiritual advisers, pastors, elders, or trusted godly people, who aren't impressed by your business card. Ask them to pray for and with you. Seek people who quietly and powerfully walk with God and will call you out if they see pride sneaking in or your spirit growing cold.

And don't forget your trusted peers, friends walking the same road and in the fight with you. These are the guys and gals raising families, building businesses, and trying to live for Jesus in a world that makes that harder every day. You need people who understand your life and aren't afraid to laugh, cry, or challenge you in the same five-minute conversation.

We tend to think, "Well, if they cared, they'd reach out." Maybe. Or maybe they're as isolated and overwhelmed as you are. Stop waiting for someone to check on you. You've got a phone. Use it. Reach out with a simple, "Hey bud, can we grab lunch?" or "Got a minute to chat?" That's how bridges are built. Don't wait until you're drowning. Build those relationships when the water is calm so they're strong when the storm hits.

I'll be honest with you. Some of the toughest moments in my leadership journey could have wrecked me if I hadn't had the right people around me. In addition to business coaches and networking connections, I had people who prayed for me when I didn't have the words. They reminded me who I was when I forgot and spoke life when I was buried in pressure and expectation. Those conversations didn't come from a leadership seminar. They came from an intentional connection.

If you're leading right now and feel isolated, tired, and running on empty, ask yourself: Who's in my circle? Who knows what I'm walking through? Who would notice if I didn't show up tomorrow? If that's a short list, it's time to make some calls.

No matter how driven, tough, or capable you are, God didn't design you to carry it alone. He gave you people. And He gave them *you*. The only question is whether you'll build those bridges before the weight gets too heavy. Leadership is lonely enough already. Don't make it lonelier by walking it alone.

The truth is that the enemy loves isolated leaders. He loves it when we think no one cares or understands. That's how lies grow, and burnout happens. That's how great leaders go silent and stop showing up where they're needed most.

So, fight back. Build your circle. Reach out first. Let God surround you with the people who won't just cheer you on, but carry the weight with you when the middle gets heavy.

Trust me, it will get heavy. But when it does, you'll have a circle of builders, not just fans. Instead of watching you struggle, they will support you. That's how leaders finish well.

Before building a circle, let's get something straight: not everyone deserves a seat at your table. Leadership is already hard enough without surrounding yourself with people who bring the emotional equivalent of a wet blanket to every conversation. Let me simplify this: You need people who build you up, not tear you down. Your support system should include people who:

- Speak the truth even when it's uncomfortable
- Encourage your calling, not just your comfort
- Pray for you when you're not in the room
- Show up when it matters, not just when it's easy

Let me be crystal clear about who should not be in your support system: negative people. Period. These people masquerade as realists. "I'm just being honest," is code for doubt, fear, and a nasty flavor of cynicism that disguises itself as wisdom.

Here's a story to help you understand what I'm talking about. I had a friend I'd known for a long time. We'd been through a lot. But he had to play devil's advocate whenever I talked about the business I was building. *Every time.* It didn't matter if we had a significant win or were doing something truly impactful; he'd find a way to poke holes in it. And after a while, I'd had enough.

So, one day, I told him, "Look, I don't need a devil's advocate. I'm already fighting battles you don't even know about. And if you can't speak life into this thing, we probably don't need to talk about it anymore." I meant it, and it rocked him. I don't think

he knew what to do with that feedback. It took him almost two years to come around. But you know what he told me when he did?

He said, "Dan, you were totally right. I didn't realize how negative I sounded. I hate devil's advocacy now. I didn't know how poisonous my presence was for people. You telling me that changed my life."

You can't afford to have people in your life who drag the whole environment down every time they open their mouths. My goal was to protect my atmosphere. In the process, I accomplished that goal and did my friend a favor, too. He changed because of my influence.

Look for people whose motivation comes from believing in you and not bitterness. There's a difference between challenging you to grow and constantly poking holes in everything God's trying to build through you. One brings life. The other drains it. If someone always brings doubt to the conversation, that's not discernment. That's discouragement disguised as maturity.

Here's the rule: Stay positive or get out. That might sound harsh, but what's harsher is carrying the weight of leadership while dragging a group of people who secretly hope you fail, just to feel validated and superior in comparison.

You don't need a fan club. You need people of faith and grit and people who will fight for your purpose with you. You need people who celebrate your wins and help you grow through your failures. You grow when your people look you in the eye and say, "You're better than this," and "God's not done with you yet."

Take inventory. Who's in your corner? If someone in your circle drains your energy, questions your purpose, or makes you feel like you're never doing enough, create distance. You're not being unkind. You're being a good steward of the assignment God gave you. You've got too much at stake to let toxic voices talk you out of the vision.

So, build wisely. Surround yourself with believers, not doubters. Builders, not critics. Encouragers, not energy vampires. Leadership is lonely enough without dragging around people who aren't called to go where you're going.

That's not pride. That's protection.

Staying Encouraged When You're Tired, Burned Out, or Done

Sometimes, leadership wears you out. We all feel tired at the end of the day, but this is different. I'm talking deep, soul-level exhaustion that doesn't disappear after a nap or a long weekend. Fatigue like this builds up from months, sometimes years of pressure, decisions, disappointments, and just trying to hold it all together while leading people, keeping faith, and putting food on the table.

If you've ever led anything for long, you've been there. You've had the moment where you're driving home with nothing but road noise, wondering, *how much longer can I keep this up?*

Here's what no one tells you: Encouragement isn't optional, it's fuel. And if you don't learn to encourage yourself, you'll run out of gas faster than you think. Sometimes, that encouragement comes from others like friends, family, team members, and the church community. But, if you've been in a leadership position, you know this: Sometimes, no one else shows up with the encouragement you need.

You've got to know how to speak life over yourself. You've got to remind yourself who you are, who God is, and what He's already done. One of the best ways I've learned to do that is by keeping a *God-did* list. It's exactly what it sounds like—a list of things God's already done in your life. The list includes the prayers He answered, the wins you've seen, the miracles you prayed for but didn't recognize when He came through and the moments He showed up when no one else did.

My list has everything from drivers who turned their lives around after one safety meeting to times we passed audits we shouldn't have to nights when Jenna looked at me and said, "I'm proud of you." I even wrote down the time one of my kids gave me a crooked little hug and said, "You're the best dad ever," right after a day I felt like the worst one on earth.

When you're tired, your memory gets fuzzy. You forget the faithfulness and what God's already done. But the *God-did* list will remind you, if He did it before, He'll do it again.

Encouragement comes from spiritual reminders and being human, unplugging, stepping away from the noise, and finding a way to reconnect to your purpose again. That brings me to a little story.

My family and I once were in San Diego at a beach house. We were right on Mission Beach. Our feet immediately sank into the sand when we stepped out the front door. There was nothing between us and the ocean except the boardwalk. Big windows opened up to the breeze, ocean views, and the sound of waves. It was one of those perfect family vacations—just my wife, our four kids, and the rhythm of waves, sun, and rest.

I love San Diego. I always have. The military bases, which I deeply respect, the farmers' markets, especially the one in Ocean Beach, and that warm, breezy weather make it one of my favorite places on earth. Every time we go, we plan the trip to coincide with a market day so we can get fresh food at the start of the week. It's become a Greer family tradition.

Here we are on this fantastic vacation. Our days were filled with wetsuits, boogie boarding, bike rides, skateboarding, family meals, and laughter. I'd take breaks and open my laptop to knock out some work occasionally—because, well, I love what I do. Somewhere midweek, Jenna looks at me and says, "You haven't stopped working this whole trip."

Now, I love that woman more than words can say, and this was before she read Elena Cardone's *Build an Empire*, so she didn't get it at the time, but she meant it with love. She was concerned. She wanted me to rest. What she didn't realize was, I *was* resting.

Working *on* the business instead of *in* the business is rest. That's when my soul lights up, and I reset. I get space to dream, refine, think, and build without pressure and out of joy. I think a lot of leaders are wired like that. We all recharge differently. While some folks go on vacation to escape their work lives, people like me go to reimagine it, to reconnect to the *why* behind the work.

I wasn't ignoring my family. I played. I boogie-boarded and rode bikes. And I took time to write, plan, and work on myself and the business. That's what filled me up. Now Jenna gets it. When she plans trips, she looks for ways to give me *work joy space*. She knows I can't go seven days off the grid without starting to twitch. And she loves me enough to plan for that.

The truth is that leadership burnout doesn't always result from too much work. Sometimes, it's the result of too little purpose. When all you do is grind and never create, you lose your soul in the process.

You need to find what fills your cup. And what fills your cup might not be rest to other people. That's okay. Whether it's a tractor ride, a walk through the woods, a sunrise with a strong cup of coffee, or scribbling on a whiteboard while your daughter draws a smiley face in the corner, don't underestimate those moments. They're more than breaks. They're lifelines.

The hard truth is that you're still someone's example, even on your worst day. That's pressure and purpose. You're showing up when it's hard, preaching louder than you think, staying faithful when empty, and shaping the people who look up to you. When you encourage yourself instead of waiting for someone else to do it, that's leadership at its best.

So yeah, you'll have tiring days. You'll have days you want to walk away. But before you do, take a breath. Make your *God-did* list. Open the Word. Go for a drive. Sit in silence. Laugh with your family. Work on what excites you. And remember, you're not done.

God's still working. He hasn't brought you this far to let you burn out. You've got what it takes. And if you stay in the fight, He'll ensure you finish well.

Leading in the Middle with Grit and Grace

There's a weird stage in leadership development that nobody trains you for. It's not the beginning when you're clueless, but everyone's nice to you because they know you're new. And it's not the top where you've got the title and the parking spot with your name on it. It's the middle—that space where people expect you to lead, solve problems, and have answers, but they don't give you authority, support, or half the information you need to succeed. It's like trying to build IKEA furniture with no instructions. Someone is yelling, "You're doing it wrong," and knows you're missing some bolts and screws. Welcome to the middle.

Isaiah, one of my previous bosses, taught me a valuable lesson. I wanted to make big changes fast. Frustration set in, and that's when Isaiah pulled me aside. He said, "Dan, this DOT thing you're doing … you're like the ship's rudder." At first, I thought, "All right, nautical metaphors, here we go." But then he hit me with this.

He said, "If you try to turn a giant ship too fast in the middle of the waves and wind, you will capsize. Sure, we could throw down the anchor and yank this boat around as fast as we want to—but we're going to lose half the cargo, knock people overboard, and maybe sink the thing altogether."

Then he looked me dead in the eye and said, "But if you act like the rudder, if you apply constant, steady pressure in the right direction, that ship will turn. It won't be fast or dramatic. But it will be effective. And when it finally turns, it will be magnificent." And he wasn't done.

He said, "Dan, you already know this won't be easy. Do you want to be the guy who makes the change? It's going to take time. You will have to fight through frustration. You'll have to put things you'd rather not deal with first. But if you want to lead well, you've got to be the rudder. You've got to keep steady. That's the only way this thing turns."

At the time, I didn't realize how biblical that was. But it's straight out of James.

OR TAKE SHIPS AS AN EXAMPLE. ALTHOUGH THEY ARE SO LARGE AND ARE DRIVEN BY STRONG WINDS, THEY ARE STEERED BY A VERY SMALL RUDDER WHEREVER THE PILOT WANTS TO GO.

—JAMES 3:4

The rudder is the smallest part of the ship, but it, not the sail, the hull, or the guy in the crow's nest, determines the whole direction. Here's what hit me later: The rudder doesn't get attention or glory, but it gets the job done.

Leading in the middle is functioning like the rudder. You apply consistent pressure. You keep your integrity when others start cutting corners. You stay in your lane when the wind shifts and people panic. And yeah, sometimes a few fish smack into you along the way. The current is tough, and the resistance is real. But you hold your direction because you know that what you're turning is worth it. That's the picture of leadership people rarely see.

From the outside, it looks like you're going about your day. But inside, you're working overtime to hold steady, stay kind, speak the truth, and lead well. That's where grit and grace come in. That's where authentic leadership is forged. It's the tension between grit and grace. The space demands you carry the weight of what must happen, even when you're unsure if you're allowed to move the pieces. You're translating the boss's vision while defusing the team's frustration and still smiling like you slept more than four hours last night. (You didn't. We know.)

Leading in the middle means being stuck between what needs to be done and what people are willing to do. You see the fire before anyone smells the smoke. You've got a fire extinguisher in hand, and someone's asking if they can take their break early. You're trying to keep the peace, move the mission forward, and ensure nobody lights the metaphorical dumpster on fire.

It takes grit. It's not the kind you find in motivational Instagram posts next to a picture of a wolf in a blizzard. I'm talking about the grit that gets up early, stays late, and keeps leading when nobody's applauding. It takes grit to deal with the fifteenth excuse of the day without flipping a table or carrying someone else's load without throwing it back in their face next week. Grit says, "I'm not doing this for recognition. I'm doing this because I was built for it, even if I do have a little cry in the truck after work."

But grit, by itself, will make you mean. That's where grace comes in. Grace keeps you from becoming a grumpy tyrant with a clipboard and a chip on your shoulder. It reminds you that the person who dropped the ball might just be going through something. Grace says, "Yes, I'm going to hold you to the standard, but I'm not going to shame you in the process." Grace helps you lead humans, not just employees.

It's not soft. It's strength under control, like a bouncer at a church potluck, firm but kind. Grace gives you room to breathe and gives others room to grow. It helps you not to take yourself too seriously. Let's be honest; sometimes, we're one urgent meeting away from losing it, and grace is the only thing between us and a sarcastic meltdown.

So, how do you lead with grit and grace in the middle of the mess?

First, stop thinking you need a title to make a difference. Leadership is about more than being at the top of the organizational chart. It's about showing up like it matters even when it feels like it doesn't. I've seen guys without a title lead circles around people with fancy name tags and company trucks. You don't need a crown to carry weight.

Second, excellence isn't something you wait for. It's something you pursue. You don't get ready when you arrive, you arrive ready. Treat your current role like it's preparing you for the next one because it is. How you handle small stuff in the middle determines whether you'll ever be trusted with more.

Third, learn to lead up without brown-nosing your way through every meeting. No one respects the guy who agrees with everything the boss says just to stay on their good side. Real leadership is speaking the truth with respect. Offer solutions, not just complaints. Support the mission, even when you've got critiques about the methods. Be the person your boss knows will bring honest and loyal opinions to the table, preferably without a side of snark.

Remember to lead the people who do the work because drivers, field techs, and admin staff are the engine of any business. If your company were a truck, they're the transmission, axles, and motor oil holding the whole thing together. Honor them. See them. Know their names. Ask how their weekend went. Say, *thank you* more than you think you need to because you'll never lead well over the long haul if you forget to serve the people in the trenches with you.

Leading in the middle means living in the tension. It means holding the line without holding grudges, being consistent without becoming a control freak, and being willing to step up, speak up, and sometimes shut up when wisdom says now's not the time.

And yeah, it's exhausting sometimes. But if you're in the middle right now, feeling stuck between expectations and limitations, don't underestimate the impact you're making. The truth is, you're probably the glue holding the whole thing together.

And someday, when things finally click and people start asking, "How did this culture shift? How did we grow like this? How did this thing hold together when everything was falling apart?" they'll realize it was you.

It was you exercising your grit and grace centered with your faithfulness in the middle. And no, they may not throw you a party, but heaven's already clapping.

Final Thought: The Middle Is Where Legends Are Made

So here we are. This is the end of the chapter, but it's not the end of your story. This is the middle. And now, I hope you've realized it's not bad.

The middle is messy, quiet, and confusing. It's full of second-guessing, gut checks, and sleepless nights. It's where no one's clapping, but you show up anyway. And yet, it's the place where more than systems and strategies are built. The real stuff, your character, faith, resolve, and calling are also built.

I've been there. Heck, I lived there for longer than I thought I'd survive.

Isaiah, the boss who told me I was the rudder wasn't wrong. I followed his advice, kept steady under pressure, doing what I could with what I had—just that small force beneath the surface, trying to keep a 4,800-vehicle company from capsizing. And you know what? I did it. Quietly, steadily, and unseen, but effective.

Accepting the promotion to DOT manager would have meant uprooting my family and moving to Houston. As much as I would have enjoyed that job, I knew I couldn't sell out what mattered most. I watched a coworker take the position while I packed my bags and went home without promotion, recognition, or a clue about what God was about to do.

And that was the turn. The same God who let me walk away from that title was already laying the foundation for Eclipse DOT. I didn't see it at first. I knew compliance, safety, operations, and people, so I started helping a few companies here and there. I also knew how to *care*. Slowly, what began as a favor turned into a side hustle, which turned into a business and a mission.

Now, we've helped thousands of companies pass audits with flying colors and built training programs that make a difference. We've turned chaos into clarity, paperwork into protection, and confusion into confidence.

Eclipse DOT was born because God used the middle to get me ready. He used silence and frustration, as well as Joe, the boss who tried to get me fired.

If you'd told me back then that I'd one day be running a company where I could make a $100,000 mistake and survive, I would have laughed so hard I'd have spit out my gas station coffee. I've made multiple six-figure mistakes in the same year, and we're not just standing, we're growing.

When God prepares you in the middle, He's prepping you to survive the storm and preparing you to captain the ship. And sometimes, when you feel like He's gone silent, He's letting you build the foundation strong enough to carry the weight of what's next.

Listen. I get it. The middle can feel lonely. You'll wonder if anyone sees you, if it's worth it, or if anything will ever shift. I'm telling you right now: It will. Rediscover your circle. Pray harder than you've ever prayed before. And when it feels like you've got nothing left, keep moving forward. One step, conversation, and whiteboard doodle at a time.

- Even if you feel like the rudder, quiet, unseen, and doing all the work while someone else gets the credit
- Even if no one's clapping, except maybe that one sarcastic golf clap you give yourself in the mirror
- Even if your only audience is your own reflection and the God you're begging for a sign (*Anytime now, Lord. Burning bush? Talking donkey? I'll take anything with subtitles.*)

This is where legends are made. So, the next time you're in the quiet or the struggle, remember: God is great, all the time. And all the time, God is great.

This middle you're walking through is not the end. It might be overlooked in your biography, but it's the chapter of your life that forged the fire inside you. It's the beginning of your legacy. When the fruit shows up, the team is strong, and the purpose is clear, you'll look back at this moment with fresh eyes. The mess and misunderstandings of leading in the middle will make sense. You'll say with a grin, "That's where the legend began.

Key Takeaways from Chapter Ten

 **You're the bacon strip in the leadership BLT.** Top brass and shop-floor boots may not mingle, but everybody notices when the bacon's missing—stay crispy.

 **Invisible weights are still gains.** Nobody sees the 2 a.m. mental spreadsheets, but those reps build leadership muscle the gym can't touch.

 **Isolation ≠ exile—it's God's private workshop.** Quiet cabs and late-night offices are where He rewires your spark plugs for bigger hauls.

 **Perspective is a torque wrench.** Understand both the crew's gripe and the boss's budget, and suddenly the bolts quit stripping.

 **Conversation beats consternation.** One "Tell me what you're seeing," can turn breakroom mutiny into co-pilots on the mission.

 **Critics come with the cargo.** When the folks you bleed for question your motives, remember—Jesus fed 5,000 and still got side-eyed.

 **Middle seasons are forge seasons.** Joseph had prison, David had caves, Moses had sheep; you've got spreadsheets and driver files—same God, same refining fire.

 **Silence is R&D for calling.** Prayer walks + whiteboard scribbles = next-level strategy; doom-scrolling = brain fog thicker than Denver smog.

 **Build a pit crew, not a peanut gallery.** Truth-tellers tighten your lug nuts; devil's-advocate spectators can watch the race from the cheap seats.

 **Run your "God-Did" highlight reel.** Nothing kills doubt faster than replaying last season's miracles on the jumbotron.

 **Grit keeps the throttle down; grace keeps you from mowing people over.** Hammer the mission, hug the humans.

 **Legends are welded in the middle.** Hold steady, keep steering, and one day folks will say, "That quiet rudder turned the whole ship."

Chapter 11 | The Tension Between Grit and Grace

Welcome to the Tug-of-War.

It's time to discuss the challenge leaders face every day. They need to be *strong enough to stand and soft enough to stay.* You'll see what I mean.

Leadership isn't clean, easy, or cozy. It's more like treading water in freezing waves while someone's yelling at you to stay calm, breathe, and save the guy who's panicking next to you. Welcome to the tension between grit and grace.

If you've never watched the movie *The Guardian* with Kevin Costner playing Ben Randall and Ashton Kutcher as Jake Fischer, pencil it into your weekend plans. It's a leadership masterclass disguised as a rescue swimmer movie. Ben Randall is the legend. He's saved more lives in the water than anyone else. But after a career-ending injury, he's pulled from the ocean and sent to teach at the Coast Guard's Aviation Survival Technician A-School—the service's grueling rescue swimmer training program.

That's where he meets Jake, a young, talented, prideful recruit looking to break all of Ben's records. Ben is hard on him—ruthless, even. From Jake's view, the man hates him. But what appears to be cruelty is actually belief. Ben isn't trying to destroy him. He's trying to prepare him, because he knows the sea doesn't care about your records— it only responds to your readiness.

One of my favorite scenes is a moment early in training. A massive, ripped recruit freezes during a water tread and gets cut. A mountain of muscle—gone. Ben shrugs and says, "Muscle doesn't float." Oof. That line hits hard in leadership as well. Grit isn't about looking strong. It's about *staying steady under pressure.*

That scene hits differently because I've watched my oldest son go through nearly the same thing. He's going through one of the most brutal training pipelines the military offers: Army diver school. (Yes, the Army has divers. I didn't know that either. Shout-out to Uncle Sam for keeping secrets.)

Phase one is known for breaking people physically, mentally, and spiritually. Every week, guys and gals drop. Not because they're weak—some of these guys look like superhero prototypes. My son described one guy in his class as an absolute beast. This guy did fifty pullups in a minute and cranked out one hundred fifty pushups in another. His runtime was somewhere between *holy cow* and *get this man a cape*. While my son was proud of hitting ten pullups (he got his upper body strength from me—not exactly Olympic material), this guy dominated until they hit the water. That's when everything shifted.

Here's what my son told me: "Water is the great equalizer." That beast couldn't handle it. The pool unders, the hour-long weighted treading drills, broke him.

You may be wondering, what's an *under*? An under is a dive training exercise. Trainees swim from one end of the pool to the other, fully submerged, without surfacing for air. Then you do it again, and again—sometimes with gear and sometimes while already physically smoked. It's a physical and mental test. Can you remain calm when your body is screaming for oxygen?

That beast of a man couldn't handle the unders. And in the Army diver program, there's no gentle exit. They won't kick you out unless you're unsafe. The process is self-selected. It's called DOR (Drop On Request). You quit yourself. You walk up to the instructor, hand them your helmet, and say, "I'm done."

That incident demonstrates the tug-of-war between grit and grace in real time.

Leadership, like diver school, weeds out the unqualified and reveals the unwilling. Many people want the reward but can't handle the pain. They appear to be leaders, but they sink when things get uncomfortable.

My son isn't the strongest. He'll tell you that himself. But what he has is faith, grit, and a stubborn refusal to quit. He's found grace in the water, grace to keep calm, support his team, and trust God when his body wants to give up. And he's found grit that shows up when everything hurts, and quitting would be much easier.

I've learned more about leadership from watching my son go through that than from half the books I've read. Most people don't think they can learn from their kids. But if you're too proud to learn from someone younger, you've already lost the leadership game.

This chapter is about the tension between being strong, yet not bitter, and gentle, yet not passive. It's about having the grace to be humble, the grit to keep going, and the courage to admit that sometimes your greatest teachers bear your last name.

Jesus led this way. Ben Randall modeled it on the screen. My oldest son is living it out in the deep end. And now, it's our turn, because leadership isn't about being the loudest in the room. It's about being the calmest in the chaos, which takes grit and grace working together.

Grit Without Grace—The Bulldozer Boss

False Belief: "Being a strong leader means never showing weakness."

Let's clear something up right out of the gate. Being tough doesn't make you a great leader. If your version of leadership is barking orders, controlling every outcome, running people into the ground, and acting like emotion is a weakness, you're bulldozing.

And sure, grit is essential. You've got to have thick skin. You've got to stand firm when everyone else is folding. But leading with grit and no grace is like building sandcastles with a flamethrower. You leave scorched earth behind, no real legacy, and a team that obeys out of fear, not conviction.

Back to Ben Randall in *The Guardian*.

Ben is preparing recruits through pressure. The reality of Ben's rationale was revealed in the 2 a.m. hypothermia training.

Picture the scene. It's pitch dark and cold. The instructors and the commander roll in to wake the recruits, only to find them standing in a pool full of ice. Jake's out of the water, soaking wet, giving CPR to a dummy. The rest of the team is shivering, treading water. Their lips are blue, and their bodies are locked in full-on survival mode. The commander loses it. "You were just supposed to *teach* them about this!" Ben doesn't flinch. "They'll know all about it in about a minute and a half. Permission to continue." That's the moment.

Leadership isn't always pretty. Sometimes it's standing waist-deep in the pain with your people. Ben didn't tell them how hypothermia felt. He let them experience it. And when he got back into that water after the commander left, the recruits shouted, "Hooah!" They saw the purpose behind the pain.

And that, my friend, separates a bulldozer from a builder. I didn't always get that right. Let me take you back to a day when I showed up with grit and forgot the grace entirely.

East Texas, DOT Style

I worked in compliance for a company, traveling from yard to yard and resolving issues. I pulled into the East Texas division, and it immediately felt different. This wasn't my first rodeo, but it was one of the messiest.

When I visit a yard, I usually observe the situation before speaking. I watch the drivers to see who's checking their trucks, who's skipping inspections, and what the load securement looks like. I try to read the culture before I confront it. But this yard was next-level lackadaisical. Sloppy straps, no hoods popped, and a truck getting ready to roll out with a trailer that screamed *CDL-required*. I caught the driver at the gate, started a casual conversation, and asked to see his CDL. It was just a standard driver's license, and he had no med card. He wasn't even on the company's approved driver list. That's when I snapped. I was hot, literally and figuratively.

I stormed into the division manager's office like a bat out of DOT hell. I laid it out: "Your guy's not qualified. Your equipment's not safe. He's not on the driver list. He doesn't have the right license. He doesn't have a med card. And he's about to leave this yard illegally."

This manager was about 5'6" in height but 3'6" in leadership presence. He wore a giant belt buckle, but it didn't seem to be backed up by much. He puffed his chest like a little Chihuahua and yelled, "Get the hell out of my office!" to the driver. He told him to roll out anyway!

So, now I'm even more fired up. I square off, voice raised: "If you leave this yard, we will have bigger problems than that job site!"

We're in a full-on standoff. The driver listens to his boss, the guy he sees every day, not the DOT guy in the nice shirt from corporate. And just like that, I lost the moment because I came in full of grit and left no room for grace. When you do that, people don't hear your wisdom. They just feel your wrath.

So, I'm stomping around the yard, East Texas heat cooking me from the inside out and writing down every violation I can see, fast and furious-style. I was five pages deep in problems when my phone rang. It was the president of the company.

I answer, hot. "What do you want? I'm down here in a yard full of DOT violations and leadership dysfunction."

ALL GRIT, NO GRACE = AFTER-SHOCK PAPERWORK.

232

He lets me vent for a second. Then calmly says, "Yeah, you're right. There are major problems, and right now, you're one of them."

Gut punch.

He continues: "You're trying to force change without earning trust. I need you to go back in there and apologize, not because you were wrong about the compliance issues, but because you overstepped your bounds. You took his authority when you should have partnered with it."

Oof. That was a hard pill to swallow. But it was precisely what I needed.

I went to lunch and cooled off. When I returned, I asked the division manager for a few minutes to talk. He was cooled down, too. We chatted. I owned my part. And over the next six to eight months, we built something strong.

It wasn't instant. Trust never is. However, when I left that company, the same manager brought me into the new company he was working for to help them with compliance. They paid me to come down, train their staff, and speak to their team. Not because I yelled louder, but because I learned to lead better.

I don't tell that story to pat myself on the back. I tell it because it's proof: Grit without grace gets you nowhere fast. You can be 100 percent right and still be one hundred percent ineffective if your delivery feels like a sledgehammer to someone else's pride.

Listen. I get it. Leadership is frustrating. People ignore instructions. Corners get cut. And it's easy to default into *because I said so* mode. But that's not how Jesus led. That's not how Paul wrote. That's not how great legacies are built.

Paul says in Galatians 4:16, "Have I now become your enemy by telling you the truth?" He wasn't asking sarcastically. He was wrestling with the reality that truth can create tension, even when spoken from a place of love. And that's why grace matters just as much as grit. Truth without grace feels like judgment. But grace without truth? That's what comes next, so stay tuned.

Here's the warning: Grit alone might get you compliance. But it won't get you commitment. It might win the argument. But it loses the relationship. And that relationship might just be the key to a breakthrough on your team.

So, here's your checkpoint, leader: Are you standing in the icy water with your team, earning their respect? Or are you standing on the deck, shouting orders, wondering why nobody follows?

If you want a lasting impact, if you want legacy-level leadership, you need grit to say the hard things and grace to deliver them in a way that people can receive.

GRACE WITHOUT GRIT—THE DOORMAT LEADER

Somewhere along the line, somebody started confusing leadership with customer service. "Be nice." "Don't make waves." "Keep everyone happy." And somehow that turned into leaders walking around like part-time guidance counselors and full-time doormats. Grace without grit isn't leadership. It's babysitting grown-ups and calling it management.

I've met these leaders. I've *been* this leader. They avoid hard conversations like they're made of lava. They hand out second chances like Tic Tacs. They smile, nod through red flags, and then wonder why the team's falling apart. They think they're keeping the peace. But they're letting the whole culture burn down while roasting marshmallows and calling it team-building.

I remember letting this soft, squishy leadership take over. We had a guy on staff— we'll call him Todd. (If your name is Todd, don't take it personally unless this hits too close. Then maybe do some reflecting.) Now, Todd was slick. He always had a story and a reason when things went wrong. If excuses were Olympic events, he'd be on a cereal box.

I kept making excuses for him. "He's just getting up to speed." "He's going through a rough patch." "He's got potential." In the meantime, he missed deadlines and dropped balls. Other teammates quietly picked up his slack like unpaid babysitters.

And what did I do? I praised them for being flexible. Meanwhile, I said nothing to Todd because I didn't want to damage the relationship. I damaged it anyway.

When the truth finally came out, it was like popping a zit that had been festering for six months. It was messy, painful, and avoidable. Grace without grit isn't gentle. It's cowardly. It feels nice at first, but it rots the foundation.

Here's the worst part, and I'm going to be honest: I wasn't just failing as a leader. I was disobeying God. I knew I was supposed to address it. I knew what needed to be said. But I let fear put on a fake Jesus costume and tell me that grace means silence. Nah. That isn't grace. That's fear in a bathrobe.

Let's not forget. Jesus flipped tables. Paul called out Peter to his face. Real leadership doesn't hide behind kind words and awkward silences. It shows up, speaks up, and holds the line with love, but without backing down. So, here's the reality: Grace without grit doesn't fix problems, earn respect, or raise the bar. Gritless grace builds a culture where everyone feels safe, until everything starts falling apart.

So, here's your gut check, leader: Are you leading? Or are you just babysitting grown adults with bad habits?

Leadership is a lot of things—humble, loving, patient—but it's never passive. If you're letting standards slip to maintain peace, you're not leading. You're managing comfort, and comfort doesn't build anything worth following.

If you want to be a real leader, you need grit to say the hard stuff, grace to say it with heart, and guts to stand in the tension without flinching. It's not always easy. But if leadership were easy, we'd let interns do it.

Nice leaders make people smile. Bold leaders change lives. This hit me personally. Back in high school, my big dream was to fly helicopters. I would enlist in the Army, enter Warrant Officer School, and become a rotor-wing pilot. I had taken my flight physical and passed all the pre-enlistment requirements. I had it all lined up. Then I met Jenna.

We were high school sweethearts. Halfway through senior year, I'd made the call. I was staying. I walked away from the Army dream to build something different. A family. A life here. I've never once regretted that decision. But the desire to fly? That never left.

Later, I had a rare opportunity to intern with a local helicopter company. This was rural Colorado. There wasn't another outfit like it for miles. They weren't offering a paycheck, just a chance to be near the equipment, learn the systems, and get a foot in the door. I turned it down because they weren't going to pay me.

I told myself that I had too much going on. My time was too valuable, and it wasn't smart to work for free. But I lacked the grace to humble myself, walk into something uncomfortable, and gain knowledge without compensation. I failed to say *yes* when God opened a door, even if it didn't come with a check attached. I wasn't mature enough to understand that I wouldn't have worked for free, I would have been working for opportunity. And I missed it.

I regret that decision, but that's not why I'm telling you about it. Years later, I realized it taught me that grace without grit is passivity that looks like patience. And grace without grit is fear, but it looks like maturity. What feels safe keeps you stuck.

Grace, in that moment, told me, "It's okay. Protect yourself. Don't sell yourself short." But what I needed was grit. Grit to go for it. Grit to be uncomfortable. Grit to say, "This might not be perfect, but it's worth the risk."

Leadership without grit is like trying to drive uphill in neutral. You can be the nicest person in the world and still lead your team straight into mediocrity.

Grace is good. We need it. But grace without grit is how people stay stuck for decades. That's how families drift, businesses plateau, and churches die slow, quiet deaths. Leaders are too scared to confront the issues that are killing the culture. Let me bring it even closer to home.

I've watched people I love refuse to confront something for twenty years. Decades-old hurtful conversations, betrayals, and unresolved family drama are never faced. Ironically, they tell themselves they've let it go and forgiven the offender. But they haven't. They've just avoided it.

Now they're walking around with hardened hearts and bitterness, thinking they're being Christlike for staying quiet. They're hiding, but they're not healed. Forgiveness doesn't mean you forget what happened. Forgiveness means you release it. And grit helps you face it.

We confuse peace with passivity. We think turning the other cheek means turning off our voice. But that's not strength, that's silence. And Jesus didn't model silence. He modeled wisdom. He spoke with authority, asked bold questions, and challenged power. Later, Paul captured that spirit perfectly when he wrote, "Speaking the truth in love" (Ephesians 4:13).

If you're leading anyone, a team, family, marriage, or church, you need grace and grit to speak truth in love. Grace enables you to love people. Grit equips you to challenge them. Grace forgives, grit confronts.

So, here are the questions you've got to ask yourself:
- Where are you confusing grace with silence?
- What opportunity are you letting pass by?
- What conversation are you avoiding?
- What boundary do you need to draw, but you've been too afraid to say it?

You weren't put on this earth to stay quiet and play nice. You were put here to lead, influence, and call people into something better. So, yes, lead with grace. But don't forget the grit that moves the mission forward. And grace makes the journey worth it.

Strong but not Bitter

Let's clarify: Strong leaders don't need to be loud or angry. They don't need to walk around with a chip on their shoulder, barking orders like they're auditioning for a reboot of *Full Metal Jacket*. You can be strong without being bitter. Be firm but not harsh. Be bold without being a jerk.

The strongest leaders I've met had nothing to prove. They weren't obsessed with being noticed or ensuring everyone knew they were in charge. They walked in purpose, and people followed. Strength doesn't need a microphone. It carries weight on its own.

But bitterness yells, snaps, and hides behind the word *boundaries* when it's a shield for unresolved pain. Bitterness tries to mask itself as toughness, but it's hollow, edgy, and sharp. It eventually turns strong leaders into cynical ones.

Strong leaders don't lead to prove they're strong. They lead because the mission matters more than their ego. Do you want to see that in action? Let's go to the last five minutes of *The Guardian*.

Jake Fischer is now a full-fledged rescue swimmer. He's on a mission in the Bering Sea, one of the most dangerous places to fly. He's out there because Ben sent him. The same Ben who trained, pushed, and called greatness out of him.

He was sent to Alaska because Ben knew he could handle it. But here's where it gets heavy. Mid-rescue, Ben and Jake are both in the water with a survivor. Waves are crashing. The helicopter is straining against the wind. They've only got a few seconds to hook the line and haul them up, and Ben knows he won't make it.

He doesn't say it out loud, scream, or panic. He calmly unhooks himself from the line, *lets go,* and gives his spot to the survivor. He gives his legacy to Jake. And he goes under. He's gone. There was no spotlight, grand goodbyes, or ego-filled speeches about how much he's given through the years. His quiet strength was his final act of service, a sacrifice only someone who truly understood leadership would make. That's strong, but not bitter.

He didn't throw shade or try to sabotage Jake because he was breaking his records. He didn't need applause or a medal. He was steady to the end because he wasn't leading for credit. He was leading for impact. That's what real leaders do.

I've seen the opposite, too—people let their position puff them up. Watching someone younger or new rise, people they are supposed to be building, often produces resentment for some people. That's not strength. That's fear in a leather jacket.

Bitterness turns leaders into gatekeepers. They stop mentoring. They withhold knowledge and hoard wisdom they should be passing down. Their mentality is that if someone else wins, they lose.

But when you know who you are and whose mission you're on, you can lead from confidence, not control. You don't tear people down. You raise them up. And when it's time for them to pass you, you cheer because it means you did your job well.

That's how I want to lead. That's the man I want to be. I want to lead with strength and never from bitterness. I want to pass on everything I know to the next generation and not be afraid if they outshine me. Leadership isn't about how bright you shine. It's about how many people you light up along the way.

If Ben had let bitterness win, Jake would have quit halfway through training. The team would have collapsed. And lives would have been lost. Instead, Ben stayed strong and calm and let his legacy live on in the next guy.

So, let me ask you:

- Are you strong, or are you just angry?
- Are you steady, or are you stuck in resentment?
- Are you building people up, or are you holding them back?

The difference between strength and bitterness is intention. Bitter leaders protect their pride. Strong leaders protect their people. If you're called to lead—if you're in this to make an impact—then let go of whatever chip is on your shoulder, and start leading like someone not afraid to be outshone.

Pass the mic. Share the wisdom. Stand in the storm. And when it's time, be willing to let go of the line so someone else can rise. That's not weakness. That's legacy.

Gentle But Not Passive

Let's be honest. *Gentle* isn't a word most people associate with leadership. Upon hearing it, you might picture a soft-spoken shepherd or a quiet soul who's always saying *yes* and never steps on anyone's toes. The word just doesn't scream *power*, does it? That's because we've misunderstood it.

Gentleness means restraint, not weakness. It means knowing you could steamroll someone in a conversation but choose to guide them through it. It means you could shut a situation down with authority, but you hold steady, speak calmly, and help someone grow instead of backing them into a corner. That's not passive. That's powerful.

Some of the most passive people I've met have been the most aggressive in the room. They're constantly correcting, demanding, and puffing out their chest. But the moment a real problem comes up, they disappear. They confuse force with strength and volume with leadership. Yelling louder doesn't mean you're leading well. It just means you're losing control. True gentleness is rare, and you remember it when you see it.

One of the best examples of gentle-but-not-passive leadership is when Jake arrives late to class. He's been out all night with a girl he met at the bar, and Ben knows it. This isn't a one-time slip, it's a pattern. Jake's talent is undeniable, but he's got one foot in and one foot out. He's still more focused on impressing than becoming someone worth following.

Ben doesn't yell or throw a fit in front of the group. But he does something that stops Jake in his tracks. While the recruits are outside doing early-morning physical training—running, pushups, all the sweaty stuff—Ben casually walks over to Jake's locker, opens it, and starts going through his things. Slowly. Quietly. With purpose. Right in front of him.

Jake's face shifts from cocky to confused to completely exposed. "What are you doing?" he asks.

Ben doesn't even look up. He just says, "Looking for something to tell me why you're here."

The room goes silent. He's not digging for dirt. He's not embarrassing him. He's asking what every leader needs to ask their team at some point: Why are you *really* here? Are you chasing glory? Looking to prove something? Or are you willing to sacrifice for something bigger than yourself?

Ben never raises his voice. He doesn't slam the locker or storm out of the room. He let the moment and its weight hit Jake where it hurt most—his pride. That's gentle leadership.

Gentleness doesn't avoid confrontation, but it also doesn't crush someone to make a point. It draws the line without drawing blood. It invites reflection instead of forcing compliance. And here's the crazy part. It works.

That one moment begins to shift something in Jake. You can see it. He starts waking up. Not just physically, but emotionally and spiritually. He begins to realize this isn't just a physical test. It's a test of character. And Ben, without shouting or shaming, starts chiseling away at the ego to make room for growth. That's what gentle-but-not-passive leadership does.

It doesn't let things slide, look the other way, or humiliate. Gentle leadership teaches through presence, not pressure—through clarity, not chaos. And yet, there's no passivity in that moment. He's not sugarcoating anything or letting it slide. He confronts it directly with clarity, purpose, and respect.

Too often, we think gentleness means letting things go. We feel pressured to give people another chance. We try to understand and remain patient instead of acknowledging that all is not well. But that's not leadership. That's fear pretending to be grace.

I've been there. I've hesitated to address something because I didn't want to hurt the relationship. I've talked myself into waiting *just a little longer* for someone to self-correct, even when deep down, I knew they wouldn't. And every time I waited too long, it cost more than it would have if I had handled it earlier. I've learned that gentleness is not about avoiding hard conversations. It's about having them without damaging the person on the other end. Sometimes, that means you sit across from someone and say, "I care about you too much to let this continue." Not yelling, shaming, or pretending is necessary. The truth delivered in love is enough.

I don't recall my dad ever raising his voice. If he did, it must have been serious, because I don't remember it. He led our home with calm authority, not intimidation. And that was a lot more powerful than I realized at the time.

You always knew when he was disappointed in you, not because he yelled or made a big scene. He'd ask questions that made you sit with your decisions for a while. Those questions stuck with you and quietly said, "You know better."

Growing up, my parents were generous but had some firm expectations regarding independence. If you wanted a cell phone, you paid for it. If you wanted a car, you bought it, paid for the gas, and covered the insurance. There were no handouts, just opportunities to take ownership. Honestly, I'm grateful for it. That mindset helped shape who I am today.

So, at 16, I had a truck, a real beauty, if you squinted and had low standards. When Dad and I brought it home, we discovered there weren't even brake components on the back axle—not worn down or missing. Gone. Guess who learned to install brakes that week?

Now, fast-forward a bit. I was job hunting one day. I pulled out of a business parking lot in front of a cop. As luck would have it, my truck stalled in front of the officer. He pulled me over and wrote me a ticket for *impeding traffic*—some technicality, but I deserved it. I could have waited, but I got impatient. That one was on me.

I paid the ticket and moved on. I didn't tell my parents. After all, I paid for everything related to my truck, so what did it matter? But if I'm being honest, it wasn't about the money. It was about my dad's driving record.

My entire life, I'd heard how clean his record was. He never sped or got a ticket. He'd only been in a couple of accidents involving animals, not other drivers. He took pride in that. Not in a braggy, arrogant way (okay, maybe a *little*), but in a way that made you want to rise to that standard.

So, when I got that ticket, I felt like I'd blown it. I didn't want to see the disappointment in his eyes, so I handled (buried) it. That was the end of the story until about a year and a half later.

My mom called me out of the blue one day and said, "Did you ever get a ticket?"

"Yeah. Why?"

"Well, your dad just found out from the insurance agent. He went to bat for you— told them no way, impossible. He's never been that upset before, not at you, at them. But he didn't know you had a ticket. And now he's just confused why you never said anything."

I told her the truth. "I didn't want to disappoint him. I felt like I let him down."

She paused for a second and said, "You need to go talk to him."

So, I went home and sure enough, Dad was in the garden. That was his spot. Anytime he needed to cool off or think something through, he went out to weed. I found him out there, pulling weeds as if he were on a mission. And I walked up, bracing for a complicated conversation.

But what happened next? That's what I'll never forget.

He looked up at me and, without anger or sarcasm, calmly said, "Why didn't you just tell me?"

Then he said something that still gets me: "That officer probably expected you to fight that ticket. You didn't even give it a chance. If you had told me, I could have helped."

His presence and wisdom were sufficient to communicate his message. It reminded me that I didn't have to carry things alone. That was gentle leadership.

He set the standard for gentle leadership. He didn't let the matter slide, but he didn't make me feel small or shame me. He simply invited me to be honest, and showed me that gentleness is about walking through challenges together, not avoiding the issue.

I haven't always led my kids that way. I've been quicker to correct, louder to respond, and faster to become frustrated. But every time I think about that day in the garden, I'm reminded of how powerful a calm question can be. A steady presence can do more than a strong reaction ever will. That's the leader I want to be—gentle, but never passive.

Jesus modeled gentle leadership better than anyone. He didn't avoid confrontation. But He never led with cruelty either. He knew when to speak gently and when to speak firmly. He knew when to comfort the hurting and when to challenge the proud. He didn't swing a hammer at everything. He spoke with authority, but He listened intently. He was the King of Kings, yet He washed the feet of His disciples. That's not passive. That's the definition of strength under control.

I believe the best leaders, especially the ones building teams, companies, or families with lasting impact, are the ones who know how to stand their ground without losing their heart. They don't make a scene, give in, or disappear when the pressure's on. They hold the line, stay present, and lead with conviction wrapped in compassion.

You can be direct without being demeaning. You can be soft-spoken without being spineless. You can be gentle, but not passive. So, if you're reading this and you've been avoiding something, perhaps with your team, in your marriage, or with someone you're mentoring, I want to challenge you to reconsider how you show up in that relationship.

Don't wait until it explodes. Don't mistake your silence for spiritual maturity, and don't let your patience become a permission slip for poor performance. Gentleness doesn't mean you let people walk all over you. It means you stand firm and invite them to walk with you instead.

I'd rather follow a leader who speaks calmly and acts courageously than one who shouts every day and never changes a thing. I want to be that leader, too, one who looks you in the eye and tells you the truth without tearing you down. I want to be the leader who shows up in the cold, gets in the water, and says, "You're not alone, but you can't stay here." That's leadership that transforms people. That's gentleness, with guts.

The Book of Daniel

If you thought I would write a leadership book with a biblical tie-in and not discuss the book of Daniel, come on. It's named after me. Of course, it's my favorite. I'm not just saying that because I enjoy seeing my name in bold font (although I do). I love this book because it's a blueprint for leadership when things get weird, hard, and lonely. Let me explain.

Daniel didn't lead a church. He wasn't secluded in a monastery writing Proverbs 2.0. He led in Babylon, a culture with zero interest in his values. Daniel's beliefs, background, and even his diet were problems to solve or habits to be broken. Sound familiar?

That's where many of us lead today, not in Babylon, but in boardrooms, oil fields, shops, schools, and companies where faith isn't the default. Holding the line gets you eye rolls. Integrity makes you *difficult*. Excellence is annoying to people who prefer average. Honoring God quietly gets treated like rebellion.

And that's why I love Daniel. He shows us how to lead when the room doesn't cheer you on. He didn't lead in a comfortable environment. He wasn't a pastor tucked behind a pulpit or a guy who went viral for saying something inspirational. No, he was a godly man in a godless system. Kings who didn't share his faith promoted him. People who didn't understand his convictions surrounded him. Jealous coworkers constantly set him up to fail, yet he never lost his composure.

He was never too harsh, nor too soft. He had the grit to stand his ground and the grace not to become bitter. That's the leadership I want in my life. Let's look at how that plays out.

When Daniel arrived in Babylon, they tried to change everything about him—his name, language, habits, and even his food. The king's officials rolled out the royal menu—meats, wine, all the rich, sacred-to-the-wrong-god stuff.

Daniel doesn't throw the plate across the room and yell, "You'll never take my dinner roll!" He pulls the guard aside and says, "How about this? We eat vegetables and drink water for ten days. Then you decide if we look worse or better."

That's not weakness. That's wisdom. That's grit that doesn't need to be shouted, and grace that doesn't mean surrender. And God honors it. That decision, handled with calm conviction instead of noise, sets Daniel and his crew apart. They look better than everyone else. They gain favor because God doesn't just bless obedience. He honors how we carry it out. But it didn't stop there.

Later in the story, we see Daniel's friends, Shadrach, Meshach, and Abednego, standing before King Nebuchadnezzar, being told to bow down or burn. Again, their answer holds the tension between grace and grit so perfectly, I wish every modern leader had it tattooed on their soul.

IF WE ARE THROWN INTO THE BLAZING FURNACE, THE GOD WE SERVE IS ABLE TO DELIVER

US FROM IT, AND HE WILL DELIVER US FROM YOUR MAJESTY'S HAND.

BUT EVEN IF HE DOES NOT, WE WANT YOU TO KNOW, YOUR MAJESTY, THAT WE WILL NOT

SERVE YOUR GODS OR WORSHIP THE IMAGE OF GOLD YOU HAVE SET UP.

—DANIEL 3:17–18

They didn't throw accusations, insult the king, or arrogantly predict victory. They simply trusted, not in the outcome, but in God with them in the fire. And when the furnace was turned up, He met them there, not before or after, right in the middle. Grit got them thrown in. Grace let them walk through it without the smell of smoke. And faith? Well, it flipped a kingdom.

Later, the same pattern repeats when Daniel himself is at the height of his influence. Some jealous coworkers (I won't name names, but let's just say I've worked with a few of those in my day) come after him. They can't find fault with his work, so they go after his worship. They get the king to sign a law that no one can pray to anyone except the king for thirty days. Classic setup. They knew Daniel wouldn't compromise, and he didn't disappoint.

But here's what's wild: Daniel doesn't go full protest mode. He doesn't panic, call a press conference, or stage a march. He goes home, walks upstairs, and opens the window, just like he always did. He prayed with the same posture he had before the law. That's grit and grace, the leadership that emerges when death is on the line.

When Daniel was thrown into the lions' den, even the king, the same guy who signed the law, was sick over it. He was inconsolable and couldn't eat or sleep. At first light, the king ran to the lions' den.

> WHEN HE CAME NEAR THE DEN, HE CALLED TO DANIEL IN AN ANGUISHED VOICE, "DANIEL,
> SERVANT OF THE LIVING GOD, HAS YOUR GOD, WHOM YOU SERVE CONTINUALLY, BEEN ABLE
> TO RESCUE YOU FROM THE LIONS?"
> —DANIEL 6:20

And Daniel—full of grace, even then—doesn't throw shade or say, "Told ya so." He doesn't flex. He doesn't gloat. Instead, he responds like a man anchored in truth and forged in faith:

> DANIEL ANSWERED, "MAY THE KING LIVE FOREVER!
> MY GOD SENT HIS ANGEL, AND HE SHUT THE MOUTHS OF THE LIONS. THEY HAVE NOT HURT
> ME, BECAUSE I WAS FOUND INNOCENT IN HIS SIGHT.
> NOR HAVE I EVER DONE ANY WRONG BEFORE YOU, YOUR MAJESTY."
> —DANIEL 6:20

Let's break that down:
- *Respectful:* "May the king live forever!" He honors the position, even after being thrown to the lions.
- *Faith-filled:* He gives all the credit to God. No ego. No self-promotion.
- *Vindicated:* He declares his innocence—not just before the king, but before the King of kings.

Boom. That's how you lead with grit and grace. You honor the process, even when it's unfair. You stay faithful, even when it hurts. You speak the truth with humility, even when you've earned the right to throw stones.

Ultimately, God gets the glory, because it was never about the platform. It was always about obedience.

This whole book, Daniel's entire story, is one big picture of how grace and grit don't cancel each other out. They complete each other. Grit without grace becomes aggression, and grace without grit becomes passivity. But together, they change nations, rescue cultures, and rewrite legacies. And maybe most importantly, they ensure you survive Babylon without becoming Babylon.

So if you're standing in a furnace right now, or staring down some lions, remember this: You don't have to flip the table or cave in. You just have to keep showing up with the window open and your heart set.

Grace in your heart. Grit in your hands. And God in your corner. That's how you lead like Daniel.

TOOLBOX OF TENSION

FIX THE WORK, KEEP THE WORKERS.

Practical Tools to Lead with Grit and Grace

Living in the tension between grace and grit sounds nice on paper, but it's much messier in real life. You've got deadlines, stress, and eyeballs watching your every move. You're trying to lead your crew, company, kids, or congregation with wisdom. People expect you to stay cool, speak the truth, stay humble, and not yell when someone backs a trailer into the side of your building. These are the times when tools matter.

Here's a practical list of things I use to stay anchored when I'm pulled between the urge to bark orders and the conviction to lead like Jesus. I don't always get it right. But these tools keep me from derailing.

Pray before reacting.

I know, it sounds simple. But this will save you from saying things you can't unsay. Before you send the email, light someone up in a meeting, or write a response in all caps, take a minute. Ask God to give you peace, perspective, and the proper posture. Grit says, "This needs to be addressed." Grace says, "Let's make sure we do it the right way."

Clarify expectations with compassion.

Don't assume people know what's in your head. Don't assume they're slacking because they're not doing it your way. Communicate clearly, then follow up with care and attention. I've learned that most people don't need harsher correction. They need a leader who tells them what's expected and helps them get there.

Stand firm on your values, but stay open to feedback.

This is a big one. Grit says, "This is who we are." Grace says, "And we're still growing." Don't let feedback shake your foundation, and don't let pride make you blind either. Even your critics can be teachers. Just don't let them sit in the driver's seat.

Practice pausing. Then respond. Don't react.

When emotions are high, it's easy to fire off the first thing that hits your brain. Grit without patience can lead to impulsiveness, which in turn ruins relationships. Breathe. Step away. Go weed the garden if you must (shout-out to my dad). But don't respond in the heat. Let the truth settle before your words do.

Speak the truth in love. (Ephesians 4:15)

Truth without love is a hammer. Love without truth is a hug that leads nowhere. Leaders are called to do both. Whether confronting a team member, correcting your kid, or calling someone higher, truth and love should go out holding hands, not one dragging the other behind.

You don't need to win every argument to win someone's heart.

This one took me a few years (and probably a few unnecessary debates) to learn. But it's true. People remember how you made them feel long after they forget what you were *right* about. Grace means choosing a relationship over ego. Grit means saying the hard thing anyway—but in such a way they'll still want to come back to the table.

Leadership isn't about always getting it perfect. It's about showing up daily, being willing to grow in strength *and* tenderness. So grab your tools. Tighten your grip. And lead like someone who isn't afraid to sweat and serve, because the world doesn't need more leaders who dominate. It needs more leaders who discern. And that, my friend, takes both grace and grit.

Wrap Up

You've made it this far into the chapter, and I hope one thing's become clear: Grace and grit were never meant to compete with each other. They're meant to hold the rope together—one strand strong, the other steady. Pull too far in either direction, and you start unraveling the leadership tension you were built to carry. We've seen what it looks like when leaders live on one side of that rope.

We've seen grit with no grace—leaders who bulldoze everyone in the name of *being right*. We've seen the yelling, control, pride, and fallout. And let's be honest, we've all been that leader at some point. I know I have.

That time I marched into that yard in East Texas, lit up a division manager for sending an unqualified guy out in a CDL-required truck, and left the whole place in a tailspin. My heart was right, but my mouth wasn't. I brought grit, but not grace. I spent the next eight months rebuilding a relationship that could have been established in a single lunch meeting if I'd started with humility. We've also seen the flip side, grace with no grit.

We've seen leaders who are too nice to speak up. They avoid every tough conversation. They'll smile while the company culture slowly catches fire. They let things slide in the name of kindness but are slow to realize the damage they're doing by not taking a lead.

I've been that guy too. Remember when I skipped the helicopter internship in high school because it didn't pay? Man, I told myself it was about boundaries. But the truth was, I didn't have the grace to humble myself and learn. I mistook comfort for calling. And I let a massive opportunity fly by (pun intended).

But then there's Daniel. And Ben. And my Dad. And my oldest son. They all show us what leading in the middle of the tension looks like.

Daniel didn't scream when the food didn't align with his faith. He didn't demand, rage, or act like a victim. He made a quiet, confident offer. "Let us eat our way, and judge by the fruit."

He displayed grit in his convictions and grace in his delivery. And God's favor was the result.

Daniel displayed the same grit and grace in the lions' den. Shadrach, Meshach, and Abednego did likewise in the furnace. They didn't threaten, they refused to bow and trusted God with the outcome. Grace. Grit. Glory.

Then there's Chief Ben Randall, already soaked to the bone, standing in the hypothermia pool at 2 a.m. He didn't shout from the sidelines. He *led from the water*, and when the commander questioned him, he didn't argue. He simply said, "They'll know all about it in a minute and a half. Permission to continue."

And there's my dad, never needing to raise his voice, but somehow still more powerful than a bullhorn. The man could pull weeds in a garden and correct your entire heart at the same time. His questions pierced more than punishment ever could. I still carry that quiet authority with me, and I still try (and sometimes fail) to pass it on to my kids.

Which brings me to this conversation I had recently with my oldest son: He's deep in the pressure cooker of Army diver training. Surrounded by guys with egos the size of cargo planes. Training is brutal. Emotions run high. He told me that one night, after dinner chow, he didn't want to deal with the drama bubbling up in the team, so he took a different path back to the barracks. Just needed some space.

I asked him, half-joking, "Would it hurt your feelings if a couple of those ego-driven guys dropped out?" He didn't laugh. He shook his head.

"No, Dad. I don't want anyone to DOR. There's enough success here to go around. And I probably won't be stationed with any of these guys. But knowing my luck, it'll be the loudest one who ends up on my team."

That's when it hit me. He had every reason to write those guys off—to wish them failure. Their quitting would improve his chances. But he didn't. That's leadership. That's grace. He chose honor when irritation would have been easier. That's grit. He is staying the course, even when the people around him don't make it easy.

And that's what I want for you—a life marked by consistency, courage, and compassion. You *can* lead like Daniel. You *can* lead like Ben. You *can* lead like Jesus. It won't be easy. But it will be worth it.

This Chapter's Challenge:

Look for one moment to show more grit where you've been silent, soft, or afraid to lead.

Look for one moment to show more grace, where your tone, timing, or tenderness could create more trust.

Grace without grit is just a smile; grit without grace is just noise. But together, they make you a leader worth following, and even more importantly, they make you a leader worth becoming.

Key Takeaways From Chapter 11

 **Bench-press truth, wrap it in kindness.** Grit says, "Fix it." Grace says, "Let me show you how."

 **Bulldozers bulldoze … then wonder why no one's left.** Muscle without mercy scorches teams quicker than Texas asphalt in July.

 **Doormats get walked on, not followed.** Permanent niceness lowers the bar until excellence trips over it.

 **Strong does not equal salty.** Real power is Ben Randall letting the rookie take the hoist line—steel backbone, zero bitterness.

 **Gentle is not the same as jelly-spine.** Daniel opened the window and prayed anyway—that's restraint with teeth.

 **Water is the great equalizer.** Fancy résumés sink fast when the pool unders start—grit keeps you afloat.

 **Truth in love beats truth in ALL CAPS.** Pray, breathe, then hit send—your keyboard doesn't need a sledgehammer.

 **Your circle sets your tone.** Gatekeepers hoard wisdom; legacy builders toss life vests and say, "Jump in."

 **Run the "God-Did" replay.** Past rescues fuel present courage when the waves get rough.

 **Grace + grit = cultural superglue.** One strand holds standards, the other holds hearts—pull either, and the rope unravels.

 **Lead like the rudder, not the foghorn.** Quiet, steady pressure turns the ship; volume only scares the seagulls.

Chapter 12 | Leading with Humility

The Text That Almost Killed Me

Now let's be honest. When your phone buzzes ten times before 5 a.m., you're either dealing with an emergency or that uncle who thinks the moon landing was faked. This time, it was neither.

I was half-asleep, barefoot, and taking my glorious morning leak when I finally checked the chaos lighting up my phone like a DOT officer's clipboard during Roadcheck Week. I read through the list of messages:

- One from my brother (probably a meme)
- One from my mom (definitely praying for me)
- Three from company drivers who all believed that their text was the most important thing on earth
- One from a division manager (yikes)
- One from the safety director (double yikes)

I scrolled through the mess like a man flipping through a stack of unpaid bills. Most of it was chattering, and nothing appeared to be earth-shattering. Then, the phone buzzed once more.

This one stopped me mid-stream. This one was from *El Presidente*.

That was my nickname for the company president. It was like a cool spy codename without the tuxedo, secret mission, or suave confidence. I felt pretty vulnerable standing there in my undies, reading a text from the big guy. I was more fearful of what was to come than I was when I received a letter from the IRS (Internal Revenue Service) last week.

"Dan, are you in town?"

Huh? That's ... random. Also, ominous. I replied, "Yes, sir! I'm home right now getting ready to head in."

"Great. We need to meet this morning. It's important."

Important? IMPORTANT?

If you want to get a man's blood pressure up, send him a text at 5:14 a.m. saying, "It's important." My heart dropped like a tire coming loose on a mountain pass—sudden, violent, and about to cause a whole lot of damage. I just stood there, staring at the screen, fully expecting the following text to say, "Bring your badge and a box." I typed back fast:

"I can be there as early as you need me. I'm at least forty-five minutes out. I can leave in five."

"Good. See you at 6:15 in my office."

That was it. He didn't leave any emoticons to let me know there was nothing to worry about—cold, direct, executive ambiguity.

I slapped on deodorant, brushed my teeth, threw on some clothes, and kissed my wife while she was still asleep. Jogging into the kids' rooms like a dad going off to war, I quickly kissed their foreheads, trying not to wake them. All the while, I was fully convinced I was about to be fired and possibly exiled from the industry.

Then I jumped into my truck and drove like a man possessed, dodging deer, elk, and yes, the occasional wild turkey (not the liquid kind). Every bump in the road felt like judgment. Every mile became a marker for my brain to whisper, *You're done for, buddy.*

I pulled into the office at 6:08 a.m. There wasn't a soul around, and only three vehicles were in the lot. Three. Not good. *He didn't want witnesses. He's going to fire me in private so I don't make a scene.*

I ran to my office, grabbed a notebook, and tossed my backpack in the corner like it was holding contraband. Then, I bolted across the building to the *presidential wing*. That was my unofficial name for his office. My office is located at the opposite end of the building, but the mahogany throne in the marble-tiled corner, which my boss occupied, created a striking contrast that made the space feel like the White House.

I slowed down at the door, catching my breath like I hadn't run the 40-yard dash in work boots. It was 6:14 a.m. My palms were sweaty. My heart was racing. I knocked, walked in, and what I saw stopped me cold in my tracks. The president, VP, and some guy I had never seen before were seated at the table.

"Oh great. Here's my replacement. They didn't even wait till lunch to introduce him."

I sat down in the hot seat. You know the one. It's the chair you occupy while flanked by authority figures. It's like you're in a crime drama and they slide a folder across the table saying, "We've got some questions."

No one said a word. Awkward smiles and the tension of a thousand bad dreams replaced conversation. I sat there like a middle schooler in the principal's office, probably for saying something like *butt nugget* during morning announcements. (Which, for the record, still feels like a solid use of vocabulary.)

Finally, the VP leaned forward.

"Thanks for coming in early today, Dan. We have some news you need to hear before you hear it from someone else."

Great. Here comes the axe. At least tell me what I did wrong. Let a guy learn something on the way out. He kept talking.

"You've been traveling a lot the last couple of years. We've been talking to every division manager you've visited."

Oh no. I must've ticked off one of the cocky ones. Maybe I called their operation sloppy. Perhaps they didn't like my beard. Was it the time I brought up how many expired fire extinguishers they had—who knows?

I braced myself for impact. Then the twist came. "What we heard surprised us, in a good way. Every division said the same thing: If they had to hire someone to run their team, they'd pick you."

Silence. I didn't know whether to cry, laugh, or check if there was a camera crew about to yell "Gotcha!"

Then the president spoke.

"Dan, I want you to represent me and the VP when you go to our divisions. You've a reputation for serving people and building trust. And we've never given this level of authority to anyone, but we think you're the right person."

I blinked.

"To be honest, sir, when I got your text, I was sure I was being fired. Then I saw the empty parking lot, and I knew I was being fired. Then I walked in and saw a stranger, and I was sure I was being replaced. So, it might take me a minute to process what you just said."

They laughed. The mystery man was a new hire they wanted me to meet. He was passing through before a flight, which was why the meeting was so early.

Before I walked out, the president stopped me, looked me in the eye and said, "Dan, do you know why we picked you? It wasn't just because you're good at what you do. It's because you don't act like you're better than anybody. Drivers, safety guys, clerks— you talk to them all the same. That's rare. That's humble. And that's why I trust you to carry my name."

I walked out of that office with the offer and a lesson I'll never forget: Humility opens doors that pride can't even knock on. Sometimes your lowest moment is God positioning you for your highest. He has been waiting for you to show Him you can handle the weight without letting it go to your head.

What Is Humility Really

Humility is often misunderstood. For years, I assumed it looked like the quiet guy in the meeting—head down, nodding occasionally, taking notes like he's transcribing the gospel. He doesn't push back, doesn't stir the pot, doesn't speak up. And because he's not causing problems, we call him humble. But that's not humility. That's being quiet, and sometimes, it's hiding. Genuine humility is something else entirely.

Humility is walking into a room fully confident in who you are, with no need to convince everyone else. It's not about shrinking back, playing small, or pretending you don't have ideas, wisdom, or experience. False humility is acting like you're less, so people will like you more. Humility doesn't require being the smartest voice, the loudest presence, or the most successful person in the room. Instead, it makes space for others to shine, even when you're fully capable of leading the conversation.

The Merriam-Webster Dictionary defines humility as *freedom from pride or arrogance.* That's a clean definition—neat and polished.

But let's be real. Humility sounds more like a Sunday school virtue than a leadership tool. It's not something you preach about—it's something that gets forged in fire—the real kind. Like when someone says something wrong in a meeting and everything in you wants to correct them and show your brilliance, but you choose to remain silent. Or when you just scored a huge win, the applause is still ringing, and something inside you whispers, *don't take all the credit.*

Now, people love to quote C.S. Lewis with, "Humility is not thinking less of yourself, but thinking of yourself less." It's catchy, and it *sounds* like Lewis, but he never actually said that. What he *did* say, though, might be even better. In *Mere Christianity*, Lewis described a genuinely humble person like this:

> *"He will not be thinking about humility:*
> *he will not be thinking about himself at all."*
> —C.S. Lewis

That's leadership. Genuine humility isn't pretending you're a nobody. It's being so secure in who you are that you don't have to make it about you. That sticks. It reminds us that humility is refusing to make yourself the center of all things, not about superficially denying your value. And if I had to throw my definition into the mix, it'd be this:

> *"Humility is knowing you can do just about anything, but*
> *recognizing someone else might be able to do it better,*
> *and being totally okay with that."*
> —Dan Greer

That's the part that rubs many leaders the wrong way. Leadership attracts doers, fixers, and builders. People like you and me are wired to solve problems and move fast. That's a gift, until it becomes a competition. Without humility, all that drive turns toxic.

Ambition can quickly become a game of one-upmanship. The race for credit gets us focused on the reflection in the mirror instead of the mission. Before you know it, you're not building a team, you're building a stage.

I've caught myself doing it. I'm most susceptible after a big project wraps up. Everything went right, and people are throwing high-fives and thank-yous my way. Then, there's this voice whispering to me. *That was all you, Dan. They couldn't have done it without you.* And if I'm not careful, I believe it. There's danger in frequently being right and usually having the answer. Eventually, you stop listening, and worse, you stop learning.

I started young, too. As a kid, I had to be part of every conversation. It didn't matter who was talking—parents, grandparents, distant relatives, or strangers—if there was a story being told, I was jumping in with a better one. At least, that's what I thought. Looking back, most of my *better* stories were half-truths, embellished, or just plain made up.

When I was about twelve, a relative visited us. She had everyone's attention the moment she started talking. Her stories, wisdom, and presence fascinated me. I wanted so badly to be like that—to impress and be liked by her. I thought the only way to do that was to match every story she told with one of my own.

So, story after story, I one-upped her without realizing it. She'd talk about a camping trip. I made mine longer and more intense. She'd talk about an injury I'd talk about a time I almost broke my leg. Did any of it really happen? I don't even remember. But in my mind, it had to be said.

Later that day, my mom calmly and softly pulled me aside. That was my first clue she was about to drop a truth bomb on me. She said, "Son, you have two ears and one mouth. That means you're supposed to listen twice as much as you talk. God designed you that way on purpose." She wasn't mad or embarrassed. She was parenting with a dose of holy wisdom.

Then she added something I'll never forget. "You don't have to outshine everybody else. Let them have their moment in the sun. Your stories and your time will come. And when it does, you won't need a spotlight, because the light will already be in you."

That was the first time I truly heard the word *humility* without her even saying it. She was right. True leaders know when to speak and when to listen. They don't jump in to compete. They show up to contribute.

That lesson stuck with me, and I've seen it play out repeatedly in leadership. You can always spot the moment a leader drifts away from humility. Their world gets smaller. Their team gets quieter. Bold thinkers stop offering ideas because they're tired of being ignored or corrected. It's not worth the effort. The office becomes a stage, and everyone else just plays backup.

Humility starts when curiosity outsizes commentary.

But a humble leader invites people to the table, not to sit there and nod, but to speak. They listen, ask questions, and hand the mic to someone else when it's their turn to shine. They celebrate when someone else has the correct answer. They're more obsessed with results than credit. And when a better idea shows up, they don't squash it. They build on it. That leadership isn't soft or passive. It takes more strength than pride ever will.

Staying humble when people start clapping is more challenging than it appears. It takes wisdom to say, "I'm honored, but I'm still learning." It takes character to keep pointing back to the team instead of the mirror. Humility keeps you grounded in your calling.

You remember where you came from. You remember the late nights and early mornings. You remember the mentors who believed in you before you even believed in yourself. You remember the coworkers who carried more than their share without ever asking for applause. And when someone hands you a platform, you use it to lift others higher, not just to raise your profile.

A wise leader once told me, "You'll know you're doing it right when people trust you with things that matter, not because they fear you, but because they know you care about more than just yourself." Humility is leadership without the need for a spotlight, influence without ego, and strength without swagger.

Not surprisingly, the most humble people I've ever met are also the most powerful. They build leaders by building people. Good teams, a title, and a successful year lead to what I want for you—a legacy of leadership built on humility, not hype.

Why Humility Is Crucial in Leadership

That two-ears-one-mouth conversation with my mom when I was a kid stuck with me. At the time, I just thought I needed to shut up more. But she was teaching me humility without speaking that word. She introduced me to what I'd later recognize as the foundation of leadership. True leaders don't chase the spotlight, they shine it on others. They don't speak to be heard, they listen to understand. They don't need to outshine anyone to know they matter. Now, decades later, sitting in that early-morning meeting with the president and VP of the company, that lesson came full circle.

They weren't promoting me because I was the loudest, nor were they giving me more responsibility because I demanded it. They trusted me to carry their names into the field because they knew I could do it without making it about myself.

They watched how I treated people—those in charge and those in coveralls. HR reps, safety guys, dispatchers, and drivers received the same courtesies—especially the drivers who had just finished a fourteen-hour shift and needed grace more than another policy shoved in their face.

They saw how I handled conversations, even when I could have dominated, but didn't. They observed me listening, staying late, and making space for people and their needs. People follow trust, and trust is built on humility. A donut offered in a breakroom, a returned phone call, and encouraging words when someone doubts themselves are the building blocks of trust. Humility makes people feel safe enough to bring their best. They know the leader in the room isn't going to hog the credit or crush their ideas.

Shortly before my promotion, I was passing through one of our divisions and decided to stop in. I said *hello* to the admin team, shook a few hands, and made my way to the shop, where I spoke with one of the parts runners. He was organizing bins, head down, not even looking up when I walked in. I offered him a donut and struck up a conversation. I asked him a simple question. "If you could fix anything about how parts are ordered, what would you change?"

He paused, looked up, and blinked like I had just spoken in a foreign language. Then he said, "No one's ever asked me that before." He proceeded to share what he saw every day. And it was gold. That's humility. Not mine, his. He didn't try to impress me.

That one question sparked changes that made our systems better. Humility means you're willing to learn from anyone. If I had walked in that day assuming I had all the answers, I would have walked out with nothing. But showing up with a humble posture led to insight, influence, and trust.

Arrogance looks like confidence on the outside, but it corrodes influence from the inside. Arrogant leaders build big, shiny, and fragile glass houses. Humble leaders build strong and grounded fortresses made to last. Arrogance burns bridges. Humility builds them. Arrogance silences teams. Humility gives them a voice. Arrogance wants the credit. Humility wants the result.

I need to tell you about Barney and how I learned this lesson because of him. Now that's not his real name, but we're going with it because the guy had a law enforcement background and reminded me a lot of Barney Fife. Except, he had more ego, less charm, and walked around like the mayor of a town nobody wanted to visit. He was my boss, and he convinced himself that he was God's gift to leadership.

He strutted through the shop like he was about to break up a biker gang. Meanwhile, we were just trying to order printer ink. His voice could make a jackhammer flinch, and he loved asking rhetorical questions like they were TED Talks. "You know why this place runs so smoothly?" (He thought the answer was him. It wasn't.)

He looked like a leader. He wore pressed shirts, used big words, and used dramatic pauses effectively. But inside, he was more like a shaken-up soda can. The work culture was tense due to his explosive nature, and there was absolutely no warning before the pop.

I tried to ignore it for a long time. *He was under a lot of pressure. This is a phase we'll all get through. Maybe he's allergic to joy.* Those were some of the rationales I used to cope with it. What I soon discovered is that he didn't like the way I led.

People responded to my style. Instead of leading the old-school way, checking the traditional boxes, I was building relationships. I was earning trust and creating change. Barney didn't like it one bit.

One day, he laid down an ultimatum: "It's either Dan or me." He told the president flat-out that he couldn't work with me anymore. He tried to force the boss's hand by painting me as the problem.

I had every reason to go on the defensive. Every reason to throw verbal punches. The facts, performance data, and team support were on my side. I could have gone to war, but I didn't. I stayed quiet, consistent, and humble.

When the president heard the ultimatum, he looked at Barney and said, "Then it's Dan." That was it. Barney was given the choice to resign or be fired. He chose to resign, saying, "That's what a real man does."

If I had gone into that situation with arrogance, defending myself by tearing him down, I believe I'd have lost. I might have lost the job, but losing trust, respect, and the future I was being prepared for would have been devastating.

Humility saved my job. More importantly, it protected my family from a season of hardship. That's why I don't talk about humility like it's a feel-good leadership slogan. I talk about it like it's a lifeline, because it is. Humility is staying grounded when you've got every reason to float away on your success.

Humility keeps you teachable after you've been promoted and preserves your honor when you've been wronged. It's how you stay influential when others start raising torches and pitchforks. You don't build humility by reading about it. You build it by choosing it every single time you don't have to.

That morning, as I sat in the president's office, listening to him explain my new role, I felt as though I was being entrusted with something of great value. I walked out, not thinking, *look what I did,* but praying, "Lord, help me carry this well. Help me never forget how I got here. Keep me grounded. Keep me humble. Let me be a leader people trust, not because I'm perfect, but because I serve."

Arrogance vs. Humility: Spotting the Difference

My promotion came with a surprising tension. The higher you climb in leadership, the easier it is to let humility slip, not because you stop caring, but because you start winning.

People start listening and seeking your opinion. They use your name in meetings you're not even in. And before you know it, you start believing your own hype. You start thinking, *I've got this. I already know. I've figured it out.* That's where arrogance creeps in.

It doesn't walk through the front door, kicking stuff over. It slips in quietly, wearing your wins like a name tag and whispering things like, *they need you,* or *you know more than they do,* or the classic, *this place wouldn't run without you.* It sounds like confidence and feels like control. But it's a slow leak that drains the trust you spent years building.

At first, you think you're just being efficient, taking charge, and leading the way. But eventually, you start noticing the tense silence. Your team waits to see how you react before they speak. People say *yes* a little too quickly. Feedback dies in the hallway before it ever reaches your desk.

You don't notice it right away because you're still getting results. But results without a relationship start a countdown to collapse. I've felt it and caused it, and I've had to face it head-on. Arrogance sometimes shows up with a smirk.

Once, I caught myself cutting someone off in a meeting before they finished their thought. I didn't do it out of malice. I was sure I knew where they were going. I *yeah yeah yeah'd* their idea and tossed out my version instead. I thought I was being helpful and efficient. But after the meeting, one of my team members pulled me aside and said, "Dan, I don't think you meant it the way it came across, but I think you just made them feel like their voice didn't matter."

That hit me right in the gut, because they were right. Arrogance makes us so confident in ourselves that we stop leaving room for others to contribute their ideas. And even if we're right, we're still wrong if people stop feeling heard. That's why I started paying attention.

Do I talk more than I listen? Do I shut down ideas before they're finished? Do people only bring me half the truth because they're worried about how I'll take it? These are the dashboard warning lights that say, "Pull over and check your leadership before it catches fire."

I've watched great leaders lose their edge not because they failed, but because they succeeded without humility. And I've watched teams loaded with talent quietly disengage while their leader gave TED Talk-style monologues and wondered why nothing ever changed.

You can still shake hands, lead meetings, and hit your key performance indicators. But if your people stop trusting that you see them, it's over. The hardest part is recognizing that stepping up can sometimes be a form of arrogance when you're in it. But under the surface, the very influence you worked so hard to build is slowly slipping through your fingers. That's why we have to stay on guard. Arrogance doesn't just show up in the people above you. It can rise right under your nose, too. And I hate to say it, but I helped create it.

An employee we'll call Jeff was my second hire, but the first real employee once the business had a solid foundation. I'd hired a buddy before Jeff, and while he was a good guy, I jumped the gun. My company wasn't ready to support both of us. So, when Jeff came along, he became my first true teammate.

He came from a sales background, but I hired him to help with compliance. I figured, "Hey, if I can learn this stuff, anyone can. It's not rocket science. It's DOT science. Which is like rocket science but usually with more paperwork and fewer explosions."

At first, Jeff was humble and eager, but a little slow. He was hired for forty hours a week, but I don't think he hit that mark once during his first year. He frequently needed a Monday morning, Friday afternoon, or a Wednesday off. Sometimes he asked for all three in the same week. At the time, my business could absorb it, so I made it work.

He was improving, slowly but surely, and I wanted to reward that. So, I gave him raises. In the first six months, he earned $2 more an hour. That would have blown my mind as an employee. I figured it would inspire him and show him that I believed in him.

It did, for a while. However, as his confidence grew, so did his sense of entitlement. One day, he walked into my office and said, "Dan, I want a $5 an hour raise." I blinked.

"You've been here like a year and a half. You've already gotten four bucks in raises. You're doing good, and I appreciate it, but five bucks?"

He answered, "You couldn't operate without me. I'm worth that much."

Interesting logic. We negotiated and met somewhere in the middle. I told myself that he was just ambitious, and he's growing. But the pattern had started.

Six months later, he came to me again. "It's been six months. When do I get my next raise?"

What the heck? Who told this guy that raises were an automatic semiannual event? Oh, wait—I did—not with my words, but with my actions.

In addition to the *request* for a raise, his tone was shifting. After three years with me, he came to my office and told me he felt he was taking a step backward because he was handling more compliance tasks again, rather than commission sales. Never mind that he'd just gotten a $5,000 raise. Never mind that he was still making monthly recurring commissions that put his paycheck on par with mine, and I was the owner.

He didn't care about that. He cared about Friday night, the next drink, the next party, and a *deserved* bonus. Meanwhile, I was working to replace team members who had left, some of whom, I later learned, left because of him. I refused to see it at the time, but I couldn't ignore the trend.

Two more people quit within a week. And during exit interviews, both said nearly the same thing. "Jeff is overwhelming. He demands respect but takes zero responsibility. If he wants to act like the boss, let him do it."

That hit hard. I knew then I'd let it go too far. I had been rewarding arrogance without meaning to. I'd mistaken confidence for contribution. And I'd ignored the signs because I didn't want to deal with the mess. But I owned it.

We picked up the slack. I stepped in and started rebuilding the team from the ground up. Despite it all, I gave Jeff a bonus during that transition because I knew he'd be losing some commission income. I wanted to show gratitude, even as I tightened the ship.

Then came the final straw. The day after Thanksgiving, he called in sick. And the next day, he asked to meet. I figured he had something to say. I wasn't expecting this. "Dan, you have two options. Either you give me a $25,000 raise or I quit. But I'll stay through Christmas and New Year's to get the holiday bonuses you usually give out."

Let that sink in. The guy's paycheck was already mirroring mine. I'd given him raises, bonuses, flexibility, and trust. And here he was, giving me an ultimatum, dangling his loyalty like bait long enough to grab a bonus check on the way out.

I didn't flinch. I said, "Sounds like your last day is tomorrow. Pack up your stuff. Ship back the company equipment—both laptops, the monitor, and anything you bought on the card. I want it all back by the end of the day." And that was that. (My wife still doesn't know this story. So, if you ever meet her, don't tell her. She might still throttle the guy from five hundred miles away.)

Here's the lesson: When you stop leading with humility, you start expecting things that aren't owed to you. You confuse reward with entitlement. You stop thinking about the team and start calculating how the team can serve you. And if you don't catch it, if no one around you calls it out, you'll begin to believe you're the reason everything works.

But let me be very clear. Arrogance always has a cost. If you don't pay attention, you won't just lose opportunities, you'll lose people, culture, and trust. That's why we have to watch for it in our teams, peers, and most importantly, ourselves.

Humility builds something that lasts. Arrogance demands something that eventually collapses. If I hadn't seen it up close, I might've missed it in the mirror. That's why I had to get honest with myself, and why every leader I've ever respected has had to do the same. If we're not consciously choosing humility, arrogance will do the choosing for us.

I don't care how high up the ladder you've climbed. If you lose the trust of your people, you're not leading anymore. You're just occupying a position. I never want to be that guy. And I don't want that for you either. That's why I built a habit I call the Humility Audit. It's a regular gut check to keep my ego in its place before it costs me more than I'm willing to lose.

The Humility Audit: How to Check Yourself

It didn't start as a system. There wasn't a moment when I sat down and said, "You know what this leadership journey needs? A Humility Audit." There wasn't a whiteboard, brainstorm, retreat, or TED Talk. It started with me sitting in my truck with a pounding headache from another long day, realizing I was dangerously close to becoming the leader I swore I'd never be.

I had a great team—incredible people. Folks who bought into the vision showed up early, stayed late, and carried the weight as if it were their own. Somewhere along the way, I noticed a shift, not in them, in me.

I stopped asking questions because I was so sure I had the answers. I stopped fully listening because I could finish their sentences. I started measuring my leadership by the scoreboard, not the condition of the locker room. And worst of all, I stopped seeing the subtle ways pride was poisoning my influence.

That's when I realized I needed a system. It didn't need to be formal or a framed poster with a mountain and an eagle and the word *integrity* under it. I needed something tangible—a rhythm, a habit, and a gut check for my soul. So, I built one—the Humility Audit.

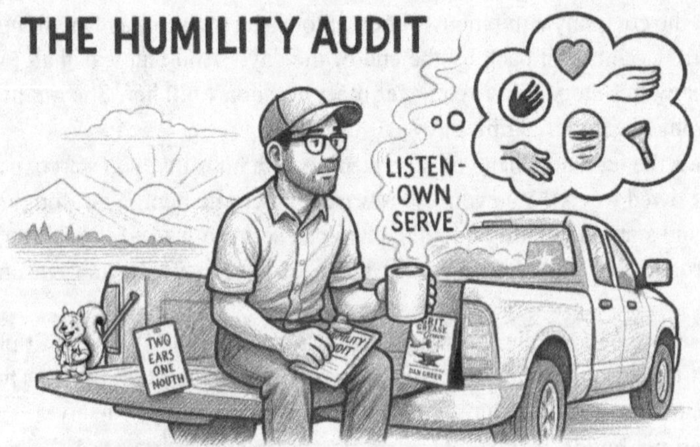

Influence starts with a gut-check, not a mic-check.

It's saved my leadership more times than duct tape, coffee, and awkward apologies combined. Seriously. The Humility Audit is like a spiritual oil change for your ego. It's a quick little check under the hood to make sure you haven't started thinking you're the most intelligent person in every room. (You're not. And if you are, you're in the wrong room.)

It's not formal. It's not typed up on company letterhead. It doesn't require a conference, a PDF, or a journal with a leather strap that smells like cedar and insecurity. It's just me being honest with myself daily—sometimes hourly—always before it's too late.

It's crucial to audit your humility regularly, as your influence doesn't crumble all at once. It erodes slowly. And I could feel it happening in me. I had started believing my own highlight reel. I started seeing the compliments as confirmation that I was the glue, the engine, and the guy who held it all together. But that wasn't humility. That was pride on a pedestal. So, I got to work on myself, because if I couldn't keep myself in check, I didn't deserve to lead anyone else.

The audit isn't complicated. It's not passive reflection, where I sip tea and think about the clouds. It's a raw, unfiltered look at my day, tone, and posture—what I said, how I said it, and what it cost.

Sometimes it happens at night, when the house is quiet and my brain won't shut off. Other times, it's in the middle of the day, right after a meeting where I bulldozed someone and instantly felt that gut punch that said, "You just missed it."

And sometimes it happens in my parked truck with the keys out of the ignition and total silence. Staring at the steering wheel, I'm praying, *Lord, did I lead like the man You want me to be today? Or did I just lead like the guy I think I am?*

That's where the real work begins—no spreadsheets or team huddle. Five brutally honest questions keep my leadership from drifting into arrogance, and my heart from drifting away from humility. This is the Humility Audit, and here's precisely how I do it.

I walk through five real questions every time:

1. Did I intentionally listen to the people I led today?

The answer to this question goes beyond, "Was I in the room?" and "Did I nod along while thinking about dinner?" I mean, did I *really* listen?

- Did I put the phone down, look them in the eye, and hear what they were saying?
- Did I ask a follow-up question because I was curious, or because I felt like I had to look engaged?

It's even trickier to listen in virtual meetings. Ask yourself:

- Did I stop typing that email while someone was talking, or was I multitasking like a productivity ninja while pretending I cared?
- Was I present, or did I do that thing where someone asks a critical question and I respond with, "Wait, sorry. What did you say?" while frantically closing three tabs?

If I'm distracted, I'm not leading. If I'm checked out, so is my team. And if I didn't truly listen, then I didn't lead.

2. Did I give credit or quietly hoard it?

- When something went right today, did I call it out and say, "That was all them," or did I secretly hope someone would clap for me instead?
- Did I give my team the credit they earned, or did I polish the win and take credit for it as if it were mine alone?

And here's the part that hurts a little more.

- When things went wrong, did I protect my team, or did I throw them under the bus to save face?
- When a client called frustrated, and I knew one of my people had dropped the ball, did I say, "Thanks for your patience, we're working on it," or did I say, "Yeah, that's on our team. I'll get on them," just to dodge the discomfort?

If I threw someone under the bus today, I'm the one who should have been hit by it. And if I let someone else on the team point fingers instead of taking ownership, I missed a huge moment to lead with integrity.

A real leader squashes blame games fast, because giving credit isn't just about clapping for people when they win. It's about covering them when things don't go perfectly.

That's how you build loyalty. That's how you build trust. And if I didn't do that today, I've got work to do tomorrow.

3. Did I own anything?

- Did I admit I was wrong today, or did I come up with a pretty good reason for why it wasn't technically my fault?
- Did I take a breath and say, "That one's on me," or did I launch into a polished explanation that made it sound like the universe just conspired against me?
- When someone challenged me, gently or directly, was I teachable? Or did I get defensive? If I can't be corrected, I can't be trusted.

If I'm always the smartest guy in the room, I'll eventually be the only one left in it. Owning my part isn't optional. It's the price of leading anything that matters.

4. Did I lead people or just manage them?

- Did I invest in someone today?

And I don't mean, "Did I throw them a quick *good job* before heading back to my inbox?" I mean, did I take time to teach someone something they didn't know before?

- When they hit a wall with a task, did I show them how to do it patiently, or did I just sigh, take over, and knock it out myself?

We've all done that. We tell ourselves it's faster if I just do it, and it is for now. But next week? They'll still need your help. And the week after that, they'll need it again. Eventually, you'll resent them for not knowing what you never actually taught them.

If I didn't give someone the time to grow today, I didn't lead. I managed. I need to slow down long enough to lead and not just delegate.

Leadership isn't about controlling outcomes. It's about building people who can carry the weight without you. If I treated people like tools instead of teammates today, I failed the mission.

And no spreadsheet or scorecard makes up for that.

5. Did anyone feel smaller because of me today?

This one hits hard, and it should, because it emphasizes the importance of valuing the people you lead.

- Did someone walk away from me today feeling unseen?
- Did my tone shut them down?
- Did my sarcasm sting more than I meant it to?
- Did I one-up someone in a meeting just to make sure everyone knew I was smarter?

I never want to be that leader. My goal is to never talk down to anyone. Period.

Most of us have been pulled over or know someone who has been pulled over by that officer who looks down over their glasses like you're some half-functioning adult, and hits you with the classic, "Do you know why I pulled you over?" You know the tone—the one that already assumes guilt and hands out shame with the citation.

I'm not saying officers shouldn't pull people over. Heck, I've trained enough drivers to know some of them need to be pulled over. But you always remember how that moment made you feel.

So, here are the questions to ask:

- Did I make someone feel that way today?
- Did someone come to me with a genuine question or need, and I responded like they were dumb for not knowing the answer?

I promise you this. They'll remember it if you did. And they'll probably think twice before ever asking again.

If someone felt smaller, embarrassed, or unseen because of me today, then I've got some work to do. And it starts with a simple conversation that most leaders are too proud to have.

"Hey, I'm sorry. I could have handled that better."

This isn't soft leadership. This is real leadership. If I'm not careful, my influence turns into intimidation, and people start following out of fear instead of trust. That's not the culture I want. That's not the leader I'm called to be.

Here's the second part of the audit, and this one's critical: How often should you run it? Every. Dang. Day. I'm not kidding. You check your bank account, don't you? You check your tires before a long haul. You check your meat before throwing it on the grill. You better believe I'm checking my humility before I lead people who are counting on me. I check it:

- After wins
- After conflict
- After someone compliments me publicly (I double-check it)
- After I say something that felt *off* in a meeting

I don't want to wake up one day and realize I've become a leader people only follow because they have to, not because they want to.

I never want my pride to compromise my team's trust, and I never want to stand before my wife, kids, employees, or God and pretend to be humble when I haven't checked my heart all week.

So, I run the audit every day. And when the answers suck, I deal with it. I apologize and reset because true humility isn't about staying perfect. It's about staying aware and being honest enough to course-correct before your people start doing it for you.

And let me be clear. This isn't a one-time practice for bad seasons. It's a daily practice for healthy leadership. It's a habit worth developing and a posture of humility. It's a system of staying grounded in a world that constantly wants to inflate you.

So that's how I do it. I ask five brutally honest questions and answer them truthfully, blocking out any influence from my ego. If you won't check yourself, trust me, someone else will. By the time they do, it might be too late to fix what you broke while you were too busy being impressive.

So do the audit. Every. Dang. Day. Then lead with confidence, because you've done the work to stay grounded in humility.

Humility Is Influence in Action

I used to think influence came from experience, titles, and how many people nodded when you spoke in a meeting. I figured if you won every argument, had the best plan, and fixed the biggest mess, people would automatically follow you. Turns out, that's not influence, and it sure isn't leadership.

One of my favorite quotes says, "If you're leading without followers, you're just out taking a walk." I'm pretty sure I first read that in one of John Maxwell's books, although I recall him saying he didn't know the origin of the original proverb either.

Either way, it stuck with me because it's true. It's a gut check most leaders never take, and some desperately need.

What I've learned, what this whole chapter has been building toward, is this: Influence doesn't come from being right. It comes from being real and in a place of humility.

Sitting in the president's office before sunrise that day, my racing heart convinced me I was done. I was bracing for the hammer to fall, certain I was getting fired for caring too much, saying too much, doing too much. Instead, they trusted me more than anyone had before. They didn't say it out loud, but I could feel it. What gave them the confidence to hand me more responsibility wasn't my performance. It was my posture.

They'd watched me show up without asking for credit, stay late, talk to the guy in the shop, and ask questions no one else bothered to ask. They saw me walk into offices and not just speak to managers, but learn from janitors, HR clerks, the guy sorting paperwork, and the safety guy who didn't use two words if one would do. They saw humility in motion. I didn't nail it every time, but I was willing to sit lower so others could stand taller. That's what builds influence.

Do you want people to follow you? Then listen to them. Show up early. Stay late. People remember who shows up. Protect your team, especially when it's inconvenient. Give someone else the credit, even when you secretly wish someone would pat you on the back.

People don't follow perfect leaders. They follow leaders who are willing to put themselves second for the good of the people in front of them. That's humility, and that's influence in action.

I get it. It doesn't always feel like it's working. Humility rarely looks glamorous in the moment. You won't always be thanked and noticed. Sometimes, it feels like you're carrying the weight while others ride the wave. However, I've learned that humble leaders always outlast those who are proud.

When you lead with humility, you're building something deeper than loyalty. You're building trust. And trust is what keeps people walking with you when everything else gets hard. It's what holds teams together when things go sideways. It's what makes your voice worth following long after the meeting ends.

That promotion? In my experience, it's never felt like a reward. It's felt like a responsibility. Not a raise in status, but a reminder: You're here to serve, not sit at the top. I've learned that real influence only works when you hold it with open hands. Trust doesn't come from being impressive. It comes from showing up when no one asks, listening when no one expects it, and carrying weight that isn't always yours to carry.

I didn't walk out of that office feeling like I'd won something. I walked out feeling the weight of being a leader people want to follow, not because I say the right things, but because I do the right things when no one's watching. That's what humility builds. And that's what builds influence that lasts—not in the spotlight with praise or status, but quiet strength that serves, listens, and stands in the gap when others shrink back.

If leadership is influence, then humility is the engine that keeps it running. I'm still learning, screwing things up, doing the audit, and praying I never forget where I came from or who I'm called to serve. I never want to take a walk alone, thinking I'm leading, when I could have walked beside people who trusted me if I'd just had the humility to slow down and invite them.

Leading with Quiet Strength and Giving Credit Where Credit Is Due

Sometimes the best example of humble leadership doesn't come from a boardroom or a business meeting. Sometimes, it comes from the passenger seat, driving home with your wife as the kids nap in the back seat and the sun's setting over the dashboard.

Jenna and I were just talking the other day. It was a conversation you don't plan, but naturally unfolds. We started reminiscing about when the kids were in elementary school. Life was a blur of backpacks, permission slips, half-eaten granola bars, and PTO (Parent Teacher Organization) carnivals. And man, Jenna was all in.

Now, if you don't know this about my wife, Jenna doesn't *kinda* do anything. Whether it's decorating a room for VBS (Vacation Bible School) or helping a friend plan a birthday party, she doesn't dip her toe in. She cannonballs into the deep end every time.

She's the person who will spend weeks building foam-board mountains, painting jungle vines, and hanging hand-cut stars from the ceiling for preschoolers who will barely remember any of it. But it matters to her that it's just right. And somehow, she pulls it off so well that other teachers take tours through her VBS rooms every single year. Yeah, it's that kind of excellence.

So naturally, when our oldest was in kindergarten, and the PTO put out a call for volunteers for the Halloween carnival, Jenna raised her hand to run a game room. Which meant she didn't just run it, she *owned* it. She planned, designed, and built props for it. She secured prizes and decorated every vertical and horizontal surface, possibly even the janitor's closet.

She went to carpet stores to get old rolls to turn into trees. She visited appliance stores and gathered cardboard to build backdrops and mountain scenes. She was hot-gluing, crafting, cutting, painting, and assembling, all while juggling toddlers, laundry, and dinner prep with one hand.

On carnival night, that room looked like something Disney would have hired her to replicate. But here's the kicker. Jenna had to step away from the room for part of the evening. During that time, another mom, who had arrived late for her shift, stood at the door, greeting people, walking them through the room, and taking full credit for every inch of it.

"This was my idea." "Oh yeah, I designed that wall!" "Thanks! Yeah, it took forever to pull together."

Jenna came back, saw it happening, and didn't say a word, not because she hadn't noticed; she had, and it stung. She remained quiet because she showed up to serve that night, not to receive credit.

Honestly, that moment infuriated me. I mean, come on! I watched her pour her heart into that room. She carried that carnival on her back for weeks. She put in more time and effort than most of the PTO combined, and someone else was out there basking in the spotlight like she was just stepping in to take a bow on Jenna's stage.

It made me want to jump in and say something. But Jenna smiled and rolled with it, not because it didn't matter, but because it wasn't the point. She was there for the kids, community, and something bigger than her ego. If someone else needed the recognition that badly, she was willing to let them have it.

That strength and quiet, grace-filled confidence is rare. Most of us would have pulled that mom aside and said, "Hey, you didn't even show up on time, and now you're pretending you planned this?" We would have had every right to say it. Jenna's response was more powerful. She didn't let someone else's ego rob her of her purpose. She knew who she was and what she contributed. She knew that the people who mattered, her kids, friends, teachers, and everyone who saw the work behind the scenes, knew it too.

What stuck with me even more than that night was what she did on all the other nights. There were plenty of times she wasn't the project lead. She was an extra pair of hands, stapling decorations or gluing together props. People would walk in and say, "Wow, Jenna! This is amazing! You're incredible!"

She'd smile and say, "Oh, thanks, but I just helped. Kay did the heavy lifting. I was just on the crew." She deflected praise just as easily as she could have absorbed it. She gave credit without hesitation, performance, or insecurity. People started trusting her more. They invited her in earlier and leaned on her more deeply. They knew she wasn't there for herself. She was there for the mission. And when she showed up, it wasn't about being the star; it was about making the whole team better.

By the time our youngest graduated fifth grade, the school threw Jenna a going-away party. It was a full-blown, heartfelt, hallway-hugging, teary-eyed goodbye. They didn't do that for the principal, but they did it for Jenna. People never forget how you make them feel. When you lead with humility, give credit where it's due, and show up without needing a spotlight, people follow you. That's influence.

As we drove and talked about all this, I felt convicted. I've been both of those people. I've been the one who worked hard and got overlooked, and I've been the one who took more credit than I deserved, whether I meant to or not.

When you're in leadership, it's so easy to convince yourself that you've earned it. You're just owning your win and it's okay to soak up the praise because you do work hard. People who make the most profound impact don't need to be noticed to feel fulfilled. They don't need to be applauded to know their worth. They consistently demonstrate excellence, integrity, and humility, like my wife, Jenna. She didn't teach me humility with a quote or a lecture. She taught me with hot glue, cardboard trees, and a smile in the face of someone else taking the bow. She showed me that the most influential people in the room are often the ones who say the least and do the most.

People want to follow leaders who stay late to clean up the mess, and still give someone else the credit for the party.

Final Challenge: Be the Humblest Person in the Room

If there's one thread that ties this whole chapter together, one thing I hope you didn't miss, it's this: Humility isn't a leadership strategy. It's a way of life.

It doesn't matter if you're leading a company, a classroom, or a PTO carnival— it's how you treat people that builds lasting influence. I've seen it in the boardroom, when the president of a multi-million-dollar company told me that what made me worthy of more responsibility wasn't my performance, it was my posture.

I've seen it in my wife, watching her glue together cardboard trees and staying silent while someone else took the credit, because she showed up to serve, not to be seen.

And, I've seen it in my son Billy, who reminded me there is enough success to go around without him needing anyone else to DOR from diver's training.

And that, my friend, is humility. He wasn't thinking about climbing to the top by stepping over others or worrying about how he looked in comparison. He just wanted everyone to succeed, even those who made it difficult for him.

That's mature, heart-driven leadership. He didn't learn it from a leadership seminar. He learned it in the quiet moments; watching, listening, and seeing how real strength shows up with sleeves rolled up and ego tucked in. That's the leader and father I want to be. That's what I hope this book helps you build into your life.

After the meetings are over, the carnival's cleaned up, the team goes home, and your son has earned his place on the battlefield of life, what will people say about your leadership? Were you impressive? Did you always have the answers? Did you look good in a blazer? Or will they say:

- You showed up for people who didn't expect it."
- You gave credit when you could have taken it.
- You led with open hands and an honest heart.
- You made us feel seen.

That's the influence that echoes. That outlasts the title and the nameplate on your desk. That's what your kids carry with them when they face their own crossroads.

So here's my final challenge to you: Be the humblest person in the room. Not the quietest or the softest. Be the one who listens most intently, shines the light on others, and still does the audit, even after the applause.

Be the leader who doesn't just demand trust, but earns it daily. Be the one who leaves people feeling stronger after talking to you, not weaker. Teach with grace, listen with patience, and lead without needing to be the hero.

If there's anything I've learned from the boardroom to the barracks to the PTO, it's this: The most humble people I know are also the most powerful.

- They don't lead with noise. They lead with presence.
- They don't hog the spotlight. They create room for others to shine.
- They don't need to be the center of the story. They build stories that matter.

Walk in humbleness and readiness carrying the influence the world needs.

Key Takeaways from Chapter Twelve

 **Spotlights are optional; headlights are mandatory.** Show up early, light the way for everybody else, and let the applause chase you down the hallway later.

 **If your phone blows up at 5 a.m., assume it's God checking your pride—** not HR serving pink-slip pancakes. Keep calm, zip up, and answer humbly.

 **Humility isn't thinking you're small—it's refusing to elbow for center stage.** Confidence whispers, "I'm ready." Arrogance screams, "I'm owed."

 **Credit is like hot coffee—pass it around before you burn yourself.** Give it away fast and often; you'll still smell like the roast.

 **Your two-ear, one-mouth ratio is not a suggestion.** Listen like there's gold in every sentence, because occasionally there is.

 **Do the daily Humility Audit before somebody else does it for you.**
- Did I really listen?
- Did I hog credit or hold umbrellas?
- Did I own my junk?
- Did I build a person, not just a plan?
- Did anyone walk away smaller?

 **Raise others, not prices.** Want more authority? Lift teammates higher. The promotion text comes when you're too busy serving to expect it.

 **Arrogance walks in dressed as *efficiency*.** If you're finishing everyone's sentences, you're probably finishing their trust, too.

 **The strongest leaders run on quiet octane.** They wash feet, glue cardboard trees, and still clap loudest when someone else takes the bow.

 **Enough success exists for everybody—stop needing someone to DOR so you can dominate.** Root for the room; it proves you're bigger than your ego.

 **Be the humblest human in every meeting.** Not the softest, not the shyest— the one who listens longest, learns fastest, and leaves others taller.

MULTIPLICATION > ADDITION

Chapter 13 | Multiplying Leaders: The Legacy Move

Legacy doesn't just happen. You build it with dust and levers.

You've got to promise me something. When this story hits, don't act like I never told you. You'll be tempted to say, "No way that happened." But it did. And now it's in print, so there's no backing out.

When I first learned to run a motor grader, one of those big, low-riding Caterpillar beasts that look like it belonged in a Transformer movie, I didn't learn from a YouTube tutorial or fancy-pants simulator. Nope. I learned the old-school way: by standing on the step, clinging to the side like a cat on a screen door, watching real-deal blade hands do their thing while I inhaled more dust than a vacuum cleaner.

I'm not exaggerating. I'd spend hours standing outside the cab while that machine crawled along at two and a half miles per hour. There I was in my overalls with a mouthful of gravel dust and a dream. This thing didn't have controls. It had a cockpit. Picture this:

- A steering wheel
- Twelve levers
- A throttle
- Two brake pedals

- A panel of other switches that probably launched satellites or opened garage doors in Nebraska

It looked like someone had duct-taped a spaceship to a bulldozer and said, "Good luck, rookie." I was hungry to learn. Not snack-before-dinner hungry. I'm talking did-leg-day-and-skipped-lunch hungry. I asked every operator questions:

- Why'd you move that lever?
- Why'd you feather the blade there?
- Why'd you cuss just now?
- Was that the lever's fault or yours?

These guys loved it. They wanted me to get it. Every one of them took time to show me, explain it, break it down, and then hand over the wheel. They'd let me try it out, then sit in the truck and watch me from a distance while I puttered along like a toddler learning to ride a bike. Only this one came with a 40,000-pound blade.

After thirty minutes, they'd come and offer feedback. "Hey, you shaved the crown off the whole road," or "Congratulations, you made a ditch where we didn't need one," or the classic, "Don't ever do that again."

But they always did it with a smirk. Why? They were doing more than running machines, they were building me.

Now let's change gears for a minute (see what I did there?).

Picture a massive, high-gloss poster: I'm standing like a boss, ball cap tilted forward, arms crossed, in a cloud of swirling dust. Behind me? A lineup of yellow beasts—dozers, excavators, skid steers, maybe a wheel loader revving just because it can. The lighting is dramatic. Dust is swirling. It's basically the cover of a construction-themed superhero movie. And underneath it, in bold letters, you can read from the parking lot:

"STAND IN THE DUST. BECOME THE BEST."

I know, this might sound like something you'd see on a motivational poster. But this was far more significant than one of those sad little printouts tacked above a busted time clock in the corner of a breakroom that smells like burned popcorn. I'm talking global domination. This poster isn't hanging in *one* office. It's in *every* equipment dealership and rental counter *worldwide*.

Walk into the lobby of the biggest Cat, Deere, Case, or Komatsu dealer on the planet, and there it is, right next to the coffee machine, glaring down at every fleet manager, shop lead, and first-day operator like it's saying, "Hey rookie! You ready?"

But here's the truth behind the poster. The guys who taught me didn't do it for show. They didn't mentor me because it was part of their job description. They didn't get extra pay, fancy titles, or a shout-out at the company Christmas party. They just did it because that's what real leaders do. They multiply.

They saw a young, green, cocky kid (yes, me), trying to act like I knew what I was doing, and instead of letting me sink, they stepped in. They showed me how to grease the fittings correctly, how to listen before speaking, and how to think like the person responsible for the entire operation, not just his piece of the puzzle.

They didn't stand above the dust yelling down instructions. They stood in it with me. That's leadership that sticks. That's the legacy you build with calloused hands and diesel in your lungs. That's what multiplies.

So yeah, put the poster everywhere. Hang it in lobbies, dealerships, job trailers, rental yards, and anywhere people still value hard work and helping the next guy win. Leadership doesn't happen in corner offices. It happens right there in the dirt—boots on, sleeves rolled, legacy in progress. I wanted to be multiplied.

That's rare, by the way. Most folks want to *inherit* greatness, not *earn* it. They want to skip the step where you eat dust, sweat through your shirt, and look like an idiot for a week straight.

I was speaking at an event one day. The room was standing-room-only packed. It felt like a fire marshal's nightmare and a speaker's dream. It's super cool to be the one at the mic.

Anyway, I'm talking about leadership, growth, and business, you know, the good stuff, and I start rattling off some of the books that have changed my life. Books that helped me go from burned out and maxed out to building businesses that thrive and people that shine.

I'm watching as a few folks in the crowd start scribbling those titles down like I just handed them the secret formula to Coca-Cola. Afterward, a couple of people came up, and one guy, super casually says, "Hey, do you make notes on all those books you read? Because I'd totally buy those from you."

I looked at him, smiled, and said, "Heck yeah, I make notes. But trust me, you wouldn't get a quarter of the value from my notes as you would from the actual book."

Then I gave him the real prescription: "Go buy it on audio and listen to it." Then, when you realize it's as much gold as I told you it was, buy it in hardcover and read it while you listen to it. Then, make your own freaking notes."

Quit looking for the shortcut. Stop hoping someone else's sweat will give you six-pack results. If you want legacy, if you want to be a leader worth emulating, you have to do the work.

Greatness? It doesn't come in a box set. It comes with blisters, repetition, and awkward first tries. And if you're lucky, it comes with someone willing to teach you. That, coupled with your willingness to show up and learn, is a winning combination.

Most people are scared of hard work because (brace yourself) it looks a lot like hard work. As Thomas Edison (Or maybe my grandpa—who knows anymore?) once said, "Opportunity is missed by most people because it comes dressed in overalls and looks like work."[5]

---

[5] It is widely attributed to Edison, but there's no concrete evidence he actually said or wrote those exact words.

But the legacy of those blade hands didn't end with them. It lived on in me and in every road I helped build. Within a month and a half, I was running finish grade before the asphalt crew came in. Me. The guy who started out standing on the step like a tourist in a theme park.

I was neither the smartest nor the strongest. But I was willing to learn from everyone, and they were willing to teach. That's what multiplying leaders looks like. Leadership is about being good at what you do and helping someone else become great, even if they do it better than you did. That's where we are going to dig in this chapter.

Fair warning: It's not going to be easy. It's going to feel like stepping off the blade and letting someone else take the levers. But it'll be worth it, because that's how you build something that lasts longer than you do.

Legacy isn't about what you *leave behind.* It's about who you *bring forward.* Ready to get dusty?

Why Multiplication is Better than Addition

If You're the Only One Swinging the Hammer, You're Going to Get Real Tired Real Fast.

Let's do a little leadership math. Don't worry. I'm not about to turn this into algebra class. I promise there will be no quizzes, no weird Xs and Ys, and no need to solve for anything except your future.

And before we proceed, let me say this. To every high school teacher who said, "You'll use this someday," I love you, but you were full of crap. Not once have I had to graph a parabola to win a client. What the heck is a parabola? No one has ever burst into my office demanding I solve for X before renewing a DOT number.

They also told me, "You'll never get paid to stare out a window all day."

I did that for over a decade as a driver and a heavy equipment operator. I was a man with a seat, a windshield, and a whole lot of thoughts. I wish I could go back to those teachers and say, "Maybe you didn't make the smartest predictions, but I found a way."

Windows became my classroom. Dusty roads became my books. And I got paid well—*decently*, I might add—to stare out a window while thinking through leadership problems, family decisions, and most importantly, how *not* to get the grader stuck again. (I got it stuck. Again.)

It's funny how life turns out, huh? Some people get leadership training from Ivy League professors. I got mine from an old diesel rig, a thermos full of gas station coffee, and a grader that had a personal vendetta against soft shoulders. But I'll tell you what. Those quiet moments behind the glass shaped me. They forced me to think, lead, and figure out how to fix problems when no one answered the radio, and the only other guy on site was twenty miles away and didn't believe in phones. That's real leadership training brought to you by dirt, diesel, and the occasional shovel.

Here's the deal: Addition grows teams. Multiplication grows impact. Both are useful and necessary. But only one turns your Monday meetings into a movement.

Addition says, "I need help. Let's hire someone." Multiplication says, "I see potential. Let's build someone."

Let me put it another way. Addition is like building a wall brick by brick. You lay one brick, then another, then another, and eventually, *ta-da*, a wall! But here's the problem: If you're the only one laying bricks, and you catch the flu, take a vacation, or finally get to that beach in Maui your wife's been talking about for three years, guess what happens? That wall won't build itself. At best, construction stalls. At worst, the wall crumbles like a graham cracker under a toddler's foot.

Now, imagine you taught three people how to lay bricks, and they each teach three more. And those folks start saying things like, "Hey, we could probably build a second wall over here."

Boom.

You're not just building anymore. You're multiplying. You've moved beyond getting more done to creating something that lives beyond you.

When I started my first company, I didn't have a dream of stacking piles of cash to swim in like Scrooge McDuck. Don't get me wrong. Money's a great byproduct. But the pursuit of money has never been the *why*. For me, my motivation has always been to serve as many people as possible and impact as many lives as I can.

The other day, one of my team members looked me dead in the eye and said, "I'm going to sell you. I'm going to sell your time." I kid you not. I almost spit out my London Fog tea, and if you know me, you know that's sacred. Steamed Earl Grey with a bit of local honey and high-protein milk frothed just right is what a hug would taste like if it were served in a mug.

So, here I am, holding back a full-blown mouth volcano while this guy says he's going to sell *my* time. I looked at him and said, "Hold up. How about I train *you* so we can sell *your* time instead?" That's what multiplication looks like.

I don't want to be the bottleneck. I want to multiply my time, not rent it out like a party clown with a balloon bouquet. I want to be the leader who gets more done in a day than most people do in a week. Scratch that—a month. Most days, I do. Not because I'm Superman. I've built a team of leaders who know how to get stuff done without waiting for me to tell them what size wrench to grab.

If you're only selling your own time, if you're the only one laying bricks, your impact has a cap. You'll build a wall, sure. But when you pour into others, train them, and trust them, you don't just build walls, you build houses, then neighborhoods. Then one day, you're looking across a whole community of leaders you helped raise up.

At Eclipse DOT, my goal has always been simple: Train our people so well that they can go anywhere and treat them so well that they never want to leave. And with a few bumps along the road (because, hey—people are still people), we've done that.

Some folks worry, "But Dan, what if you train them too well and they leave? Or worse, start their own business and take your clients?" And to that I say, if I train someone to lead so well, they go out and thrive on their own. That's not a threat to my legacy. That *is* my legacy. That's multiplication. That's the move. And here's where it gets real.

Jesus, our ultimate leadership model, could have just healed people, dropped wisdom like a divine mic-drop, and gone on His way. But He didn't. He looked around at this ragtag group of misfits. Some couldn't fish right, one had anger issues, one was stealing from the squad fund, and Jesus said to Himself, "Yeah, I'm going to build the future through them."

He trained, trusted, and launched them. He created followers who became leaders who would multiply His mission. That's multiplication. It's not always clean, safe, or efficient. But dang, it works.

You've got to decide: Do you want to be the hero of every story? Or do you want to be the reason dozens of other leaders rise?

Look, I get it. Multiplication takes more upfront effort. It means slowing down to explain things. You have to watch someone mess up what you could have done in five minutes. It forces you to hold your tongue when they do it differently than you would have.

It's like teaching your kid to mow the lawn. Sure, you could do it in twenty minutes and have those clean diagonal stripes you're proud of. But if you don't teach them now, you'll still be mowing that yard when you're eighty-seven with a bad back and a lawn chair bungee-corded to the zero-turn.

Addition gets it done. Multiplication keeps it going. When you multiply, you're not just getting help, you're building a legacy. You're turning your impact from a solo act into a full-on movement.

So, what's it going to be? Are you stacking bricks or raising builders? If the thing you're building depends on you showing up every day, it's not a legacy, it's a hostage situation.

It's Not Easy, and That's the Point

Leadership Isn't a Drive-Through. It's a Slow-Cooker

You could do it faster yourself. You know it. I know it. We've all had those moments when someone's halfway through a job and you're thinking, *I could have finished this, gone to lunch, and taken a nap by now.* Have you ever watched someone spend forty-five minutes setting up a printer? It's painful. You pray for the ink cartridge to explode so you can call it a loss and move on.

That's the tension. Leadership isn't about efficiency. It's about effectiveness. Effectiveness means mentoring when it would be easier to muscle through it. It means slowing down, explaining things, letting them try, allowing them to make mistakes, and then gently (or not-so-gently) helping them course correct.

It means accepting that they might fail. And here's the kicker: That's not a bug in the system. It's a feature. The first time I taught someone how to back a trailer, you'd think I was asking them to land a jet on a moving flatbed.

Once, when I was knee-deep in CDL training, I'd been flying all over the country helping companies train their drivers, and this trip landed me in Chicago. The company flew me in to work with their team of six guys and one gal. They all had their permits and had been driving a little, but they needed help tightening things up before testing. I was there to whip the team into shape in just three days.

This was right after my oldest son shipped out to the Army for basic training. My heart was a jumble of emotions, including pride, excitement, and every other feeling imaginable. I was flying home after the Chicago training to load the family and blasting off to Pismo Beach, California, for another week of training. From there, we would drive to Fort Leonard Wood, Missouri, to see him graduate. My schedule was packed with family and purpose, so it was all good.

Back to Chicago—on day one of training, we hit it hard. We covered everything from inspections to techniques to how to avoid sweating through your clothes while learning under pressure. I told them, "At the end of today, your brain's going to feel like mashed potatoes. You're going to swear up and down there's no way you're going to remember any of this. Then you'll go home, get some rest, and show up tomorrow like a dang superhero, and it'll all start to click."

And wouldn't you know it? By the end of the day, everyone was mush. Heck, *I* was mush. I'm from Colorado, where humidity is 0 percent, and ninety-eight degrees is considered a scorcher. It was 101 degrees with a humidity level of 92 percent in Chicago. That isn't weather. That's boiled air.

When day two rolled around, everyone was crushing their pre-trip inspections, so we moved into the backing portion of the training. That's where one of the team members, fresh out of the Army, started struggling.

She couldn't quite get the trailer to do what she wanted. And listen, I've taught many people, and I know when someone's overwhelmed, overthinking, or simply over it. She was frustrated, but I could tell, she wanted it. She wasn't a quitter. She needed a nudge in the right direction.

So, I climbed in the cab with her and gave her some pointers. I broke it down and explained how the trailer reacts, when to move slowly, when to hold the wheel, and when to breathe. Sure enough, she began to understand.

Later that day, I told one of the other trainees, "Hop in the cab with her. But don't coach. Your job is to encourage. Stay calm. Tell her she's got this." They did. And she nailed the backing.

Fast-forward a couple of months. She went in for her CDL test and crushed it—100 percent on the pre-trip and 100 percent on the backing. I was so stoked I about fist-pumped a hole through my phone when I heard. But wait, it gets better.

That same company sent one of their leaders through our Train-the-Trainer course a little while later. He said something I'll never forget. "Dan, I'm going to do exactly what you teach us because I know it works. I've seen it with my own eyes."

That trainer? He has now trained five more drivers, and every single one of them passed their CDL test on the first attempt. That is multiplication. That's what happens when you invest in someone, even when it would have been faster to jump in and do it yourself. It took time, patience, and me not flying off the handle when trailers zigged instead of zagged. But it paid off.

One leader became a trainer. That trainer created five more licensed drivers. And every one of those drivers will now impact lives, serve companies, and maybe train someone else down the line. That's the power of slow-roasted leadership. That's what legacy looks like.

It's not about how fast you can crank out results. It's about who you raise up, and who they raise up after that. It's marinated and smoked at a low and slow temperature. Leadership is the brisket of life. And yeah, it's going to take some time. But if you're in this game only to get it done fast, you're not leading. You're sprinting. And no one follows a sprinter. People watch from a distance, hoping they don't pull a hamstring.

Multiplying leaders isn't a one-week mentorship plan. It's a years-long commitment to walk with people through their mess, not just manage their performance. It's saying, "I'm not just here for what you can do. I'm here to help you become who you're meant to be."

And let me say this clearly: If you're constantly frustrated because nobody does it like you do, maybe you haven't slowed down long enough to teach them how to win. Or maybe you haven't been willing to let go of the reins long enough for someone else to find their stride.

Look, I get it. It's hard, slow, and messy. But so is farming, raising kids, life, and anything that matters. Easy doesn't build leaders; easy builds dependency.

And let's not pretend you were fantastic from the start either. I don't care how confident you are now. When you first sat in the seat of that rig, you weren't great. You were nervous and green. And you probably ground more gears than coffee beans. But guess what? You got better because reps produce results. Your people need to know you've made mistakes too, not because it lowers your credibility, but because it raises their hope.

You've probably heard it said that *rough seas make experienced sailors.* I like to say that driving big rigs over mountain passes, down narrow canyon roads, with potholes big enough to swallow a tire and blind corners that make you clench your teeth—*that makes experienced drivers.*

Leadership works the same way. The smooth stretches don't sharpen your team. It's the rough spots, the ones with a 6 percent downgrade and no guardrail, that teach people how to think, react, and grow under pressure.

So, when it feels hard, takes longer, costs more, and tests your patience, remember this: That's not a sign you're doing it wrong. It's proof you're doing it right, because legacy leaders don't just build things. They build people, and people take time.

Hey, life is messy. But that's what makes it fun. Learn to love the mess because God usually brings the message through the mess if you let Him.

You're not just shaping employees. You're shaping leaders. And you're not just building careers. You're building a legacy. So keep showing up. Keep teaching. Keep handing over the wheel, even when it's uncomfortable, even when they stall it, grind the gears, and panic halfway through the turn. If you're the only one driving, no one else is learning. And if no one else is learning, your impact ends with you. But if you multiply, impact keeps going.

Look, I get it. The idea of multiplying leaders sounds fantastic when you're sitting in a padded chair at a leadership retreat with an iced coffee in one hand and a fresh notebook in the other. People say things like "Pour into others." "Replicate yourself." "Raise the next generation of leaders." It sounds like a spiritual experience. But in reality, it's not always inspirational. It's usually perspirational.

Do you want to know what multiplying leaders looks like? It looks like repeating yourself for the fifth time to someone who still isn't getting it, but you believe in them enough to say it a sixth time. It looks like letting them lead a meeting though it makes you cringe a little. It looks like watching them try and fail, then pulling them aside after and saying, "Let's talk about it." It's messy, awkward, and slow. It will test your patience and expose your pride. But if you do it correctly, it will grow your influence in ways you can't imagine.

This isn't theory or fluff. This is authentic leadership, forged in long days, significant risks, awkward conversations, and genuine care. So if you're ready for that, let's dive in and be honest. Leadership is easy until people get involved. You can read all the books, write all the values on the wall, even draw out your vision on a whiteboard like a motivational Picasso. But none of that matters until you lead humans.

Humans have opinions, make mistakes, and learn according to their unique growth curve. They have weird ways of doing things that are somehow both completely wrong and kind of genius. That's the hard part. And that's where authentic leadership begins.

See, the goal of becoming a great leader isn't exclusively to grow your business. It's not even to build a great team. The real move, the legacy move, is to create leaders. Not followers. Not task-doers. Not note-takers. Leaders are people who think, lead others, and might outgrow you. That's what this section is about.

I've learned these lessons the hard way, with boots on the ground, duct tape in one hand, and frustration in the other. I've screwed up in ways that would make an OSHA (Occupational Safety and Health Administration) rep flinch. I've doubled back more times than a GPS in the mountains. I've stared at my phone like it personally offended me and nearly Frisbee'd it across the shop floor (twice). But I've also seen people I trained go out and smoke it beyond what I ever thought possible. And that is what awakens your soul and reminds you why it all matters.

So, if you're looking to multiply leaders, here's what it's going to take:

- Letting go of control
- Getting over your ego
- Coaching in the mess
- Cheering when they outshine you
- Learning to lead people into the life they're meant to build, even if it looks nothing like yours

1. Train Them to Replace You (Yes, really)

I accidentally started one of the smartest moves I've ever made. It started with a guy asking if I'd hit my head. I'd just launched our Train-the-Trainer program. I'm fired up. I've got systems, a process, the whole nine yards. It's working. Then the phone rings.

It's a customer I'd worked with before. He's a straight shooter. Smart guy, but he's confused. You could hear the hesitation in his voice, like he wasn't sure if he was calling a training company or walking into a pyramid scheme.

He said, "Dan, I don't mean this in a bad way, but aren't you kinda putting yourself out of business?"

I paused, and then I laughed out loud, because here's the thing: he was right. We train CDL drivers. And now, I was teaching other people to train their own CDL drivers. It looked completely backward, like selling flashlights that come with instructions on how to build your own.

Who does that? "Here's a light. Also, here's how to never need me again." It doesn't exactly scream smart business, right? But I told him the truth. "I hope so. I hope I put myself out of business doing this."

I'm not in this to build a castle with a drawbridge and my name on the banner. I'm in this to create a movement. There are too few drivers for too many open jobs. And there are too many people sitting on the sidelines waiting for someone to say, "Hey, you've got what it takes."

And guess what? I can't be everywhere. I'm not Jesus or Batman. (Although if I had to pick, I'd go Batman. Cooler gadgets and way less pressure.) But if I train 1,000 trainers, and each of them trains 100 people in their lifetime, that's 100,000 people getting new careers, new confidence, and new lives—not because I showed up, but because someone I trained did.

Now listen, I fully admit I'm not a math guy. So, if that number's off, please don't email me with a spreadsheet. Just round up. It sounds cooler anyway. The point is this: If I'm the only one who can do what I do, I've failed. Authentic leadership is about being the best and building people who no longer need you.

That's why I started this whole thing. Not so I could have my face on more fliers, but so the message could go further than I ever could alone. Some of these trainers are better than I am. They teach more smoothly, lead sharper, and connect faster. And I'm over here cheering like a proud dad in the bleachers, with a foam finger in one hand and the camera in the other (still on selfie mode), wondering why the footage is just my nose and confused breathing.

If your people never surpass you, you haven't built leaders. You built shadows. So yeah, train them to replace you. Give them the playbook. Hand them the mic. And when they take the stage and crush it? You sit your proud little self-down, drink your fizzy water, and say, "That's my guy right there."

That's what legacy looks like. Legacy is not, "I built it." Legacy is, "I built the people who built it."

2. Don't Be the Counselor (A Real Life Case Study on how to Ruin Influence with One Phone Call)

We were gearing up for a big family trip, flying cross-country to visit my oldest son during his four-day Army weekend. He hadn't seen his siblings in six months, and this wasn't a casual getaway. It was a mission—a Greer family reunion with military precision. The plan was tight, bags were packed, flights were booked, and everyone was buzzing.

Now my two older kids are in high school. My son is a veteran of this system. He grabs the required absence form, gets all his teachers to sign it like a pro, walks it over to the school counselor, and bam—approved. No questions asked. "Tell your brother thanks for serving."

Now, enter my daughter. She's got the same family, form, teachers, and trip. She gets all her signatures, turns it in, and instead of a stamp of approval, the counselor calls my wife. And this woman, God bless her over-inflated sense of authority, says, "Your daughter's absence is not approved. You'll have to change your trip."

Ohhh boy. Let me pause here for a moment and say this: Thank God my wife answered that phone. Had I picked up, there might've been a small mushroom cloud rising from the high school admin office. My response would have gone something like: "I'm sorry. What planet are you on where you think you get to tell me how to raise my kids or plan my family's schedule?" She probably would have been Googling *how to file a restraining order against a patriotic dad* by the time I finished.

But my wife was graceful, poised, and Ninja-like. She smiled, nodded, and said, "Well, I think my daughter's going to have the one-day flu next week. Thanks for your time." Mic. Dropped.

Now, I'm not against schools. I love teachers. I respect the heck out of anyone pouring into the next generation. They are saints in sneakers. But this? This was not leadership. This was a power trip with a nametag. And you know what? We do this all the time in business as well.

We say we want to develop people. We say we believe in them. But the moment they do something we don't understand, or heaven forbid, something that goes against our little control bubble, we pull the *counselor card*. "That's not approved." "You didn't ask permission." "Let me micromanage that until your soul dies." This occurs when ego, rather than leadership, takes the lead. If your team has to ask permission to think, you're not leading. I've been there. I've let my pride lead. I've stepped in and taken control because it made me feel important.

That counselor didn't care about my daughter. She cared about her power. Her *perceived* control and approval stamp. When leaders operate from that place, whether in school, a shop, or a staff meeting, they kill trust faster than a social media trend.

So let's make this super clear: If you're leading with ego, your people will learn to hide. If you're leading with control, your people will stop growing. If you lead with trust, even when it costs you comfort, they'll thrive under your watch.

Don't be the counselor or the guy who shuts it down because it didn't go through your inbox first. Be the leader who's more concerned about growth than control. Let them take the trip. Let them stretch. Let them go, even if it makes you uncomfortable. The leaders you're trying to develop don't need permission. They need someone willing to let go of the wheel.

3. Empower, Don't Enable (Yeah, You Might Feel Like a Jerk Doing This)

Being helpful to the point of sabotage is one of the hardest leadership traps. It sounds noble on the surface.

- "I want to be there for my team."
- "I like to support my people."
- "I don't mind helping. It's faster if I do it."

Yeah, it's also the fastest way to train a team that can't do jack without you holding their hand. Here's how it played out recently for me.

One of my team members called and asked, "Hey Dan, how do I do this?" Now, I enjoy helping my team. I do. I want them to win, and I want them to feel supported. But something in me paused. Instead of hopping on a call or doing a screen share to solve the problem for her, I asked, "Did you check the framework we built?"

Silence. You could almost hear her blinking on the other end of the phone. She said, "Well, I was trying to figure it out on my own first." Which sounds admirable, right?

But, we built the freaking framework for this exact reason. We didn't spend hours documenting systems and processes for fun. We did it so no one had to guess, wing it, or call and interrupt my day while I'm elbow-deep in twenty-five other things.

So, I said, "Awesome. Go check the framework first, then call me back if you're still stuck." I'm not going to lie. I felt like a jerk, because my knee-jerk instinct is to swoop in, fix it, and be the hero. But leadership is about building people who don't need a hero.

Enabling sounds like support, but it creates dependency. Empowering feels a little harsh, but it develops leaders. One makes you feel good in the moment. The other prepares them to run things when you're not around.

Let's take it to the jobsite. Imagine you're teaching someone to lay bricks. Enabling is when you hand them the brick, mix the mortar for them, point to where it goes, then

hover while they set it. If they screw up, you snatch it back and fix it.

Empowering is saying, "Here's how to string a line. Here's how thick the mortar should be. Watch me lay a few. Now you try it. And if the wall leans a little, we'll fix it later. Keep going." Empowering is letting them build crooked before they build straight.

You can't empower someone if you're afraid of feeling like the bad guy for five minutes. Saying, "No, go figure it out first," makes you feel like a jerk sometimes.

Would you rather feel like a jerk for thirty seconds or keep doing the same task for them every week for the rest of time? That's what will happen if you don't make them think for themselves. I'll take the jerk-feeling, thank you very much.

You know what else helps? Shutting up. I'm serious. When they call for help, ask questions:

- What have you tried?
- Where did you get stuck?
- Did you check the process?

Then shut up. Let them fill the silence. Let them think. Let them *struggle* for a second, because that's where leaders are made. Perfectly scripted how-tos with you spoon-feeding answers and hand-holding that eventually turns into handcuffing won't cut it. If you're a predictable answer key, don't be surprised when your team fails to learn how to solve anything.

Empowering might not always feel good at the moment. You'll feel like a jerk. They might grumble. But give it a beat, because if it makes them better, stronger, faster, and more confident, be the jerk with purpose. There's a difference between task rabbits and leaders. Leaders need space to lead.

Fast-forward to another teammate—someone who had been with me a little longer. We finished our daily huddle. Our Eclipse DOT huddles are concise and to the point. Sometimes people bounce out of them like a jackrabbit being chased by a coyote.

This team member disappeared after the meeting. Just like that—gone. Radio silence. About thirty minutes later, she says, "Hey Dan, you got a second? I need help with a permit." Now I light up. "What? You're pulling a permit? That's awesome. I didn't even know you were working on that today!"

We hop on a quick call, and she shares her screen to show me the process. She's already halfway through. Doing great. Then she hits a snag and asks what she's doing wrong. I look at it and casually ask, "Hey, what state's this for again?"

She answers, "New Mexico."

I nod. "Cool, and where's the starting address?"

Without hesitation, she said, "Texas."

I said nothing as I stared at the screen. That silence was golden. You could see it happen in real time, like watching a lightbulb flicker, buzz, and finally light up. She stared for a second, then smiled, laughed, and said, "Ugh. I really hate you, Dan."

Said with love, of course, and a healthy dose of "I can't believe this is what I asked you for." I laughed and said nothing. I stayed on the call and let her resolve the issue. Then, she finished the permit while I slipped into the background and continued to my work.

When she wrapped it up, I popped back in and said, "See? You got this." And she did. I didn't fix it for her. I didn't jump in. I gave her the space to realize she already had it in her. That's the difference between control and coaching. Control says, "Let me." Coaching says, "You can." So the next time someone asks you for help, don't assume you need to carry it for them.

Sometimes a pause, a question, and silence are all they need to find their own answer. And when they do, you'll both walk away smiling, with them saying something like "I hate you" through a laugh. You'll smile and go back to work, because that's leadership done right.

4. Embrace the Mic-Drop Moment (Especially Important When You're the One Who Screws It Up)

Let me take you back to the moment I accidentally rescheduled an entire company. Yes, you read that right. I didn't reschedule a team or a calendar invite. I rescheduled *the whole company.*

I had taken on this brand new role managing DOT compliance. Fresh and fired up, I was eager to prove I was a team player. My overachiever mindset screamed, *I'm going to show them they picked the right guy.*

I got this calendar invite for the quarterly, all-hands-on-deck, full-company, iron-your-shirt-and-don't-say-something-stupid meeting. Even the guy who lives in spreadsheets suddenly finds a personality, and someone always says synergy like it's a magic word that'll fix our budget. It's not the casual weekly check-in where people show up with bedhead and muted mics. No, this was the real deal. It was in person at a rented hotel conference room with linens on the tables and those chairs that look fancy but feel like plywood after ten minutes. They even had a full-on breakfast spread—eggs, bacon, tiny yogurts, and those mystery Danish pastries that somehow disappear first. This was that meeting.

The company president appears in a tucked-in shirt, all buttoned up, as if we're about to sign a trade agreement with Switzerland. You *pretend* to take notes in case someone important is watching, and let's be honest, everyone's watching.

The invite said 7:30 a.m. Now, I'm new in the role and want to show I'm sharp and reliable—someone they can count on. All right, got to be early. Can't be late. Got to show them I'm the guy who's five steps ahead. Better back that baby up to 6:30 so I've got time to beat traffic, find parking, shake hands, eat bacon, maybe even make a good impression.

So I open up Outlook like a responsible grown man, click the little time box, and slide that meeting from 7:30 to 6:30 a.m. Easy. But there was one problem. It was a shared invite—with everyone—across the entire company. And instead of adjusting it on *my calendar* like any normal, sane person would do, I unknowingly rescheduled the whole dang company to 6:30 a.m. I didn't even realize it. I clicked save and walked away like, "Boom. Look at me, all prepared."

Meanwhile, emails started flying. Phones started buzzing. Someone probably thought there was a daylight saving glitch. One guy legitimately asked if the building had changed time zones. It was chaos. And I, completely unaware of the digital disaster I'd unleashed, was casually going about my day like I hadn't ruined everyone's morning.

I didn't get a pop-up warning such as, "Are you sure you want to wake up six hundred employees at the crack of dawn?" Nope. I clicked, saved, and walked away like a hero. Then the messages started rolling in. Slack, email, and text all say things like, "Uhhh … Dan? Why the heck is the meeting now at 6:30?" "Is this a joke?" "Are we trying to run a bakery now?"

My phone lit up like a Christmas tree. I had no idea what I'd done. For a split second, I thought maybe this was a prank *on me.* But no. This was my fault. And now, I had to own it. I was mortified.

Here I was with a brand new role and responsibility, and I single-handedly jacked up the most high-stakes, once-a-quarter, bring-out-the-breakfast-casserole meeting the company had. The one they rent hotel space for. The one with name tags and awkward networking. The one where people practice what they're going to say before they speak. And I moved it for everyone.

I thought I was toast. But when I walked into that meeting with coffee in hand, crow in my throat, something unexpected happened. People already knew me. I wasn't the new guy anymore. I was the guy who screwed up the meeting time. Which, strangely enough, made me one of them.

Here's the best part. After it was all said and done, my manager pulled me aside and said, "Hey Dan, any chance you could make another glorious blunder like this for our annual meeting in a few months? We could use a spike in attendance like that. Let us know what *accidental* chaos you've got planned. We'll budget for extra muffins."

I couldn't believe it. My total blunder ended up driving the biggest meeting turnout we'd ever had. Here's what that moment taught me: You don't lose leadership by messing up. You lose it by hiding from the mic when it's your turn to own it.

I could have blamed the software, played dumb, pretended it was some executive decision, and ducked out of the spotlight. Instead, I walked in, laughed at myself, took the hit, and showed them that I don't have to be perfect to lead. And neither do you. Leadership isn't about flawless execution. It's about honest influence. It's about raising your hand and saying, "Yeah, that was me. Won't do it again. Let's roll."

Your team doesn't need a perfect leader. They need a real one—someone who can laugh when it gets awkward, own it when they blow it, and still walk up to the mic like, "Welp … that one's on me. Let's get to work."

So, the next time you drop the ball or, say, reschedule an entire company-wide meeting by accident and make 647 people think they're late for a funeral, own it. Smile, shrug, and bring donuts. Humility doesn't disqualify your leadership, it deepens it. And if you can lead with your humanity showing, they'll follow you a whole lot farther than if you pretend to be flawless.

5. Coach for the Win (Even When They Don't Know They're Ready for It)

I'm going to tell you about a guy on my team who started just wanting a paycheck and ended up becoming a business partner. I won't name names, but if you've been around our crew, you know who I'm talking about.

When he first joined, he was solid. He showed up, clocked in, and did his thing without drama or complaints, and no drive. He wasn't lazy. He was stuck in that mindset of just being at work to collect a paycheck and not get yelled at. We've all seen it. Maybe we've even lived it. You're doing enough not to get fired, but not sufficient to make a dent. Then something shifted.

I didn't hit him with some Tony Robbins pep talk or sit him down and say, "Son, I see potential in you." You know what happened? He watched. He watched me grind, dream, and build. He saw the business I was building, but more importantly, the life I was creating. He saw how I traveled with my family, celebrated wins, poured into people, and made a living doing something I *actually* gave a crap about.

Slowly but surely, the guy who once said, "I'm just here to work," started saying, "Hey, how can I do more?" He began asking questions, volunteering for new responsibilities, arriving early, and staying late. At first, I thought maybe he got a new alarm clock or was trying to impress a girl in accounting.

It wasn't forced. It wasn't some motivational miracle. I didn't give him a TED Talk or slide a copy of *Think and Grow Rich* across his desk as if it were contraband. It was coaching by example. And here's the funny part: I didn't even know I was coaching. I was doing what I do, working hard, building something meaningful, and trying not to screw up too publicly. But once I saw that spark? That tiny flicker of, *I think I want more,* I turned on the heat like a dad with a fresh grill and something to prove.

I started giving him more ownership, letting him lead small projects and coaching him after meetings. I would ask questions like, "Why did you handle it that way?" and "What do you think we could have done better?" At first? He hated it. He didn't want to reflect. He didn't want feedback. He tried to win without watching the film. But I didn't let up, because I knew something he didn't know yet: Coaching isn't just about correcting mistakes. It's about calling out more discipline, focus, and impact, more than they thought they were capable of.

Over time, he rose. He began leading others, running meetings, and acting like an owner before his name was ever on the documents. Now, he's not just *on* the team. He *is* the team. Honestly, there are days when he handles things better than I would have. He makes decisions more quickly and leads more effectively. Sometimes I hear about a problem *after* it's already solved, and the solution was better than what I would have recommended.

And you know what? That's not a threat. That's legacy, because that's what authentic coaching does. Coaching extends beyond simply completing tasks and developing skills. It unlocks something in someone they didn't even know was there.

Here's the part that still blows my mind. When I got ready to spin off a part of one of my companies, the part I was done with—the one I'd lost the fire for—he was ready. He stepped up, and I let him. Today, he's a part-owner of that new company. He's building it, running it, and owning it, literally and figuratively. He started showing up, asking questions, and caring, he was rewarded. Now don't get me wrong. I'm not saying you should run out and start giving away shares of your company like Oprah handing out iPads.

"You get equity! And you get equity! And you get your own LLC!"

What I *am* saying is this: As a leader, you get to watch other leaders rise. And that's the real reward. It's not always about the profit. Sometimes the reward is the pride of watching someone grow into a role they didn't even know they could handle. Sometimes it's about building a business and realizing that along the way, you built a person.

So don't wait until someone begs for mentorship. Start coaching *before* they even know they want it. Coach in the small stuff. Coach through your example. Coach when it's uncomfortable. Coach when they're just in it for a paycheck. If all you're doing is correcting screw-ups, you're not coaching. You're just managing chaos.

But if you lean in when no one's watching, start asking better questions, and believe in people before they believe in themselves, you might build a partner. You saw something in them and stayed long enough to pull it out, not because they were born for it or because you gave them a title. That's leadership coaching, and that's the stuff that lasts long after the paycheck clears.

BUILD THE LIFE YOU LOVE. LOVE THE LIFE YOU BUILD.

6. Build the Life You Love (And Help Others Do the Same)

What's the point of building great leaders if you're still miserable in your own life? What's the point of multiplying your team, scaling your business, and training your people if you secretly hate the thing you've built? If you're not happy with the life you're building, start building a new one. Leadership is about growing others and leading *yourself* into a life worth waking up for. What do I mean by a life worth waking up for? I'm not talking about yachts and six-figure watches.

A life worth waking up for is being able to take your kids on a trip without checking your email every twelve seconds. It's having dinner with your family and tasting the food because your brain isn't stuck in task mode. It's building a life that feels like freedom.

Here's the twist most leaders miss: You don't inspire people just by training them. You inspire them by living a life that makes them say:

- "I want to taste what he's tasting."

- "I want to wake up with that fire."
- "I want to lead like that, and live like that."

That's what happened with the team member I mentioned earlier. At first, all he wanted was a paycheck. But then he saw what I was building. He saw me leading, laughing, working hard, but not being owned by the work. He saw me live on purpose, and it ignited something in him.

Your team, your family, and the next version of yourself are all watching. If what you're building is broken, leaving you burned out, bitter, or bored, tear it down. Build something better. It's not too late. You don't need to throw your life away. You need to pick up the hammer and build again. Start simple:

- Redefine success.
- Say *no* to stuff that drains you.
- Say *yes* to things that light you up, even if they're inconvenient.
- Surround yourself with people who inspire you to be your best, not those who guilt you into staying small.

And if you've already built a life you love, live it out loud. Let others see it. Let them borrow your courage until they find their own. Let them believe, through watching you, that they're allowed to dream again. Legacy isn't only what you leave behind. Legacy is also the permission you give others to build a life worth following.

So, build it. Love it. And lead like it matters because it does.

Building Others Through Faith-Fueled Leadership

(Because Multiplying Leaders Without Faith Feels Like Guesswork)

If you're going to discuss multiplying leaders and leaving a legacy, but you leave out faith, you're not building something that lasts. Sure, you can create a business and influence. But without faith, you'll miss the depth. That's why, for me, faith-fueled leadership isn't a side note. It's the whole framework.

Faith-fueled leadership considers what's eternal and the impact that still echoes when you're not in the room or on this side of heaven. I want to build better employees. But more than that, I want to help raise people who walk in integrity, lead with courage, and make decisions that honor God.

You can teach skills all day long, but if there's no character under it, it's just a matter of time before it cracks. Faith isn't just what we carry in our quiet time. It's how we lead. It's how we show up when the storm hits, respond when someone fails, and it's the foundation underneath the framework. Leadership through a faith lens is counterintuitive. It's not about holding onto power. It's about giving it away.

Jesus didn't walk around proving He was in charge. He didn't say, "Bow down, I'm the guy with the clipboard." He washed feet. He sent people out. He built people up.

That's multiplication, legacy, and faith in action. Look, I know it's more comfortable to keep your faith in the *personal* box. I've been there. You feel like it doesn't belong in the leadership conversation. But if your faith is genuine, it will affect the way you lead. Period.

When someone makes a mistake, respond with truth and grace. When the pressure's on, you pray before you panic. When your team watches how you live, they don't just see hustle, they see hope.

Here's why faith-fueled leadership is so fulfilling: It builds people with purpose. They learn that they matter, not because of what they produce, but because of who they are. It reminds them they were made on purpose, for a purpose. They see how even their biggest screw-ups can turn into future sermons if they stick around long enough to grow through it.

I don't want my legacy to say, "Dan built great companies." That's fine. That's cool. But that's not the goal. I want it to say, "Dan built great *people*. And while he was at it, he pointed them toward something eternal."

Companies come and go. But faith-fueled people live forever. So no, I don't separate faith from leadership. I fuel my leadership with it. And if I've multiplied anything worth celebrating or helped build anyone who now leads well, it's because I asked God to be in the driver's seat. I showed up to do the work with my hands open.

Multiply What Matters

Leadership is about who's following you and who's growing because of you. Let's go full circle here. Remember how this chapter started?

I was hanging off the side of a motor grader like a goat on a cliff. I had no safety harness, no training manual, and no clue what I was doing. I was white-knuckling the step and inhaling more dust than a Hoover, absorbing everything those blade hands were doing with twelve levers and what looked like a spaceship's control panel; it fascinated me.

I didn't just watch. I asked questions, stayed late, and learned from all those guys. Eventually, they let me take the controls. That moment made me a better operator and a better leader because it let me learn. They let me suck at it. And they coached me anyway. Instead of saying, "You're not ready," they said, "Climb up. Let's find out."

Eventually, I wasn't just riding the step. I was running finish grade before the asphalt crew rolled in. And later, I became the guy teaching others how to run that same machine. That's multiplication, legacy, and exactly what leadership should look like—willingness to hand off the sticks and cheer someone else on.

You've read the stories—some funny, some humbling, and some that still make me want to disappear into the floorboards. Remember the time I accidentally rescheduled a 7:30 a.m. quarterly company-wide meeting for the entire organization, including the president, the janitor, and probably the ghost of a former employee, to 6:30 a.m.? Yeah. That one.

As embarrassing as that moment was, it had a multiplied impact. People showed up early. They talked about it for weeks. And someone said, "Dan, any chance you can sabotage the annual meeting too? We could use another attendance boost." You're welcome, corporate America.

Here's what I'm trying to say: You're here to build a team and multiply leaders. You're here to create something that outlives your checklist, outshines your credentials, and outlasts your name badge. You don't need a title or a pulpit. You need a willingness to let other people climb the steps. Let them ride alongside you. Let them watch, ask, try, and fail. Let them run the machine while you sit in the truck and hold back the urge to scream.

And when they jackknife the trailer, forget to click *save*, or schedule a team meeting during your dentist appointment, don't take over. Coach them. Laugh with them. Let them become the leader you'd want on your team. If your leadership always centers on you being the hero, you're not multiplying. You're micromanaging. Trust me. Nobody builds legacy by hogging the remote.

So, here's your challenge. Are you ready?

- **Find someone this week who's still riding the step.** Find someone who isn't shiny yet, doesn't believe in themselves but shows up anyway. Notice them. Invest in them. Hand them a tool and say, "Let's figure this out."

- **Coach before they ask.** Don't wait for them to beg for help. Don't wait until they crash and burn. Start coaching when it's inconvenient, messy, and they think they're not worth the time.

- **Pray for them.** Seriously. Ask God to show you who's ready, even if they're only clocking in for a paycheck. Ask Him for eyes to see beyond the tasks and into the calling. You might be the only person in their life who sees it.

- **Celebrate their wins like a lunatic.** Wave that foam finger. Send the over-the-top text messages. Reach out with random fist bumps in the hallway. Let them know you're watching, and you're proud.

All this matters because if all you're doing is building systems, your work ends when you do. But if you're building leaders, your legacy lives on long after you shut off your laptop.

You don't need to be the most intelligent person in the room, but you need to be the one who makes room for someone else to grow. You don't need to be perfect. You need to be authentic, willing, and able to let go of the mic and relinquish control of the mission.

So, stop waiting for permission. Don't wait for the perfect moment. Multiply what matters now, because real leaders build people, hand off the sticks, and cheer from the steps. They own their mistakes and teach others how to avoid making the same ones. They point people toward purpose, even when it means they lose the spotlight. And when the people you've poured into start rising, when they run faster, lead better, and do it all with grit and grace? That's not a threat. That's the point.

I'm not building this so people remember my name. I'm building people so *God's* name gets known.

That's legacy.

Key Takeaways from Chapter Thirteen

 **Addition hires hands—multiplication unleashes leaders.** A bigger crew moves dirt; a crew of builders moves mountains.

 **Train them to outshine you.** If your protégés can't replace or eventually lap you, you're not leading—you're hoarding.

 **Quit being the human answer key.** Point them to the playbook, ask a question, then shut up. Struggle is the secret sauce.

 **Celebrate like crazy.** Foam fingers, dad-level fist pumps, awkward hallway high-fives all make their wins louder than yours.

 **Own the oops—publicly.** If you reschedule a six hundred-person meeting by accident, laugh, apologize, bring donuts, and move on. Humility deepens trust.

 **Faith is the foundation.** Skills handle the job; character and a whole lot of Jesus keep it standing when the wind hits.

 **Enable ≠ empower.** If they can't act without pinging you, you've created hostages, not heroes.

 **Legacy isn't about having your name on the wall;** it's about their names on the roster. When ex-employees thrive, you did it right.

 **Messiness is mandatory.** Dust, missed shifts, and crooked walls are welcome signs that learning's happening. Embrace the chaos.

Chapter 14 | The Leaders You Run with Define the Leader You Become

Build Your Circle, Change Your Legacy

The Wake-Up Call

Jenna and I flew down to Cancun, Mexico, for what turned out to be hands down one of the best masterminds I've ever attended. Unreal content and top-tier delivery made it an event that punches you in the gut—in a good way. Hang tight, because this story doesn't start with the fireworks. It begins with awkward silence and overpriced airport food.

We flew in a day early. If you know me at all, you know I like to reverse-engineer everything. I was there to learn more than what was presented in the sessions. I wanted to study how the whole event was run—logistics, flow, speaker transitions—heck, even how the emcee handled a mic fumble. I've been called to host and lead live events, so I wanted to see how the pros did it. Objective observers might say that I was creeping in the background with a notepad and too much caffeine.

I should mention that this was not a cheap ticket. We paid *way* too much money for this mastermind. Scratch that—when you get the right transformation, it's never too expensive, but I digress. Again.

This mastermind group hosted several events throughout the year, one of which took place in Cancun. So, we jumped on a jet, landed at a killer all-inclusive resort, and kicked off what we thought would be a people-filled, heart-centered, let's-do-big-things experience.

Our dinner on the first night was at a restaurant on the resort property. Tables were arranged in clusters of ten. Jenna and I picked one, and soon others joined us. Here's where things get interesting. I decided to shut up and observe. Pro tip: You learn more by listening than by flexing. What I saw was a table full of highlight reels.

Everyone at that table was peacocking. They tossed out revenue numbers like they were playing Monopoly with fake bills. They seemed to be pretending to be rolling in it but ordering nothing but lemon water at an *all-inclusive* resort. I'm thinking. *You're out here draped in more designer labels than a fashion blogger during Paris Week, but scared to order a steak that's already paid for?*

It was like watching people indulge at a buffet and then skip dinner to count calories and show off. The math wasn't mathing. And the energy was faker than a gas station Rolex.

I kept quiet. Watching. Listening. Thinking, *these aren't my people.* They weren't bad people, but they were all trying to be someone. And I'm out here trying to be who God made me to be—flaws, farmer tan, and all.

The next day, we hit the sessions. Absolute fire, *life-changing* content shifted my mindset. My health improved significantly after I lost thirty pounds, simply by reevaluating my diet. I've kept twenty off to this day. The other ten still stop by like an old friend after enjoying a good brisket.

Approximately six to seven hundred people attended this event. The energy was wild at this jam-packed event. The content was easily ten out of ten. But I struggled with the people and the community.

I went home and called my coach. I said, "I got so much from the content, but I connected with only one person. Everyone else felt miles away in values and vision."

She said, "That's interesting, because I remember what you said about that first night at dinner. You said you didn't want to say anything because everyone was showboating." She paused. "Not because you couldn't speak. But because you *chose* not to."

And man, that hit me like a slap from a southern grandma. That's when it clicked: It wasn't that I didn't belong in rooms like that. I was supposed to *build* a new, better, and real one. I was supposed to create a circle where you could drop the act, ditch the ego, and get honest about your faith, business, calling, and mess. It would be a place where iron sharpens iron, and if you're full of crap, someone loves you enough to call you on it. Their purpose isn't to tear you down. They know you value honesty because growth comes from being challenged by people who care more about your future than your feelings.

This was to be a circle where we don't compete, we sharpen. That was the moment I stopped waiting for the right room to show up, because God told me to build the dang room myself.

Why the Right Circle Beats Solo

Going solo to an event sounds strong, but it's overrated. I flew down to Phoenix, Arizona, by myself, to attend a three-day business summit, one of Grant Cardone's events. I went to check it out, and I went VIP style. I spent real money, got the lanyard, swag, access, catered meals, early entry, and the whole deal. I was all in. It was fire.

The sessions were packed with gold. I had pages of notes. Ideas were hitting me like dodgeballs in middle school gym class—rapid-fire and from every direction. But I had no one to talk to about any of it.

Between sessions, while other folks were huddled around tables with their teams, mapping ideas out on napkins and firing each other up, I was alone. I was sitting in a comfortable seat, holding a nice notebook, staring at a multitude of ideas with nowhere to take them.

And I remember this moment vividly. A woman sitting a few rows away from me ran a tree care business out of Atlanta. She brought a crew, two or three people who got it. They were writing notes and talking strategy. You could see the wheels turning. They were building something right there in real time. They were in it together.

Meanwhile, I'm over here re-reading bullet points and quietly arguing with myself. *Should we try this? Nah. Maybe. Actually. Probably. But also, no. Crap.* I wasn't alone because no one wanted to be around me. I was alone because I'd convinced myself that there's something noble in carrying the weight of growth by yourself. It was as if being the only guy at the top somehow proves you deserve to be there.

But that's not strength. That's pride dressed up in ambition. And it's lonely as hell. When you're solo, everything is heavier. There's no one to challenge your thinking, no one to tell you when your great idea is nothing but a caffeinated impulse. No one is there to help you shape that spark into a real fire.

I can't tell you how many ideas I've had sitting in VIP chairs with nobody to pressure-test them. I never share my many dreams because I was missing voices that could help sharpen them. That moment in Phoenix made something clear: You can buy the best seat in the house, but without the right people beside you, you're simply a well-fed spectator.

This was before Jenna and I went to Cancun together. She's been my person in the room so many times. She gets it. She asks the hard questions, helps me keep the main thing the main thing, and simply keeps me from getting distracted by shiny crap that doesn't matter.

These days, I take people with me to events. Sometimes I even foot the bill, because it's that important. Having someone next to you who knows your vision, wants to see you succeed, and will speak up if you're drifting is priceless. That's why I stopped building big things alone. Going solo might help you learn, but the right circle enables you to lead.

The Power of the Right People

Have you ever looked around and thought, "Man, I'm surrounded but not supported?" Yeah, me too. That's when I realized, it's one thing to be in a room full of people. It's another thing to be in a room full of the right people.

You want people who do more than clap when you win. They call you up when you're off. These people love you enough to challenge your blind spots and pray over your breakthroughs.

I used to think I needed a massive network, but what I needed was a handful of warriors with wisdom, grit, and faith. Everyone needs people who see who I am, who I could be, and refuse to let me settle for less. So let me introduce you to my inner circle. These folks have shaped me, stretched me, and kept me grounded while I tried to launch to the moon. This is a select group of people, and it's not easy to make the cut. Here they are and the reasons they're rockstars in my eyes:

Jenna, My Secret Weapon and Unofficial CEO of Sanity

The one person who's been a constant in my life is Jenna. She anchors my circle. She's been with me on my leadership and business rollercoaster, and my what-if-we-did-this-crazy-idea moments.

This woman is more than the glue that holds the family together. She's the epoxy that holds me together when I'm spiraling through a dozen business ideas before breakfast. She's the first person I want to talk to when something big happens. And she's the first to gently tell me, "You might want to pray about that one, babe." Her advice grounds me when I start planning to buy another domain name, launch another company, or build something totally off the wall.

Jenna loves me, gets me, and chooses to be with me. Now that's miraculous. I can bounce any idea off Jenna and know I'll get an honest response rooted in wisdom and love. Sometimes it's, "Dan, that's brilliant." And other times it's, "You need sleep and food. Then we'll talk." Either way, she's not hyping me up with fluff. She's grounding me with truth. And when it comes to protecting her people, Jenna is fierce.

She takes up my offenses faster than a lawyer on retainer. If someone throws shade my way or tries to take advantage of me, she's got the whole courtroom drama already scripted in her head. And if she had a gavel, believe me, justice would be served with a smile and a lemon bar.

She reads the room when I can't. She hears my silence and knows when something's off. Somehow, she balances being an incredible mom, running a household that never stops moving, attending our kids' events, and supporting everything I do, while also being my sounding board, encourager, and best friend. But what really gets me is how she shows up in pivotal moments.

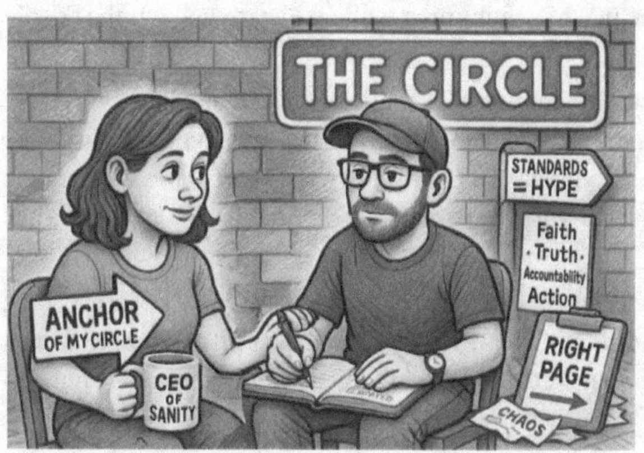

I'll have worked myself into a full-on overthinking tornado. The whiteboard is filled up with a half-drafted plan. My mind is racing a mile a minute, and she looks at me and calmly says, "Have you prayed on this?" It stops me cold every time, because no, I hadn't. I was too busy doing to be still and listening. And that one simple question, asked with zero judgment and total love, reroutes my whole spirit. Jenna grounds me in business, and she grounds me in faith.

Sometimes I'll look up in the middle of the day and realize that while I'm building businesses, chasing big dreams, leading teams, and trying to change the world, she's in the background making all of it possible. She's not in the spotlight. She doesn't need a title. But make no mistake. This entire operation is stronger because of her.

When I feel like I'm carrying the weight of the world, she reminds me I don't have to carry it alone. When I forget to celebrate the wins, she's the one pointing them out. When I'm discouraged, she gives me space, prayer, and a warm hug that says, "You've got this, and I've got you." She's steady. She's wise. She's fiercely loyal. And she's mine.

If your circle doesn't include someone who believes in you like Jenna believes in me, start there. Build with someone who's got your back, your heart, your blind spots, and occasionally, the spiritual two-by-four that reminds you to get back on your knees.

I say it all the time: I may be the voice people hear, but Jenna's is the voice I listen to most. Every good leader needs a Jenna in their corner.

James, The Steady Flame with a Leadership Engine

James is more than a good leader. He's the guy who makes you reevaluate your whole calendar, tighten up your to-do list, and ask yourself, "Have I done anything productive today, or have I been staring at my inbox pretending to work?"

He started out working fleet—boots on the ground, sleeves rolled up, and handling real-world operational chaos that most people couldn't survive for a week. He didn't complain or cut corners. He mastered operations. From there, he didn't climb the ladder. He launched off it.

He worked his way up to COO of a major company. It wasn't one of those companies where everyone has a fancy title and nobody knows what's going on. This was a real operation with real pressure and specific performance metrics. He thrived, led people, built systems, and kept the machine humming while still caring about the people who kept the wheels turning.

Then, because being COO wasn't enough of a challenge, he stepped into a VP role at another large company with a crystal-clear fast track to the presidency. That's like someone saying, "Hey, we love how you juggle flaming swords. How about we light the stage on fire too?" And James is the guy who would say, "Sounds fun! Where's the torch?"

What sets him apart isn't the titles. It's how he carries himself. James doesn't come in hot. He comes in steady, focused, and clear. He's got that rare gift where he listens first, speaks with precision, and when he drops wisdom, everyone in the room shuts up and takes notes.

When I talk to James, I always walk away better. He doesn't hype you up with fluff. He sharpens you with truth. He does more than nod along. He challenges your thinking. He affirms your ideas and helps you refine them. He points out what could go wrong and helps you map out how to get it right.

Sometimes it feels like being around the guy gives you a leadership energy boost. I swear there's caffeine radiating off his calendar. One conversation with him, and suddenly I've gotten new ideas, a more efficient system, and the courage to take a risk on something I was overthinking two hours ago.

James is the leader everyone needs in their circle—

solid, sharp, grounded, and growing. If you ever get the chance to talk with him, listen carefully. Listen to what he says and pay attention to how he thinks. The way James approaches leadership is how great companies get built and people grow. In my circle, that presence isn't optional; it's essential.

Tucker, The Sales Sniper with a Servant's Heart

Most of us have met someone and instantly think, "Yep, this guy gets it." That's Tucker.

We met at a high-level event I'd paid a lot of money to attend. The cost of admission went beyond the snag-a-free-pen event. It was an investment with VIP seats, high-caliber people, and big opportunities. But instead of sitting front row, wide-eyed, and taking notes like a good little student, I was standing in the back of the room doing what I always do—dissecting everything.

I wasn't just listening to the speakers. I was watching how the whole experience was built. I soaked in everything—the flow of the event, the emotion behind each story, the placement of the speakers, the timing of the music, and the way they were guiding belief and behavior.

At one point, I leaned over to this sharp-looking sales guy named Tucker and said, "I know why they brought that last guy up. He was there to break a false belief, probably something like, 'Success is only for people with connections or a perfect background.' He told his story, got vulnerable, and boom—his belief shattered. But why this next guy? His energy feels different."

Without missing a beat, Tucker looked at me and said, "Oh, that one's easy. He's here to break the belief that leaders have to be loud, polished, or charismatic to make an impact."

Boom.

That moment hit hard. If you've never studied events like this, you might miss it. Great speakers aren't just telling stories. They're dismantling limiting beliefs sitting in the audience's heads. One by one, they knock down the lies holding people back.

And Tucker saw it as clearly as I did. That's when I knew this guy wasn't just attending the event. He understood the architecture behind it. He saw how it was engineered to shift minds and open wallets. He didn't just get the message. He got the mechanics behind the message.

In that one sentence, he nailed it. I didn't need a ten-minute explanation or a drawn-out debate. He just understood the psychology behind the stage. Tucker wasn't just in the room; he got the room, and he got the game behind the game. I knew I needed to stay connected. Later, I reached out and said, "Hey man, I'd love to talk sales strategy sometime—maybe bounce a few ideas around."

His response? "Bro, you push me forward constantly—of course, I'd love to chat. Let's do it." That's Tucker. No ego or fluff. No "Let me check with my team and circle back." Absolute, grounded confidence and a let's-grow-together-mindset.

Tucker is sharp. He could close a deal in a windstorm with one phone call. He's skilled and humble. He's not proving he's the best. He's becoming the best. And he's doing it with purpose, integrity, and a lot of heart.

What sealed the deal for me, though, wasn't the way he saw through the event psychology. It wasn't even his sales chops (which are top tier). It was Tucker's faith, his drive, and his care.

This guy cares. He's open, honest, and he'll tell you about his struggles while still encouraging you through yours. He's not pretending to be perfect. He's relentlessly honest. In a world where people are more polished than authentic, Tucker leads with something more substantial than strategy. He leads with heart and conviction.

Every time we talk, this rapid-fire mix of bold ideas, truth bombs, and deeper conversations leaves me sharper, more grounded, and more fired up to lead. He's the guy who follows up after a big discussion with, "Hey man, I was thinking more about what you said. Here's another take I think could help."

He shows up for the highlight moments and the quiet ones. That's rare.

So if you're building your circle, your tribe of warriors, leaders, and fire-starters, find your Tucker. Find someone who gets it, sharpens you, loves Jesus, tells the truth, and believes in the power of doing life and business the right way.

And Tucker, if you're reading this, sorry, brother. You're in the circle for good now.

Alejandra, The Leader People Would Willingly Follow into a War Zone

Alejandra is an absolute beast in the road works world. She displays the hardhat, grit-under-the-fingernails, let's-get-it-done leadership style. She built her company from nothing. Without a silver spoon, lucky break, or corporate safety net, she relied on hustle, vision, faith, and relentless execution.

She survived in a male-dominated, rough-around-the-edges industry, and she thrived. She didn't knock on the door. She built the whole building.

But what makes her rare is that she leads her people, not just the business. Her leadership isn't loud or flashy. She doesn't rely on some rah-rah motivational poster to generate results. She leads with quiet confidence, deep respect, and fierce loyalty.

One day, we were chatting, and she pulled out a photo of her core team. These people have been with her since day one. She couldn't even get the words out without her voice cracking and her eyes welling up. She was proud of what she built, but she was overwhelmed by who stayed.

That's when I saw it clear as day: Alejandra is more than a boss. She's a leader people love to follow. You don't get that loyalty with a paycheck or a job title. Only a servant-hearted, people-first, integrity-rooted leader can cultivate followership like that.

Her team doesn't follow her because they trust her. She's been in the trenches with them. She shows up and leads by example. She knows her people by name, remembers their kids' birthdays, and still finds time to innovate, scale, and crush business goals while staying deeply human in every interaction. She leads with strength, and she loves without limits.

People don't just want to work with her. They want to build alongside her. That's the difference. And from a leadership perspective, she's wicked smart, strategic, and visionary. She doesn't get caught up in minutia. If there's a better way, a more efficient path, or a chance to build something great, she's on it. She leads with excellence and empathy, not ego.

Alejandra is a leader I want in my circle because she knows how to grow a business, and she knows how to grow people. She embodies everything that matters most in leadership:

- Grit
- Grace
- Loyalty
- Vision
- And a heart that stays rooted, even when the pressure's high

So, if you're building your circle, don't just fill seats. Find your Alejandra. The leader who talks about integrity and lives it when no one's watching. She doesn't care about a title as much as she cares about building something that lasts.

People like that are rare. They don't chase clout; they carry character. They're not just valuable; they're vital. I've already got her on my radar. She doesn't even know she's being recruited yet. But when the time's right, the door is open, the seat's saved, and The Circle's ready.

The *right* circle isn't about popularity; it's about purpose. And finding yours? It's worth every ounce of work.

Not All Circles Are Equal

Some so-called leadership communities are merely multi-level marketing schemes, dressed up in fancier suits with slick branding and no substance. They talk a big game, leadership, growth, purpose, community, but peel back the curtain and it's just a money printer disguised as mentorship.

There's one group to which I gave way too much of my time and money. I won't name-drop, because this isn't about throwing shade. It's about calling out reality. I've been to multiple events. Sat in their sessions. Took notes like I was cramming for finals. I gave them my attention, my energy, and yep, my card number.

They ran a 45-day *leadership experience*. That's what they called it.

Experience? I've had better experiences waiting at the DMV.

No kidding. I got more practical, heartfelt, kick-in-the-pants wisdom from one twenty-five-minute podcast than I did from their entire high-gloss, lights-and-lasers, name-tag-and-networking marathon.

And the kicker came at the end of it all, when I thought maybe, *just maybe*, we'd get something real—boom. "Would you like to become a certified coach under our program and share our leadership philosophy with others?"

Translation: Wanna sell our stuff for us and pay for the privilege?

It didn't matter if you had *fruit* in your life—and I don't mean the bowl of bananas on your kitchen counter. I'm talking results like changed lives, developed teams, and established businesses—evidence that your leadership extends beyond your echo chamber. But nope. It didn't matter if you'd only ever led your dog, your fantasy football team, or your buddies when you convinced them to do a group juice cleanse.

As long as your check cleared, congratulations. You're now a certified leadership coach. It was like a leadership-themed time-share pitch with Bible verses sprinkled in for flair.

Now let me be clear: That might work for some people. Maybe they're just starting out. Perhaps they need a plug-and-play system. Maybe that belonging feels like momentum. But me? I'm not after hype. I'm after honesty. I want a circle that's not impressed with what I say on stage, but is invested in how I live off it. I'm not looking for 100,000 fans. I'm looking for a few dozen warriors. I'm looking for people who've been through fire, don't flinch when you're bleeding, will pray with you, fight for you, and still have the guts to say, "Bro, you're slipping. Tighten it up."

That's not something you find in a flashy event. That's something you build slowly and intentionally. It's messy and real. I want a circle where the number of zeros in your bank account is of less value than those you display when nobody's looking. Instead of asking, "How big is your following?" I want people to ask, "Who are you when the lights go out and the real you walks in?"

I don't want to be the biggest fish in the room, but I don't want to be stuck in a kiddie pool with people who haven't even launched their first idea either. I need a circle of people who are moving, building, thinking bigger, failing fast, and learning faster. These people aren't afraid to call you out because they've been called out themselves. They love Jesus, lead with integrity, and live in the trenches, and do more than post about it.

So yeah, not all circles are equal. Some are elevators. Some are echo chambers. And some are just mirrors for your ego. Build the kind that makes you better.

How to Build a Real Circle

Warning: Building a circle is not for the faint of heart or anyone who thinks networking means handing out business cards while pretending hotel coffee doesn't taste like your worst decisions.

Building a real circle is brutal. It can punch you in the wallet, test your soul, and keep you up at night. If you're lucky enough to find a solid circle already built by someone with integrity, alignment, and a backbone, jump on it. Creating one from scratch is like building a barn with a popsicle sticks and staples. It's possible, but stupid hard.

I tried to find one. I paid more than I care to admit trying to plug into other people's *leadership collectives* and *mastermind ecosystems.* What I found out is that most of them let anyone in, as long as the card swipes clean. It didn't matter if you had wisdom or just Wi-Fi. No fruit? No problem. Just post some motivational nonsense and tell everyone you're a *coach.* If they're not disqualifying people, that's your sign to disqualify *them.* If everyone's welcome, standards aren't.

So, eventually, I stopped trying to squeeze into rooms that weren't built for people like me. I didn't need another *leadership experience* that felt more like group therapy for wannabes. I didn't need another coach turning me into a clone of them.

So, I did the only thing that made sense. I built what I couldn't find. Not out of ego, but because I knew there had to be more. It wasn't easy, but the easy path rarely leads to anything worthwhile.

It wasn't built with vision boards and pep talks. It was constructed with midnight whiteboard marathons, more windshield time than a long-haul trucker, coffee that tasted like disappointment in a cup, overpriced name tags, and awkward dinners where I prayed the chicken wasn't still frozen inside. It was built with gut checks, quiet prayers, and clarity that only comes after the tenth wrong room.

Failure? Oh, I had that in bulk. Before I found the right people, I found a ton of the wrong ones. I recall an event that promised to change my life. It changed my bank balance—six grand gone in three days. Their big idea was clap when the music hits, tell everyone how powerful the content was, then go back to your mediocre results.

One breakout session was a guy reading slides straight from a book I'd already read. Somehow, he made it worse. I didn't know it was possible to murder a bestseller, but this guy gave it a full-on crime scene. I walked out wondering if I'd paid for a conference or a hostage situation with snacks. The whole thing felt like a time-share pitch with name badges.

Another time, I joined a high-level coaching group that claimed to be all about kingdom-first business growth. That sounded like my jam. However, once I got in, I quickly realized that it wasn't about building leaders. It was about building hype.

Nobody asked if you'd ever led a team through a hard season or even finished something you started. It didn't matter if you knew how to treat people right, make hard calls, or stand firm when things got messy.

All they cared about was if your credit card cleared and your Instagram feed looked inspiring. You could have been living in chaos, leading nothing, and faking everything, but if you smiled big and posted enough motivational quotes, they rolled out the red carpet.

It was all sizzle, no steak. All surface, no substance. And for a guy like me, who's built stuff the hard way with boots on the ground, callused hands, and sleepless nights, that's just not going to cut it.

And don't get me started on the *bro-down* weekend where we were supposed to forge lifelong bonds over campfires and content. We forged something, but it smelled more like Axe Body Spray and desperation. One guy tried to pitch his crypto app over lunch, as if it were a youth group mixer. Another was more interested in creating shirtless content for his Instagram than discussing leadership. I left that one early.

But I didn't quit, because I wasn't chasing clout. I was chasing *alignment.* And then, I met Tucker, the same Tucker I mentioned earlier.

It was a high-end event at the VIP-only lunch. I was doing my usual thing, standing in the back of the room, arms crossed, decoding the whole strategy like I was getting paid to audit it. Then this sales guy leans over and, without missing a beat, breaks down the speaker's belief framework faster and sharper than I did.

I raised an eyebrow and thought, *Well, dang. This dude's got it.*

Now look—he was clearly part of the sales crew. But something about him didn't match the mold. He wasn't cornering people into buying things they didn't need. He wasn't sniffing around for commission like a dog at a cookout. He wanted people to walk away with what they *needed,* not what made his numbers look good.

That's rare. Most salespeople at those events are all flash, fake smiles, and pushing deals that only benefit themselves. But this guy Tucker, he was different. He wasn't selling. He was serving. That's when I knew he's wired like me. A week later, I texted him: "Hey brother, let's grab lunch. My treat." He said *yes.*

He didn't know I was bringing my wife, Jenna, the human b.s. detector. I didn't tell her anything. I just said, "Come meet a guy. See what you think." I didn't need a second opinion, I needed *the* opinion.

We talked about life, leadership, sales, and faith. When we got in the car afterward, Jenna looked at me and said, "You stay close to him. His faith, his drive—that's rare. That's gold."

Boom. Game over. He was in.

But let me be clear. Tucker didn't just walk into my circle. I built a space where people like him *wanted* to be. That's the secret most people miss. You don't find great people by luck. You attract them by being the person who deserves that level of relationship.

Real leaders see each other. And when you spot one, you don't wait. You pull up a chair and make room for them. And this wasn't a one-off. It's been a process. I've prayed through it and paid for it. I've been burned more times than I can count, and people have flaked, failed, and faked their way out. And still, I kept building, because now and then, you meet a James.

You know you have to say hello to the guy across a lacrosse field, cheering with intensity and joy. You learn he's not only there for the game. He's there for his niece and nephew and drove four hours to watch them play. He doesn't say much. But when he does, it's wisdom laced with kindness and straight fire.

That's how circles are built, not in conference rooms, but in life moments.

You find an Alejandra, a leader who could outwork a room of CEOs but still knows every employee's birthday. She doesn't need a stage. She *is* the stage because people gather where she goes. Her presence demands excellence without ever having to raise her voice. You don't teach that. You recognize it, and if you're smart, you keep her close.

You find a Jenna—your anchor and filter. The one who helps you see what you're too tired, busy, or stubborn to see. She'll pray with you and punch you in the arm if you start believing your hype.

That's how circles are built—one conversation, one prayer, and one gut check at a time. Can you create your own? Sure.

Just be prepared to burn your budget chasing the wrong people in the wrong places. Expect to lose time, sleep, and your voice in conversations that go nowhere. Plan to drive nine hundred miles, sit through a meeting with a guy pitching the next big thing, and realize halfway through his breath smells like broken promises and burnt toast. Be aware that you will question your discernment skills after someone you thought was solid turns out to be all talk and no traction. And yeah, you'll drink enough terrible coffee to question your life choices.

But if you want a real shortcut, find one that's already been built the hard way. Find one that's been vetted, tested, forged in fire, and built on genuine faith, not just slick branding and empty promises.

And when you find it, don't pitch your product. Don't puff up your story. Show up real—no spin, no sales hat, and no performance. Real recognizes real. And when it does, no slick sales pitch or polished follow-up replaces what happens next.

You don't chase clout. You chase calling. Link arms with people who've got scars to prove they've been in the fight. That's how you know it's real. That's how you know it's worth it.

Why Faith Belongs at the Table

Too many folks are out here trying to build God-sized visions without inviting Him to the table. That's like trying to run a diesel truck on Kool-Aid. It's not going to work, friend.

I've been to those *faith-driven* leadership groups that talk a big game. They toss around buzzwords like *kingdom-minded* and *purpose-driven*, but when you start digging under the hood, you realize they just bolted a Jesus sticker onto their business plan, as if that makes it holy. They're not leading with faith, they're using it for branding. And I don't know about you, but I don't want to be in a group that squeezes God in between PowerPoints and product pitches. I want Him baked into the foundation.

I remember reading the story of Hobby Lobby's founder, David Green. This guy or one of his people prays over every store before it opens. Not quietly either. We're talking full-on, hands-on-the-doorframe, invite-the-Spirit kind of prayers.

I had to ask myself, *do I pray like that?* Do I go beyond praying at home and before dinner, and pray over business decisions and leadership challenges? And more importantly, do I surround myself with people who would stop a meeting to say, "Hey, let's pray about this."?

That's The Circle I want—one where faith is the first thought and not an afterthought. Faith is the filter, framework, and fuel through which all decisions are made.

I don't mean we beat people over the head with Bible verses, try to scare anyone into holiness, or hand out salvation packets like it's Halloween. I mean we live out genuine faith that shows up in how we treat people, run our businesses, and lead when nobody's clapping. We pray first and plan second.

That's why Jenna and I started a nonprofit ministry, *God First. Life Next.* We saw too many people doing the opposite of what the name says; putting life first and wedging God into whatever space was left over. Newsflash: God is the main course, not a condiment for your leftovers.

If you're seeking or building a leadership group, here's my advice: find one where they pray out loud and nobody flinches at the word *Jesus.* Look for an environment where wins are celebrated, and losses are covered in prayer. Find a group with people who will text you and say, "Hey, I prayed for you this morning," and mean it, not because it looks good, but because they care.

The strongest leaders I know are the ones who've walked through hell and came out praising anyway. They didn't use faith as a flex, they used it as a lifeline. They've failed more times than I've even tried, but they're still standing, still praying, and still believing. Those are my people. They aren't afraid to pray and don't flinch when the fire comes. They know that if God isn't first, nothing else works.

That's The Circle I built on purpose with prayer, pain, trial and error, and a zero-tolerance policy for fake faith and plastic smiles.

So, if you find a circle built on genuine faith, forged in truth, and fueled by people who give a rip, don't hesitate. Grab a seat. And if you're still searching, I might already be building the one you've been praying for.

The Cost of Staying in the Wrong Room

We've talked about the cost of finding the right room—the bad coffee, the wasted travel, and the conferences that made your bank account cry. But we haven't talked about the silent killer: staying in the wrong room too long. That's where the real cost shows up.

Most people don't stay in the wrong room because they're dumb. They stay because they're comfortable. They know it's not the right fit. They're not being challenged, and as a result, they're not growing. But it's familiar, safe, and they already paid the fee, so they might as well see it through, right?

Wrong. Comfort is a heck of a liar. It'll whisper, "You're doing all right," while you're slowly drifting further from who you're called to be.

Imagine you join a leadership group. It's not toxic or harmful. It's *fine*. Group members clap at the right moments, say all the buzzwords, and even quote John Maxwell from time to time. But deep down, you know this isn't it. You know you're meant for more.

But you stay because you're loyal. You've made friends, and starting over sounds daunting. Now, fast-forward a year, and you're still there. You're still the sharpest one in the room and still pulling others up while nobody's pulling you. You're the go-to guy in a room where no one goes anywhere. So, you pat yourself on the back for being generous, but deep down, you're exhausted. You weren't made to drag everyone uphill forever.

And that brings me to a story from one of the most outstanding leaders I've ever known, my Grandpa Phelps. Now, Grandpa Phelps didn't run a Fortune 500 or produce a podcast. But the man had more wisdom in his pinky finger than most gurus pack into a three-day seminar with laser lights and a fog machine.

One day, when I was about eight years old, I was in the shop with him, trying to help. By *help*, I mean getting in the way like only an eight-year-old can. I was struggling to move this long, greasy, knotted-up chain across the floor, pushing it with all my little kid might. Sliding it, shoving it, frustrated as all get out.

Lead by pulling—don't exhaust yourself pushing.

Grandpa Phelps turned around, raised an eyebrow, and said something I'll never forget: "Boy, you can't push a chain." Then he grabbed the hook end of it, gave it one tug, and it followed him across the floor smooth as butter. That was it. No lecture. No whiteboard.

"You can't push a chain."

That line has haunted me in the best way ever since, because here's what I've learned: You can't push people who don't want to move. You can love, encourage, and pray for them. You can model leadership, but you cannot make someone grow.

I've tried. I've wasted months, sometimes years, dragging folks into their potential and pushing them toward purpose while they're making excuses. Every time, I ended up frustrated, burned out, and wondering why I felt so stuck.

I'd forgotten Grandpa's lesson. You can't push a chain. And you sure as heck can't grow if you're constantly tied to people who don't want to move.

The Wrong Room Will Cost You More Than Money

It'll cost you time, energy, momentum, and vision. But worst of all, it'll cost you who you could have become. While you're being loyal, not offending anyone, and being careful not to rock the boat, there's a version of you who's bolder, stronger, and more on fire for your mission, and is being delayed. You stayed where you didn't belong. It's like training for a marathon on a treadmill that won't turn on. You're moving and sweating. But you're not getting anywhere.

Here's the gut punch. You don't see the full cost of the wrong room until years later, when you realize you've plateaued. You look around and think, "Why am I still here?" You realize all the growth you missed out on wasn't stolen. You sacrificed it. And for what? Familiarity. No thanks.

The Circle You Choose Determines the Pace You Grow

Are you being pulled, or are you doing all the pulling? Are you growing, or merely staying busy? Are you surrounded by people who sharpen you or by people who smile while you slowly settle?

The wrong room won't kill you overnight. But it'll lull you into mediocrity. I don't know which is worse. So yeah, finding the right room is hard. But staying in the wrong one? That's the most expensive mistake a leader can make.

The Circle That Shapes You: Finding the Right People for Growth, Grit, and Godly Leadership

Do you want to become a better leader, nurture a stronger marriage, or grow a business that honors God and doesn't run you into the ground? Then you've got to stop doing life alone. The most important decision you'll ever make as a leader, besides surrendering your life to Christ, is deciding who you let in your circle.

The people around you will either fuel your fire or snuff it out with a wet blanket and a Bible verse taken out of context. They'll either push you toward your calling or pull you back to average. And the longer you stay around the wrong folks, the harder it is to hear what God's saying.

So, What the Heck Is a Mastermind?

First, a mastermind is not a bunch of dudes in robes quoting Tony Robbins in a candlelit barn. It's not a yacht club for CEOs or highlight reel influencers. It's not even a new idea.

Back in the 1930s, Napoleon Hill called a mastermind *two or more people working in perfect harmony for a definite purpose.*

Long before that, Jesus said:

FOR WHERE TWO OR THREE GATHER IN MY NAME, THERE I AM WITH THEM.
—MATTHEW 18:20

That's what I'm after. And my definition is simple:

"A mastermind is a group of people who show up on purpose, for a purpose—faith, leadership, family, legacy—whatever God's put in their hands to build."
—Dan Greer

The keyword is *intentionally*. You don't fall into a mastermind. You build it, or you find one built the right way, and join it.

Who You Let In Changes Who You Become

You've heard it before: "You're the average of the five people you spend the most time with." This isn't some cheesy quote you slap on a coffee mug or a motivational poster with a mountain on it. It's true.

If you run with five gossipers? You'll be fluent in drama by next Thursday and probably leading the prayer chain that somehow turned into a rumor mill. Hang with five people who dodge responsibility, blame everyone else, and only show up when there's free food. You're going to start thinking that showing up is optional, and mediocrity is a lifestyle.

But if you lock arms with five God-fearing, purpose-driven, no-excuse-making, truth-speaking leaders, you'd better buckle up. Your standards will rise, your goals will grow teeth, your excuses will get uncomfortable, and your life will shift faster than a hot rod on race day.

Your circle becomes your mirror, and eventually, your future. Their habits rub off on you, their mindset creeps in, and their words start to echo in your own. So, if you don't like where you're headed, don't just look at your calendar. Look at your crew.

Over time, their habits become your habits. Their

mindset becomes yours. You start to think like them, talk like them, and lead like them. That can either be a blessing or a complete gut punch. Let's not sugarcoat it. This works both ways.

Hang around the wrong room long enough, and suddenly, shrinking your dreams feels wise. You'll start dialing down your purpose, as if it's too loud for the group. You'll bury your big ideas so Karen doesn't feel threatened at the potluck. You'll start playing small, not because you lack ambition, but because no one else brought a shovel big enough to dig deep.

And here's the worst part: You'll slap a noble label on it and call it *loyalty*. But let me be clear: It isn't loyalty if it's killing your calling. That's not loyalty. That's slow death by small talk, stale donuts, and coffee that comes with a side of shame. It's nodding your head at the same tired conversations while your soul's over there screaming, *We were made for more than this!*

Don't stay stuck just because you're scared to outgrow somebody else's comfort zone. That's like keeping training wheels on your Harley because your buddy's still riding a tricycle.

God didn't call you to play chameleon. He didn't knit you together in your mother's womb so that you could blend into beige conversations and beige dreams. He called you to boldly and faithfully lead, and yeah, sometimes with a voice that turns heads and makes the room a little uncomfortable.

Authentic leadership doesn't whisper. It walks in with purpose, speaks with conviction, and carries a plunger, because sometimes you have to clean out some crap before progress can happen.

Real Talk About Masterminds

You've already been in one. You just didn't call it that. Think about it:

- The 4-H crew at the county fair learning grit and responsibility was a mini-mastermind.
- That firehouse full of volunteers training to serve their community was a circle of purpose.
- That Bible study where people sharpen each other instead of just quoting bumper-sticker verses is a mastermind.
- A family dinner where everyone's chasing goals and calling each other up counts as a mastermind, too.

Any group with alignment, action, and accountability is a mastermind. But once you leave that room, campfire, or conference, *that fire dies*, unless you are intentional about keeping it stoked. That's what I wanted to change and why I started building my own.

I was sick of surface-level content, hype without heart, highlight reels, and handshake pitches. I needed encouragers who would pray without being asked—ones who would check my blind spots and call out my crap with love and truth. I wanted people who weren't in it for the badge, but the battle.

Building that circle is hard. It costs you. But when you find it, you don't just rise, you become who God made you to be.

The Circle That Pulls You Higher

Growing up, my family was all in with The Grange. If you've never heard of it, don't worry, most folks haven't. But back in the day, The Grange was a lifeline. Farmers from the North and South leaned on each other to survive after the Civil War. Over time, it evolved into a tight-knit, family-driven organization that fought for things that mattered, like launching 4-H, rural mail delivery, and now, high-speed internet for the forgotten corners of America.

My parents were highly involved. We traveled the country to attend national conventions, and I loved it. Every time I left one of those gatherings, I was fired up, inspired to lead the charge back home. I'd scribble down new ideas, dream big plans, and think, *This is it. This is going to change everything.*

And then I'd walk into our tiny local Grange meeting. About a dozen folks, bless their hearts, retired, rewired, and old enough to have voted for Lincoln. One guy still used a flip phone. Another lady once asked me if Wi-Fi was a new brand of fertilizer.

The whole crew looked like they'd just finished reruns of *Matlock* and were only there to wrap things up before the potluck started. Heaven help us if we were late for lukewarm green bean casserole and suspicious Jell-O with mystery fruit floating in it.

I'd sit there, fired up with fresh ideas, and they'd be discussing whether to use a 20-cent or 21-cent stamp on the next newsletter. Let's just say the energy gap was noticeable. The excitement faded, not because the ideas weren't good. I wasn't surrounded by people who were chasing the same dreams.

That cycle? Oh, it's real. And it still shows up in my life like clockwork. Ask Jenna. She knows the signs. I'll hit a mastermind, get fired up like someone dumped jet fuel on my soul, and come home talking faster than a cattle auctioneer with a caffeine addiction. Two months later, that flame flickers.

At first, she lets it slide—probably hoping it's just a low day. But then, without fail, she drops the soft-but-loaded line: "Babe. It's time. Call someone. Get poured into. I don't care what it costs. You need your people."

Translation: "You're gettin' cranky, your fire's running low, and I'm not about to let you turn into one of those grumpy old guys from the potluck meetings."

She's always right, because leaders don't run on autopilot. We're not machines. We're more like wood-burning stoves. If you stop adding logs, the fire dies.

We don't need hype. We don't need hustle. We need fuel, fire, and people—the right people. You know them by the grit in their souls, faith in their bones, and enough fire to light you back up when yours starts fading.

Don't Lead Alone. Jesus Didn't

Let's just go straight to the top here: Jesus didn't lead alone. He could have. He was the Son of God, after all. But He chose to build a circle with twelve guys and a few close friends—a team. None of them were perfect people—far from it.

Peter was impulsive. Thomas second-guessed everything. And Judas? Well, he's the guy who would sell you out for gas money and a half-eaten sandwich. Still, Jesus led with them, not above them. He taught, challenged, and prayed with them. He even washed their filthy feet. He could have dropped sermons from a mountaintop and mic-dropped His way out. He didn't. He pulled up a chair and gave each disciple a seat at the table.

So, Jesus, the Son of God, Savior of the world, and the miracle worker who walked on water, needed a team. What in the holy DOT regs makes us think we can solo this leadership thing? Sure, you might be the one with the vision and pushing the plow. But that doesn't mean you're supposed to carry the whole dang farm on your back, milk the cows, and fix the fence before breakfast.

Leadership isn't a one-person rodeo. It's a team sport. Even Jesus didn't do it alone. So why should you? Lone-wolf leadership isn't heroic. It's exhausting, and even worse, it's dangerous. Nobody's walking with you to warn you of pitfalls. And if you're surrounded by people who clap for your compromise but never call you to rise, that's not a circle. That's a trap.

Leaders Grow on Purpose

Leadership isn't a destination you arrive at. It's something you *choose* every day, especially when it's hard. You've got to build growth into your rhythm, or you'll wake up stagnant, stuck, and wondering where the fire went.

So, I built The Circle. And no, it's not for everyone. It's not a networking group. It's not a place to chase clout or collect participation trophies. It's for gritty, called leaders who are still fighting for purpose—even when no one's clapping.

If that hits something deep in you, you can learn more at realdangreer.com. But don't just click. Count the cost first. Then step in.

And it's got levels, because leadership doesn't come in one-size-fits-all:

- Just starting your journey? There's a circle for you where you can build bold habits, deepen your faith, and lead with integrity from day one.

- Been in the game for a while, but feel like your fire's flickering? There's a circle to reignite your grit and remind you who you are.

- Already built something big, but still hungry to grow? There's a high-level circle for you, too, because real leaders never outgrow growth.

But here's the deal: You apply because finding the right people is more important than filling seats. I don't care about your title. I care if you're willing to be sharpened. I don't care if you've made millions. I care if you've still got that fire to grow. I care if you're the leader who shows up, takes action, tells the truth, and leads with faith.

If that's you, welcome to The Circle. If that's not you yet, no hard feelings. But don't be surprised when your fire flickers while others are lighting torches.

So here's the gut check:

- Who's in your corner?
- Who's calling you out and calling you up?
- And if you don't have that crew yet, what's holding you back?

The next breakthrough in your life, leadership, business, and faith depends on you choosing better people to surround you. And maybe that starts right here. Pull up a chair. The table's set. Let's go.

Key Takeaways From Chapter 14

The leaders you run with define the leader you become. Build, or leave the room. If the crowd's all flex and no fruit, quit waiting for your people, and create the space yourself.

Solo is overrated. VIP seats mean nothing without teammates to sharpen the ideas you scribble down.

You can't push a chain. Stop dragging folks who love neutral. Find engines, not anchors.

Your five voices are your future. Hang with people whose habits, faith, and standards you want to rub off on you.

Faith is the framework, not the garnish. If a group flinches at open prayer, that's your exit cue.

Comfort is a sneaky dream-killer. Staying in the wrong room out of loyalty keeps the next-level you on ice.

Iron sharpens iron, and sparks welcome. The right circle loves you enough to applaud your wins and challenge your blind spots.

Celebrate big and, compete small. Cheering loudly for others muscles envy out of The Circle.

Character is greater than credentials. Titles impress but fruit convinces. Vet people by outcomes, not optics.

Jesus rolled with twelve—so should you. Even the Son of God chose community over lone-wolf leadership.

VISION MATTERS, BUT IGNITION IS LEADERSHIP.

Chapter 15 | Nobody Follows a Parked Car

Movement or Stuck?

I was sitting in the Durango airport, one of the smallest commercial airports you'll ever see. It's got three gates, no moving walkways, no fancy lounges, and no overpriced airport salad bars. We don't even have a jet bridge. You walk out the door onto the tarmac, follow the painted lines like you're in a real-life game of airport hopscotch, and climb a set of stairs or a ramp to board the plane. It's amazing. I wouldn't trade the simplicity of the small-town experience for the world. It's enough to get you where you're going and fits me. No fluff or chaos. Get in, get out, and get to work.

I travel so much that the TSA agents know me better than some of my extended family do. I walked in the other day, kicked off my boots, and tossed my bag on the belt when one of them said, "Morning, Dan. Where are you leading folks this time, and when's your wife expecting you back?"

We laughed. Then another agent leans over and says, "Hey, I saw that video you did about leadership not being about barking orders. My boss should probably watch that one twice." Then he whispered, "Also, that bit about DOT compliance and duct tape? That one had me wheezing." (Yes, this is my shameless plug—@realdangreer. In addition to leading leaders, I'm entertaining airport security one reel at a time.)

Look, I don't mind the jokes, because whether it's in a boardroom, a barn, or the TSA line, I'm living what I teach. Leadership doesn't turn off when you land. It doesn't pause because your bag didn't make it. And it certainly doesn't park in economy because things got hard.

Anyway, I was flying out for a client job. It was two and a half days of on-site work, but I blocked out three on my calendar. I didn't think I'd need that much time, but I wanted freedom to overdeliver if needed. That's something I've learned about leadership. Leadership means doing more than enough to get by. It means building margin so you can serve beyond what's expected.

My wife Jenna dropped me off that morning. I can't say this loudly enough: She's the real MVP (Most Valuable Player). Bless her heart. We've been in one of the busiest, most chaotic seasons of our lives, and she's been rock solid through it all. She holds down the fort at home, pours into the kids, supports my crazy schedule, and somehow still manages to smile through it. She's put her dreams on pause so I could chase this mission God laid on my heart, and she does it with more grace than I deserve. That woman's love is a full-on superpower.

So, she dropped me off, gave me one of those you-got-this looks, and off I went. I breezed through security. TSA in Durango is two friendly people and a conveyor belt, and made my way to the one table in the entire airport that has a power outlet. Yep, there's only one. But I'm a seasoned traveler here. I know the prime real estate.

I tossed my phone on the wireless charger, cracked open my tablet, snapped on the keyboard, plugged into my setting-the-stage playlist (everything from Tracy Lawrence to AC/DC—don't judge), and boom—I'm working. I'm replying to emails, knocking out tasks, and getting ahead before I even leave the ground. It took me thirty seconds to get locked in and productive.

A lady sat down across from me. She pulled out her laptop, followed by a mouse, a mouse pad, a water bottle, a notebook, and a pen. Then, she repositioned her chair, slid the computer a little to the left, too far, back to the right. Okay, next she tilted the screen, took a sip of water, wiped the table, looked around, and adjusted the chair again.

I felt like I was watching someone choreograph a dance to start working.

By the time she finally looked ready to get something done, they called our flight. I watched as she carefully and neatly packed it all back up in reverse order, like it was some ritual. Then it hit me.

I used to be her.

I used to spend a lot of time getting my setup right. The lighting needed to be perfect. My favorite pen, the right playlist, a fresh cup of coffee, a clear desk, and a distraction-free environment all had to be in place. Basically, the stars had to align, and only then I might be ready to work. I called it getting organized, but the truth is, I was procrastinating in style. I wasted so much time. The setup became the excuse for not starting. And it always felt justified, because it looked productive. But that was performance, not progress.

That moment at the airport reminded me of something I've had to learn over and over again: You don't need a perfect setup to make progress. You need to start.

And, if you don't want to do something, you'll find every excuse not to do it. We've all done it. We've rearranged our calendars, reorganized our desks, and alphabetized the sticky notes. We've done everything except the task that needs to be done. We delay, distract, and set ourselves up for paralysis. Leadership doesn't work like that.

Leaders don't follow the most polished plan. They follow motion, consistency, and people on the move.

So, if you've ever found yourself stuck in setup mode, spending more time preparing than producing, consider this your loving, sarcastic reminder from a guy who's been there: Nobody follows a parked car. They follow the one who turns the key, hits the gas, and figures it out on the road.

Now that you've got the engine warmed up, let's talk about what leadership in motion looks like. All the ideas, insights, and stories in this book come alive, making their way off the pages and into the real world.

I get it. You might be feeling a little overwhelmed right now. That's normal. It's expected. You've been handed a book full of conviction, challenge, grace, humor, systems, soul work, and plenty of gut punches. You've been stirred, stretched, and maybe smacked around a little in the best way possible. But this moment right here is about possibility, not pressure. I want you to picture something.

You walk into a room and there it is: a massive oak table, longer than you can see. It's sagging under the weight of a feast. Silver platters. Steaming bowls. Roasted meats glistening with juice. Fresh-baked bread. Your favorite dessert, *the one your grandma used to make.* There are dishes you've dreamed of, ones you've seen on TV, and a few that make your mouth water from the smell alone.

Overwhelm shrinks with action. Start by taking action.
Pick a plate. Finish it. Repeat.

The air? Unreal. It smells like a bakery, a steakhouse, a backyard barbecue, and a world-class dessert shop all at the same time. This isn't stress, it's *glory*.

At the head of the table is one chair, and your name is on it. You walk over, grinning like a kid on Christmas morning. You sit down, lift the lid on the first serving bowl, and can't believe this is yours. You load your plate and dig in. It's perfect. It's everything you hoped for.

You lean back, thinking, *Man, I'm full. That was incredible.* Then you spot a little note tucked under your plate. The message reads, "You may not leave the table until it's cleared."

And then, you feel two massive hands rest on your shoulders. Looking up, you see a dude in a tuxedo who is as big as John Cena. He is an imposing character with no smile, has arms like tree trunks, and is at least seven feet tall in your imagination. He stares at you while gently pushing your chair back in. What once felt exciting now feels heavy. That table full of food now looks like a burden.

Welcome to leadership overwhelm.

That's what it feels like when you finish a book like this, or come back from one of those fire-breathing conferences where the speakers are so good, you forget to blink. You've got 2,000 ideas, eighty-seven notes scribbled on napkins, and one question bouncing around your brain like a fly in a coffee cup. *Where the heck do I even start?*

And that, my friend, is precisely where most people stall out. Not because they don't care, but because they never shift from inspiration to implementation. They stare at the table. They glance over their shoulder. They see that giant of a guy, and they freeze. Paralysis by analysis sets in, and they conclude that if they can't eat the whole feast immediately, it's better not to start at all. But that's not how leaders roll. Let me offer you an alternative perspective on this dilemma.

You don't eat the whole buffet at once. You select a few courses and servings to put on your plate. You can even choose to eat nothing but pie if that's what you want to do. Then, one bite at a time, you eventually eat what's on your plate. Implementation of effective leadership strategies is similar. Look at all the options before you. First, pray, and then choose which action items, conversations, policies, and systems you will take on.

When you finish, hand the empty plate to the giant behind you. He'll smile, and you won't know for sure if he's proud of you or severely constipated. Either way, he's glad to help.

Then, you grab a fresh plate and repeat the process. With every plate you knock out, the table shrinks. The overwhelm fades. And that massive, intimidating mountain in front of you looks a lot like a hill God built for you to conquer.

Most people don't quit, because they never started. But you have a system. So start small and start now. Eat the pie.

There's an old saying that goes, "If you have to eat a frog, do it first thing in the morning. And if you have to eat two frogs, eat the bigger one first."

Now, some folks say Mark Twain said it. Others say that's a load of bull. Either way, the point stands, and it's a good one. Do the hard stuff first. Don't dance around it. Don't check your email, straighten your desk, or color-code your to-do list. Eat the frog. Take on the tough conversation, make the call, fix what's broken. Leaders don't become great by avoiding frogs. They become great by swallowing the hard stuff before breakfast.

Translation? Get the hard stuff out of the way early. Stop staring at it. Stop decorating your to-do list with it. Eat the dang frog. And if you've got an elephant to eat, the same rule applies. One bite at a time. One plate at a time.

Look. You will not implement everything in this book today. I don't expect you to. Honestly, I hope you come back to it in six months, a year, or five years, and something new resonates with you right where you need it most. That's how you know it's alive in you.

I hope you dog-ear it, re-read it, and argue with it. I hope you buy the audiobook and listen to it while you read, because let's be honest, hearing me say this stuff out loud hits different. I hope you highlight more than a middle school science book that you weren't supposed to write in, but did anyway. And I hope it messes with you, in the best way, because real leadership books don't just teach. They stick, challenge, whisper when you're alone, and shove you when you're stuck.

This isn't just a book. It's a conversation you'll keep having with yourself until you become the leader God envisions you can be. But you've got to do *something* with it *now*. Even if it's only one step.

Leadership is moving through the storm and not waiting until it passes. And trust me when I say this: Your team doesn't need a perfect plan. They need to see you take the first step. Once you do, they'll follow. Remember, nobody follows a parked car.

But leadership doesn't end when the wheels start turning. What truly builds trust is how you drive when no one's watching, when it's slow, quiet, and there's no applause. It's in those unseen moments, long after the spotlight fades, that you keep steering steady in the same direction, day after day. That leadership doesn't make headlines, but it makes all the difference.

I didn't learn that from a leadership course or a keynote. I learned it from my former leader, Isaiah. If that name sounds familiar, it's because I introduced him to you earlier.

I had just stepped into a dumpster fire. DOT compliance was an afterthought at best. This company had grown rapidly, hired top talent, and had built an impressive fleet. But when it came to DOT, they were running ninety miles an hour in the dark, with no headlights, no brakes, and a paper trail that looked more like a scavenger hunt.

The files contained more spiders than documents. DOT policies were outdated or missing entirely. Compliance? Let's just say we were flying under the radar so hard, it was a miracle we hadn't been grounded. It felt like management had handed me the keys to a freight train already halfway off the rails and said, "Good luck!" This was an urgent situation and things needed to change quickly.

I wondered if I'd made the biggest mistake of my life. The stakes were high. I felt the pressure in my chest. That voice inside started whispering: *You're not ready for this. You don't know enough. You're going to blow it.* And right when that inner spiral hit full spin, Isaiah walked in.

He sat down across from me like it was just another Tuesday. I, on the other hand, had about forty mental tabs open and was praying none of them crashed mid-conversation. The conversation we had in the humblest of offices completely changed the way I lead. He dared to say what I needed to hear, not what I wanted to hear.

When he said he needed me to be the rudder of this company, I had no idea what he meant. I'm a truck guy, not a boat guy. But when he explained how critical the rudder is for determining the direction of a boat, it everything changed.

"When it moves, even just a little, everything else follows. Apply steady, consistent pressure in the right direction, and eventually we'll get exactly where we need to go." Isaiah was giving me permission to go slowly, but never stop.

One man with a simple message delivered one of the most powerful leadership lessons I've ever heard. I didn't know it at the time, but the Bible speaks *directly* about this.

OR TAKE SHIPS AS AN EXAMPLE: ALTHOUGH THEY ARE SO LARGE AND ARE DRIVEN BY STRONG WINDS, THEY ARE STEERED BY A VERY SMALL RUDDER WHEREVER THE PILOT WANTS TO GO. LIKEWISE, THE TONGUE IS A SMALL PART OF THE BODY, BUT IT MAKES GREAT BOASTS... THE TONGUE IS A FIRE.

—JAMES 3:4-6

You often don't realize you're steering it until years later, when the ship finally turns, and you look back and think, *Man. I didn't even know we were moving.*

But here's the flip side. That same rudder can do damage. That's the warning in James. The tongue, like the rudder, is small, but it can *burn a forest down*. It can *wreck a culture*. It can *derail trust*, all with one careless swing. That's why what Isaiah said mattered so much. Pressure applied with wisdom, humility, and direction, takes people somewhere worth going.

So, when I sat in that chair, with Isaiah calling me to be the rudder, I heard more than a metaphor. I heard a mission. I've never forgotten that. When I wanted to quit, I remembered that rudder. When no one noticed my work, I remembered that rudder. When progress was slow, I remembered that rudder. When leadership felt lonely, heavy, and thankless, I remembered Isaiah's words and continued to apply pressure.

So if you're in a season where it feels like nothing's changing, hear me. You don't have to be loud or in the spotlight. You just have to be faithful. Steady pressure turns ships. Quiet leadership creates lasting change. And small acts, done daily, move mountains. Be the rudder. Hold the line. Turn the ship.

And sometimes, after you've been the rudder for a while, holding steady and pushing through the quiet stretch, what you need next isn't more consistency. I was sitting in the front row at a Russell Brunson conference, carbonated water kicking in, notebook open, heart open too, if I'm honest. I'd been grinding hard that year, growing businesses, raising a family, building something that mattered, and I needed a little fire. A little reset. Maybe even a little kick in the rear.

The room was buzzing. You know that electric energy you feel when you're surrounded by people who want purpose, growth, and impact. Entrepreneurs, builders, leaders—we are all looking for the next thing to stretch us.

One big-name speaker after another stepped on stage and delivered their big stories. It was challenging to take notes with all the slides and sound bites flying by at a rapid pace. Then one guy walked on stage, clothed in jeans and a T-shirt, with a quiet confidence that said he didn't need flash to deliver the truth.

He stepped up to the mic, looked out at the crowd, and simply said, "Do hard things." That was it—three little words with no fanfare or fluff. Then he repeated it. Slower this time. Like he wanted it to land. "Do hard things. Every single day."

I remember leaning back in my seat and waiting for the rest of the message. But that *was* the message. That was the whole thing. And then he explained why. He said most people, about 99 percent, spend their entire lives trying to make things easier, smoother, and safer. They float, cruise, coast, and avoid resistance at all costs. Doing hard things requires something most people aren't willing to give—effort on purpose.

He said, "If you're willing to do what most people won't, you'll live a life most people never will." That's when the whole room got quiet, a *conviction* silence, that moment where it stops being about a conference and starts being about your life.

I sat there, pen frozen in my hand, thinking about all the times I'd waited too long to make a move. I remembered all the things I *knew* I needed to do, but talked myself out of. I thought about the conversations I had postponed, the systems I had kept putting off fixing, and the leadership decisions I had delayed, which were because they were uncomfortable or messy. That moment reminded me that leadership doesn't live in the easy. It lives in the *stretch.*

Doing hard things because you're a leader becomes permission for others to move too. That's what leadership is. It's going first, stepping into the tough stuff before anyone else will. It's showing up when it's inconvenient. It's choosing courage over comfort, and doing it consistently.

The speaker on that stage didn't influence me because he had a catchy phrase. He influenced me because he lived it. And leaders who live it create motion everywhere they go.

So, when I got home from that conference, I made a commitment: *Do one hard thing every day.* Model leadership as a dad, husband, friend, and man by doing hard stuff. The more I lead, the more I realize this: Leadership is evidenced by being followed *on purpose.* The only way people follow you on purpose is if they see you doing the hard thing when it would have been easier to stand still. If you ever forget, just remember the simplicity of the guy on that stage, living life in motion.

What's Your First Move?

Writing this book has been a wild ride and, I've enjoyed every minute. But here's the crazy part: I gave you way more than I ever thought I would. And that's coming from a guy who didn't finish reading a book from about third grade until somewhere deep into dad life. Seriously, I wrote book reports based on the back cover content and chapter titles, and somehow managed to squeeze out an A+. Don't tell my mom or my teachers. They still think I was a child prodigy. But here I am, *writing* a book. And more than that, you're *still reading it.* What a time to be alive.

Now, I hope you didn't cherry-pick your way through this book like I did back then. There's way too much gold in these pages. At this point, you probably know more about me than my relatives do, maybe even more than my brother does. Again, don't tell Mom. She might be a little bummed that you're ahead of her in the *Dan trivia* game.

But seriously, you've made it here, and I'm proud of you. Most people don't. Most buy a book, skim a chapter or two, then toss it under the truck seat, where it stays until trade-in day. Or it sits on their nightstand collecting dust. But not you. You've come this far. Don't let that effort go to waste. Here's the thing. Leadership is about taking action.

Let me leave you with one last story. It's a great one, I promise.

A while back, I was the closing speaker at a youth conference. Now, the event had an earlier speaker, a good one, who spent her entire three-hour session over a day and a half discussing everything wrong in the world. "Don't do this, avoid that." Her stories were powerful, but something was missing. She didn't give us any direction on what to do. Now, don't get me wrong; she was excellent at highlighting dangers, but I felt like there was a missed opportunity to inspire these young people with action steps.

So, there I was, just minutes away from going in front of this sea of teenagers, who, let's be real, had probably already decided that nothing I was about to say would be cooler than whatever social media they were scrolling. Feeling the pressure, I did what I always do when I'm stuck: I prayed. *All right, God, I'm going to need some help here. What do these kids need?*

Now, God has a funny way of getting my attention. Sometimes it's subtle, sometimes it's more like getting smacked upside the head with a holy two-by-four. And clear as day, He replied, "Dan, you're going to give away some of your cash."

Well played, God. If there's one guaranteed way to grab the attention of teenagers, it's free money. And if there's one guaranteed way to catch my attention, it's God reaching straight into my wallet. He's pretty creative like that.

I stood up there with three bills—$1, $20, and $50—and asked for volunteers. Three kids eagerly joined me up front. I held out the cash, turned my back, closed my eyes, and said, "One of you, take a bill. Any bill."

Nothing happened. Crickets. I peeked and said, "Seriously? Free money! Grab one. Only one bill each, though."

On the second try, finally, someone took the $50 bill. Right after that, another person snatched the $20 bill. Finally, reluctantly, the last girl grabbed the $1 bill. I turned around and smiled, saying to her jokingly, "Well, you got the last one. There's your reward for waiting. Go ahead and sit down."

The girl with the $20 bill stayed. "Why didn't you grab the $50 bill first?" I asked. "It was more valuable."

She hesitated, then admitted, "I wanted it, but I was scared. I wasn't sure what would happen. But once the $50 bill was gone, I couldn't let the $20 slip away, too."

"Exactly," I said. "It's easier to take action once you see someone else take the leap first. There's less fear when someone else shows it can be done safely, right?"

"Yeah, totally," she said, smiling broadly. I let her keep her prize, and she bounced happily back to her seat.

Then, the young man with the $50 stepped up. "Why the fifty?" I asked him.

"You told me to!" he said.

"Nope," I replied, laughing. "I just said, take one bill. You picked the highest value. Would you trade it for another bill in my pocket?"

He shook his head quickly. "No way, you'll trick me and hand me a dollar!"

I reached into my pocket and pulled out a $100 bill. His eyes widened. "Man! I should have traded!" he said, laughing.

"Too late now. You missed your chance," I teased. "But look, your action, the courage to grab the $50 first, led the others to act. You set things in motion. You took the risk first, so your reward was highest."

Last, I brought back the girl who grabbed the single dollar. "Why did you wait so long?" I asked gently.

"Because everyone else took the better bills first," she said quietly.

I smiled warmly. "You waited to see what everyone else did. You hesitated. Is that how you want your life to be? Always waiting and getting whatever's left?"

She shook her head firmly. "No, definitely not."

"Exactly. Don't let fear or hesitation hold you back. Leaders go first. Leaders act boldly and inspire others to move forward."

And that, my friend, is precisely my message for you. After reading this book, you've learned what it takes. You've heard the stories. Now the question is, what are you going to do?

Are you going to take action? Will you join or build your circle of leaders? Will you lead through service, practice extreme ownership, and inspire others, or will you wait, watching opportunities pass you by?

Don't wait. Go first. Be the rudder. Nobody follows a parked car.

Now you're at the end of the book. This is usually where an author neatly wraps things up, provides a checklist, a tidy action plan, and maybe even a pat on the back. But leadership isn't neat. It never has been, and I'm not about to pretend otherwise.

So, let's skip the fluff. You don't need another workbook. You don't need extra hours in your day. You don't need permission. You need action—one bold and messy step right now.

You've journeyed through influence, ownership, grit, humility, and faith—all the beautiful truths of leadership. Maybe the guidance in this book inspired you. Perhaps it overwhelmed you. Possibly it woke something inside that's been silent for far too long. But none of that matters unless you do something about it. So, what's your next move?

Notice, I didn't ask what your *perfect* or *someday* move is. I want you to decide what move you can make right now. Perhaps it's finally time to schedule that tough meeting. Maybe you should send a text apologizing for your mistake. Perhaps it's about creating a system to bring order out of chaos. Possibly it's stepping outside tomorrow morning and walking the yard with your team. Maybe it's sitting down with your family tonight and reminding them who you are and what you're building together.

Whatever your next move is, it's time to make it.

I tell you this as someone who's stood exactly where you are, unsure, overwhelmed, afraid, and chose to move anyway. Every breakthrough I've experienced began the moment I acted. Oftentimes, those steps were uncomfortable and imperfect. But the goal was consistency—doing the next right thing, until something shifted.

So, as you close this book, don't just highlight the good lines or nod and say, "That was pretty good."

Move. Lead. Act. Don't do it to impress anyone. Do it because this is who God called you to be.

Our world needs more examples—leaders who walk the walk, act when it's hard, put their rudder in the water, and go first. You're one of those leaders. You're part of that rare 1 percent who refuse to settle. Step up, lean in, and choose action.

So, let's go. Let's build businesses worth talking about. Let's nurture families that thrive. Let's develop teams that follow because of trust, not obligation. And let's do it with grit, faith, joy, with a bit of grease on our hands.

Keep moving forward, one hard step after another. Because, as you've already learned, nobody follows a parked car.

Before you close this book, there's one last thing I need to tell you. It's a truth I've lived over and over again:

You can learn something from anyone if you're paying attention.

That's it. You've reached the end, but here's the irony: This isn't an ending, it's your beginning. Leadership doesn't start when you're handed a title. It starts the moment you open your heart, your eyes, and your ears, and admit you don't have all the answers.

Some of my greatest leadership lessons weren't learned in boardrooms or at seminars. I learned them in the back lot, talking with drivers covered in diesel and dust. My wife taught me leadership lessons, holding our family together while I chased dreams. My kids reminded me that curiosity is a powerful force. Even strangers unknowingly taught me lessons I desperately needed. If you're humble enough, hungry enough, and willing to listen, leadership will find you.

There might be an Isaiah, quietly telling you to be the rudder, not the sail. A soft-spoken speaker simply saying, "Do hard things," may awaken you to a simple yet powerful strategy. The driver texting you late at night because you're the person they trust is teaching you a valuable lesson about leadership. Authentic leadership is decisive and needed now more than ever.

We need leaders who choose impact over spotlight. Build people up, not burn them out, and nurture families grounded in love rather than performance. Leaders who make choices rooted in prayer instead of panic are a treasure to those they seek to lead. People need leaders who understand the value of lifelong learning. The one-and-done mentality won't cut it.

That's the vision I'm fighting for—the future I'm praying for.

In a noisy world, authentic leadership cuts through. Not because it's louder, but because it's lived.

So here's to your next step. Your first bold move. Your hardest decision. The awkward conversation. The overlooked moment. The open heart. The quiet courage. The steady grind. Here's to chasing leadership with grit, with faith, with joy, and maybe even with a bit of grease on your jeans. (Yes, honey, I still don't know how it got on the throw pillows. My bad!)

This journey has been incredible. I've poured my heart onto these pages, and I'm truly honored you chose to join me. Now, as we close, I'd like to do something a little different. I want to pray for you. If that's not your thing, no worries. You can close the book now and share it with someone else. But if you're comfortable, join me in prayer.

BLESSING THE READERS

Heavenly Father,

Thank You for this incredible reader, for their courage to seek growth, their commitment to push forward, and their perseverance in reaching this very moment. God, I pray You strengthen their heart and deepen their resolve. Fill them with boldness and clarity to step confidently into the leadership role You've specifically designed for them.

Father, open their eyes to see influence everywhere and in everyone around them, recognizing their power to shape lives positively. Instill within them the discipline and courage to take extreme ownership in all they do, owning their decisions, actions, and impacts fully.

Lord, guide them as they build their brand as a leader, one that is authentic, reliable, and trustworthy. Help them to lead honorably, even when no one is watching, knowing that genuine leadership is lived consistently behind closed doors.

Heavenly Father, remind them daily of the incredible power of prayer, that their strength and direction flow from staying closely connected with You. Teach them the humility and strength of servant leadership, empowering them to put others first, knowing their most significant impact is through genuine service.

Give them vision, God, whether it's their own or one they choose to embrace fully. Equip them to own and pursue that vision passionately, positively, and powerfully, influencing others along the way. Father, comfort and strengthen them in those moments of loneliness that often accompany leadership. Remind them that You are always near.

Help them navigate the tension between grace and grit, striking a balance between compassion and firm resolve. Let humility be the foundation of their leadership, allowing them to grow and multiply new leaders around them, not simply growing themselves.

Encourage them to build and nurture their circle, surrounding themselves with people who uplift, challenge, and inspire growth. Finally, Lord, move them to action—real, intentional, courageous action that creates lasting change.

Bless them richly, beyond anything they could ask or imagine. Guide every decision, every step, every conversation, and every encounter. Turn their challenges into victories, doubts into clarity, and efforts into meaningful impact.

We thank You, God, for every lesson learned, every obstacle overcome, and every triumph experienced on their journey. Let Your grace and wisdom flow through them, shaping them into the impactful, authentic leader You've called them to be a beacon of hope, integrity, and inspiration.

We ask all this in the powerful, matchless name of Jesus. Amen.

Now, go out there and lead. Your story is just getting started.

About the Author

Dan Greer is what happens when you mix five generations of grit with a God-given calling to build leaders and fix broken systems.

His roots run deep in Southwest Colorado. Dan is raising his kids on the same **chunk of dirt** he grew up on—the very land his family homesteaded back in 1902. That ground has seen cattle, crops, and now, kids learning what it means to lead with character. Dan's not just rooted, he's relentless. He's a builder by nature, a problem solver by trade, and a coach by calling.

Dan is the founder of Eclipse DOT (www.EclipseDOT.com), an international company that equips businesses with fleets to operate smarter, scale faster, and build stronger leaders. But when Dan saw a gaping hole in the industry—no real tools for compliance professionals managing multiple companies—he didn't wait for someone else to fix it.

He built DOT Docs (www.DOTDocs.com). DOT Docs is not a band-aid nor a knockoff. It's a ground-up solution for the people in the trenches. DOT Docs made compliance so simple even a driver could do it—and Dan can say that, because he used to be a driver, and still is, from time to time.

Dan's not a coder—he's a problem solver—a visionary who creates tools real companies actually use. When the industry couldn't solve the problem, he rolled up his sleeves and built the system everyone wished they had.

As a business coach, Dan works directly with leaders who use vehicles in their businesses, helping them unlock growth, simplify operations, and activate their teams. He's helped companies double their revenue over twelve months in as little as three days by aligning leadership and eliminating friction. His coaching doesn't just inspire—it transforms.

But business isn't the only place Dan invests. He is also the founder of **God First, Life Next** (www.GodFirstLifeNext.org), a nonprofit movement calling people to put God at the center of everything. Through devotionals, resources, and real-life stories, Dan and his team help people flip the script—living with faith as the foundation, not an afterthought.

For Dan, this isn't theory—it's personal. Years ago, he made God the CEO of every business and nonprofit he leads. That shift changed everything. Decisions got clearer, stress got lighter, and purpose became the bottom line. To Dan, leadership without God at the helm is like a truck without a steering wheel—you might move, but you won't go where you need to.

Dan is a solution finder, a systems thinker, and a leader's leader. He sees what's broken, builds what's needed, and equips others to lead well—even in the chaos. Whether it's people issues, compliance confusion, or culture drift, Dan brings the grit, the grease, and the grace to get things moving.

He's also a dynamic, high-impact speaker known for keynotes and trainings that blend faith, business, leadership, and real-world stories that stick. Whether he's on stage, in a boardroom, or out in the yard, Dan connects.

If you're ready to scale your business, develop leaders, or bring clarity to your chaos, then you want Dan in front of your team.

To book Dan for a keynote, workshop, or executive training—or to explore the tools he's built for business owners and fleet leaders—visit:

- ☞ www.RealDanGreer.com
- ☞ www.EclipseDOT.com
- ☞ www.DOTDocs.com
- ☞ www.GodFirstLifeNext.org

And watch for his next book. If this one fired you up, the next one's coming in hot.

And when he's not leading companies or speaking on stage, you'll find Dan out on that same chunk of dirt, teaching his kids the kind of lessons no boardroom could ever give—lessons in grit, grease, and grace.

"....BETTER A LITTLE WITH RIGHTEOUSNESS THAN MUCH WITH DISHONESTY."— PROVERBS 16:8

Top off your tank with the right fuel.

More Resources

Want to keep the fire going? Whether you're looking to sharpen your leadership, equip your team, strengthen your faith, or bring Dan in front of your people—here's where to go next.

Websites

Leadership, coaching, and speaking: www.RealDanGreer.com
Fleet-focused growth and solutions: www.EclipseDOT.com
Compliance made simple: www.DOTDocs.com
Faith first, everything else next: www.GodFirstLifeNext.org

Book Dan to Speak or Train Your Team

From keynotes to custom workshops, Dan delivers real-world leadership and systems that get results.

Visit www.RealDanGreer.com/speaking or email dan@realdangreer.com

Podcast: *Forged*

Raw, real, and faith-filled leadership forged in the trenches. Listen on all major platforms or at www.RealDanGreer.com/podcast.

YouTube Channels

Leadership, business, and personal growth: Real Dan Greer
DOT training and field-tested insights: Decoding DOT

God First, Life Next

If this book spoke to you, you'll love the weekly devotionals at **God First Life Next**. These are short, straight-to-the-point devotionals built to help you start your week anchored in faith. Every Monday, you'll find fresh encouragement to keep God first—because when He's in His rightful place, everything else falls into place.

Sign up at www.GodFirstLifeNext.org.

The Inner Circle

If you're ready to go beyond books, podcasts, and keynotes—and actually lock arms with Dan and other growth-minded leaders—apply to join the **Inner Circle**.
This is where the conversations go deeper, the accountability gets stronger, and the growth gets real. It's not for everyone, but if you're serious about scaling your business, leading with faith, and surrounding yourself with people who push you higher, this is where you belong.

Apply today at www.realdangreer.com/inner-circle/

Social Media

Instagram: @realdangreer
Facebook: @realdangreer
LinkedIn: Dan Greer
TikTok: @realdangreer

Other Publications

Dan's next book is already in the works—built to take leaders, trainers, and teams even deeper. Sign up for updates or get early access at www.RealDanGreer.com